Making Human

CONFIGURATIONS: CRITICAL STUDIES OF WORLD POLITICS

Patrick Thaddeus Jackson, series editor

# Making Human

*World Order and the Global Governance of Human Dignity*

Matthew S. Weinert

University of Michigan Press
Ann Arbor

Published in the United States of America by the
University of Michigan Press
Manufactured in the United States of America
⊗ Printed on acid-free paper

2018   2017   2016   2015      4   3   2   1

A CIP catalog record for this book is available from the British Library.

Library of Congress Cataloging-in-Publication Data

Weinert, Matthew S., 1970–
    Making human : world order and the global governance of human dignity
/ Matthew S. Weinert.
        pages   cm. — (Configurations: critical studies of world politics)
    Includes bibliographical references and index.
    ISBN 978-0-472-07249-1 (hardcover : alk. paper) — ISBN 978-0-472-
05249-3 (pbk. : alk. paper) — ISBN 978-0-472-12084-0 (e-book)
    1. Globalization—Social aspects.    2. Security, International—Social
aspects.    3. Human security—International cooperation.    4. World
politics.    5. World citizenship.    6. Civil society.    7. Humanitarianism.
8. Human rights.    9. Political ethics.    I. Title.
JZ1318.W444      2015
341.4'8—dc23
                                                              2014027611

*For Viet*

The world finds nothing sacred in the abstract nakedness of being human.

—Hannah Arendt

The idea of humanity remains a "blank space" on the "emotional map of the average person."

—Norbert Elias

. . . imagining possibilities in terms of broad abstractions— world order, international society, the global village, the family of humankind, and so on—involves the risk that these abstractions have little positive consequence for the faces and the names of the humanity on whose behalf we might speak.

—Jayan Nayar

If we accept that the meaning of the concept of mankind is nothing but the sum total of its different usages, we can conclude that the only perennial part of its meaning lies in the very aspiration to universality embodied in the consistent effort to transcend the particular circumstances of its articulation. At the heart of these attempts we find nothing but circularity: human beings are members of mankind by virtue of being human, and they are human beings by virtue of being members of mankind.

—Jens Bartelson

The concept of an all-inclusive humanity, which makes no distinction between races or cultures, appeared very late in the history of mankind and did not spread very widely across the globe. What is more, as proved by recent events, even in one region where it seems most developed, it has not escaped periods of regression and ambiguity. For the majority of the human species, and for tens of thousands of years, the idea that humanity includes every human being on the face of the earth does not exist at all.

—Claude Lévi-Strauss

# Contents

# Foreword

Matthew Weinert has produced in this book a remarkable study of the slow emergence of an operative concept of "humanity" in world politics. That this concept is operative does not mean that it is universally accepted or perfectly enforced; rather, the concept figures into and helps to shape a variety of global initiatives in the contemporary world, from international legal proceedings to the ways that the United Nations Security Council evaluates threats to international peace and security. Demonstrating that the concept is now more prominent than it was in previous eras and how it has become so is the burden of Weinert's account.

Weinert demonstrates this development in a manner befitting the best kind of theoretically rich, configurational social science. Beginning with a detailed discussion of the concept of the human being in the philosophical literature and developing his account particularly through a close engagement with the work of Hannah Arendt, Weinert spells out five component mechanisms that can contribute to the process he calls "making human": recognition, resistance, reflection, replication, and responsibility. Specific combinations of these components help to explain both progress toward and the challenges facing the articulation of a meaningful notion of humanity. Serving to explain the critical junctures in the story are the incomplete manifestation of these components in the early days of the UN Security Council and during the Eichmann trial—along with the political projects and obstacles that prevented them from playing a more prominent role—and their implementation in some of the recent decisions of the International Court of Justice.

While applying critical constructivism to the notion of world society, Weinert's book also develops a distinct way of accounting for the global pattern he has in mind. As he states in his introduction, "To explore the potentialities of world society, one must begin not merely with the individual person but with the problem of the human being." Here we have the basic constructivist—or, perhaps better, postessentialist—insight about the non-naturalness of our basic notions, connected not just to the ways that they themselves are generated in practice but also to the broader social contexts they inhabit. As a process, humanizing produces not merely human beings but the very notion of human society, and that notion is, in turn, implicated in the production of standards of individual dignity. There is nothing vicious about this circle, since Weinert privileges neither the micro individual nor the macro society; instead, the process itself takes center stage in the account.

The implications of Weinert's study are profound. The emergence of a notion of humanity would change how large swaths of world politics operate, because whether they accept or contest this notion, they are forced to grapple with it. If Weinert is correct, a basic shift in our ways of thinking about ourselves may be underway. This cannot fail but have implications for the study of most of the topics on the agenda for research in international relations, and for that reason alone, Weinert's book repays careful reading. In addition, the book provides an outstanding example of how one does configurational research on normative concepts, by carefully laying analytical mechanisms onto a complex actuality so that critical junctures can be glimpsed.

Patrick Thaddeus Jackson
Series Editor, Configurations

# Preface and Acknowledgments

Intellectual work often emerges from or intimately relates to the wellspring of personal experience. As a first-time homeowner who lacks the skills to beget my vision of domiciliary perfection inspired by *This Old House,* I am compelled to hire laborers to maintain my nearly hundred-year-old house: electricians, insulators, masons, plasterers, plumbers, roofers, window installers, and sundry tradesmen (and men they have all been). But I have come to be rudely initiated into the world of contractors and subcontractors; "rudely" seems to be the only apt way to characterize dishonesty, ineptitude, tardiness, and even theft. Frustrated, I began to describe these various personages as a vile lot—necessary evils, as it were.

Yet the issue ran deeper than mere bad luck. My own dehumanizing language, born out of disgust, eroded my trust. The wounds of suffering injustice plunged me into an ugly abyss: I projected onto the *whole* of workmen the contemptible behaviors of a *few*, and in the spirit of dehumanization, these became characteristics of a "type" of human being. Damningly, I began to doubt *their ability* to transcend *my* narrow and negative understanding of them. If this is true of workmen, I wondered, might it also be true of others "we" come to abhor? Thinking of Armenians and Jews, Tutsis and Tamils, Bosnian Muslims and blacks, women and LGBT persons, I asked, how do those we have marginalized, oppressed, and dehumanized become, once again, fully human?

It occurred to me that my questions reversed an idea I first encountered as a college sophomore while reading Hannah Arendt's *The Origins of Totalitarianism.* She provocatively described the Nazi regime as engaged in the "production of living corpses" (1973, 447–57). A bit of sleuthing later in life revealed that Arendt, a Jew forced to flee her native Germany and then interned in the Gurs concentration camp in southern France, initially opined that "nobody wants to know that contemporary history has created a new kind of human being—the kind that are put in concentration camps by their foes and in internment camps by their friends" ([1943] 2007, 265). By the time *Origins* was first published in 1951 (initially under the title *The Burden of Our Time*), she recognized that her earlier view required precision. In the eyes of their captors and torturers, the imprisoned were only human by virtue of scientific classification; rather, as *animal laborans*, they were constructed *out* of human existence as a social designation. Might what she framed as the methodic production of living and actual corpses—the "killing of juridical man," followed by the "murder of moral man" and the annihilation of individuality, which made easier the inevitable slaughter of the body—be thought of in the reverse, that is, as making human?

Finally, after more than two decades, I am able to offer a response.

Many debts were incurred in the production of this book—far too many to acknowledge, as is usually the case. Very special thanks go to Alice Ba, Will Bain, Gretchen Bauer, Linda Bishai, Janice Bially Mattern, Lisa Burke, Bob Denemark, Jack Donnelly, Kara Ellerby, Jamie Freuh, Alan Gilbert, Patrick Hayden, Tom Keating, Tobias Lemke, Jenny Lobasz, Jim Magee, Bill Meyer, Cornelia Navari, Nick Onuf, Rajdeep Pakanati, Claire Rasmussen, Sudeshan Reddy, Brett Remkus, Andrew Ross, Jennifer Sterling-Folker, Ann Towns, Nancy Wadsworth, Amentahru Wahlrab, Daniel Whelan, Lauren Wilcox, and several anonymous reviewers for providing eminently helpful comments and posing learned questions.

Several others deserve special mention. Bob Murray bravely tackled the first full draft of the manuscript with his usual wit, insight, and penchant for asking difficult but necessary questions. He inspires in many ways, not least through his professional achievements, which prod me toward trying to become more of a specific kind of human being: a scholar. Mehrnaz Mostafavi's boundless intellect, insightful ruminations, and Socratic questioning always sharpened my ideas; her professional devotion to human security, evidenced by her laudable work in the UN Human Security Unit, motivates. Elizabeth Feary repeatedly tested her mettle and thus always led by example. Lauren White and Leslie Cohn kept me on track in ways they may not realize. Lauren Balasco, Kelly Ehrenreich, Ashley Lavery, Olivia Lucas, and Nick Wicks provided research assistance of exceptional quality and care. Patrick Jackson first saw promise in the idea. He introduced me to Melody Herr at Michigan, who proved an early, enthusiastic advocate. Patrick was always generous with giving time he never seemed to have; his scholarly example, combined with Melody's meticulous and critical reading and multiple expressions of genuine care, always rescued me when I foundered on the shoals of inarticulateness and diffidence. Susan Cronin and Kevin Rennells superbly assisted throughout the production process. I could not have conjured a better team of supremely attentive professionals with whom to work.

Several chapters initially appeared as papers at various conferences: the 2010, 2011, 2012, and 2013 International Studies Association conventions in, respectively, New Orleans, Montreal, San Diego, and San Francisco; the 2010 and 2012 meetings of the International Studies Association–Northeast in Baltimore, Maryland; and the August 2011 World International Studies Conference in Porto, Portugal. The University of Delaware generously awarded me two Summer Scholars research grants to fund research assistants and a travel grant to present my research in Portugal. UD's Department of Political Science and International Relations absorbed costs associated with my conference activities and thus deserves special thanks. To the department's administrative support staff—Lynn Corbett, Barbara Ford, Nancy Koeller, and Cindy Waksmonski—I extend my deep gratitude for their infinite goodness and for putting up with me all these years.

To my family, I owe much, much more. Acknowledgment of and thanks for their enduring support seems paltry compensation for decades of advice and an unwavering ability to overlook my multiple shortcomings. Only now, as we age and infirmities gradually intrude on family life, do I understand the profundity of how their unassuming leadership by example has enabled me toward becoming the self I aim to be.

Finally, toward understanding that making human is not only a sociopolitical process but an enduring subjective labor, often born out in the confines of our private lives, no one has helped me more than Viet Đinh, who makes me more human each day and to whom this book is dedicated.

# Introduction

## The Question

(Blue) ants. Apes. Bloodsuckers. Cockroaches. Dogs. Monkeys.
(Capitalist) pigs. Swine. Vermin.
Diseases. Infections. Parasites. Plagues. Scourges. Viruses.
Barbarians. Degenerates. Savages. The uncivilized.
Chinks. Dykes. Fags. Gooks. Gringos. Guineas. Honkies. Huns.
Injuns. Krauts. Niggers. Polacks. Paddies. Spics.
Three-fifths.
Man.[1]

What a litany of epithets we have fabricated to capture the extent and degree to which we have held others in such shocking disregard. Some were preludes to violence, others to enslavement, internment, or imprisonment; still others were the salvo to extermination. Together, they constitute, along with so many other terms of opprobrium, a lexicon of dehumanization. Respectable society wishes the terms to disappear. But the words—weapons, really—remain.

Thus a question arises: how do the marginalized, excluded, and dehumanized ever become (re)integrated into the human family? The question, of course, implies there is a human family. While the idea may be normatively attractive,[2] buttressed by the scientific dictum that all *Homo sapiens* are human, the social deployment of difference jettisons biological sameness. Color, ethnicity, gender, ideology, intelligence, nationality, occupation, physical capabilities, political affiliation, race, religion, sexuality, and sundry other signifiers have been used to justify colonization, discrimination, disenfranchisement, enslavement, ethnic cleansing, the forced removal of children from their families, genocide, homophobia, human trafficking, imperialism, internment, lynching, miscegenation prohibitions, misogyny, pogroms, purges, racism, segregation, sexism, sexual violence, sterilization, torture, and wars of extermination. Unlike the cosmopolitan thesis that "all human beings possess equal moral status" (Hayden 2005, 3; cf. Pogge 2002, 169; Barry 1999, 35–36), dystopic, dehumanizing practices suggest that being human and the human being are social constructs.

By human *being*, I refer to intersubjective understandings and standards that determine who is human. These, in turn, are both informed by and limit being *human*, meaning all those activities, affiliations, identities, memberships, programs, and projects that give our particular lives meaning. Stated differently, being human refers to the various modes of becoming individual selves in ways that accord with the social yardstick of the human being. On this reading, dehumanization stems from incongruity between one's particular mode of being human—say, to take some obvious examples, being a Jew in Nazi Germany, an ethnic minority during the violent disintegration of Yugoslavia, or female or homosexual in several parts of the world—and prevailing conceptions of human being.

Given multiple analyses of dehumanization,[3] this book investigates the reverse: humanization. Since history illustrates that we cannot assume membership in the so-called human family, our political analyses must begin not with a liberal exaltation of the individual person or a cosmopolitan aggregation of all human beings into an amorphous category of "humanity" but, rather, with the problem of being human: that is, with the awful truth that we live in a world in which countless "types" have been singled out, detached in varying degrees from the so-called human family, and at times eliminated.[4] Though we may agree with the cosmopolitan thesis, if we "put cruelty first" (Shklar 1982, 1984; cf. Young 1990), we must consider how the dehumanized come to be viewed, accepted, and treated as fully human. The problem, in other words, is to discern how we "make human" in sociopolitical life. This book tackles that issue.

## The Argument

Much of the work of making human occurs, I suspect, at the micro level of the individual: it includes, for example, sympathizing with those who suffer; engaging different others; curbing our biases for the purposes of cooperation if not harmony; and tolerating, not fearing or stigmatizing, and perhaps even appreciating difference. In this view, empathy and introspection deliver us from solipsistic fear and disgust of others not like us. Yet we do not (or cannot) always extricate ourselves from socially and doctrinally sanctioned prejudices that partly constitute our worldviews. Thus the problem of making human extends beyond interpersonal relations and appears as a social and political phenomenon. Might there be, then, processes that perform the work of humanization—that, in other words, substitute for our individual failings?

My response to that question centers on five processes that operate within and through (international) institutional sites: recognition of the individuality of the other, resistance to forms of oppression and discrimination, reflection on the moral worth and status of others, replication (of prevailing mores), and responsibility for self and others.[5]

### Recognition

In 1929, an exceptional case came before the Privy Council of Canada. *Edwards v. Attorney General of Canada*, also known as the Persons Case, pivoted on whether women were included under the designation "qualified persons" in a section of the British North American Act of 1867 regarding eligibility to serve in the Canadian Senate. A year earlier, the Canadian Supreme Court unanimously answered the question in the negative, and the plaintiffs appealed to the prime minister's august body of advisors. The Privy Council examined prior legislative acts and judicial rulings and interrogated the Supreme Court's reasoning that a long history of women's exclusion from public life—extending as far back as the Roman Empire—justified its decision. The lords remonstrated, "[C]ustom [the exclusion of women] would have prevented the claim [of women's inclusion] being made, or the point being contested. Customs are apt to develop into traditions which are stronger than law and remain unchallenged long after the reason for them has disappeared. The appeal to history therefore in this particular matter is not conclusive." All the council could determine on the basis of evidence was that "the exclusion of women from all public offices is a relic of days more barbarous than ours."

The council also studied "internal evidence derived from the Act itself," including use of gendered pronouns and the gender-neutral term *member*, neither of which was probative, and specific invocations of the term *male* as opposed to *female*, which proved material. In two sections of the act, language expressly limited the right to vote in provincial elections and eligibility to hold office to "male British subjects." Thus the council reasoned that had the framers of the act wished to exclude women from senatorial office, they would have employed definitive, not generic, terminology in the relevant section. But even if exclusion was the intended effect, the lords had to consider the abolition between 1916 and 1922 of all provincial restrictions on the franchise and the right to sit as members of dominion and provincial legislative bodies. The council therefore concluded that women were persons.

Kathleen Lahey's *Are We "Persons" Yet?* applies the rationale of the decision to the paradox that sexual minorities in Canada "could have 'equality' without full 'rights' and sometimes 'rights' without 'remedies'" (1999, xv). She argues that "in law-based state/societies, exercise of 'rights' of many kinds is really contingent upon admission to the category of 'legal persons.'" Lahey traces the concept of legal personality from its emergence in Roman civil law and its deployment over time against "Jewish persons, queers, women, racialized slaves, and other groups" to its "emergence in liberatory documents of 'modern' states such as the fourteenth amendment to the US Constitution and the 'Persons' case in Canada in 1929." She finds that "whenever states have made serious efforts to protect disadvantaged groups from hatred and discrimination, they have begun safeguarding the fundamental incidents of legal existence—'legal personality.'" These incidents include rights to enter and participate in the affairs of state, to move freely about in public, to "structure a life without violence or appropriation of property," and to enter into legally recognized relations sanctioned by property law, contract law, and family law."

In 2011, Hillary Clinton, then US secretary of state, acknowledged the law's role in instigating social change in her groundbreaking speech on "gay rights as human rights." "In many places," she noted,

> including my own country, legal protections have preceded, not followed, broader recognition of rights. Laws have a teaching effect. Laws that discriminate validate other kinds of discrimination. Laws that require equal protections reinforce the moral imperative of equality. And practically speaking, it is often the case that laws must change before fears about change dissipate.

But reliance on shifts in legal structure, Clinton averred, cannot be the sole tactic to combat discrimination. Conversations—"a constellation of conversations in places big and small"—must take place, ones that emerge from "a willingness to see stark differences in belief as a reason to begin the conversation, not to avoid it." I suggest that we should not limit these conversations to dialogic interaction between at least two persons. Rather, we should enlarge the notion to include conversations we have with ourselves—what we might call "thinking"—which I capture with reflection on the moral worth and status of others as a process of making human.

From these two examples, we derive three interrelated understandings or practices of recognition: recognition of attributions of legal personality, of rights and their extension to the marginalized/dehumanized, and of the interlocutory capacities of distinct and diverse people. All suggest a broader notion of recognition as an intersubjective activity concerning the acceptance of the individuality of the other, or, alternatively phrased, equal regard in conditions of reciprocity.[6] Recognition embodies the human need for validation by others,[7] which has been variously phrased: Martin Buber (1950, 140) characterized it as "the need of man to feel his own house as a room in some greater, all-embracing structure in which he is at home, to feel that the other inhabitants of it with whom he lives and works are all acknowledging and confirming his individual existence," G. A. Cohen (1988, 139) as a "need to know who" one is and how one's multiple identities connect oneself with others. Both renderings acknowledge the self as relational—that is, as embedded in networks and relationships characterized by interdependence and dependence. Put differently, "the self has no 'separate, essential core, but, rather, becomes a self through relations with others'" (Hekman quoted in Robinson 2011, 4).

## Resistance

For some, recognition of either their full human status (e.g., Tutsis in an ethnically charged Rwanda or Bosniaks in Serb-dominated territory) or an identity component of the self (e.g., being a woman in an androcentric world or being nonheterosexual in a heterosexual one) proves to be a struggle "in connection with something of specific intrinsic worth" (Hegel 1952, ¶351). The point suggests that not all violence or forms of resistance should be condemned, which Didier Fassin (2010, 84), following Walter Benjamin, maintains: "if 'lawmaking violence,' which is 'executive,' and 'law-preserving violence,' which 'serves it,' are pernicious, [Benjamin] writes, then by contrast, violence exerted over other men for a superior good may be necessary, since it is respectful of life, not as 'mere life' but as 'that life that is identically present in earthly life, death, and afterlife.'" We need only think of struggles against the South African system of apartheid or Jim Crow laws in the United States to underscore the point.

Drucilla Cornell suggests that we should think about resistance as struggles "against the appropriation of the Other into any system of meaning that would deny her difference and singularity" (1995, 78). For Cornell, resistance as a praxeological endeavor aims to expose and oppose practices and institutions hinged on blindness to exploitation or founded on violence against others. As a psychological exercise, resistance demands that we question inherited, ostensibly naturalized and settled concepts and that we work to "loosen" their meanings by wrestling with convention, "expand[ing] our sensibility, and re-imagin[ing] our form[s] of life" (Cornell 1995, 76). Resistance is thus code for "consciousness raising" insofar as it aims to denaturalize truths assumed to be timeless by exposing them as products of prevailing understandings situated within particular social and power configurations.

Resistance may take several forms. First, it may mean confrontation. It could involve physical protest, such as the suffragette marches, the Stonewall riots of 1969, or the militancy of groups like ACT UP. It could appear in the guise of legal activism, such as with the push for marriage equality in courts.

Second, resistance may be understood as a self-affirmational performance that actualizes potentialities of existence. Examples are Rosa Parks's now iconic seating that unleashed a civil rights movement, LGBT pride parades that exhibit and celebrate a right to "Be," or, as happened in 2013, "drive-ins" during which Saudi women flaunted the injunction legally prohibiting them from driving automobiles (Hubbard 2013).

Third, resistance may be construed as an alterior narrative posited against a dominating (silencing) discourse. As Hannah Arendt puts it, "[W]e humanize what is going on in the world and in ourselves only by speaking of it, and in the course of speaking of it we learn to be human" (1968b, 25). In some cases, the subject of discourse (race, gender, sexuality, religion) is clear. Even so, it is not something to be simply appended to a dominating discourse, as Jacqui True (2011, 76–77) has argued with respect to gender and research designs; neither should gender "be studied as the diffusion of just another international norm, since gender together with race and other social categories are part of the discursive structure of all norms." Instead, serious and sustained inquiry into the roots of dehumanization needs to be conducted. Likewise, "progress" on matters pertaining to the rights of LGBT persons, Secretary Clinton noted (2011), "starts with honest discussion"[8] between all persons on all sides of the issue. The point is not to force changes in belief (no one, Clinton mused, "has ever abandoned a belief because he was forced to do so") but to foster an understanding that "universal human rights include freedom of expression and freedom of belief, even if our words or beliefs denigrate the humanity of others," and to inculcate knowledge that "while we are each free to believe whatever we choose, we cannot do whatever we choose, not in a world where we protect the human rights of all."

In other cases, the subject may not be so readily apparent. In October 2013, Human Rights Watch issued an investigative report on six US drone strikes in Yemen—one in 2009 and the others in 2012–13—that resulted in the deaths of at least fifty-seven civilians. *Between a Drone and Al-Qaeda: The Civilian Cost of US Targeted Killings in Yemen* maintained not only that the drone strikes have killed many more civilians than the United States has acknowledged[9] but that some of the attacks violate international law. Two of the attacks indiscriminately killed civilians, while the others "may have targeted people who were not legitimate military objectives or caused disproportionate civilian deaths." While the bulk of the report concentrates on facts (of the attacks, obligations under and prohibitions specified by international law, and US policy) and makes recommendations to the American and Yemeni governments to ensure future compliance with international law, an NPR reporter, Carrie Johnson (2013), characterized the report as trying "to humanize the victims" by naming them and detailing the (very human) activities in which they were engaged when killed.

Even if the term *humanize* does not appear in the document, attention is given to conveying details of the victims in a way that counters the dehumanizing silence of the Obama administration. But if Washington's muteness deliberately reinforces the perception that those killed are terrorists, the administration likely banking on a public not intent to inquire any further about "those kinds of people who probably deserved to die," the suggestively silent prepositional *between* of the report's title compels us to ask, "What exists between a drone and al-Qaeda?" Yet that is the wrong question, the subtitle beseeches. If we substitute "who" for "what," we discover laborers who shielded themselves from hot summer sun after a long day's work (Johnson 2013).[10] We find the charred, fragmented remains of twelve villagers, including three children, "dusted with [the] flour and sugar that [they] were bringing home from market"—literally (and figuratively), as the report mentions, "breadwinners for more than 50 people in one of the poorest areas of Yemen" (Human Rights Watch 2013, 53–54). We find the student who borrowed his uncle's car, which he used as a taxi to earn extra money for his family and help pay the medical expenses of an ill relative. We find children at play and farmers tending to animals. In short, we find scenes of everyday human life. We also find the positing of an alterior narrative that, to anticipate an argument in chapter 3, has humanized "collateral damage" and, in doing so, revealed the moral bankruptcy of a term that serves as another mode of dehumanization.

*Reflection*

Broadly defined, reflection on "our most basic notions of what it means to be human" aims to disclose and clarify the "historical narratives" that are "basic to identity and human self-knowledge, collectively and individually" (Smith 2007, 243), the point of which is, in Iris Marion Young's critical, emancipatory formulation, to project "normative possibilities unrealized but felt in a particular given society" (1990, 6). Inwardly manifested as introspection, reflection takes the self as its subject. Outwardly directed with others as its subject, reflection re-presents the world and others in thought, the danger of which is always that "the other is met not as the other, but merely as part of the monological self" (Buber 1965, 206). Thus reflection should never be an end point but only a beginning for engagement with and in the world.

To put a finer point on it, reflection, even as an introspective exercise, is not mere solipsism. The language we use, whether in dialogue with others or in thinking, is "part of an activity" or "a form of life" (Wittgenstein quoted in Onuf 1989, 44) that reproduces the myriad of social structures and conventions from which language emerges and the self whose very construction derives from particular deployments of language. Reflection marks the beginning of a transformative process: as it foregrounds the historical narratives that have shaped our (dehumanizing) understandings of and practices in the world, it forces us to "'see' the world differently" (Cornell 1995, 78–79) and thus conditions us to question our moral sensibilities. For instance, how we respond to rape depends on how we "see" women and men: if we define rape as something that happens to women, we miss sexual violence enacted on men (see Carpenter 2005). If we construe the sexual exploits of men during war as instances of "boys being boys," we miss rape's use as a weapon of war. Likewise, how we respond to the demand for legal recognition of same-sex relationships depends on not only how we see LGBT persons but how we understand the very notions of love and marriage that have been portrayed in arguments against marriage equality as the province of procreative heterosexuality. In this view, our moral identity, conceptions of ethical behavior, and ways in which we care for others are "not secured in advance, but develop subject to a process of self-reflection" (Beiner 1997, 20).[11]

Revisions of our ethical imaginations and moral sensibilities may be most stable and significant in their impact when articulated in law. I draw on the 2003 *Lawrence v. Texas* reversal of the 1986 decision in *Bowers v. Hardwick* to illustrate. If the *Bowers* Court narrowly interpreted the question before it to ascertain whether "the Federal Constitution confers a fundamental right upon homosexuals to engage in sodomy," the Court in *Lawrence* averred that the justices' prior concern "disclose[d] their failure to appreciate the liberty at stake" (*Lawrence v. Texas* 2003, 2(b)). The earlier Court was found to "overstate" the historical grounds adjudged to justify moral disgust with and restrictions on male homosexual activities. Yet the *Lawrence* justices argued that sodomy laws were not historically "enforced against consenting adults in private" but were deployed to counter "predatory acts against those who could not or did not consent." By omitting this key piece of historical evidence, the *Bowers* majority could define "'the alleged right to commit homosexual sodomy' as a configuration of body parts" (Kaplan 1997, 222), as Justice Blackmun's dissenting opinion in *Bowers* noted, and the justices could thus permit their disgust to outweigh the key issue at stake: "the richness of a relationship will come from the freedom an individual has to choose the form and nature of . . . intensely personal bonds . . . [and hence] the fundamental interest all individuals have in controlling the nature of their intimate associations with others."

The *Lawrence* justices could appeal to seventeen years of social, legal, and political changes that manifested "an emerging awareness that liberty gives substantial protection to adult persons in deciding how to conduct their private lives in matters pertaining to sex" (*Lawrence v. Texas* 2003, 3(c)). Contextual factors permitted the Court to reflect on the stigma sodomy statutes imposed and to determine that, ultimately, it was "not trivial" but, to anticipate an argument in chapter 2, substantially demeaned "the dignity of the persons charged," by demanding "notation of convictions on their records and on job application forms, and registration as sex offenders under state law"—all of which diminished their standing in society and impinged on their ability to live self-determined, self-fulfilling lives.

## Reproduction or Replication of Norms

Despite a tendency to couch norms with terms such as *shared, moral,* or *good,* I, like Klotz (1995, 14), hesitate to do so, because the relational contexts within which norms operate, not to mention their (potentially unethical) origins or deployment, may neuter those more agreeable qualifiers. Feminist, critical, and poststructural theories draw attention to the fact that norms may be imposed on others.[12] Norms and their associated, undergirding normative beliefs that signal what actors deem is right to do (Crawford 2002, 86–98) may confront others as objective barriers to their humanization. Further, even in instances in which norms are emancipatory in constitution and intent, particular meanings and applications of them may clash with local understandings and blind societies to other forms of exploitation and violence (True 2011, 75–78).

Still, norms perform central roles in humanization. First, norms may be crafted in direct response to the second-class status and/or suffering of others, such as abolitionist (e.g., Crawford 2002, 159–200) or antiapartheid (e.g., Klotz 1995) norms, notwithstanding any unintended, oppressive effects they may produce.[13] Second, norms may stem from disgust or disapproval of difference and hence attach conditions to emancipation and humanization. In international relations history, perhaps the most famous instance of such a norm was the nineteenth-century "standard of 'civilization'" that tethered the recognition of non-European polities to changes in their domestic social, political, and legal systems. Finally, norms and normative beliefs may also humanize and emancipate through their use in ways that subvert or alter official or dominating understandings of different, marginalized others.

Consider how proponents of marriage equality (re)appropriate concepts and practices of love, care, commitment, and family from a heteronormatively restrictive framework; such are the normative values of human *being*, not monopolistic possessions of certain categories of persons. Navi Pillay, UN high commissioner for human rights and key architect of the UN Free & Equal campaign for LGBT rights, has somewhat shifted the rhetorical grounds on which she has championed rights for LGBT persons. Her first statement (2010) on the issue focused entirely on legalistic issues stemming from systematic discrimination and violence. But as many states have resisted the importation of LGBT concerns under a human rights rubric, she now frequently refers to the "humanity" of LGBT peoples and their experiences by underscoring the presence of same-sex relationships across time and space, appealing to basic human experiences of love and difference, and referencing changing attitudes as integral to the human condition. Ignacio Saiz (2004, 65) charts a similar trajectory in the international arena: "The sexual rights discourse builds on the limited articulation of sexual rights at Cairo and Beijing, as well as on existing case law on sexual orientation and standards regarding. It embraces a more affirmative and emancipatory vision of sexuality, seen not just as something to be protected from violence or other interference, but also as a social good to be respected, protected, and fulfilled. The principles underpinning these rights have variously been identified as 'autonomy,' 'empowerment,' 'bodily integrity,' and 'respect for sexual and family diversity.'" I am not suggesting that rights-based equality arguments recede into the background; they do not. Yet they increasingly share the stage with liberty-based ones that, as a function of reflection on lived human experiences, underscore autonomy and difference as core elements of the human condition (see Yoshino 2007).

The emphasis on human experience and, less obviously, individuality highlights the infinite possibilities inherent in creating a life meaningful to oneself. Put in pedestrian language, no two persons are the same. Even if deep, sustained similarities may be discerned between at least two people in behaviors, practices, identities, and life projects, the ways in which those individual persons experience, interpret, and enact such categorically differ. Dignity and liberty, as conceptual categories of social positioning and deep normative commitments, demand, at minimum, that we permit others to pursue their life projects and, at maximum, continued interrogation of social practices and institutions to determine if they substantially infringe on modes of human development and expression that are at root nonharmful to others.[14] By focusing on dignity and what it means to be human, we disentangle ourselves from universal, essentialist constructions of sexuality, sexual orientation, and gender identity and permit a more open and fluid dialogue that centers first and foremost on social constructions of the human being and the degree of liberty required to construct individually meaningful lives.

## Responsibility

Responsibility as a process of making human may be thought of as responsibility to self and to others. Self-responsibility entails obligations to care for one's interior life (e.g., the emotional, intellectual, psychological, and spiritual dimensions of our lives) and body, to explore the potentialities of Being constrained by the presence and capacity of others to do the same, and to accept the consequences of one's actions and decisions.

William Paul Simmons argued this point with respect to human rights law and the marginalized other. One of the three modalities he identifies for reconstructing human rights to more fully respond to the needs of the marginalized and oppressed involves self-responsibility in the form of ascribing one's identity and identifying one rights (2011, 129). For too long, he maintains, human rights law "often disregarded" and even "silenced" the voices of the disempowered, marginalized, and suffering; human rights theorizing has usually emanated from abstract universalisms, not "from the voices of the Marginalized Other" (3). Many feminist, critical, and poststructural theorists anticipated the argument. Balakrishnan Rajagopal (2003, 12), for instance, noted that "the idea of human rights has proved to be blind to the tremendous variety that human-rights struggles take in the form of social movement resistance in the Third World," especially with respect to gender,[15] development, and democracy.

Self-definition as a form of self-responsibility finds a parallel in the taking of responsibility for others, especially when our practices stem from the needs of those for whom we care. The other two modalities Simmons (2011, 129) identifies involve "patient listening to the voice of the Other" and working in solidarity "with the Other to build the life-project that the Other is unable to complete because the Other is outside the system." By solidarity, Simmons, borrowing from Enrique Dussel, means "'the affirmation of the exteriority of the other, of [her] life, [her] rationality, [her] denied rights'" (11). The first counters patronizing tendencies that some have charted in human rights discourse and practice, while the second builds coalitions between diverse people.

Yet responsibility is Janus-faced. Following Foucault, Iver Neumann and Ole Sending (2010, 115) read the exercise of self- and other-directed forms of responsibility in terms of a sociopolitical transformation in which power no longer simply appears as an external force that compels an individual to do or refrain from doing something but, rather, operates through individuals as self-regulation. In this view, individuals morph from being objects of regulation to being subjects with rights (120). The freedom of rights-bearing individuals, put differently, is maintained within social limits as long as individuals act responsibly, that is, in accordance with social rules and norms. Hans-Martin Jaeger (2007, 266) traced that transformation with respect to security (humanitarian intervention and human security) and development (from macroeconomic development to a micro focus on human development). He characterized the shift toward the individual as marking "a change from a 'macroeconomic' and political rationality of the welfare state to a 'microeconomic' and depoliticized rationality of 'human resource management,' choice, and responsibility." On the one hand, the shift empowers, just as it contributes to a notion of self-sustainability and responsibility as components of what it means to be human and how to be human—a life lived in accordance with social standards and norms. On the other, the shift implies that failure to exercise rights responsibly or to manage one's life in accordance with prevailing norms invites surveillance and policing. Cognizant of this duality, Foucault (1986, 51–53) framed responsibility not as "an exercise in solitude" but as "a true social practice[,] . . . a recognized hierarchy [giving] the most advanced members the task of tutoring the others." For him, responsibility is "the attention one devotes to the care that others should take of themselves, [which] appears then as the intensification of social relations."

Care and power are thus mutually implicative and constituting. Care as a manifestation of responsibility to others permeates much of human life (see, e.g., Tronto 1993; Held 2006; Engster 2007; Benedict 2009). An ethics of care construes the self as relational—that is, not as a priori given but as a product of ongoing relations with others (see Robinson 2011, 4). This "relational ontology" acknowledges that interdependence and dependence—and hence hierarchy (no matter how ephemeral) and power—are pervasive features in human life; consequently, "the practices of care through which we fulfill our responsibilities to particular others" must feature in our political analyses and should not be relegated to the private realm. As Robinson has persuasively argued "relations of care and intimacy are of great political significance in that their form and nature are determined by relations of power that play out in a variety of contexts—from the household to the global political economy" (5).

## Book Outline

Chapter 1 locates theoretical antecedents of the processes of making human produced by the tension between social understandings of human being (or what it means to be human) and ways of being human. Specifically, I draw on the work of Gerritt Gong, Martin Wight, and Hannah Arendt. Gong (1984) studied the development of a standard of civilization and thus was concerned with analysis on the second (state) and third (system) levels, not the first level. However, the standard included certain prohibitions on interhuman practices—slavery, suttee, and polygamy. Confronted with such "uncivilized" behavior, European colonialists demanded that others meet conditions branded as signifiers of civilization. Wight (1992) engaged the matter by constructing a theory of humankind around the problem of the barbarian. The bulk of the chapter, though, mines the work of Arendt, whose writings, as indicated in the preface, prompted me to ask questions regarding what it means, politically and socially, to be human in a dystopic world.

Chapter 2 picks up on a foundational Arendtian claim. Based on the interwar experiences of minorities in Europe and the Jews in the Holocaust, she deemed expulsion from political community as the cardinal offense against human dignity. For her, human dignity entailed status as a member of an organized political community, the primordial obligation of which is to defend inhabitants and their rights. Belonging, I ascertain, is a first step toward the realization of dignity. The chapter surveys several key studies, from which it derives two core understandings of dignity as status and value. The remainder of the book examines how status and value are accorded, defended, and developed by international bodies, with primary focus on the United Nations, its organs, and affiliated agencies. I then shift my focus to the UN Charter, to illustrate how this document, often construed as the blueprint of sovereign state-based postwar international relations, likewise erected pillars on which a post-Holocaust humanitarian world order concerned with defense of the human person and human well-being may be supported.

Chapters 3–6 assay international practices of making human, as political/diplomatic response to egregious human suffering (chapter 3), conceptual reconfiguration of the notion of security (chapter 4), and legal discourse and practice (chapters 5–6). Chapter 3 considers how the UN Security Council has confronted the problem of dehumanized bodies. By tracing a nonexistent or parenthetical concern with victims early in Security Council operations to more robust responses to threats to or attacks on the human person, I underscore how this premier international body contributed to the project of making human by broadening its calculus of maintaining international peace and security. Chapter 4 furthers the thematic linkage between making human and security by examining the emergence and development of the human security concept within the UN system. Chapters 5 and 6 treat examples from international law: chapter 5 explores the development of international criminal law, while chapter 6 examines the International Court of Justice's grappling with the issue of self-determination and the meaning of peoples, most recently articulated in the case concerning Kosovo's unilateral declaration of independence. Both chapters manifest new conditionalities for making human, the latter by what I pithily call suffering for sovereignty (*repression* as a perverse precondition for making human), the former by delegitimizing and punishing severe violations of human dignity (*retribution* and *restitution* as making human). Drawing on a plethora of primary documents (e.g., UN reports and resolutions and international court and tribunal judgments), *Making Human* maps a distinctive, if inconsistent, tendency within the discourse and practices of international organizations and states to make human and deepen and broaden what Ruti Teitel (2011) has called humanity's law. But if she focuses on a paradigmatic shift in international relations and international law away from an exclusive focus on sovereignty and toward concern with human well-being, *Making Human* explores the very problematic, very social construction of the human that underlines the shift. The practices and processes of making human, I conclude, provide keys to understanding, theoretically and practically, how we might construct a world order in which individual human beings are accorded dignity, secure in both their rights and their personhood.


## Case Selection

To make the argument, I might have examined obvious sets of cases, such as immigrant struggles to assimilate in multiethnic societies, the treatment of indigenous peoples in the United States and Australia (among others), the reintegration of Japanese Americans into American society after their internment during World War II, blacks in postapartheid South Africa, or African Americans in the United States. I may have framed this study in terms of postconflict reconciliation and reintegration processes—for example, post-Holocaust European Jewry or Tutsis in postgenocidal Rwanda—that alert us to procedures that foster forms of "social learning" (e.g., Aiken 2010, 166) or to how social healing is promoted through reparations, apology, forgiveness, and accountability (e.g., David and Choi 2009). Likewise, I might have studied making human as an adjunct of the human rights story. Or I may have pitted processes of making human in conversation with social movements, such as the abolitionist (e.g., d'Anjou 1996; Daget 1980; Davis 1984; Walvin 1980), women's (e.g., Butler and Scott 1992; Lahey 1999; MacKinnon 2006), or gay rights movements (e.g., Bawer 1993; Warner 1993; Wintemute 1995; Lahey 1999, 2010; Nussbaum 2010), which demonstrate, among other things, how affirmative conceptions of self, coupled with acts of resistance, underscore elements of a common humanity in ways that foreground and undermine systems of exclusion, marginalization, and oppression. Yet no justification for case selection would have deflected criticism of authorial discretion, the effect of which would be to silence other pertinent instances of inhumane treatment and imply, no matter how unintended, the importance of certain cases over others.

Limiting the study in any such fashion would have failed, in my view, to adequately capture the human experience, even though we may glean salient lessons from in-depth case analysis. We, as individuals, are congeries of identities, not indivisible entities as the etymology of the word *individual* (the *in-dividual*) suggests (Booth 1993, 78). Our multiple identities consequently expose us to varying, overlapping degrees of inclusion/exclusion and acceptance/rejection given particularities of context. For instance, while a white woman in the United States may earn seventy-seven cents on the dollar compared to white men in the same profession (earnings for African American women and Latinas trail; see Fitzpatrick 2010), that woman may face no other discernible form of discrimination. In some societies, white men may possess socioeconomic privileges that nonwhite men may not. But in nineteen states in the United States, some white men, homosexual ones, may be fired by their employer or expelled from rental housing on grounds of sexual orientation (ACLU 2011), while black heterosexual men legally cannot be.[16]

We need not stop at what American jurisprudence calls suspect classes.[17] Other pertinent, if mutable, identifiers may play a role in one's dehumanization. Argentine and Chilean dictatorships in the 1970s staged disappearances of political and ideological opponents. The Khmer Rouge in Cambodia targeted, among others, those it perceived to be "contaminated" by Western culture: for example, the bespectacled, speakers of foreign languages, and those employed in particular occupations such as banking and education (see Quinn 1989). To add to that improbable list, the UN Security Council has concerned itself with the protection of journalists and humanitarian relief workers, not because they constitute what municipal legal systems call suspect classes (they do not), but because their targeting is related to such signifiers.

Even a cursory accounting suggests that individuals are besieged on the basis of their identities—no matter how ephemeral or immutable, self-ascribed or other-imposed. This reveals an ambiguity or tension that animates, if not defines, our social existence: "we are always both the self we imagine and the body others see" (Marso 2012, 167; see also de Beauvoir [1948] 1994). Dehumanization, in its myriad of forms and degrees, magnifies specific aspects of another's Being that observers find abhorrent or threatening, so much so that those elements come to define, precisely and monolithically, a person and, in many cases, a people. Dehumanization may manifest, at one extreme, as the use of an epithet that demeans or degrades another and, at the other, as the denial of citizenship (Sokoloff 2005) or even, physically, as the camp—that is, the stigmatization and removal from society of a mass of bodies whose identities have been turned into a scarlet letter. When fixation on an identity signifier engages sociopolitical institutions to regulate, segregate, trade, sell, incarcerate, intern, expel, or exterminate, we have reached the height (or depth, as it were) of dehumanization and political evil: the superfluity of others (see Hayden 2009).

Still, my approach may invite skepticism. Catharine MacKinnon (2006, 3) intuited an inherent circularity in humanization: "Seeing what subordinated groups are distinctively deprived of, subjected to, and delegitimated by, requires first that they be real to power: that they be first seen as human."

Jens Bartelson (2009, 177–78) echoes her view, at the heart of the idea that "human beings are members of [hu]mankind by virtue of being human, and they are human beings by virtue of being members of [hu]mankind." Yet while we find "nothing but circularity" in the cosmopolitan mindset, Bartelson appreciates that the circularity has "allowed for a gradual extension of membership in the face of radical otherness and difference, to the point of making diversity a constitutive feature of humanity." From this central feature follows "the only moral precept . . . from the social ontology of world community": that is, "the requirement of mutual respect in the face of human diversity."

*Making Human* responds that we may cut through the circularity by transforming cosmopolitan critiques into an inquiry. If cruelty reveals that being human and the human being are subject to the vicissitudes of power and prejudice, how might we understand their manufacture? To wit, resistance, struggles for recognition, and certain modalities of self-responsibility fracture and open up political spaces controlled by dominating selves in ways that do not depend on a prior acceptance of the other as human but, rather, underscore the ways the other *becomes* human in the eyes of dominating selves.[18] Likewise, the exercise of self-responsibility and the reproduction of prevailing normative standards reveal fully human capacities for acting in community. However, as relationships between the processes are complex, mutually implicative, and overlapping, teasing each one out in their specificity is an exceedingly difficult enterprise. Consequently, cases aim to illustrate more the interlinkages between and the interplay of the processes—that is, how they operate in tandem—and less their individual contours and mechanics.

While an inquiry of this sort avails itself of broad historical coverage, I limit my investigations to post-1945 for two reasons. First, a series of movements—from the Nuremberg and Tokyo tribunals to the International Criminal Court, from decolonization to human rights, from state security to human security, from state development to human development—appear to challenge the edifice of a state-centered conception of international relations by appealing to a more primordial, more fundamental unit of international political analysis: the individual. Harold Jacobson (1982, 320) describes post–World War II developments as adding up to "a historic consensus . . . on the meaning of human dignity and justice, and thus on the overarching goals of international and national policy and on the broad outlines of world order." Ruit Teitel (2011) perceives in such developments the emergence and evolution of a law of humanity in real policy and legal, not merely philosophical and aspirational, terms. While temporally delimiting this study no doubt fractures the proverbial whole story, the limited time frame allows us to conceive of an economy of making human in the wake of a devastating war in which the human potential to annihilate itself (or at least others) en masse—whether through camp or (mushroom) cloud—fully revealed itself and therefore made imperative the need to center the human being and human dignity in international relations.

Second, while the processes of making human predate the UN Charter, the Charter provides a blueprint for incorporating them into analysis of contemporary world politics. The Holocaust and the experience of two world wars brought to bear on international relations a distinct concern with human welfare, and this concern palpably weaves through the Charter from the preamble through Chapters XII–XIII on the trusteeship system. Chapter 2 of this book explores this theme and sets up the argument that logics, languages, and practices in world politics have, in varying degrees, tethered the dignity and worth of the human person to broader concerns of international stability. Successive chapters demonstrate the ways—sometimes rudimentary and contentious, sometimes highly formalized and determined—in which the international community has effectuated or attempted to effectuate those provisions of the Charter.

By treating humanization as a sociopolitical phenomenon or a congeries of practices rather than a discrete psychological or interpersonal experience, I am able to link the central focus of this project—how we make human—with a problem in the academic discipline of international relations and the wider practice of politics: translating basic human existence into a conceptual category with political import, whether it be iterated in academic discourse as a humanitarian world order, cosmopolitan or world polity, or world society or in diplomatic discourse as the human family or humanity. The point is to digest and unpack what has become a familiar trope and reconstruct it as something with political gravitas.

## Making Human and International Relations

Studying international relations (IR) from the standpoint of human beings, or with attention to how structures and systems of world politics affect and are affected by humans and their well-being, has generated considerable attention in analyses of, for example, biopolitics (e.g., Agamben 1998, 2000; Foucault 2003; Jaeger 2010),[19] care ethics (e.g., Tronto 1993; Held 2006; Robinson 1999), feminist theory (e.g., MacKinnon 2006; Reilly 2007; Tickner and Sjoberg 2011; Confortini 2012), human development and human welfare (e.g., George and Wilding 2002), human security (e.g., Hudson

2005; Bedeski 2007; de Larrinaga and Doucet 2008; Robinson 2011), human suffering and cosmopolitan harm conventions (e.g., Linklater 2001, 2009), humanity in international law (Meron 2000a, 2000b; Teitel 2011), race and international relations (e.g., McCarthy 2009), and self-determination (e.g., Knop 2002; Dahbour 2013; Sterio 2013), as well as, more generically, in studying "global politics as if people mattered" (Tétreault and Lipschutz 2009; see also Linklater 1982). This very partial list indicates the diversity of kinds of studies that entertain, in varying ways, the problem of being human in a dehumanizing world.

Other disciplines, too, have tended to the issue, including biomedicine and biochemistry, ethics, history, philosophy, and social theory, which have considered the constructedness of human nature (e.g., Smith 2007), that which makes us human (e.g., from a philosophical point of view, see Holbrook 1990; from a biomedical point of view, Pasternak 2007), and what it means to be a person and/or a self (e.g., Taylor 1989; Rouner 1992). One sociologist has indicted all social sciences, lamenting that

> while many of our . . . theories are interesting and do illuminate particular dimensions of human social life, I am not convinced that we as people actually find ourselves represented by them. When we look at the models of the human operative in, say, exchange theory, social control theory, rational choice, functionalism, network theory, evolutionary theory, sociobiology, or sociological Marxism, we may recognize certain aspects of our lives in them . . . But I suspect that few of us recognize in those theories what we understand to be most important about our own selves as people. Something about them fails to capture our deep subjective experiences as persons, crucial dimensions of the richness of our own lived lives, what thinkers in previous ages might have called our "souls" or "hearts." (Smith 2010, 2–3)

To underscore interest in these issues, the University of Pennsylvania Press began to publish a new journal, *Humanity: An International Journal of Human Rights, Humanitarianism, and Development*, in the fall of 2010.

While considerable space has opened to study the human being, approaching IR from the standpoint of first-level analysis is fraught, as the field has been dominated by what Robert Isaak (1974, 264) has called "two dehumanizing assumptions": that the object of study should be either the international system or the nation-state.[20] Combined, these two "levels of analysis" repress a third alternative: "analyzing individuals in interaction with other individuals." In 2004, Barry Buzan, a leading IR theorist, acknowledged that third alternative by recasting the rather neglected concept of world society in English School theory.[21] World society had hitherto served as a conceptual midden to account for nonstate actors (individuals, corporations, nongovernmental organizations, and the like) in the social structure of international relations. Framed by the language of common values and interests, cosmopolitanism, and solidarism, world society eventually signaled the primacy—analytical, moral, or programmatic—accorded to human beings over states (e.g., Dunne and Wheeler 1996; Mayall 2000; Brown 2001; Linklater 1998, 2001, 2009; Wheeler 2000).[22] Despite conceptual recognition of the salience of nonstate actors, world society lacked analytical import, owing to disparate understandings compounded by laudable yet ambiguous equations that "humanity is one" (Mayall 2000, 14). Recounting E. H. Carr and Hedley Bull, Buzan (2004a, 36) summarized the scrape of world society as not existing "in any substantive form," unlike the international society of states. He concluded that "its moral priority is unattached to any practical capability to deliver much world order" and that, in the end, its commitment to, say, human rights, exists "only as an ideal, not as a reality."

In place of an undifferentiated, ill-defined world society, Buzan imagined two distinct domains: transnational and interhuman societies. Transnational societies are less geographically rooted and capture associative tendencies between people based on acceptance of and adherence to norms, rules, and institutions (2004a, 210). The focus shifts away from states and individuals to a panoply of clubs, firms, lobbies, and coalitions; yet these "globalisms [if they reach that scale] tend to be separate rather than coordinated." Interhuman societies are framed around collective identities (210), which, in turn, stem from "individual-to-individual interaction" (120) that exists along a spectrum of possibilities.[23] At one extreme, we find strong, deep, enduring commitments to family, clans, tribes, and nations; at the other are shallow identity claims based on universalisms such as humanity or "the planetary ecosystem." At the same time, he admits of substantive, transspatial globalisms; certain religions (e.g., Christianity and Islam) and civilizations (e.g., Western, Confucian) inculcate shared, entrenched values and, in some cases, breed meaningful identities.

Though Buzan's concerns were structural, not normative (127–28), his reconfiguration opens theoretical doors to exploring a particular calculus of IR framed in first-level analytics that dispose of reliance on unknowables (e.g., human nature; see Jacobi and Freyberg-Inan 2012), found in early brands of realism and idealism (see Morgenthau 1962, 3–4; Waltz 1959, 16–41). If world society or interhuman domain or humanity (or, by extension, the very concept of the human being, which is at the core of these formulations) are to have any conceptual or theoretical weight, their relevance is to be found not in abstraction or presumptiveness about the inherent decency or depravity of human beings but, rather, by understanding key underlying dynamics that constitute and (re)shape them, of which dehumanization and humanization are two. In this way, pace Niklas Luhmann's hinging of world society to global communication patterns and hence its divorce from actor type (often posited as antithetical to the state) or shared normative and value commitments, we understand world society not only to have substantive form, contra Buzan's claim, but to exist as something "antecedent to states" and the international society they form. On this view, interstate societies appear as specific historical manifestations or modes of world society's internal differentiation (Kessler 2012, 81). A similar point can be made from the perspective of (de)humanization. Perceptions and fabrications of and encounters with difference have produced enduring institutionalized, if objectionable, practices (e.g., racism, slavery, imperialism, constitutionally imposed schemes of differentiation) alongside virtuous ones (e.g., charity, tolerance). These, in turn, have informed institutional structures and frameworks. Antony Anghie's *Imperialism, Sovereignty, and the Making of International Law* (2004, 3–4), for instance, considers a set of (contemporary) governance structures and practices (including good governance, human rights, international financial institutions, and the war on terrorism) "that continually repeat themselves at various stages in the history of international law," tracing them back to a colonial "dynamic of difference" that distinguished civilized from uncivilized, backward, and primitive others. Colonial and imperial systems spawned logics of superiority and hierarchy, which eventually morphed into racially constructed notions of civilization that buttressed dominating and exploitative material structures and social relations (see also McCarthy 2009, 69–95). In Marxist terms, ideas governing the meaning and status of human—a component of society's superstructure—inform structure, whether precipitant from a dynamic of difference or a cosmopolitan sensibility.

In this regard, cosmopolitanism could do more than it currently does. Its three basic premises—that individuals are the "ultimate units of moral and political concern," that all human beings possess equal moral status, and that "human status has global scope" (Hayden 2005, 11)—have prompted insightful inquiries into harm (e.g., Linklater 2001, 2011), world citizenship and democratic forms of governance, social movements, transnational challenges that evade the capacity of any single state to manage or control, postidentity politics, the reform of existing international institutions and the creation of new ones, and the generation of practices and institutions to enact cosmopolitan visions (on these matters, see, e.g., Held 1995; Barry 1999; Vertovec and Cohen 2002; Hirsh 2003; Parekh 2003; Hayden 2005; Fine 2007). Yet for feminist theorists, "cosmopolitical" visions tend to mirror "wider political, economic, cultural, and gender power imbalances" (Reilly 2007, 183) in ways that gloss over phenomenological variance in human status.

For cosmopolitanism to be a fully emancipatory political project, it must tackle racialized, economized, gendered imbalances and practices that encroach on its premises. *Making Human* thus begins with the understanding that being perceived and received as (fully) human by different others is not guaranteed, automatic, or immediate.[24] I treat "the human" as a question in the constructivist spirit of humility and self-reflexivity (Hoffmann 2009)—not because I fundamentally believe we should excise (particular) persons from our sociopolitical narratives, practices, and histories. By beginning not with the thesis of equal moral status or with a basic biological assumption of sameness but with cruelty, we strip from world society the idealistic, cosmopolitan aura that surrounds it. If we abandon the equal moral status thesis, we are forced to grapple with a more ominous proposition: that the concept of the human being has been subject to remarkable variance over time. We are compelled to manage how we might stabilize the concept and how to extend it to those not treated as (fully) human. We are, moreover, forced to recognize that humanization hinges not only on ethical considerations but also on the operationalization and deployment of power, defined broadly as "the production, in and through social relations, of effects that shape the capacities of actors to determine their own circumstances and fate" (Barnett and Duvall 2005, 3). Instead of asking rhetorically and plaintively, "Can't we all just get along?" I focus on how that has been possible. If we reframe the inquiry, the issue is not simply presumptive and aspirational (i.e., an effort to affirm that we are all members of world society) but, rather, pragmatic and historical. The declarative "We *are* morally equal" morphs into the interrogatory "*How* do we *become* morally equal and, moreover, *effectuate* such equality?" Inevitably, the matter comes down to how we make human.

I do not suggest that the argument is circular. Rather, we cannot understand one construct (world society, humanity, the cosmopolitan polity, or world order) without understanding the composition and construction of its component parts (human beings or individuals). My first and primary line of inquiry into making human can thus be read as a vehicle to critique and explore the second, concepts of world society and humanity. As chapter 1 maintains, since we cannot assume membership—the so-called human family has not been able to agree on who is "related" or by what degree and who is not—we must problematize the concept of the human and all of its inclusive iterations.

## Toward a Global Governance of Human Dignity

That being human and the human being prove not to be constants but historical contingencies subject to the vicissitudes of power and the exigencies of politics implicates, too, the instability of human dignity, which has, especially in the post–Cold War world, become a pivot on which world order turns. Confronted with, on the one hand, postmodern and posthuman critiques and, on the other, biotechnology, genetic engineering, concentration camps, exterminations, the omnipresent threat of annihilation by weapons of mass destruction, and extreme poverty,[25] some might be inclined to argue that there remains (or, more combatively, there *must be*) an essence of self and dignity preserving. The problem with our conceptions of dignity, which appear in a nearly ubiquitous Kantian formulation as "an inherent worth of immeasurable value" that derives from our ontological status as *Homo sapiens* (Smith 2010, 434–35; see also Howard and Donnelly 1986), stems from their disjuncture with historical practice. Far from being an inviolate, inveterate aspect of human life and personhood, dignity evolves within the constraints of context.

This does not mean that human dignity or living a life worthy of being lived (Weiss et al. 2010, 153) is or ought to be dictated and governed by forces external to the self. Nor does the approach in this book suggest that dignity is infinitely malleable or ambiguous. It recognizes that human dignity is significantly shaped by mechanics and determinations of sociopolitical power and processes at all levels (local, national, regional, international, transnational). While chapter 1 identifies elements of dignity as it locates antecedents of the processes of making human, chapter 2 offers a road map for understanding dignity as a social construct related to status and, therefore, as an "existential value" (Kateb 2011, 10), since threats to and subversions of dignity are threats to and subversions of our individual and species identities and existences. Successive chapters explore how practices in diverse fields contribute to and clarify our understanding of dignity.

Because of the systemic-level deployments of the processes that make human in multiple forums, I frame making human as the global governance of human dignity. By global governance, I mean the management through norms, rules, laws, structures, institutions, and power of transnational phenomenon by diverse state and nonstate actors. Throughout the book, I use the terms world order and global governance not interchangeably but relationally. By world order, Bull meant the aggregate of "patterns or dispositions of human activity that sustain the elementary or primary goals of social life among humankind as a whole" (1995, 19). In this view, order is not a static thing—say, the arrangement of decorative bottles on a window sill—but a process. Being a social construct, order is an arrangement designed to effectuate particular objectives; while this enables us to think of it in terms of regularity and predictability, which lends order a staticity that it shares with the arrangement of material objects in one's house, order is ultimately subject to human spontaneity, ingenuity, action, and interpretation. Put in the Arendtian language of chapter 1, world order is shaped by the tectonic force of natality, that is, the physiological (dis)appearances of human beings and the ways, through word and deed, they insert themselves in the world. According to this perspective, global governance is a particular historic pattern or mode of world order comprised of (varying, disparate, discrete, and sometimes conflicting) activities tending to common predicaments and problems.

Though it may be customary to think of governing in terms of world trade, aspects of the environment, global security, or nuclear energy, I stretch the term *governance* to cover a most basic presupposition: being human. Throughout history, categorization of "types" of humans constituted a primordial form of governing and managing human diversity. We may think of humanization as a primary institution of world society, by which I mean a "durable and recognized pattern of shared practices rooted in values commonly held" that eventually "play a constitutive role in relation to both the pieces/players and the rules of the game" (Buzan 2004a, 181). In other words, processes of making human fundamentally relate to how we understand and structure the broader concept of humanity. Though discrete, processes of making human exhibit what Wittgenstein called "family resemblances." Even if they may "have no one thing in common," they "are all related to one another in many different ways" (1958, ¶65, p. 31), much like the "resemblances between members of a family: build, features, colour of eyes, gait, temperament, etc. etc. [that] overlap and criss-cross" (¶67, p. 32). Chapters 3–6 explore processual interlinkages in ways that probe various tensions, mediations, and reconciliations wrapped up in the interface of an interstate postwar order and a post-Holocaust humanitarian world order. They consequently provide insight into the development of what I call the global governance of human dignity, which, in the language of Neumann and Sending, transforms objects into subjects and centers "the freedom and agency of those that are governed as both an end and as a means for governing" (2010, 9). The key points are that individuals are social beings born into preconstituted social worlds and that the contours of our lives, including what it means to be human and what constitutes our dignity, are also socially determined. The question is how.

What I propose might be read in terms of a classic "levels of analysis" framework. I begin from the premise that the social status of *human* is not always equable with the biological designation *Homo sapiens*. Socially, the status has been denied, divided, or in some manner apportioned; hence I inquire into the construction and acquisition of that status. I call this "making human." In social science parlance, such an inquiry would be deemed first-level analysis, which locates causes of events in or explains outcomes as a result of the (psychology, presumed nature or essence, or motivations of the) individual. The claim made in this book is not that *all* international events are traceable to (de)humanization but that these dynamics have been determinative in the construction and maintenance of particular systemic configurations and practices (e.g., de/colonization, slavery/emancipation, de/segregation). Further, as my cases aim to demonstrate, processes of humanization underline many key activities and decisions in contemporary international relations in ways that effectuate a post-Holocaust humanitarian world order.

I also seek to ground the notions of world society and humanity through third-level analysis, by locating causes of events in the system itself, meaning the ideational and material structures that provide the backdrop of and, in many senses, inform and animate relations between actors that comprise the system. Notions of humanity and world society, far from being tropes deployed as diplomatic or academic rhetorical flourishes, exert influence on policies and ways of thinking about contemporary international relations, especially, as I show, in international organizational environments. What is produced systemically, then, is a mode of world order that is increasingly, though not inexorably, framed in humanitarian ways.

By traversing the levels of analysis, I follow a well-worn path trod by many (constructivists, feminists, critical theorists, postmoderns/poststructuralists). Feminist scholarship, for instance, has sought to "find" women (long hidden) in international relations (see Enloe 2000); expose (masculine) gender biases that have variously silenced, erased, and oppressed different others; denaturalize biases that have come to be accepted as objective and neutral; deepen and extend knowledge by posing gender experiences and narratives that challenge accepted frameworks; and rethink political, social, economic, and legal relations, structures, and processes in ways that eschew domination and exclusion.[26] Feminism, moreover, "is about what we see in global politics by looking at and for women and gender, and what those things tell us about how the world works" (Tickner and Sjoberg 2011, 5). But it is not solely about what we see and what the world external to our bodies tells us; solipsism is not the feminist message. Rather, the declarative—an analytical rallying cry—directs us to look at the world through a particular lens, suggesting that what we see is not always what we assume to be a timeless, universal truth. Exclusionary, silencing biases have often become so deeply ingrained in systems, structures, and processes that we perceive them as natural and objective—and perhaps even as immutable. But individuals may condition (and alter) structures and systems, just as much as systems and structures condition individuals. Granted, this is a constructivist reading of feminism, but one that coheres with its core principles and methodologies, according to Catia Confortini. Both share "an 'ontology of becoming'" that aims to unpack the complex relationships between agents and the structures and social systems within which they act, even if feminism tends more overtly to critical theory's emancipatory impulse. For Confortini (2012, 21), "a critical feminist project aims at understanding both how social change happens in the context of defining structures and how such change can be emancipatory—that is, how it is effectively transformative of unjust structures." In this respect, *Making Human* shares analytical space with critical feminist theory, even if I do not restrict my inquiry to gender and women.

Despite clear affinities to feminist, constructivist, critical theory[27] and to English School approaches to international relations, I here engage not (extensively or exclusively) with any single theory but, rather converse with many. In short, this book is less about a single theory's conception of humanization and more about a phenomenon that earlier theories of international relations simply do not or inadequately capture. This is not to suggest that various theoretical approaches cannot cull or converse with particular points to enrich their own traditions. For instance, by problematizing, not assuming, the meaning of being human and humanity writ large, *Making Human* calls into question the notion of the (atomistic) human that lies at the heart of liberal theory. Given that processes of making human are always instances of the operations of power, the account offered here may find some coherence with a nonstructural realist account of international relations—the kind of constructivist realism offered by Jennifer Sterling-Folker (2005). Such an account must consider not simply the dehumanizing effects of power that stimulate imperial or aggressive ventures but also the various ways power humanizes previously dehumanized others, which, as an exploration of the consent side of hegemony, a realist might comfortably appreciate. My emphasis on the social manufacture of those concepts will thus appeal to constructivists, as likely will my position that processes of making human in the aggregate constitute a "global governance of human dignity." Further, we can draw on constructivism's concern with the coevolution of moral beliefs and the constitution of social facts. We can apply the feminist concepts of an ethic of care, empathetic cooperation, and relational autonomy and learn from feminist theory's agonizing over the lack of humanity accorded to people because of gendered (and various other) constructions. We can contribute in a critical and constructive way to the English School's largely neglected concept of world society[28] and learn, in the process, that interhuman interaction can very much alter international relations. Structurally oriented IR theories might consider that conceptions of what it means to be human and thus who is human generate sets of practices and relations that are often enforced materially. As such practices and relations unfold, normative beliefs grounded in superiority, supremacy, or outright disgust perform important constitutive roles with respect to the development of new and emendation of existing institutions, social practices, and relations in ways that directly translate into structure (see Anghie 2004; McCarthy 2009, 69–95).

The cases surveyed in this book highlight modalities of making human in specific circumstances, but always in broad brushstrokes. I eschew deep, detailed case analysis in favor of identifying (by no means inexorable) patterns and connections across time and space, even if the patterns and connections are not always consistent. Put differently, my main objective with this book is to get us thinking about the social construction of the human being and its attendant notion of humanity, not to explore specific, detailed discourses and practices among particular actors with respect to particular cases at particular points in time. In terms of world society, the continuities help destabilize the claim that it lacks substantive form; but the accumulated evidence does not lend the notions of world society and humanity fixed meanings hinged on universal, inclusive notions. Rather, their meaning and the content of their practices pivot very much on definitions of who is human, what modes (associated with activity/behavior and identity) are appropriate to being human, and how dignity is both defined and allocated. To explore the potentialities of world society, one must begin not merely with the individual person but with the problem of the human being. This, in turn, facilitates consideration of the processes by which those who are "outside" the human family become fully human and to whom dignity is accorded. A theoretical account of world society or humanity must therefore be dystopic at heart: that is, it must be attentive to the exclusionary practices of collectivities and hence to "the needs of those who are outside or on the margins" (Fine 2007, x). By accounting for the extent to which logics of inclusion/exclusion are continually at play, we disabuse ourselves of the theoretical reflex that automatically affixes cosmopolitan, solidarist presuppositions to world society.

Robert Fine (2007, x) has, in a similar vein, critiqued cosmopolitanism for "not being cosmopolitanism enough" because it "attaches [itself] to an already strong and confident sense of belonging . . . It leaves intact a conventional notion of belonging, in which individuals know intimately the contours of their world, and it only supplements this sense of belonging with a universal element." Yet he acknowledges that cosmopolitanism's appeal and, arguably, world society's attraction has "to do with the idea that [while] human beings can belong anywhere, humanity has shared predicaments and we find our community with others in exploring how these predicaments can be faced in common." Fine's approach is problem-solving theory focused on the management of shared predicaments and, simultaneously, critical theory focused on dynamics of membership; cases explored in this book, as diagnostic moments in the evolution of world order and world society, illustrate this approach.[29] *Making Human*, as an extension of that kind of logic, begins at the proverbial beginning: that while we can belong anywhere, nowhere has proven more vexing than belonging to humanity itself.

## CHAPTER I

# Membership and Belonging

> . . . humanity, which for the eighteenth century, in Kantian
> terminology, was no more than a regulative idea, has today become
> an inescapable fact. This new situation, in which "humanity" has in
> effect assumed the role formerly ascribed to nature or history, would
> mean in this context that the right to have rights, or the right of every
> individual to belong to humanity, should be guaranteed by humanity
> itself. It is by no means certain whether this is possible.
>
> —Hannah Arendt[1]

> . . . the isolate can always be annihilated by anyone who looks
> seriously at the phenomenology of how selves get created.
>
> —Wayne Booth[2]

Judith Shklar (1982,1984) challenged liberalism to put cruelty first, while
Iris Marion Young (1990), in proposing a conception of justice, began with
domination and oppression. These choices were, to use Shklar's terms (1998,
11), acts of "moral intuition" based on the "fear of systematic cruelty" and,
I would add, its prevalence. They also precipitated from a need to rectify
silences in political theory and philosophy concerning suffering and marginalization. If Shklar resisted claims that a proper or "noble" liberalism must
stem from purportedly universal moral or ideological aspirations, not the
reductively limited, ephemeral experiences of cruelty and oppression (1998,
13), Young found in philosophy and social theory a troubling silence regarding oppression that "happens to social groups," in part because "philosophy
and social theory typically lack a viable concept of the social group" (1990, 9).

Beginning with cruelty exposes "an enormous gap between private and
public life," which, in Shklar's view (1982, 25) renders visible previously in-
visible others and obliterates the distance between governments and their

citizens. This is not to suggest that "private life is better than public: both are equally cruel. It is rather that one has a sense of the incoherence and discontinuity of private and public experience." In the study of international relations, Cynthia Enloe (1996, 187) led a similar charge by castigating the discipline for holding that "a humanitarian, populist approach" focused on the margins is not "what a formal analysis of international politics is all about." More sympathetically stated, she determined that "most international relations analysts feel ambivalent toward human dignity's . . . relevance to their own intellectual enterprise," for in the analytical economy of "cause and effect," one must be "discriminating" (187–88).[3] But a focus on the "margins, silences and bottom rungs," long assumed to be "naturally marginal, silent, and far from power" (188), opens analysis to considering the diversity of forms and effects that power takes, which Enloe does with respect to the 1994 Chiapas rebellion in Mexico.

I do not wish to mislead the reader by creating the impression that what follows is an exploration of Shklar's brand of liberalism, Young's conception of justice, or Enloe's engagement with power. Rather, I refer to them to underscore the fecundity of beginning with cruelty and taking a humanitarian approach to international relations inquiry. I thus problematize Aristotle's key claim that humans are by nature political animals, by underscoring that who or what is human is itself a political question (Barker 1958, 5). This approach offers not a history and narrative of elites, executives, militaries, and states but a phenomenological sensitivity attuned to various ways interhuman relations affect world politics and to how interhuman relations and individual lives are substantively affected and transformed by broader decisions, processes, systems, and structures that constitute the "stuff" of formal international relations analysis. Such an approach forces us to grapple with the central moral question posed by instances of cruelty, oppression, and dehumanization: not only how do we respond to them, to which much attention has been devoted, but how do we become human?

In a sign that times are changing, Mary Ann Tétreault and Ronnie Lipschutz's felicitously entitled introductory international relations textbook *Global Politics As If People Mattered* first appeared in 2005 and was updated and reissued in 2009. They attempt to explain and convey an understanding of global politics by situating ordinary people, not political, economic, or cultural elites, at the center of inquiry (2009, 1). But even ordinary people must be analytically parsed; differences in context, capacity, capability, experience, history, identity, and the like account for substantial variation in how ordinary lives are lived and how ordinary peoples are perceived, especially when confronted by sites, practices, and holders of power. Hannah Arendt put it much more bluntly: "the world [finds] nothing sacred in the abstract nakedness of being human" (1951, 295).[4] To make sense of the world and the human beings within it, we must perforce trade abstract universalisms for "classes and ranks" and "social privilege and prejudice" (Arendt [1944] 2007, 279).

Tétreault and Lipschutz intuitively know this. No matter how ethically appealing it may be to aggregate human beings into an inclusive conception of humanity, classifications are analytically necessary if one aims to consider "the differential complexity" of the societies in which we live—"not social relations as such or the institutions that comprise them, but the extent to which human ingenuity and complex organization have made it possible for some people and societies to dominate others" (2009, 186). Ordinary people—social individuals,[5] on their reading—appear throughout their text as socially signified groups: classes, laborers, wounded warriors, members of nations and ethnic groups, and the poor and hungry, among others. This chapter builds on differential complexity by exploring antecedents of the processes of making human to capture the peculiar logics, languages, definitions, rules, ceremonies, techniques, relations, and systems that not only aggregate entities into particular groupings but condition how we think of collective membership.

Membership in any imagined cosmopolitan polity is by no means automatic, in part because the very meanings of the notions "human" and "humanity" are contested—which is not to say aleatory and infinitely elastic. I do not outright reject universals—in this case, the notion of a human being and its collective analogue, humanity. Rather, my argument cognizes the particularity of universals: that their content depends on how we, individually and collectively, answer questions regarding membership in our respective communities; the degree to which difference is perceived to undermine or threaten the specific forms of our collective existence; who is morally constituted as an inviolable being worthy of dignity and hence membership; and why. Universality and particularity are thus not mutually exclusive but mutually constitutive and interdependent. Erin Daly (2013, 20) writes with respect to dignity that the "best way to harmonize the universal and the particular is to suggest that dignity is how we describe the essence of what it means to be human, but that the right to dignity is how we describe what legal claims people can assert to insist that their humanity be recognized." This explanation anticipates an argument I present in chapter 2. Both Daly and, from a more critical standpoint, McCrudden (2008) argue that dignity is constructed by courts, not a timeless essence to be found; as such, it is subject to variance.

Still, while thinking in terms of the constructedness of membership may not be foreign to many of us—immigration laws, nationality and nationalism, racial categorization, religion, and the concept of identity itself produce and are productive of us/them dichotomies—thinking individually of our humanness (and our dignity) as constructed and subjected to terms of membership very well might be. As our identities are social in nature, they remain subjected to the perception of and reception by others. Put in different idiom, that which *Becomes*—a self, individuality—is in the dehumanizing act already presumed by others, and it is this presumption (dehumanization as an act of overt reification) that arrests *Becoming* into an existent *Is*. To spin Descartes a bit, we think and therefore think that we are. Yet who, what, and how we "are" are in varying degrees contingent and contested matters, both individually and socially.

Martin Wight (1992, 49) intuited the problem and framed it for an international relations audience: "[I]f international society is not co-extensive with the human race, then what of the human beings and societies which are external to it? This is not an abstract question; it has been, and may again be, highly concrete." Whereas his response to that question is conceptual and theoretical, Gerritt Gong's is historical and practical. Both offer compelling accounts that create space for considering the kinds of questions I entertain, but it is in the work of Hannah Arendt, the main focus of this chapter, that we find further guidance on how we may do precisely this.[6]

## Being Inhuman in a Human World

The issue of membership in and the expansion of international society from its European core has long preoccupied some scholars of international relations, chief among them English School theorists (e.g., Wight 1977; Bull and Watson 1984; Gong 1984; Watson 1992; for a critique, see Jones 1981). Because the discussion has largely resided within the state-centric frameworks of international system and international society, it has focused almost exclusively on second- and third-level analyses. World society, the third of the English School's now-famous conceptual trilogy, remained largely neglected until the 2004 appearance of Barry Buzan's *From International to World Society?*, which breathed new life into an underutilized concept. But in doing so, as briefly discussed in the introduction, Buzan replaced the triad with three domains: the interstate, transnational, and interhuman, each defined ontologically in terms of its central actors (2004a, 261; on his structural account of the interhuman dimension, see 118–28, 258–61). Yet like most homocentric approaches—for example, cosmopolitanism and human rights—Buzan assumes membership in the interhuman, even if he charts variation in types or depths of commitments and exchanges between people along a spectrum of "universally shared identities which could vary from the minimum recognition by all humans of each other as like-units (paralleling pluralism among states), to the advent of a world civilisation linking all humankind together in a complex web of shared values and elaborated identities" (135).

While his reconstructed trilogy offers a productive research program, the problem of the human being and being human remains, as it does with leading cosmopolitan accounts (e.g., Held 1995; Nussbaum 2002; Kuper 2006). The human being, being human, and humankind are not objective, natural realities. Rather, they are constructions stemming from networks of discourse and practice that produce and are produced by specific meanings of the terms shaped within context. Identity may be the predicate of being human, but the real grammar lies in the underlying mechanics by which we accord the status (invariably in degrees) of human being to diverse others. A comprehensive account of international relations, if it is to be responsive to global dynamics of (dis)integration, perforce must consider the ways we as social selves negotiate the terrain of difference and thus how we come to recognize bodies as persons.

Yet while identity ensures membership in particular groupings, it does not guarantee membership in humankind. Gong and Wight employed the language of the "uncivilized" and the "barbarian" to capture a particular sort of being—one not yet quite fully a human being in a sociopolitical sense—and how that being is, to use Wight's expression, digested by the international society of states. The predicament finds descriptive resonance in the Greek. Whereas *zoē* refers to biological life common to animals and humans,[7] *bios* pertains to a distinctly human life lived in community (if not always in communion) with others, and the latter is characterized by a myriad of forms, projects, and identities that are shaped by self-definition, speech, action, and interaction with others. Several salient questions arise: How and by what processes and activities does *zoē* subvert the boundaries of its existence? When and under what conditions is *zoē* accorded the status of *bios* and equipped with all of the rights, privileges, and possibilities equable with that civilized self?

Gong's *The Standard of "Civilization"* (1984) explores one nineteenth-century diplomatic and legal response to the problem: a mechanism by which European states could demarcate the boundaries between a civilized self from an uncivilized, even barbaric, non-European, non-Christian other. Gong identifies "civilization" as code for a set of benchmarks including "protection of basic rights of . . . citizens, standards of honesty and efficiency in administration, capacity to adhere to rules of international law and to enter into diplomatic relations, and avoidance of slavery and other odious practices similar to those which European states expected of each other" (viii, 15). If subjects met and adhered to these benchmarks, they theoretically could be granted full admission into the European society of states. The standard was thus a regulatory or governance norm that structured "decision-making and policies at all levels" (True 2011, 76–77).

Yet the standard of civilization was not mere mimicry; its replication demanded the internalization of European norms and institutional procedures to the extent that Hedley Bull considered the brandishing of such norms as "equal rights of states to sovereignty, of peoples to self-determination, and of persons of different race to individual rights" (Gong 1984, ix) by Africans and Asians as marking the apogee of "barbarian" socialization and their constitution as human in a European—hence acceptable—mold. But as Gong notes, the standard was not solely unidirectional; it "also represented a code of expected 'civilized' behavior which Europe imposed upon itself," embodying both "humanitarian sentiments and codes of *noblesse oblige*" (6). In this regard, it was what Jacqui True (2011, 76) calls an embodied norm, meaning one "internalized in bodily practices [that] constitutes the subject and his or her recognition by others."

Even if the standard prohibited suttee and polygamy and thus proved regulative of human activity, it was nevertheless a tool of interstate relations. Gong alerts us to recognition as an evolving process by detailing how particular countries navigated, managed, and inculcated the standards, sometimes successfully (Japan and Siam) and sometimes not (the Ottomans and China). In chapter 6, I pick up on this theme and provide a contemporary, if obverse, gloss on the standard.

Like Gong, Wight (1992, 50) treated the very tension at the heart of the expansion of international society—confrontation with and recognition of the other—by framing a "theory of [hu]mankind" around the "barbarian." Pithily, he noted that "non-self governing peoples, colonial populations, were barbarians who had been absorbed into international society but not yet been digested." Each major tradition of international relations (or the three traditions of English School theory) answers differently the question of digestion: a realist (Machiavellian or international system) "theory of barbarians" translates into exploitation because "barbarians have no rights"; a rationalist (Lockean, Grotian, or international society) theory translates into trusteeship, since "barbarians have appropriate rights"; and a revolutionist (Kantian or world society / cosmopolitan) position maintains that barbarians "have equal rights" even if their content is contested (82–83). I here survey each tradition briefly.

In realism, the barbarian comes "to be" in international relations as an instrument of the powerful—and thus never as fully human. From this follow four interrelated doctrines, described by Wight. First, "civilization has the absolute right to expand itself" (55). This veritable law of the stronger, Wight muses, effectively creates an insider civilization that realists would not normally admit exists but that is produced when civilized insiders confront differentiated others who are then posited as uncivilized, presumably weaker outsiders. Second, "barbarians have no rights" or "are outside the law" (57). The combination of the first and second doctrines produces a third: "barbarians may be exploited." The fourth doctrine—that "barbarians are not human"—offers at least three possibilities of fate: "if tractable and muscular, they will be enslaved [think of Nazi, Soviet, and Maoist labor camps]; if intractable and useless, exterminated; and if there are too many to be exterminated and they are difficult to organize they will be segregated [think of the Bantustans in South Africa]" (62). In the realist world, digestion of the barbarian is a misnomer, for incorporation merely involves chewing and spitting out the remains of what was, in biological fact, only a *Homo sapiens*.

Rationalists accept the realist doctrine that civilization has the absolute right to expand, but they ascertain limits on that right. Responding to Spaniard treatment of indigenous populations in the New World, Vitoria appealed generously, if naïvely, to the *jus gentium*, or law of peoples (a more expansive notion than today's narrower translation as law among nations). Not only did he condemn the conquest, but he maintained that the *jus gentium* bestowed equal rights on Spaniard and native alike (Wight 1992, 71). While Spaniards possessed rights to travel and settle abroad and a corresponding obligation not to eviscerate native societies, natives possessed rights of landownership and a corresponding obligation not to inhibit foreigners from settling, trading, or even proselytizing. Once the rights of the former were infringed on, however, the right of self-defense kicked in—in which case Vitoria seemed not to appreciate that "laissez faire [really] meant the right of the stronger" (Wight 1992, 70).

Grotius translated Vitoria's *jus gentium* as the "society of mankind bound by a general law" (Wight 1992, 72). The Grotian framework could be depicted as three concentric circles, with the general law or *jus gentium* occupying the outermost circle, a mediate circle of a European law of nations, and an interior circle representing the state and its municipal law (Wight 1992, 73). Thus Grotius could condemn Muslims' poisoning of waters as "'contrary to the law of nations, not indeed of all nations but of European nations and of such others as attain to the higher standard of Europe'" (Grotius quoted in Wight 1992, 73). Kant replaced Grotius's geographic formulation with a cosmopolitan vision evocative of Vitoria, but one in which the *jus gentium* was confined to "conditions of universal hospitality," which practically meant "the right of a foreigner not to be treated with hostility . . . upon the soil of another" (Wight 1992, 74–75).

Nevertheless, despite Kantian cosmopolitanism, the broader distinctions inherent in a differentiated, (i.e., racialized) approach to civilization was gradually inscribed in international law (see Keene 2002, 101–19; Anghie 2004). James Lorimer, a Scottish natural law theorist, wrote of a tripartite division of humanity in the 1883 edition of *The Institutes of the Law of Nations:*

> . . . civilised humanity, barbarous humanity and savage humanity. Civilised humanity signified the nations of Europe and the Americas, which were entitled to full recognition as members of international society. Barbarous humanity was synonymous with the independent states of Asia—Turkey, Persia, Siam, China and Japan—which were entitled to partial recognition. And savage humanity encompassed the rest of humankind, which stood beyond the pale of the society of states, although it was entitled to "natural or human recognition." (Lorimer quoted in Bull 1995, 36–37)

Not until Locke and Burke, however, did a more comprehensive rationalist doctrine emerge—one that theoretically took into account the possibility of full equal rights yet rested ultimately on managerial relations of command and control. While both men appealed to the notion of trusteeship, Locke viewed it as an institutionalized form of assistance and rule on behalf of the other (regardless of whether such assistance and rule was wanted or needed). For Burke, though, trusteeship became "a right of empire" (Wight 1992, 76). In their respective schematics, the barbarian retained rights, but certainly not ones equable with the European core. Moreover, these rights were circumscribed and ultimately held in trust, subject to the rule and administration of the trustee. Yet who was fully digested remained, on the rationalist view, a matter of subjective taste or judgment.

Of the three traditions, revolutionism is wed to a universal, inclusive conception of humankind, and it is within this framework that Wight— who calls it a "political philosophy of the outsider or barbarian, which has since been called anticolonialism" (1992, 86; see also Fanon 1963)—outlines processes by which *zoē* morphs into *bios.* In rationalism, the metamorphosis wholly depends on the goodwill of dominant actors in international society;

in revolutionism, it is a matter of self-assertion—freedom, egalitarianism, and "revisionism [of the contemporary order] and interventionism" to assist those struggling for liberation and against aggression, each rooted in profound "resentment against those from whom [equality] had to be asked" (Wight 1992, 86–89). Dissident demands find support in (European) revolutionists who "go out, with missionary fervor, to convert barbarians and bring them into the fold." But this troubles Wight because "barbarians are brought in as reinforcements against [or instruments for] somebody else" (97–98). Strikingly against the grain of the revolutionist belief in the universality and formal equality of humanity, such a view, he censured, has led, in practice, not to "government of people" but to "the administration of objects" (98), which comes close to realist instrumentality and rationalist trusteeship (see Bain 2003). Of course, in the revolutionist approach, the barbarian does not become an instrument of the powerful but comes to represent a cause célèbre of the human ability to subvert the dominant order of things.

Subversion is theoretically (not to mention practically) significant. Contrary to English School accounts that define world society in terms of "shared norms and values at the individual level" (Buzan 2001, 477), Wight centers the concept of world society around tensions, fissures, contradictions, and disjunctures stemming from marginalizations and exclusions that precipitate from (highly skewed and particularistic) interpretations of or conditions placed on presumably universal values. The terrain on which such battles are fought is one of membership in humanity, which, in turn, hinges on who is worthy of being conferred the status of human.

## Being Human in an Inhumane World

From Wight and Gong, we can extract two salient processes of making human: replication of prevailing norms and resistance. *Zoē* either imitates and internalizes particular standards imposed on it[8] or resists and becomes *bios* by exposing injustices, advocating reform, or subverting the dominant order. But barbarians[9] no longer appear on the international scene as primitive peoples subjected to the pedagogy of the "civilized," even if new tribes are found deep within secluded geographical enclaves (see Phillips 2011). If we recode the term *barbarian* to signify not just totalitarians (e.g., Nazis) and terrorists[10] but also undesirable others, our interlocutions reveal a proliferation of barbarian forms generated by racial or ethnic hatred, religious tensions, factionalism, political/ideological strife, sexualities, corporeality (e.g., the fat or obese, the diseased), the female, the veiled (Erlanger 2011), the nonveiled,[11] the immodestly dressed in Orthodox religious communities (see Kalman and Reynolds 2011), and sundry other reasons. Becoming/being a barbarian is always a matter of perception—one person's religious savior is another's zealot/fanatic, one's cockroach or vermin or plague is another's victim whose personhood, which has been obliterated "through several perversions of power" (Hayden 2009, 3), demands defense. The condition I describe is one of "real worldlessness," which Arendt characterizes as "always a form of barbarism" (1968b, 13).

Worldlessness underscores Arendt's conclusion that the most fundamental human right is the "right to have rights" or "to live in a framework where one is judged by one's actions and opinions," which means "a right to belong to some kind of organized community" (Arendt 1973, 296–97; see also Birmingham 2006).[12] If the history of the Jews and the plight of minorities during the interwar period taught Arendt anything, it was that "the world [finds] nothing sacred in the abstract nakedness of being human" (1973, 299);[13] for her, only living *in* community as a free, engaged, social self could protect the natural human condition of plurality and, with it, individuality, action, and discourse. As will be explored in the following pages, this particular concern long occupied Arendt and assumed the form of two intellectual pursuits: one focused on the pariah (see Arendt [1957] 1997; [1943] 2007; [1944] 2007), the other on totalitarian rule and its penchant for producing "living corpses" (Arendt 1973, 447–57; see also 1963a).

The following subsection explores the pariah theme, with special attention paid to the act of resistance as a self-creative performance as evidenced by Rahel Varnhagen, a Jewess who hosted one of the most prominent nineteenth-century Berlin salons. Given the inability of the pariah to fully overcome her status, I explore two implications: first, making human requires publicity; second, Arendt's conception of natality must be revised to include an intersubjective dimension that appreciates and fully incorporates the publicity requirement. To ground my demand to conceptually stretch natality, I briefly examine two instances that Arendt found noteworthy and that give depth to making human and making humanity: the creation of a new category of crimes against humanity after World War II and the experience of the revolutionary council system.

### From Zoē to Bios, or from Pariah to Person

Whereas Aristotle distinguished between biological and sociopolitical life, Foucault called such a distinction into question precisely because "the simple fact of life" now "resides at the heart of modern politics" (Vaughan-Williams 2009, 22). For Foucault, biopolitics, or "attempts to govern whole populations" through a variety of institutions and regulations to augment health, (re)productivity, and public hygiene, ruptured or transformed politics because of its attunement to the corporeality of *zoē*. Giorgio Agamben (1998, 9) disagrees, arguing that "what characterizes modern politics is not the inclusion of *zoē* in the *polis* . . . nor simply the fact that life as such becomes a principal object of the projections and calculations of State power." Rather, for Agamben, *zoē* has always figured in political life—even within the Aristotelian framework—for the *polis* was constructed on and thus defined by an "original" biopolitical act that excluded *zoē* (1998, 6, 15–29; see also Vaughan-Williams 2009, 22). Exclusion—the ban—is the foundational constitutive political act.

That the *zoē*/*bios* distinction is insufficiently nuanced to describe the complex relationship between politics and life permits Agamben to introduce a conception of "bare life" to signify those caught in a "zone of indistinction" between *zoē* and *bios*—a zone and a status that may be extinguished by sovereign command. Vaughan-Williams (2009, 24) summarizes bare life as "a form of life . . . amenable to the sway of sovereign power because it is banned from law and politics and subject only to the whims of that power." Yet Agamben inadvertently tends to erase conceptual clarity. On the one hand, he argues that "we all potentially run the risk of becoming bare life" (1998, 111); on the other, he describes "the 'body' [as] always already a biopolitical body and bare life" (187). He adds that "nothing in it [the body] or the economy of its pleasure seems to allow us to find solid ground on which to oppose the demands of the sovereign power." As the phenomenon of bare life (as an analytical category, a perception, and an experience of politics) increasingly collapses the diversity of human experience into a sovereign power trap, it forecloses or at least severely constrains the possibilities of an emancipatory politics; hence it robs itself of analytical power if the whole of human experience can ultimately be subsumed under it.

But Agamben is not immune to liberation. In *The Coming Community*, he locates emancipatory potential in what we might call "the performative": that is, not in universal principles, such as human rights or the inherent moral worth of the individual, but in what he variously calls "whatever being" (1993, 1), "whatever singularity" (85), or "being-as-such," all of which mean "the simple fact of one's own existence as possibility or potentiality" (43). "Whatever being" is a single human being possessed with a potential to become *someone* other than its unadulterated, born self. Arendt (1973, 455), I think, is more eloquent and direct on this point: "Actually the experience of the concentration camps does show that human beings can be transformed into specimens of the human animal, and that man's 'nature' is only 'human' insofar as it opens up to man the possibility of becoming something highly unnatural, that is, a man."

Yet the performative, or what we might reframe here as the tendency to become a self, troubles the state: it "cannot tolerate [it] in any way" (Agamben 1993, 86). "The state," Agamben avers, finds objectionable the fact "that the singularities form a community without affirming an identity, that humans co-belong without any representable condition of belonging." "[W]hat is important [for the state]," he explains, is never the singularity as such, but only its inclusion in some identity, whatever identity." Identities are self-conscious, self-selected modes of belonging that affirm an existence and ways of human *being*, but they can also be dehumanizing traps: convenient, essentialized shorthand to make sense of the diversity of the human condition, they can be, more nefariously, the basis on which diverse others can be monitored, restricted, and possibly eradicated. Identities, whether self-ascribed or other-imposed, are Janus-faced: the essential building blocks of our social selves also might become the grounds of our oppression and dehumanization.

Arendt shares Agamben's general ambivalence and disquiet. According to Bonnie Honig (1992, 220), "Arendt's actors do not act because of what they already are, their actions do not express a prior, stable identity; they presuppose an unstable, multiple self that seeks its, at best, episodic self-realization in action and in the identity that is its reward." Put back in the language of Agamben, only "whatever being," in the sum of its many singularities, can challenge sovereignty and reveal the limits of sociopolitical power—in conditions in which freedom and action remain possible. Only in the totalitarian regime or in the concentration camp can power exert such determinative, controlling sway over life; perhaps this is why bare life is frequently explicated with reference to Auschwitz or Guantánamo Bay (e.g., Passavant 2007; Vaughan-Williams 2009; Fassin 2010).[14] Even then, power is constrained by the physical limits of policing.[15] Thus, while the state presumably cannot tolerate a myriad of life forms, it must. Invoking bare life as a totalizing concept ultimately proves insufficient to explain a vast range of human experience, for each "whatever being" exists with other "whatever beings," and in the performance of self-creation and self-exhibition, it explores, expands, and tests existence as possibility or potentiality. Bare life, being under constant surveillance, simply cannot do so.

If we read Agamben with (or against) Agamben, it appears that he at least implicitly recognizes the potential analytic trap that bare life represents, if not the circularity of his argument: we are all at risk of devolving into bare life, yet the body is already bare life. This position tells us very little about the human condition. Are we to ascertain that we lack any control over our bodies and our destinies and that being human is purely a product of sovereign determination or the machinations of power wherever exercised? The "whatever being" concept, by retreating from the totalizing nature of bare life, suggests that we do possess varying degrees of control over our lives—so much so that the possibilities of democratic politics inheres in the performances of "whatever being." Here we find congruity with Arendt's treatment of the pariah.

Max Weber adapted the Portuguese term *paria*, which had been used to refer to the so-called untouchables in India, and applied it to Jews in Europe. For Weber, the term *pariah* signified a "'guest . . . ritually separated, formally or *de facto*, from [his or her] surroundings'" (Weber quoted in Momigliano 1980, 314).[16] Arendt arguably advanced the term, making it more prominent, in her 1957 biography of Rahel Varnhagen, who, otherwise devoid of many rights and excluded and shunned by society as a Jewess, presided over one of the most celebrated and popular Berlin salons in the late eighteenth and early nineteenth centuries.[17] If the parvenu (the upstart or social climber) "seeks an assimilation that can never be complete, . . . the self-conscious pariah affirms her minority identity and the social exile it costs her" (Moruzzi 2000, 56). If the pariah elects not to erase the fate of difference and thus to affirm an authenticity of self and experience, the parvenu consciously shuns a likely fate of exclusion through assimilation—which is really done by denying oneself. The parvenu was the Jew who converted to Christianity, married into acceptable society, and shunned association with other Jews—all in an effort to escape the perfidy of Jewishness. The parvenu was emphatically not a sycophant: Arendt reminds us that "[n]ineteenth century Jews, if they wanted to play a part in society, had no choice but to become parvenus," that "belonging, in fact, was promised precisely to [the Jew] who had 'annihilated' himself as a 'sensuous individual,' in his sensuous specificity, with a particular origin and a particular situation in the world" ([1957] 1997, 238, 183). Belonging was synonymous with self-abnegation.

Rahel Varnhagen, though she tried to annihilate herself, carved out an alternative space. In and through her salon, through acting the part of "whatever being" (or self-affirmational singularity), Rahel not only grasped her Jewishness but helped constitute (and understand) herself. Rahel's salon—attended by elite Berlin society, including prominent princes, politicians, diplomats, Junkers, aristocrats, businessmen, and intelligentsia, many of whom were, publicly, ardent anti-Semites (Arendt [1957] 1997, 126)—proved the vehicle for Rahel to extricate herself from the pariah/parvenu dichotomy and hence from the confines of the bare life that poorer and Orthodox Jews of the time were relegated to live. Anti-Semites could commingle with Jews in the salon, where "each person was worth neither more nor less than he himself was able to validate by his cultivated personality" (Arendt [1957] 1997, 126); put colloquially, one temporarily abandoned one's social identities at the door and, in the space of the salon, exhibited, performed, and created oneself as an individual in a kind of second birth.

The Jewish salon was an avowedly unique social institution. As Arendt notes, it provided "a social area outside of society," and "Rahel's garret room in its turn stood outside the conventions and customs of even the Jewish salon." Arendt further explains,

> The Jewish salon . . . was the product of a chance constellation in an era of social transition. The Jews became stop-gaps between a declining and an as yet unstabilized social group: the nobility and the actors; both stood outside of bourgeois society—like the Jews—and both were accustomed to playing a part, to represent something, to expressing themselves, to displaying "what they were" rather than "showing what they had"; in the Jewish houses of middle class intellectuals they found solid ground and an echo which they could not hope to find anywhere else . . . [P]recisely because the Jews stood outside of society they became, for a short time, a kind of neutral zone where people of culture met. (Arendt [1957] 1997, 127)

Neither fully private nor fully public, the salon might be described as a nonspace: liberated from the confines of the private and divorced from society's impositions, prejudices, and conventions, it was thus located somewhere in between. The nonspace provides a stage, a geography, to explore the potentialities of human *being*. Didier Fassin (2010, 85–86) lyrically captures Arendt's framing of the larger issue.

> On the one hand, life, "limited by a beginning and an end, follows a strictly linear movement whose very motion nevertheless is driven by the motor of biological life which man shares with other living beings and which forever retains the cyclical movement of nature." On the other hand, life, "specifically human, is itself full of events which ultimately can be told as a story, establish a biography." Referring to Aristotle . . . [Arendt] therefore opposes "this life, *bios*," with "mere *zoē*," history and language establishing what is the human proper. Within

a few short years, Arendt thus proposes two quite distinct readings of life. The premises are identical: life as a natural phenomenon is differentiated from life as a historical phenomenon; biology is contrasted to biography. However, the relation between the two is, in one case, conflictual and tragic; in the other, it is harmonious and reconciled.

It is worth emphasizing that the body, in both biology and biography, remains the medium of the performance we call living. It is both object and subject; it is enacted and acted on. While life "as a kind of praxis" (Arendt 1958, 97) may be more encumbered in some respects than others (think here of Aristotle's account of the slave), those ensnared may occasionally find opportunities for expression, performance, and self-creation. So while Rahel was, by virtue of the society in which she lived, imprisoned by the shackles of her female Jewish body, she eventually utilized that which others found abject, which she reconstituted as a vehicle for temporary liberation.

Arendt may have read the transgressive, emancipatory example of Rahel's life too liberally, for she found "humanity in the form of fraternity" among "historically persecuted peoples and enslaved groups" (1968b, 13). She hypothesized that the worldlessness (the "barbarism," as she likewise called it) resulting from being expunged from this world compelled the persecuted to move so closely together

> that the interspace which we have called the world . . . has simply disappeared. This produces a warmth of human relationships which may strike those who have had some experience with such groups as an almost physical phenomenon . . . In its full development it can breed a kindliness and sheer goodness . . . [I]t is also the source of a vitality, a joy in the simple fact of being alive, rather suggesting that life comes fully into its own only among those who are, in worldly terms, the insulted and injured. But in saying this we must not forget that the charm and intensity of the atmosphere that develops is also due to the fact that the pariahs of this world enjoy the great privilege of being unburdened by care for the world. (13–14)

And this is precisely because they have been expelled by it. To describe the pariah as possessed of a "great privilege" seems aberrant, if not repugnant. Since the passage from which this quotation is extracted concerns the plight of European Jewry, we can (or must) imagine that Arendt thought of the shtetl and salon, not the camp. The persecuted, having been victimized by the dehumanizing trap of identity, have no such privileges; the world happens to them in ways not of their choosing, thus making a mockery of the claim. Yet there is something trenchant in her observation: that a responsibility to others, or what she called "positive solidarity," may develop "in dark times" (13)—that is, when the spectacle or experience of suffering overwhelm all other possibilities of living life,[18] when *bios* proves fleeting against the compulsive demands of *zoë*'s stark nakedness.

### Positive Solidarity, Institutions, and the Making of Human Beings

Making and being fully human require conditions of publicity. By "public," Arendt meant two things: appearance and the world itself (1958, 50–52): "Appearance—something that is being seen and heard by others as well as by ourselves—constitutes reality . . . The presence of others who see what we see and hear what we hear assures us of the reality of the world and ourselves" (50). The preceding claim underlines Arendt's vision of politics that rests on the socially embedded and active individual,[19] not the atomic isolate. Mere appearance is but one aspect of publicity; interpretations of what is seen and heard likewise constitute reality. The salon and the shtetl, the prison and the camp, may provide instances or spaces for (limited) forms of self-expression, which may enhance the pariah's sense of self and dignity. But neither self-creative and affirmative performances in nonspaces nor resistances to sovereign traps guarantee a public acceptance that is presupposed by Arendt's conception of the human as a speaking and acting being (176). Nonspaces do not share in a common world in an Arendtian sense, precisely because they are defined by their bracketing out from such a world.

Consequently, Arendt's emphasis on the word and the deed—which, in her conception of natality, signify a second birth—demands clarification. Human beings are born into this world in a base biological sense and thus appear as entirely new organisms or beings. That is natality's first, physiological dimension. The second, performative dimension concerns how we "insert ourselves into the human world . . . [or how] we confirm and take upon ourselves the naked fact of our original physical appearance." Though speech and action are the modes in which we appear to each other "not as physical objects" but as individualized human beings, the fact remains that even slaves could speak and act; such did not guarantee their human status—a fact Arendt acknowledges in a damning judgment of slavery as constituting the "primordial crime upon which the fabric of American society rested" (1963b, 71). Put differently, the productive potential of self-performative and creative acts is limited by the very social structures within which we exist;

we come to *Be* not only through speech and action but, ultimately, through our acceptance by and inclusion within, not bracketing out from, public life. We therefore need to stretch Arendt's conception of natality to include a third dimension: an intersubjectivity embracing not merely recognition and acceptance of the other but a range of mechanisms, techniques, processes, practices, and activities that constitute the meaning and status of the human being and, with it, humanity as a whole.

In Arendt's view, the very notion of humankind

> owes its existence not to the dreams of the humanists nor to the reasoning of the philosophers and not even, at least primarily, to political events, but almost exclusively to the technical development of the Western world . . . Technology, having provided the unity of the world, can just as easily destroy it[;] the means of global communication were designed side by side with means of possible global destruction. It is difficult to deny at this moment the most potent symbol of the unity of mankind is the remote possibility that atomic weapons used by one country according to the political wisdom of a few might ultimately come to be the end of all human life on earth. The solidarity of [hu]mankind . . . is entirely negative; it rests, not only on a common interest in an agreement which prohibits the use of atomic weapons, but, perhaps also . . . on a common desire for a world that is a little less unified. This negative solidarity, based on the fear of global destruction, has its correspondence in a less articulate, but no less potent, apprehension that the solidarity of mankind can be meaningful in a positive sense *only if* it is coupled with political responsibility. (1968a, 82–83; emphasis added)

Here we have the rudiments of a cosmopolitan politics. But if traceable to technologies that facilitate transborder linkages of peoples, humanity would conceptually and practically be fragmented, contingent on and determined by access to technology. If traceable to the means of mass destruction, to which we might append terrorism, environmental catastrophe, genocide and ethnic cleansing, extreme poverty, endemic disease, and malnutrition (for superb treatment on several of these issues, see Hayden 2009), humankind appears to be nothing but an inadvertent effect. As residue, humankind lacks capacity to self-define; it is merely one object among others defined primarily by its capacity to be annihilated in toto.

However, negative solidarity may stimulate forms of political responsibility that would necessarily grant the notion of humankind a substance it otherwise lacks. But while fear of endangerment or mass destruction might engender an imperative to counter the sources of our potential annihilation, there is nothing inevitable about the translation of negative solidarity into positive solidarity, partly because, as Arendt mused, responsibility might prove to be an "intolerable situation" (1968a, 83). Where, one might ask, do my responsibilities to myself end and my responsibilities to others begin? How far do my responsibilities to these others extend?[20]

Answers to these kinds of questions are contextual. Positive solidarity (responsibility) emerges as conscious, though not always planned, reactions to the unpredictability and precariousness of human existence that are shaped by circumstance and volition. Arendt locates one example in the aftermath of World War II: while the Allied powers could have simply executed or accepted the surrender of former Nazi officials, the Americans insisted on criminal prosecution, which I explore in chapter 5. The decision was seismic: the willingness to abandon practices historically associated with the end of war rested on a new understanding of the human condition. The scale of Nazi crimes shattered all pretense to tradition, culture, and civilization; these crimes made us painfully aware that "the claim to global rule" pursued in the name of humanity[21] transformed it from "a beautiful dream of unity or a dreadful nightmare of strangeness" into "a hard inescapable reality" (Arendt 1951, 434). Yet if the Nazi regime restricted the status of human and, as Arendt would maintain, stripped it of meaning, Allied powers reappropriated and breathed new life into it. Telford Taylor, counsel for the prosecution at Nuremberg, reasoned that

> criminal proceedings rest on laws whose "essence" . . . "is that a crime is not committed only against the victim but primarily against the community whose law is violated." The wrongdoer is brought to justice because his act has disturbed and gravely endangered the community as a whole . . . The reparation effected . . . is of an altogether different nature; it is the body politic itself that stands in need of being "repaired," and it is the general public order that has been thrown out of gear and must be restored. (Taylor paraphrased in Arendt 1963a, 261)[22]

This view ascribes great importance to the notion of humanity as "one political entity" (Arendt 1951, 436), since a "crime against humanity" violates "'the human status' or . . . the very nature of mankind"; it is an attack "upon human diversity . . . without which the very words 'mankind' or 'humanity' would be devoid of meaning" (Arendt 1963a, 268–69). Hence Nuremberg marked a decisive turning point in international law, as it transcended the state-centrism of international relations (Arendt 1951, 436). First, it gave practical effect to what was hitherto a figment of the conceptual imagination. Law made human by recognizing the status claims of dehumanized (and exterminated) others and delineating boundaries of permissible behavior. Might no longer made right, theoretically at least. Second, enactment of the law, Arendt recognized, owed not necessarily to the states that concluded the agreements to create the tribunals but to their participants, that is, the trial judges and prosecutors who "render[ed] justice without the help of, or beyond the limitation set upon them through positive, posited laws" (1963a, 274). Interpreted uncharitably, the point ascribes to judges a legislative role, however much the judges in *Eichmann* or any of the Nuremberg successor trials resisted the characterization (274). A more sympathetic, and ultimately cosmopolitan, interpretation coheres with Arendt's political thought: law, whether municipal or international, must "be seen by a self-governing people to be 'its' law and not be imposed upon it by other instances" (Benhabib 2010, 243). Here judges and prosecutors acted as cosmopolitan agents who nurtured into adolescence a law of and for humanity by taking seriously the law as written (Meron 2000a; Teitel 2011).

The danger as Arendt saw it was to (re)nationalize such crimes—exactly for which she impugns the Israeli court in the Adolf Eichmann case.[23] Gideon Hausner, the chief prosecutor, interpreted the charges against Eichmann in national, not cosmopolitan, terms—that is, as crimes against the Jewish people, not as crimes against *humanity* (Arendt 1963a, 254, echoed at 257 and 261). Insofar as the victims were Jews, Arendt concurred that "it was right and proper that a Jewish court should sit in judgment" of Eichmann (269). But by reading the crimes in terms of a history of anti-Semitism, as if the Holocaust were the latest and most extreme pogrom conducted against the Jews, the court missed the fundamental import of what had happened: "only the choice of victims," she wrote, "could be derived from the long history of Jew-hatred and anti-Semitism." Therein lies a third novelty of Nuremberg: the real nature of the crime was universal, for the deportations and exterminations violated and attempted to eradicate what Arendt refers to as "the space between individuals" and hence to destroy publicity itself (262). Conceptually, the crime targeted human diversity; it could not simply be read in narrow terms as an attack on Jews, Poles, Slavs, Roma, homosexuals, and the physically and mentally handicapped. The crime aimed toward the creation of "One World" stripped of the natural condition of plurality (Arendt 1973, 297). Following, it seems, Karl Jaspers, Arendt argued that only an international tribunal could appropriately try Eichmann, because only it could adequately represent the wronged, that is, humanity itself (1963a, 269).

This constitutive role of international law echoes, in some important respects, Arendt's account of the development of law in ancient Greece and Rome. In the Greek case, *nomos* (law) constituted the political through circumscription of membership in the polis; the polis was defined as much by its exclusion of women, slaves, propertyless men, and non-Greeks as by its literary, philosophical, and architectural achievements. As such, not only did Greek law reject the natural condition of plurality (diversity) among human beings, but it radically curtailed the notion of human by erecting boundaries between various types of people. Analogous to city walls, law, too, bound the polis; resulting space—between poleis, between the Greek and the non-Greek world, between citizen and noncitizen—became essentially a no-man's-land, a land of violence and war. This in-between space marked precisely the *end* of politics, for it could be tamed neither by prepolitical or legislative activity nor by amity, since the Greek agonal spirit dictated that heroism and bravery be translated into competition. Competition was proof of one's existence.[24]

The Romans took a more expansive view. If law in the Greek world separated, law in the Roman world constituted and formalized relationships between peoples by binding them together in mutual recognition through mutual agreement, in community though not necessarily in communion (Arendt 2005, 179). Roman law emerged from

> a contract between two warring factions, the patricians and the plebes, that required the approval of the entire populace . . . Significant for the contractual nature of the law is the way this basic law . . . [did] not unite the quarreling parties simply by erasing the distinction between patricians and plebes. The opposite was the case: the explicit prohibition—though later rescinded—of marriage between patricians and plebes emphasized their separation even more explicitly than before. Only the state of hostility between them was set aside . . . The *res publica*, the life of public affairs, which arose out of this contract and evolved into the Roman Republic, was located in that in-between space between formerly hostile partners . . . And just as such an agreement can come about only when the interests of both sides are recognized, this basic Roman law is likewise a matter of "creating a common law that takes both parties into account." (179–80)

Like Nuremberg, Roman law constituted specific actors as it constituted a public space that, subsequently, became a public interest. *Interests*, or *inter-*

*ests*, meaning "something which lies between peoples and therefore can relate and bind them together," is specifically the hallmark of a common world that evidences an existing "web" of human relationships (Arendt 1958, 182–83).

This space was not limited to Roman society. Roman law and Roman imperial expansion *acknowledged* others and, in this way, was able, in contradistinction to the Greeks, to join and unite their colonies "in a permanent alliance" (Arendt 2005, 187). There is danger in overstating the case, however. As Owens (2007, 79) points out, the relationship was not one of equality; rather, a relationship between empire and subject was fashioned out of a choice between submission and destruction. Still, the surrendered "could retain their life, [while] the Romans, in Arendt's words, 'gained . . . a new political arena, secured in a peace treaty according to which yesterday's enemies became tomorrow's allies.'" If Greek political space ossified through self-policing its boundaries for the purpose of promoting political flourishing within the polis, Roman political space sought rejuvenation through geographic and conceptual expansion; human beings of disparate sorts could be mobilized vis-à-vis the cause of Roman imperial expansion precisely because law recognized them and gave them some space to *Be*.

Juxtaposition of, on one hand, the Nuremberg legacy that defined humanity and, on the other, the development of law in the Greek and Roman contexts reveals that while reflection on the status of being human may instigate the transformation from *zōe* to *bios* and while acts of resistance fuel the process, ascription of status in and by the law proves salient in making human. Indeed, intersubjective recognition compelled Arendt to conceive of politics as "a global dominion in which people appear primarily as active agents who lend human affairs a permanence they otherwise do not have" (2005, 97). Yet this global dominion is not the universal analogue of the Greek agora or Roman Republic from which many of Arendt's ideas spring—and thus it should not be read as an argument for a singular world state. She granted primacy to the principles behind the agora, not to the institutional frameworks that embody them or within which they may be embedded. Foundational for her are plurality, agency, recognition, freedom, equality of status and access, "the right to contribute to debate, discussion, and decision, [and] the opportunity to place oneself into the public realm—to appear as a political individual" (Williams 2005a, 201; Arendt 1958, 186–207). Ironically, then, in contradistinction to those who criticize her for idealizing a particular (Greco-Roman) narrative of the state, Arendt actually "moves away from the state as the principal political actor that is characteristic of so much of International Relations theorizing. It is the socially conditioned and located individual who is the focus of politics and the essential political agent" (Lang and Williams 2005, 5). While the state remains "vitally important" insofar as it is "a necessary condition for the fulfillment of human agency," the very potential of "its perversion into the nemesis of a proper human life" means, for Arendt, that the emphasis of politics must be placed squarely on the human being.

But sometimes one must fight for recognition—rarely is it automatic—whether that struggle is verbal or physical; and in those acts of contestation, dialogue, and concerted action, Arendt came to understand politics as an infinitely creative activity spawned by the myriad of novel ways, self-reflective and not, in which people (re)present and (re)produce themselves. She found the revolutionary council systems instructive, which also strongly suggests that we need to stretch and enrich her concept of natality.

> Since the revolutions of the eighteenth century, every large upheaval has actually developed the rudiments of an entirely new form of government, which emerged independent of all preceding revolutionary theories, directly out of the course of the revolution itself, that is, out of the experiences of action and out of the resulting will of the actors to participate in the further development of public affairs. This new form of government is the council system, which as we know, has perished every time and everywhere, destroyed either directly by the bureaucracy of the nation-states or by the party machines . . . Spontaneous organization of council systems occurred in all revolutions, in the French Revolution, with Jefferson in the American Revolution, in the Parisian commune, in the Russian revolutions, in the wake of the revolutions in Germany and Austria at the end of World War I, finally in the Hungarian Revolution. What is more, they never came into being as a result of a conscious revolutionary tradition or theory, but entirely spontaneously, each time as though there had never been anything of the sort before . . . [T]he council system seems to correspond to and spring from the very experience of political action. (Arendt 1972, 231–32)

Felicitously, the councils signaled, in Arendt's view, a search for freedom *into* politics, not freedom *from* politics (1963b, 13–52, 217–81; 1972, 231–32). As Thomas Jefferson described the councils, citizens could "continue to do what they had been able to do during the years of revolution, namely, to act on their own and thus to participate in public business as it was being transacted from day to day" (Jefferson paraphrased in Arendt 1963b, 251). Hence "the ward system was not meant to strengthen the power of the many but the power of 'every one' within the limits of his competence; and only by breaking up 'the many' into assemblies where everyone could count and be counted upon 'shall we be as republican as a large society can be'" (254).

Arendt drew two important conclusions from the council experience. First, the councils illustrated the constitutive power of selves acting in concert and hence exhibited natality's second, performative dimension. As such, they deeply implicated the third dimension of natality: an intersubjectivity that makes human by admitting multiple perspectives into political life that are otherwise excluded, defines the parameters of human being, and stretches the bounds of willingness to share the world with others. But the councils were either violently eliminated or eclipsed by emergent, institutionalized systems of rule. Thus we must take what is salient about the councils—the possibility for renewal—and embed them in our systems of government and publics if they are to flourish. Bonnie Honig draws on Arendt's reading of the American Declaration of Independence (Arendt 1963b, 192–203), which comprises all of the "basic elements" of her vision of politics.

> The Declaration is a political act, an act of power, because it founds a new set of institutions and constitutes a new political community . . . Focusing on the famous phrase, "We hold these truths to be self-evident," Arendt argues that the new regime's power, and ultimately its authority, derive from the performative "we hold" and not from the constative reference to self-evident truths. Both dramatic and nonreferential, the performative brings a new political community into being; it *constitutes* a "we" . . . In contrast to the performative "we hold," the constative reference to self-evident truths expresses not a free coming together but an isolated acquiescence to compulsion and necessity . . . Constatives are "irresistible"; they "are not held by us, but we are held by them" . . . On Arendt's account the real source of the authority of the newly founded republic was the performative not the constative moment . . . And the real source of authority in the new republic, henceforth, would be the style of its maintenance, its openness to refounding and reconstitution. (Honig 1992, 216–17)[25]

Both the specific historical experience of the council system and the necessity of renewal in political life suggested to Arendt a second insight: the need for "a new concept of the state" in which power "is horizontally directed so that the federal units mutually check and control their powers" (1972, 230). In this "council-state . . . the principle of sovereignty would wholly be alien . . . [since] power would be constituted horizontally and not vertically" (233; for a similar scheme, see Kuper 2006). Consequently, Arendt tantalizingly suggests a reformulation of international relations that is not "*super-national*" in orientation, since we do not need a "new international court that would function better than the one at The Hague, or a new League of Nations, since the same conflicts between sovereign or ostensibly sovereign governments can only be played out there all over again—on the level of discourse, to be sure, which is more important than is usually thought" (1972, 230). Rather, Arendt explains, the system is cosmopolitan and transnational: "This new form of government is the council system . . . which begins from below, continues upward, and finally leads to a parliament."[26]

The preceding remarks, from a 1970 interview, fail to elaborate in a way that would help us "reconstruct the idea of humanity" (Fine 2007, 114). Indeed, Arendt retreats to the terrain of domestic politics without further regard to the international implications of the councils that she hears as saying, "[W]e want to participate, we want to debate, we want to make our voices heard in public, and we want to have a possibility to determine [our political futures]" (Arendt 1972, 232). But the council systems, both in their specific, revolutionary incarnations and, in a broader sense, as localized forms of political action, accentuate the failure of political systems to recognize and incorporate our human capacities and ways of being. Demands for inclusion, which affirm the central importance of speech and action in public, simultaneously suggest that hinging natality on speech and action are ultimately insufficient to ensure that which our second birth presumably implies: our status as coconstructors of our intertwined political fates.


## Conclusion

Diogenes challenged the self-image of the traditional Greek male, bound as he was to particularities of place. When asked from whence he originated, Diogenes replied, "I am a citizen of the world." If the Cynics introduced the notion of the *kosmou politês* (world citizen), the Romans Seneca and Plutarch ascribed to it a gravitas that would later prove the cornerstone of Kantian ethics: "[W]e should regard all human beings as our fellow citizens and neighbors," Plutarch exhorted; our moral duties arise from the community of humankind (Nussbaum 2002, 7).

Cosmopolitanism's moral aspirationalism may attract some, but in practice, most people remain wed to particularities of identity and space. Even if we abstractly regard all others as fellow citizens and neighbors, we simply may dislike subsets of them. We may abhor their behaviors and personalities and come to loathe their presence. We may generalize based on a small sampling and come to anathematize collectives for perceived abnormalities and degrade their status or enjoin their membership or rights demands. Even if we apprehend others as fellow (planetary) citizens and neighbors, there is no guarantee that we will also apprehend any corresponding, meaningful conception of a shared "world." These multiple others who confront us might simply appear as occupants of proximate and distant territories on a map: citizens, too, but of different polities; inhabitants of a singular earth, yet denizens of disparate worlds whose very practices and predispositions reveal that they are neighbors only by dint of geography—and humans of a vastly different sort. We may share a planet, but we do not share identities. Indeed, their identities may be an affront to "us."

By beginning with the dystopic truth that human being is a socially conferred status that admits of degrees, Gong, Wight, and Arendt were able to grapple not just with a fundamental question—"What are 'we' to do with 'them'?"—but also with its corollary, "How are 'they' to be integrated with 'us'?" Encounters between Europeans and non-Europeans eventually produced a standard of "civilization" that dictated the manner by which the latter could gain entry into international society.[27] While the instruments of material power mattered in the imperial scheme, such instruments derived real strength from underlying norms and perceptions;[28] in this regard, international society began to take shape through an ongoing assessment of what it meant to be human. Rarely, as Wight explored, did social relations automatically presuppose good neighborliness or conceptions of common humanity.

Arendt's observations were more diverse and scattered, though her sharpest points appear in *The Origins of Totalitarianism*. Etiologically, the superimposition on the globe of imperial boundaries that left "'no uncivilized' spot[s] on earth" (Arendt 1973, 297), the experiences of expulsion and marginalization, and the fabrication of the technological means to annihilate humankind adduced that we lived in "One World" (299). Practically "only with a complete organized humanity could the loss of home and political status become identical with expulsion from humanity altogether" (297);[29] treatment of the stateless and hence rightless proved the truth of Arendt's assertion. Because doctrines of minority and human rights could not, in reality, protect those stripped of citizenship, Arendt reduced the most fundamental human right—that is, "a right to have rights"—into an even more primordial right: the "right to belong to some kind of organized community" (296–97), which is to say, "a right to the human condition itself" (1951, 439).

The problem created by this "new global political situation" was therefore not merely geopolitical but humanitarian, for denial of membership in and expulsion from the "One World" was equable with loss of *human* status.[30] If the problem was universal, so was the response: articulation of shared, common responsibilities,[31] which Arendt viewed as clearly illustrated by the correspondence between "the one crime against humanity [expulsion]" and "the one human right [belonging]" (1951, 437). For her, the equation encapsulated the notion of human dignity, to which I now turn.

## CHAPTER 2

# Human Dignity as Status in Community

The final issue is what dignity we are willing to give to man.

—Dag Hammarskjöld[1]

For respect for human dignity implies the recognition of my fellow-men or our fellow-nationals as subjects, as builders of worlds or cobuilders of a common world.

—Hannah Arendt[2]

In the Arendtian schematic, dignity connotes membership in political community and hence status as human. This connotation makes no claims about capacity or competence to contribute to or act in community but, rather, underscores the intersubjectivity on which dignity depends as a conceptual and practical condition. Interestingly, Arendt's first assessment of dignity was not generous: expulsion and extermination led her to conclude that dignity was "the last and possibly most arrogant myth we have invented" (1951, 439). She had a point. Practices repeatedly undermined (nay, mocked) assertions of the inviolability and dignity of human beings. Tellingly, she corrected herself. Successive editions of *The Origins of Totalitarianism* excised the line, and we find in its place an insistence that human dignity "needs a new guarantee which can be found only in a new political principle, in a new law on earth, whose validity this time must comprehend the whole of humanity" (1973, ix). Cause for the shift may be ascertained in her reflections on human rights, for even with the loss of such rights, individuals may retain their "essential quality as [hu]man, [their] human dignity. Only the loss of a polity itself expels [them] from humanity" (297).

The extremity of Arendt's position stems directly from the extermination camps.

> If a human being loses his political status, he should, according to the implications of the inborn and inalienable rights of man, come under exactly the situation for which the declaration of such general rights provided. Actually the opposite is the case. It seems that a man who is nothing but a man has lost the very qualities which make it possible for other people to treat him as a fellow-man. (300)

Thus the problem does not perforce inhere with dignity; rather, it relates to how we think about dignity. It is not immutable or natural. Dignity connotes a social status—not merely as a member of some political community, but as a human being (*bios*). Remedying and clarifying dignitary claims is work often born within and by law (see McCrudden 2008; Waldron 2012a, 2012b; Daly 2013). In this vein, Drucilla Cornell (2010, 223) argues that the political principle about which Arendt wrote to guarantee dignity is grounded in both freedom, which coheres with Arendt's thinking, and equality, which Arendt actually resisted.[3] Using the South African Constitution to develop her argument, Cornell asserts that "it is dignity as it actually functions in the state's regulation of social life in the name of equality [against apartheid, discrimination, and segregation] that is also used to stand against totalitarianism and the violation of individual freedom" (225). Jeremy Waldron (2012a, 48) echoes the point: according to the South African Constitutional Court, "the history of the country demonstrates that discrimination 'proceeds on [an] assumption that the disfavored group is inferior to other groups. And this is an assault on the human dignity of the disfavoured group.'"

To counter dehumanization, Arendt envisioned a polity clearly cosmopolitan in orientation that admitted one key human right as its "prepolitical foundation" or the basis of its new legal structure (1951, 439): "the right to belong to some kind of organized community" (1973, 297), meaning "a right to the human condition itself" (1951, 439). We may infer by her occasional use of the term *humanitas* that this polity was not a state as we currently know it—though it could temporarily take such form. The very phrase "crime against *humanity*" indicated what Arendt had in mind. Though she never explicitly defined *humanitas*, Michael Gottsegen deduces it to mean "a *willingness* to share the world with one's fellow citizens," the nature of which is communicative (1994, 58; see 58–62).[4] He continues, "[W]e share the world, and indeed constitute it as a world (as 'reality'), by talking about it with one another. By talking about it we humanize it and ourselves." In an obvious Arendtian vein, Gottsegen associates willingness with the normative vocabulary of positive solidarity, mutual respect, dialogue, forgiveness, promise making, tact, self-censorship and consideration of others, since they signify an intention "to participate in the process of mutual manifestation" (61). But willingness—to share this world with others, to recognize them as coarchitects, to see and treat them as fully human—is conditional; this is why we need an account of making human. Belonging can only be the starting point of dignity.

This chapter develops an understanding of dignity on which to rest the empirical work of chapters 3–6. It does not offer a comprehensive philosophical, theoretical, or legal exegesis on the meaning of dignity; recent exemplary works on dignity include those by Smith (2010, 434–90), Kateb (2011), Waldron (2012a), and Daly (2013). Coincident with much of this scholarship, I treat dignity as a social construct (see Waldron 2012a, 61); as such, it is existential (Kateb 2011, 10) and contextually rooted. Yet contextuality does not entail infinite elasticity, subject to idiosyncratic, malleable judicial interpretation (on this point, see McCrudden 2008). As Erin Daly (2013, 5) has cogently argued (against McCrudden), despite a diversity of constitutional and juridical deployments of dignity that bathe the term in ambiguity, distinctive patterns of meaning are discernible. Our understandings of dignity layer over time and become deeply imbricated in our practices; this permits a more comprehensive and stabilized, if never quite settled, definition of dignity. Because of this sedimentary layering effect, it is not enough to say that dignity is *X*—as in, dignity means the inherent worth of the human person—and be done with it, at least empirically speaking. For instance, societies may decide that prohibiting same-sex marriage does not affront or undermine the dignity of homosexuals precisely because the prohibition affirms prevailing morals and upholds the dignity of a community. But over time, coincident with reflection on the moral worth of others and their life projects, recognition of their individuality and their networks of relations that give life meaning, and evolved understandings of what constitutes oppression and marginalization, societies may revise their positions. Dignity is a valuable social currency whose trade fortunately or unfortunately hinges on, as Dag Hammarskjöld intuited, what dignity we are willing to give each other.

In this chapter, I first outline key recent scholarship on dignity. In doing so, I extract elements that constitute a core conception of dignity. I then shift focus to the UN Charter, as the remainder of the book examines how human status and value, two of dignity's principal motifs, are accorded, defended, and developed by international bodies, with primary focus on the United Nations, its organs, and affiliated agencies. The purpose of such an examination is to illustrate how the Charter, often perceived as the blueprint of sovereign state-based postwar international relations, likewise established pillars to buttress a post-Holocaust humanitarian world order.

## Human Dignity

In 1996, Cynthia Enloe described as ambivalent the understanding that "most international relations analysts" had of human dignity's "relevance to their own intellectual enterprise." On the one hand, this is not surprising, since dignity hardly ranked among the portentous subjects of interstate relations during the Cold War; thus, in the discriminating analytical economy of "cause and effect," dignity was omitted from scholarly consideration (187–88). On the other hand, the silence surprises, for the language and logic of dignity soon proliferated in the postwar world. The Charter of the United Nations (1945) mentions dignity in its second preambular determination to "reaffirm faith in fundamental human rights, in the dignity and worth of the human person, in the equal rights of men and women and of nations large and small," thus situating dignity as a cornerstone of the architecture of post-Holocaust international relations. The Universal Declaration of Human Rights (1948) mentions dignity five times, including twice in the preamble as "the foundation of freedom, justice and peace in the world." The International Covenant on Civil and Political Rights (1966) and the International Convenant on Economic, Social, and Cultural Rights (1966) likewise accord dignity primary place among the hierarchy of rights, from which all human rights presumably derive. Regionally, the American, African, and Arab charters on human rights invoke dignity to ground their respective conceptions of human rights and, in certain instances, to underscore the gravity of specific actions such as slavery and the slave trade (per Article 5 of the Banjul Charter) and occupation and racism (per Article 2 of the Arab Charter).

Further, the constitutions of 142 countries (including Kosovo), two territories (the British Virgin Islands and the Cayman Islands), and the Commonwealth of Puerto Rico echo, in varying ways, the commitment to dignity.[5] At one extreme, dignity is treated as a first-order, foundational principle. The German Constitution, for instance, regards dignity as inviolable and situates the state's authority in the service of its protection (Article 1). The South African Constitution proclaims dignity a founding principle of a postapartheid politics and legal order, while the Constitution of Kosovo understands dignity to be the "basis of all human rights and fundamental freedoms" (Article 23).[6] At the other extreme, dignity appears as simply one right among rights: the Constitution of Iran guarantees dignity's inviolability "except in cases sanctioned by law" (Article 22)—which arguably may be vast given the state's broad discretionary powers. Considering that dignity only appeared in many of the world's constitutions post-1945, Erin Daly

(2013, 18) avers that the "greatest legacy" of the Universal Declaration of Human Rights is the "importation of the idea of human dignity into constitutional cultures around the world," which "has created a legal basis for protection against discrimination and degradation and has helped to ensure that all peoples have access to adequate education, food, medical care, and other basic necessities."

In 1982, Harold Jacobson celebrated dignity's near universality as adding up to "a historic consensus . . . on the meaning of human dignity and justice [in ways that affect] . . . the overarching goals of international and national policy and . . . the broad outlines of world order" (1982, 320).[7] Dag Hammarskjöld, second secretary-general of the United Nations, earlier articulated such a view. For him, the UN represented a unique opportunity to construct common responsibilities, or, in Arendtian language, forms of positive solidarity. He did not understand the "One World" as a construction by internationally like-minded people who viewed the UN "as a club" to which similarly minded people "will be admitted, in which membership is a privilege and expulsion is the retribution for wrong-doing." Likewise, he rejected its construction "by force of arms" (2005, 117).[8] Rather, as he submitted at Stanford University in 1955, the "One World" is effectuated through mutual recognition and reconciliation. Nationalism and internationalism are not mutually exclusive, he maintained, but mutually implicative recognitions of "the value and the rights of the nation, and of the dependence of the nation on the world" (2005, 139), as enunciated by the UN Charter (142) and the Universal Declaration of Human Rights (51).[9] Taking a more sober approach, however, he determined that world order and the stability of the Charter-based postwar international system boiled down to one central issue: "what dignity we are willing to give" to human beings.

Tellingly, none of the aforementioned documents actually defines dignity, and they too often conflate it with bodily protection, liberty, freedom, equality, and rights. Such evasions might suggest that dignity is a historical contingency, not a constant, subject to power relations and social processes. This is not to say that human dignity is solely determined and governed by forces external to the self, but it is to recognize that human dignity is significantly shaped by machinations of sociopolitical power and processes, whether locally, nationally, internationally, or transnationally (see Howard and Donnelly 1986). Tethering a conception of human dignity to power and social relations does not insinuate that dignity is infinitely elastic or entirely ambiguous, even if defining it succinctly and conclusively eludes us. To wit, there is something stable about notions of dignity insofar as they fundamentally imply living a life worthy of being lived (Weiss et al. 2010, 153).

Leszek Kolakowski (2002, 46) observes that "it is difficult to define what human dignity is. It is not an organ to be discovered in our body; it is not an empirical notion, but without it we would be unable to answer the simple question: what is wrong with slavery?"

Similarly, Oscar Schachter maintains that while international law lacks a definitive conception of human dignity—"its intrinsic meaning has been left to intuitive understanding, conditioned in large measure by cultural factors"—we may recognize when "a violation of human dignity" has occurred "even if the abstract term cannot be defined" (1983, 849). He lists five dignitary characteristics.[10] First, the dignity and worth of the human person have something to do with "a high priority . . . accorded in political, social and legal arrangements to individual choices in such matters as belief, way of life, attitudes and conduct in public affairs." Second, dignity demands that we abandon actions that do not humiliate or demean people (850). While humiliation may be predominantly subjective—each person has a different threshold of tolerance—context, scale, and the temporality of the effects of humiliation help us define that which objectively constitutes humiliation; international courts have sidestepped the subjective issue by hinging a violation of dignity on its social dimensions, such as ability to participate in social, political, and economic affairs or restrictions on freely selected employment, place of habitation, and the like (850). Third, human dignity connotes "proper regard for the responsibilities of individuals"; that "people are generally responsible for their conduct is a recognition of their distinct identity and their capacity to make choices." Fourth, dignity entails "recognition of a distinct personal identity, reflecting individual autonomy and responsibility," which must embrace "recognition that the individual self is a part of larger collectivities" (851). Finally, human dignity pays due regard to social and economic arrangements and hence "a minimal concept of distributive justice that would require satisfaction of the essential needs of everyone."[11]

While Schachter's conception of dignity may reflect, to substantial degree, the liberal "vision of life" of individuals living "as . . . equal and autonomous member[s] of society, enjoying a full range of human rights" (Howard and Donnelly 1986, 803), this does not mean that "a life worthy of being lived" is entirely subjective, individualistic, or atomistic or that such a life is fundamentally at odds with non-Western societies: while the act of living is often left to the self-determinative capacities of individuals, exogenous systems and structures, as well as our relations with others, influence and constrain. Nor does Schachter's view suggest that dignity demands uniformly specific socioeconomic and political arrangements. Communities must answer the many questions that Schachter's conceptualization raises. What kinds of social and economic arrangements best provide for or satisfy essential needs? To what degree might collectives impose restrictions on individual autonomy in order to advance collective welfare? How are objective benchmarks that define threshold conditions of degradation and humiliation determined, and who exactly determines them? While answering these kinds of questions is beyond the scope of this study, they suggest dignity to be a set of dispositions, techniques, and practices that operate emotively, psychologically, socially, politically, economically, and legally.

Kolakowski and Schachter's conceptions of dignity rest on two presuppositions. The first is that of the equability of human beings, no matter their particular identity claims. Here, they do not reduce dignity to worth. Dignity shoulders a different burden, or performs different work. Rather, dignity signifies a more primordial ontological equality meaning that there are no valid distinctions between peoples to be made on any grounds to denigrate them, regulate their private lives, persistently humiliate them, or deny access to institutions or mal-distribute resources. Put differently, all *Homo sapiens* are human, no matter their particular identities. Second, both presuppose that dignity entails equality of status as a member of political community which permits them a "'capacity to assert claims'" (Feinberg quoted in Waldron 2012a, 50). This entails two nonmutually exclusive conditions: that one is a member of a particular community in which claims can be made, and hence which have institutions or procedures to entertain such claims, and/or that there exist agents willing to assert claims on behalf of those whose dignity has been affronted. In Waldron's estimation, this capacity to assert claims or capacity to be endowed with dignity has resulted from a vast historical feat of social engineering in the form of equalization or "leveling out" of dignity (or rank) formerly accorded to nobility (33) that we still see today as women, indigenous peoples, children, and LGBT people, among others, are accorded rights and status, and hence opportunities to realize their capacity to make claims.

Herbert Kelman captured both presuppositions and, in certain respects, anticipated Waldron's argument about dignity as status. Beginning with a Kantian idiom, Kelman understands dignity to refer "to the status of individuals as ends in themselves" (1977, 531), which he translates as acknowledgment of (personal) identity and membership in community.

> To accord a person identity is to perceive him as an individual, independent and distinguishable from others, capable of making choices, and entitled to live his own life on the basis of his own goals and val-

ues. To accord a person community is to perceive him—along with one's self—as part of an interconnected network of individuals who care for each other, who recognize each other's individuality, and who respect each other's rights. (531–32)

Developments in international criminal law (ICL), which I discuss in chapter 5, confirm the thesis. But one point bears mention. By recognizing, for instance, that the rape of Tutsi or Bosnian Muslim women not merely harmed their bodies and destabilized their psycho-emotional health and well-being, but engendered their stigmatization, humiliation, marginalization, and, too often, exclusion from their communities, ICL substantiates the understanding that dignity is a profound statement about one's status or standing in community and hence about one's ability to construct a life worthy (to that individual) of living.

Yet that dignity is both inward-directed and other-regarding, subjective and objective, makes it inherently slippery. Donna Hicks (2011) navigates between those poles to stabilize the concept. She begins with an observation based on her decades of experience as conflict mediator in Latin America, Cambodia, Northern Ireland, Sri Lanka, and sundry other places: "a violation of our dignity feels like a threat to our survival . . . Until we fully recognize and accept this aspect of what it means to be human . . . we will fall short in understanding conflict and what it takes to transform it to a more fruitful interaction" (12). Though it is not entirely clear—what constitutes a threat to our survival might turn on entirely subjective criteria—she nevertheless constructs a "dignity model" of conflict resolution centered on ten essential elements: acceptance of the identity of others; inclusion of others; safety, or "putting people at ease"; acknowledgment of others' concerns, feelings, and experiences; recognition, meaning the validation of others' "talents, hard work, thoughtfulness, and help"; fairness in the treatment of others; giving others the benefit of the doubt, which demands that we start from "the premise that others have good motives and are acting with integrity"; listening actively with intent to understand others; encouraging others to act independently "so that they feel in control of their lives"; and accountability for one's actions (25–26). Hicks's model, it should be noted, shares elements with a conception of making human: recognition of the individuality of the other; reflection on each individual's moral worth and positions; resisting one's impulses to dismiss others or view one's positions as superior; self-responsibility and exercising responsibility toward and for others; and, finally, reproducing certain basic, socially sanctioned behaviors (e.g., listening, treating others fairly). The point is to create an atmosphere of trust within which more difficult issues may be rationally and equably discussed.

Hicks's account is a praxal one, in the specific, sociological sense of the term, by which is meant "a routinized type of behavior which consists of several [interconnected] elements . . . [including] forms of bodily activities, forms of mental activities, 'things' and their use . . . [and] background knowledge" (Navari 2011, 621; see also Adler and Pouliot 2011). More pointedly, practices, according to Ted Schatzki, are constituted by practical understandings of how to do something; rules, which either explicitly or implicitly constitute activities and direct actors; and "teleoactivities," by which is meant coincidence between the goals associated with a practice and community attitudes toward it (Navari 2011, 617). Hicks's dignitary model of conflict resolution guides participant behaviors toward particular socially desirable objectives (e.g., conflict resolution, cooperation, postconflict reconciliation) that exemplify a willingness to recognize others as coarchitects (of peace) and share the world with them.

Gilbert Meilaender (2009) pushes the understanding of dignity as a set of practices by distinguishing between human and personal dignity—a differentiation continuing a tradition of thought that began with the 1486 appearance of Pico della Mirandola's *On the Dignity of Man* (see Kateb 2011, 3–10). For Meilaender, the distinction is revealed in our encounters with others as bodies. The moral task that arises from such encounters is "to recognize the person" inside the corporeal shell (Meilaender 2009, 103). In his view, the spectacle of bodies fosters an awareness of the human species as distinct from, to paraphrase his titular adage, beasts and gods; awareness and recognition, in turn, contribute to species "integrity and flourishing." Human dignity is but a "placeholder for what is thought to be characteristically human" (1), that is, not animal or divine (notwithstanding that certain species—e.g., elephants—have evolved modes of communication, social structures, and social practices). Hence we need a conception of "*personal* dignity . . . to make clear that, however different we may be in the degree to which we possess some of the characteristically human capacities, we are equal persons whose comparative 'worth' cannot and ought not be assessed."[12]

On this point, Meilaender is careful not to hang either personal or human dignity on the hook of individuality or uniqueness, since that move automatically renders suspect prosaic—that is, nonunique—characteristics of our selves. More troublingly, emphasizing our uniqueness or particularity forces us into assessments of comparative worth, "because our life is marked by [varying degrees of human] characteristic powers and capacities" (6). "Just as some of us flourish," he writes, "displaying humanity at its fullest and best, others of us have, at most, a kind of basic humanity that falls far short of the full development of human possibilities—'an anthropological minor league.'" By alternatively attaching personal dignity to equal moral status, personal dignity is supposed to shoulder the burden of and perhaps compensate for the problems associated with human dignity. Under the rubric of human dignity, our claims rest not only on the grounds that we are members of a particular species but on our ability to develop and deploy the aspects that distinguish our species from others—which has the unfortunate, concomitant effect of denigrating those species (6–8).[13] To offset the implication that some members of the species are more *human* than others, Meilaender maintains that, under a conception of personal dignity, our claims rest on our inherent and hence incomparable worth and less on our ability "to be someone" (102).

Yet our actions reveal that personal dignity does not shoulder its burden well. We assess the comparative worth of persons every day in ways that minimize the importance of moral equality. In a morally superficial sense, we attach worth to individual human beings based on our needs at any given time. For instance, a car mechanic possesses more (functionally determined) worth to us than our neighborhood handyman who has but rudimentary skills in car repair. Yet, in a worldwide neoliberal market economy, instrumental assessments based on productive power, capability, and task might render certain peoples and communities—say, female Bangladeshi garment workers—irrelevant or marginal precisely because they are perceived as replaceable. If we enlarge and institutionalize comparative assessment of worth, we begin to tread on uncomfortable, if not morally questionable, terrain. The 9/11 Victim Compensation Fund ascribed differing degrees of (monetary) worth and value to the victims of the terrorist attacks based on a complex calculus that accounted for collateral offsets, pensions, retirement funds, life insurance policies, dependents, wages earned, and potential future wages as determined by education and professional experience. Compensation packages ranged between $250,000 and $7.1 million (Rabin and Sugarman 2007, 909).[14] Individuals without dependents received less than those with them—which might be read as punitive or discriminatory toward those who were too young or not yet prepared to have children or spouses, decided not to have children, or could not conceive. Likewise, custodial staff received less than corporate executives and bond traders. While many readers might consider the 9/11 compensatory scheme reasonable (after all, the fund was akin to a life insurance policy, which is but a self-assignation of monetary worth and value of ourselves and our loved ones), we nevertheless might locate a parallel in the 1975–79 Khmer Rouge genocide: the regime exterminated those affiliated with professions (and practices) deemed too modern or Western (Quinn 1989). More abhorrently, we might also think of the internment of American *citizens* of Japanese descent whose worth to society was deemed too insignificant to prevent their internment; of Jim Crow laws in the American South ensuring that, despite constitutionally mandated racial equality, blacks were not treated as full citizens, let alone accepted as fully human; or even of women who may perform the same work as men but earn less. Alternatively, think of instances (e.g., the Nazi regime) in which whole groups of people were deemed expendable precisely because of their discounted worth. Thus, while we prefer to think that we are, ultimately, equal persons whose comparative worth cannot and should not be morally assessed, the fact is that our worth and hence our value is, in many respects, continually recalculated.

We might therefore begin from a less aspirational position. Let us return to Waldron (2012a), who proposes that dignity be disentangled from worth, which is impossible to measure, and tethered to its other intellectual lineage, status, which, though once attached to persons occupying positions of high political and religious importance and those with economic and social power, has filtered down to all types of people and hence "leveled out." His position is sensitive to both social construction and the sedimentation of meaning over time. Yet, detached from objectivist moorings (whether divinity, natural law, or reason) and tied to status, dignity appears exposed to the vicissitudes of social life—a point not missed by Waldron's critics who prefer a more conceptually stable notion (see Waldron 2012a, 79–129).

The point is well taken. Yet preference for a stable, anchored, and potentially unchanging conception of dignity expresses an aspirational condition that is not necessarily factual. Our dystopic histories destabilize meanings we attribute to dignity—whether as the high ranking accorded to nobility, or the ontological equality of simply being human. Understandable are the need and desire to concretize dignity, but neither do these cohere with its (re)apportioning nor with its specific manifestations over time and space. We thus cannot define dignity *prior* to social relations but must locate its meaning *within* them. Tétreault and Lipschutz's (2009) conception of the social individual and Wayne Booth's framing of the self as "a society of selves" (1993, 89) follow this line of reasoning.[15] For Booth, the mutually constitutive relationship between self and society indicates that dignity is properly understood as our "freedom to pursue a story line, a life plot, a drama carved out of all the possibilities every society provides . . . The carving is done, both consciously and unconsciously, by a self that is social at birth and increasingly socialized, colonized in response to penetrations by other selves." We are, as Booth remarks, "a *kind* of society; a *field* of forces; a *colony*; a *chorus* of not necessarily harmonious voices; a manifold *project*; a *polyglossia* that is as much in us as in the world outside us." This understanding of the exogenous forces that contribute, consciously or unconsciously, to our making does not unilaterally elevate them above our own efforts toward self-realization. While we may be subject to various external influences, we retain some significant control over how we interpret, utilize, and act on such influences; Booth's dignitary conception is, in the end, simultaneously individualized and socialized in ways that allow for both collective and individual determination and responsibility. In this view, violations of dignity are not only those that violate bodily integrity but also those that deny the person any meaningful, sustained, and substantive interaction with society—a matter I revisit in chapter 5 Put differently, violations of dignity deny or severely impinge on acknowledgement of (personal) identity and membership in community.

Thus far, we have an understanding of dignity as the reciprocal recognition of human status and a corresponding sense of individual value, the content and meaning of which dialectically unfold in light of tension between the imperatives of self-development and the exigencies of social constraints. Dignity thus appears as a nonrelativist, constructed concept; as such, its meaning and content are not infinitely variable, as a relativist might argue, but, rather, emerge from the values, knowledges, interpretations, and purposes identifiable with particular contexts that are not always self-referential but are substantially informed by wider normative and social structures.

At this point, I draw, to clarify, on Erin Daly's (2013, ix) distinction between "dignity as a constitutional value and dignity as a constitutional right." As a constitutional right, dignity's meaning is tied to the specificity of its appearance and thus might be tethered to particular interests, such as "property [or] protection against medical experimentation," or with "particular sectors of the population [such as] women, workers, older people, or people with disabilities" (1). Put differently, certain societies prefer to limit dignity's meaning by linking it to specific, enforceable rights. As a constitutional value, human dignity refers to "the value of a person" that, as Daly's analysis attests, strongly relates to status. Determination of the meaning and extent of value "is unique to each society and each constitution," since value "expresses the society's fundamental religious, moral, and ethical concepts. As such, it . . . depends on context and is subject to change in a changing world . . . Within [a society's constitutional] framework of interpretation, the interpretive value functions as a regulative, organizational, and integrative principle for the constitutional text" (ix).

Aharon Barak, in his capacity as president of the Supreme Court of Israel, put it differently. While the court determined that no philosophical or
moral tradition should dominate dignity's meaning, the judges intuited that
dignity concerns the recognition of individuals as free to develop their body
and mind as they see fit, as long as they do so "within the social framework
to which [they] belong and on which [they are] dependent'" (Barak quoted
in Daly 2013, x). In another case, he added that while "the sanctity and liberty of life" are at the center of dignity, "the autonomy of the individual will,
the freedom of choice, and the freedom . . . to act as a free creature" are its
foundation. "Human dignity," he explained, "rests on the recognition of a
person's physical and intellectual wholeness, one's humanity, one's value as a
person—all without any connection to the extent of its utility for others." In
this view, dignity is grounded in the sheer fact of being classified as human.
Barak adds, however, that "human dignity as a constitutional value reflects
society's understanding of [human beings'] humanity within the society." In
other words, dignity comes down to willingness to accord it to others.

Constitutions, in their generic language of equality, confer on dignity a
tremendous feat of social engineering long in the making. Jeremy Waldron
(2012a, 33) explains that the modern incarnation of dignity "involves an up-
wards equalization of rank . . . that was formerly accorded to nobility," that
the connection between ancient and historical conceptions of dignity, on the
one hand, and modern conceptions, on the other, lays in the undergirding
notion of rank. He maintains that whereas prior practices attached degrees
of dignity to status-based hierarchies (e.g., "the dignity of a king was not the
same as the dignity of bishop and neither of them was the same as the dignity of a professor"), moderns have democratized dignity and use the term
to capture "the idea of the high and equal rank of every human person" (14).
To demonstrate the veracity of this claim, Waldron urges us to "look first at
the bodies of law that relate status to rank (and to right and privilege) and
see what if anything is retained of these ancient conceptions when dignity
is put to work in a new and egalitarian environment" (14). To the extent
that dignity is a right, it is manifested as "the recognizable capacity to assert
claims" (Feinberg quoted in Waldron 2012a, 50). This argument recalls Arendt's distinction between *homo* and *persona* in *On Revolution* (1963b, 107),
in which the difference

between a private individual in Rome and a Roman citizen was that
the latter had a *persona*, a legal personality, as we would say; it was as
though the law had affixed to him the part he was expected to play
on the public scene, with the provision, however, that his own voice

would be able to sound through. The point was that "it is not the natural Ego which enters a court of law. It is a right-and-duty-bearing person, created by the law, which appears before the law." Without his *persona*, there would be an individual without rights and duties, perhaps a "natural man"—that is, a human being or *homo* in the original meaning of the word, indicating someone outside the range of the law and the body politic of the citizens, as for instance a slave.

To what extent dignity is realized is both a legal and social matter. For instance, legislators, judges, and citizens may decide that prohibiting same-sex marriage does not affront or undermine the dignity of homosexuals. But over time, coincident with reflection on the moral worth of others and their life projects, recognition of their autonomy and individuality, and evolved understandings of what constitutes oppression and marginalization, legislators, judges, and citizens may revise their positions. Some may find such variation uncomfortable, for it confirms dignity's woolliness and impresses on one that dignity is but a "place holder for the absence of agreement" (Mc-Crudden quoted in Waldron 2012b, 201).

Nevertheless, Daly finds common patterns for dignity, at least insofar as constitutions and constitutional courts around the world have deployed the term. She observes that

> dignity is fundamentally the same idea throughout the world—there is an identifiable emerging consensus that dignity is the bedrock value of human rights in any constitutional regime. Yet, in each court's hands, it is transformed by each country's constitutional culture, to produce a distinctive value suited to each society's needs. In Latin America, where the struggle for democracy has been building for centuries, it is about building a strong enough base on which democracy can stand to resist assaults, domestic or foreign. In Germany, . . . dignity makes the individual strong enough to withstand the threats of tyrannical powers that would dehumanize and deracinate him or her. In South Africa, it is . . . the promise of self-fulfillment, where the fundamental evil of the apartheid state was to limit and control the possibility of self-realization. In India, whose democracy is relatively stable and whose threats are not existential, dignity is about grappling with irrepressible, pervasive, and deep poverty. In Israel, dignity is critical to keeping the balance between a democratic and free society on the one hand and the security needs of a state under constant existential threat on the other. Far from meaning all things to all people,

dignity has a meaning that is particular to the history and present challenges of each culture. It is the flip side of "never again," the customized magic weapon conjured to combat whatever demons are in each country's closet. (2013, 4–5)

For a variation on that theme, let us return to Waldron.

> Dignity is the status of a person predicated on the fact that she is recognised as having the ability to control and regulate her actions in accordance with her own apprehension of norms and reasons that apply to her; it assumes she is capable of giving and entitled to give an account of herself (and of the way in which she is regulating her actions and organising her life), an account that others are to pay attention to; and it means finally that she has the wherewithal to demand that her agency and her presence among us as a human being be taken seriously and accommodated in the lives of others, in others' attitudes and actions towards her, and in social life generally. (2012b, 202)

How dignity is interpreted depends in part on the claims being made of it. A claim of dignity as status recognition in both its individual and community variants, to use Kelman's conceptualization, means different *foundational* things to different peoples and societies; hence variation. But without reciprocal recognition, however, the scheme falls apart. Dignity is thus, at root, social, not natural. People, Waldron argues,

> try to do all sorts of things with power, and one of the things they sometimes try to do is to treat certain people as having a status that is lower than [an animal] or treat people as though the capacities I have mentioned are unimportant and have no implications for the way those people are ruled. Because this is possible, dignity has to function as a normative idea: it is the idea of a certain status that ought to be accredited to all persons and taken seriously in the way they are ruled. (2012b, 202)

So even if there are themes or patterns that universally feature in dignity's makeup (e.g., status and value), the particular understandings of those evolve within specific contexts. Daly (2013, 20) writes that the "best way to harmonize the universal and the particular is to suggest that dignity is how we describe the essence of what it means to be human, but that the right to dignity is how we describe what legal claims people can assert to insist that their humanity be recognized." She cites a ruling by the Constitutional Court of Colombia that schematized dignity as entailing "[1] autonomy or the possibility of designing a life plan and self-determining according to [an individual's] own desires; [2] certain concrete material conditions of life; and [3] the intangible value of physical and moral integrity. As shorthand, the court characterizes these three dimensions respectively as living as one wishes, living well, and living without humiliation" (26).

No doubt, that court's rendering and shorthand are attractive and useful. While, prima facie, we may find nothing overtly problematic with the scheme, I propose instead to think of dignity as comprising the three dimensions of the interior, the corporeal, and the sociopolitical, which, in my view, make it easier to conceive of and distinguish actions that substantiate or undermine dignity. By the *interior dimension* of dignity, I mean the integrity of our psychological, emotional, and intellectual lives, capacities, aspirations, and pursuits. While we may hurt others in our quotidian lives, I restrict this dimension to deliberate and systematic assaults on the psychoemotional well-being of the individual. Chapter 5 expands on this point in the context of international criminal case law that has been concerned with mental and emotional harm resulting from criminal activity that produces "grave and long-term disadvantage to a person's ability to lead a normal and constructive life."[16] By the *corporeal dimension* of dignity, I refer to the body: both its sustenance (e.g., provisions for essential needs of life such as water, food, and shelter) and its integrity (e.g., protections from assaults such as rape, sexual depravity and violence, torture, and other forms of marking and maiming the body).[17] This dimension figures prominently into the human security agenda as explored in chapter 4. By the *sociopolitical dimension*, I refer to both the status of the human person within society and the various obligations on our political, legal, and social systems to erect schemes and processes and ensure conditions within which dignity may be realized.

Despite this analytic parsing, we must remain mindful that all three dimensions interrelate, as our bodies are *a* if not *the* primary medium through which we engage in and with the world. Existentially and phenomenologically, we are always, ambiguously, both the person we think we are and the person others see and experience (de Beauvoir [1948] 1994; Marso 2012). In this account, the body acts as a frame or parergon. It is the thing that both separates the exterior from the interior, the outside world from the self, and yet also serves as their confluence. It is thus something worthy of being protected and regulated in its own right, though how far regulations extend is a matter of great debate (witness the abortion debate in the United States—a topic well beyond the scope of this project). The body is both an inside of the self (a thing of personal ownership, a mechanism of expression, a site of personhood) and an exteriority, or an outside (i.e., an object of regulation, a subject of interpretation by others). The law protects the body as a composition of a self (protecting it, e.g., from sexual assault and violence, torture, and abuse), even while controlling it. Protection and regulation together comprise dignity's governance.

### Dignity, World Order, and the UN Charter

In light of the copious information documented in Daly's *Dignity Rights* (2013), that dignity is both an object and a subject of national governance is not debatable, though the extent to which this is true within individual countries varies considerably. Connoting value and status, dignity entails more than belonging to a political community. Greater burdens must be imposed on or associated with dignity to effectuate its core components of value and status, which, in turn, regulate activity, govern treatment of people, and imply political, social, and economic methods or systems to actualize particular understandings of it. Postwar constitutions, Daly finds, not only increasingly incorporated dignity in their frameworks but "did so in conjunction with . . . judicial review and with that, the modern conception of rights as enforceable through the judicial machinery of the state, even—or principally—against the state. This shift . . . marks the complete transformation in our understanding of rights from one that signified citizenship for the purpose of conferring and affirming state sovereignty to its present use as a nonviolent weapon to be asserted individually or collectively to limit state sovereignty" (24).

Yet the extent to which dignity is an object and a subject of international governance and a cornerstone of post-Holocaust international relations is certainly debatable. The skeptic might aver that one could not amass a breadth and depth of evidence (as Daly has done on a national basis) that clearly (and surprisingly) reveal the extent to which dignity has become a justiciable right and a constitutional value with considerable legal weight internationally. *Making Human* illustrates the salience of dignity in international relations and global governance practices and discourses. Though the next four chapters will present evidence to support the claim, the argument is made indirectly as a proposition on human status and how such status is accorded, defended, and developed by international bodies, with primary focus on the United Nations, its organs, and affiliated agencies.

But the argument goes further, as explored in this section. On the one hand, postwar international relations have remained a sovereign state-based international order as outlined and articulated in the UN Charter. On the other, post-Holocaust international relations have introduced and endorsed pillars of a world order identified with the dignity and rights of individual human beings in ways that entail restrictions on the prerogatives and machinations of the former (albeit not always or not always effectively). In terms of global governance or world order, *A Life of Dignity for All* (Ban 2013) represents the latest (at the time of writing) in a series of reports by the UN secretary-general to advance the programmatic implications of these pillars and orient activity increasingly around the welfare of individual human beings (see Annan 2000, 2005). Those reports echo the September 2000 Millennium Declaration commitment by member states to "uphold the principles of human dignity, equality and equity" (¶2). It is the perception and invocation of the UN Charter as not merely the nucleus of postwar interstate architecture but also the foundation of a world order centered on human beings that helps ground this shift toward making dignity more an actionable right and less a rhetorical appeal. In what follows, I extend arguments related to the statist view of the Charter to help make the humanitarian argument.

Dag Hammarskjöld (2005, 117) described the UN Charter as "based on . . . a working hypothesis[:] . . . that all the great nations and groups of nations must belong to it if it is to succeed. The Charter does not quite say that membership should be universal, but that is its spirit." References to "all peoples," the "human person," the "collective" and the "international," "the world," and associated terminology, along with invocation of universal principles, purposes, and objectives, lend substance to this view. Hammarskjöld, though, hones in on Article 1(2), which regards the principle of self-determination (the subject of my chapter 6) as a key ingredient for "friendly relations." In his estimation, self-determination, especially in light of decolonization over which he partially presided,[18] proved a vehicle for the diffusion of UN principles and gave "democratic ideals . . . a world-wide application." Consequently, he perceived that it "may well come to be regarded as one of the most significant landmarks of our times" (118–19).

Thomas Franck (see Chesterman et al. 2008, 4–13) calls this intended or aspirational universality aspect of the Charter "pervasive perpetuity." It is one of four elements that distinguish constitutions from other formal agreements or contracts (5). Constitutions, unlike ordinary contracts, constitute "an ongoing process of interaction and not simply a substantive set of rules. In that sense, the chosen instrument—by which the rights and obligations in an ongoing relationship are determined and agreed—becomes not merely normative but constitutive." The condition of pervasive perpetuity is grounded in a constitution's nonderogable or peremptory clauses (e.g. "there is no right of exit") and in the "web of criss-crossing mutual expectations, duties, and entitlements" that constitutions create and that "are not readily disentangled": "To permit one to exit can be seen as a derogation from the legitimate expectations of all the remaining members and as an act that may be construed as damaging the community as a whole."

To illustrate, Franck interprets the US Civil War as "fought to establish that states of the Union, once enlisted, had no right of exit." Similarly, the Charter, unlike the Covenant of the League of Nations, contains no provision for states' withdrawal, even if states may lose voting privileges and other rights of membership (Article 5) or may be expelled on occasion of persistent violation of Charter principles (Article 6), by a two-thirds vote of the General Assembly (Article 18(2)). In other words, it is the prerogative of the community of states, not the right of individual states, to decide on issues of membership. Not even South Africa during the apartheid era, which had been the target of numerous condemnations and findings that its policies and behavior displayed "continued and total disregard . . . of . . . Charter obligations" and were "'inconsistent' with the Charter and 'incompatible' with United Nations membership" (Goodrich et al. 1969, 100), was found by the General Assembly to be in persistent violation of Charter principles and thus eligible for expulsion. One may read that as an homage to venerable sovereignty construed as permissiveness and prerogative. Yet the decision not to expel may underscore the normative and pragmatic indispensability of membership in the UN system, as expulsion would, in the words of many delegates at the San Francisco conference, "'entail more drawbacks for the Organization itself [and thus for the international system] than for the state concerned'" (Goodrich et al. 1969, 98–99). Only one state had attempted to withdraw: Indonesia's attempt to do so in 1965 to protest the election of Malaysia to a temporary seat on the UN Security Council was met by a vague quip by Secretary-General U Thant that Indonesia's position "gave rise to a situation for which no express provision had been made in the Charter" (76). Neither the Security Council nor the Assembly formally entertained the matter, treating the episode as one of temporary noncooperation; Indonesia eventually retracted its position.

As further evidence of the Charter's pervasive perpetuity, Article 2(6) requires that the UN ensure that nonmember states "act in accordance with [UN] Principles so far as may be necessary for the maintenance of international peace and security." For Franck, an international lawyer, Article 2(6) does not simply block states from escaping basic international obligations laid out in the Charter by refusing or quitting membership but "purports to revoke the basic international legal principle that a sovereign state cannot be bound in law except by a free act of its own volition" (Chesterman et al. 2008, 6). Similarly, the binding powers of the Security Council as stipulated in Articles 25 and 49 signify the revocation of that conventional right and hence signal a new kind of international order with constitutional underpinnings. None of these provisions comport with "the normal expectations of treaty law," but they do "bear resemblance to a social compact or constitution" (6).

A related, second feature of constitutions according to Franck is their primacy or "legal preeminence among legal instruments" available to the communities they serve (Chesterman et al. 2008, 7). In the case of the Charter, primacy is enshrined in Article 103, which ensures that "in the event of a conflict between the obligations of the Members of the United Nations under the present Charter and their obligations under any other international agreement, their obligations under the present Charter shall prevail." One very well might argue that such a provision is conditional, activated only in the event of a conflict of obligations. This is true. But when read together with Articles 2(6), 25, and 49, the legal preeminence of the Charter cannot be impugned.

A third feature of constitutions is that they are distinguished by their indelibleness. The Charter is no different. Constitutive instruments "are not easily nipped and tucked or reconfigured to meet the needs of contemporary fashion" (Chesterman et al. 2008, 6). Aside from a series of amendments from 1963—73 that increased the sizes of the Security Council and the Economic and Social Council to accommodate a surge in membership brought about by decolonization, "there has been a notable absence of revision." Plans to enlarge the Security Council in the early twenty-first century to make it more reflective of geopolitical realities have consistently foundered (see, e.g., Blum 2005; for an alternative view, see Johnstone 2008).[19] Amendments are extraordinarily difficult to obtain: they require adoption by a two-thirds vote in the General Assembly in addition to ratification by two-thirds of UN member states, including all of the permanent members of the Security Council (Article 108). As further evidence of the Charter's indelibleness, reservations—legal mechanisms that allow states to opt out of certain provisions—are impermissible (Chesterman et al. 2008, 7), a scheme that was replicated in Article 124 of the Statute of the International Criminal Court and reflected in the 1951 advisory opinion of the International Court of Justice that no reservations could be appended to the Genocide Convention, because to do so would contravene the spirit and purpose of that convention.

Finally, constitutive instruments aspire to "institutional autochthony"— first, by establishing "the basic loci of governmental power . . . and appropriate parameters of power allocated to each" and, second, by making provisions for "the umpiring and implementing of these allocations of function and jurisdiction" secondarily assigned to the International Court of Justice (Chesterman et al. 2008, 7). The Charter "sets out the jurisdictional parameters, and delimits the functions of the principal organs through which the Organization is to operate." In support of this point, Franck cites the operations of an international civil service in the UN Secretariat, the secretary-general's powers under Article 99 and his "good offices" mediatory role, the obligatory budgetary powers of the General Assembly, and the Security Council's decisions to establish two ad hoc international criminal tribunals for the former Yugoslavia and Rwanda, as illustrations that "membership by a sovereign state in the Organization necessarily involves adherence to a system of governance that, to some degree, is capable of generating new obligations not specified in the Charter itself, and to do so without the consent of all the parties to the compact" (Chesterman et al. 2008, 9; this point is the subject of Alvarez 2006).

Of what relevance is Franck's position for our purposes? His legalistic, state-oriented, and institutional concerns seem far removed from the ones explored in this book. Yet his reading of the Charter as a constitution of international society begs inquiry: might that reading be too narrow, given the increasing degree to which the UN has focused its activities on improving human welfare and substantiating human dignity?

With regard to "pervasive perpetuity," two points bear mentioning. First, our perspective on universality need not be confined to states. The Charter opens with three rather powerful, if enigmatic, words: "we the peoples." For the American reader, those words have particular resonance, for they only slightly modify the preamble to the Constitution of the United States. In the Charter, "peoples," as a reflection of the plurality and diversity of humanity, replaces its singular form in the Constitution; in the eyes of the Americans, the new organization would be "an expression of the will of the peoples of the world . . . , primarily concerned with their welfare" (Goodrich and Hambro 1949, 89). To wit, the Charter opens the UN system to multiple kinds of actors: individuals and peoples (via Articles 1(3), 13(1)(b), 55, 73, 76, and 83(2)) and nongovernmental organizations (via Article 71 and ECOSOC).[20]

The populist or humanitarian theme is woven throughout the Charter, climaxing in Article 55 and settling in Chapters XI and XII, which treat non-self-governing territories and trusteeships, respectively. The eight preambular determinations to which governments and, presumably, peoples pledge are synthesized into four primary purposes enumerated in Article 1. These purposes include, among others, developing "friendly relations . . . based on respect for the principle of equal rights and self-determination of peoples" and "promoting and encouraging respect for human rights and for fundamental freedoms for all without distinction as to race, sex, language, or religion." In contrast to Article 1, which broadly paints the objectives of equal rights for nations, self-determination, human rights, and the resolution of international problems of an "economic, social, cultural or humanitarian character," Article 55 specifies responsibilities that the UN shall undertake and that its members, via Article 56, pledge to work toward. Such obligations encompass the promotion of "higher standards of living, full employment, and conditions of economic and social progress and development; solutions of international economic, social, health, and related problems; . . . and universal respect for, and observance of, human rights and fundamental freedoms."

The term *dignity* makes its first and only appearance early on in the Charter, as part of a second preambular determination to "reaffirm faith in fundamental human rights, in the dignity and worth of the human person, [and] in the equal rights of men and women and of nations large and small." When this determination is read with Article 1(2), dignity, worth, and equal rights are, in the Charter scheme, politically and organizationally best insured by a scheme of self-determination, which found its supreme collective expression in decolonization. Self-determination and, concomitantly, dignity, human rights, social welfare, and economic development are constituted as matters of international concern precisely because they do not serve merely as ends in themselves but are perceived as central to the cultivation of friendly and peaceful international relations.

My critic retorts that "peoples," in the plural, morphed into its collective political version, "states" (or, as occasionally used in the Charter, "nations"). Thus, while, linguistically, the Charter "constituted an important departure from past practice which had been, as in the case of the *Covenant of the League of Nations,* to refer only to states or their governments" (Goodrich and Hambro 1949, 89), the preamble, as if to dispense any doubt as to the constituents of this new organization, concludes with the solemn agreement of governments. That position is, of course, true. But some interpretive license, played out in UN work, must come to bear, which is my second point.

Let us return to Hammarskjöld's working hypothesis on self-determination, which remains relevant even in this postdecolonization era, as evidenced by the recent ascension to UN membership of East Timor and South Sudan and by Kosovo's unilateral declaration of independence. Self-determination concerns the permission of peoples to decide their political fate. The General Assembly in 1960 underscored as much by reading self-determination and Chapter XI teleologically as a "dynamic state of evolution and progress towards a 'full measure of self-government.'"[21]

But this interpretation is its sovereigntist/political form. Self-determination may be read in a more personal way: as a making of the self or a constitution of individuality/personhood through the development and deployment of one's capacities and capabilities. In Booth's idiom, self-determination involves the infinite number of ways we constitute ourselves—Arendt might subsume this under her conception of action—given the multiple interpenetrations of self into society and of society into self. For Daly, this is dignity's individuation function (2013, 32–34). The interpretation is also reflected in Charter provisions. To wit, with respect to non-self-governing territories and trusteeships, administering authorities and UN member states are bound per Article 73 to "recognize the principle that the interests of the inhabitants . . . are paramount, and accept as sacred trust the obligation to promote to the utmost, within the system of international peace and security established by the present Charter, the well-being of the inhabitants." This includes empowering inhabitants through political, economic, social, educational, and scientific means; assisting them "in the progressive development of their free political institutions"; and encouraging "constructive measures of development." Likewise evidencing this meaning are provisions on human rights, dignity, the worth of the human person, and, as the preamble notes, "better standards of life in larger freedom."

The Cold War, however, stymied much of the core missions of the United Nations with respect to reaffirming the dignity and worth of the human person as well as faith in human rights, ensuring gender equality, and promoting social progress (Annan 2000, 6). Reflecting on his millennium report entitled *We the Peoples*, Secretary-General Kofi Annan noted that he "drew on the opening words of the Charter . . . to point out that the United Nations, while it is an organization of sovereign States, exists for and must ultimately serve those needs. To do so, we must aim, as I said when first elected eight years ago, 'to perfect the triangle of development, freedom and peace'" (Annan 2005, ¶12). His later report *In Larger Freedom* was so named "to stress the enduring relevance of the Charter of the United Nations and to emphasize that its purposes must be advanced in the lives of individual men and women. The notion of larger freedom also encapsulates the idea that development, security and human rights go hand in hand" (¶14).

"In larger freedom"—three powerful, if enigmatic, words—appear at the conclusion of the fourth preambular determination. Annan interprets the phrase as implying

> that men and women everywhere have the right to be governed by their own consent, under law, in a society where all individuals can, without discrimination or retribution, speak, worship and associate freely. They must also be free from want—so that the death sentences of extreme poverty and infectious disease are lifted from their lives— and free from fear—so that their lives and livelihoods are not ripped apart by violence and war. Indeed, all people have the right to security and to development. (¶15)

His vision is at once democratic (by underscoring consent), rationalized (through the rule of law), and individuated (i.e., predicated on the autonomy and relationality of the individual). The vision implies a cosmopolitan global polity in which dignity shoulders the burden of securing, defending, and advancing status claims of individuals in international/global relations, not simply as members of states, which institutions of ICL have affirmed: an offense against dignity is one that fundamentally harms a person's status as a functioning member of community. But increasingly, in diverse issue areas, the individual's dignity and well-being, which is to say individual identity and individual standing in community, are the standards against which actions should be measured.

With respect to a second element of Franck's constitutional indicators, legal preeminence, one might propose that the purposes and principles of the Charter themselves, to which even nonmember states are bound, ascend to such primacy. Nongovernmental organizations affiliated with ECOSOC work toward the principles and objectives of the UN and may even pressure and/or shame states into doing so. UN member states may create trust funds, such as the UN Trust Fund for Human Security established by agreement between Japan and the UN and generously funded by many governments, to effectuate the purposes and principles of the UN. The Global Compact, a voluntary strategic policy initiative to align private-sector activity with UN principles related to advancing human rights, safeguarding labor, protecting the environment, and combatting corruption, also illustrates the primacy accorded to UN objectives.[22] In Franck's view, to reiterate, such organs illustrate an aspect of institutional autochthony: that "membership by a sovereign state in the Organization necessarily involves adherence to a system of governance that, to some degree, is capable of generating new obligations not specified in the *Charter* itself, and to do so without the consent of all the parties to the compact" (Chesterman et al. 2008, 9). Now it becomes clear that a range of actors become wedded to the purposes and work toward their effectuation. Technically not bound, these actors nevertheless lend normative priority to UN purposes—likely evidence that humanity is not simply the sum of its parts but a first-order value and status itself.

The Charter's potential as an instrument to make human and ground human dignity as a base of global governance inheres in its aspirational intent and vision: a "One World" (in the Hammarskjöldian sense) generated by and generative of forms of solidarity not restricted to nationalistic frameworks, though certainly inclusive of them; a "One World" guided and organized constitutionally around a set of principles and purposes that have spawned voluminous declarations, resolutions, funds, programs, offices, plans, actions, and actors to work toward their effectuation. Chapter VII and Article 55 may be construed as tools to *resist* forms of oppression, whether agentic or systemic in orientation. Various provisions that speak to human rights and fundamental freedoms, to non-self-governing peoples and inhabitants of trusteeships, coupled with provisions that address economic, social, cultural, educational, and health matters, compel *reflection* on the worth of others not like or known to us and on how best to advance self-determination in both its political and individual variants. Effective actions and programs may, in turn, be reformulated as best practices to be *replicated*. The irrevocable *recognition* of the connections between human needs and empowerment, on the one hand, and international peace, order, and friendly relations, on the other, underscores the interpenetration of the domestic and the international, the individual and the collective, the particular and the universal, in ways that highlight our shared *responsibilities*. The tethering of individuals, nongovernmental organizations, member and nonmember states, and the organization itself to local, national, international, and transnational commitments to fulfilling Charter objectives illustrates in the end that the "One World," far from being a utopian dream, is very much a reality in which we find "our community with others in exploring how [humanity's shared] predicaments can be faced in common" (Fine 2007, x).

## Conclusion

How we face such predicaments is an empirical matter. That we face them, often mediated through and by institutional mechanisms and procedures, raises the question of whether something qualitative has changed in international relations. Arendt thought that the "One World," or "the new global political situation," differed fundamentally from the humanist imaginations of philosophers, not just because she discerned its origins in destruction, but, more positively, because within the possibility inheres the realization and ef-fectuation of common responsibilities. Hammarskjöld likewise found in the "One World" a reality made possible by Charter principles and its promise of self-determination that would defend and advance human dignity.

Humanity's corporate existence manifests as a normative ideal, a regula-tive force, and an organizing logic. As a normative ideal, it informs practices with aspirational motifs such as dignity and social justice. As a regulative force, it shapes, constrains, and directs behavior, as we see in humanitarian law and the laws of war (see Meron 2000a; Teitel 2011). As an organizing logic, it becomes shorthand to use in measuring policy and practice against the ideals and motifs it reportedly represents. The next few chapters bear practical witness to such influences and manifestations.

Yet this kind of narrative does not neatly fit into conventional accounts of international relations, often marked as they are by exemplar moments in time: Westphalia, Utrecht, Vienna, Paris, Versailles, San Francisco, and, to a lesser degree, Bretton Woods and Yalta occupy the same intellectual space as the less-geographically formulated "Cold War." Each serves as shorthand to use in capturing logics, principles, and practices presumably idiosyncratic to the order that bears its name. In this view, even this ill-defined post–Cold War era, often associated with globalization, encapsulates a period marked by a history of people, movements, and ideas. Indeed, it was ushered in by a joint American-Soviet proclamation heralding a "new world order." The constructed moment is at once a historical moment, and the sum of such moments is both an articulation of humanity and the memory of humanity, in and across time and space.

This book is less a geographic moment of history and more a subterra-nean undercurrent—the documentation of a history that has affected many and been noticed by few. That is where much of international relations lies, I suspect: in the recesses and valleys of quotidian life as much as in the peaks of exemplar moments of constitution and deconstruction. For while we are drawn to the drama of natalist moments in which particular visions of order and patterns of relations are generated and effectuated or to the spectacle of destruction when orders collapse, the tensions of persistent realities may more deeply affect lives and shape orders even if there were no geographic analogues, signposts, or moments in time that we might use as convenient shorthand to signify them. We need, in short, to understand world order in human terms, which comes at a price: there may be no easily discernible eras; hence my approach may not so easily gain traction in a broader lexicon of IR. Yet a study of world order in human terms is sensitive to under-standing the capacities, tools, and mechanisms within periods of time that variously presage, express, manifest, and constitute the ways we perceive, categorize, and treat others, all of which give history and political relations their color, tone, melody, and, often, their substance.

For Arendt, imperialism, totalitarianism, and technology marked the substantive, though not theoretical, appearance of the "One World." Constructed on a singular notion of humanity, which differed from earlier philosophical imaginations that were notable precisely for their disjuncture with practice, the "One World" indicated for her a negative solidarity borne out of the destructive potentials of the modern world. Yet, consequently and somewhat dialectically, an opposing positive solidarity in the guise of forms of political responsibility may develop. For Arendt, the postwar tribunals and the emergence of a crime against humanity signaled maturation of the idea of humanity: no longer associated with a rootless cosmopolitanism, humanity both metamorphosed into an organizing principle of social relations and, in the process, acquired a reality that encapsulated the essence of the human condition of plurality.

An argument can be made that dignity, along with international peace, security, and development, is a cornerstone on which are constructed the United Nations system and, by implication, the postwar international order; Kofi Annan even identified dignity / human rights, security, and development as the triadic pillars of the UN and of all international and world order (2005).[23] The Charter, as a constitutional schematic, catalogs numerous obligations and objectives from which stem a range of plans, initiatives, programs, projects, funds, agreements, and treaties. Some are unequivocal, such as the Security Council's power to impose sanctions on recalcitrant states or to authorize the use of force. Others are rather more ambiguous and operate under spell of interpretive license: such as "to promote social progress and better standards of life in larger freedom." Given the multiple humanitarian provisions in the Charter and the opening of the UN system to diverse nonstate agents, a case can be made that the Charter is more than a blueprint for a postwar, state-centric international order. It is also one for a post-Holocaust, humanitarian world order. The process of interpreting and fulfilling those objectives, of defining and bestowing dignity on others, and of defining what it means to be human may be construed as a set of processes and practices integral to world order.

The manners by which we construct notions of the human being and humanity are, in this view, quite central to accounts of international relations. Practically, how we understand and thereby treat diverse human beings makes significant difference in how we arrange and prioritize political, legal, economic, and social principles and institutions. Theoretically translated, both humanization and dehumanization perform powerfully constitutive and regulative functions in the unfolding of world order.

## CHAPTER 3

# The UN Security Council

## *Making Human for International Peace and Security*

> The Security Council . . . requests agencies, funds and programmes of the United Nations to . . . devote particular attention and adequate resources to the rehabilitation of children affected by armed conflict, particularly their counseling, education and appropriate vocational opportunities, as a preventive measure and as a means of reintegrating them into society . . . [and to] promote a culture of peace, including through support for peace education programmes.
>
> —UN Security Council Resolution 1379 (20 November 2001)[1]

Adoption by the United Nations Security Council (hereinafter the UNSC or the Council) of Resolution 1373 in 2001, which criminalizes the financing of terrorism, and of Resolution 1540 in 2004, which requires states to erect legal and institutional machinery to combat the proliferation of weapons of mass destruction, triggered apprehension that the Council embarked on a new legislative course of action, since both impose binding obligations on states (see Szasz 2002; Alvarez 2003; Talmon 2005; Rosand, Millar, and Ipe 2007). On the one hand, such misgivings discount the obligatory powers granted to the Council per Articles 25 and 49 of the UN Charter.[2] On the other, apprehension reflects a shift in Council practices.

For much of its history, the Council responded to specific disputes between and gradually within states. Then, in the late 1990s, it began to address noncountry, non-conflict-specific issues. While this may instigate disquiet, thematic work reflects the spirit of Article 34, which authorizes the UNSC to investigate situations that "might lead to international friction or give rise to a dispute." The *Security Council Report*, produced by a nonprofit organization founded to provide "consistent, balanced, and high-quality information about the activities" of the UNSC, identifies thirty-one thematic issues before the Council. Eight are procedural in orientation and stem specifically from tasks enunciated in the Charter: admission of states to the UN; appointment of the secretary-general; elections of judges to the International Court of Justice; review of UNSC mandates; composition of its annual report; elections of temporary members of the UNSC; oversight of its subsidiary bodies; and establishment, clarification, and review of UNSC working methods. The remaining twenty-three substantive issues concern children and armed conflict; conflict mediation; conflict prevention; cooperation with regional organizations; disarmament; drug trafficking; energy, security, and climate; international criminal tribunals; justice, impunity, and rule-of-law issues; natural resources and conflict; peacekeeping; the Peacebuilding Commission; postconflict stabilization; protection of civilians in armed conflict; regional and subregional issues; sanctions; human rights; follow-up on World Summit commitments; security-sector reform; sexual exploitation; small arms; terrorism; and women, peace, and security.[3]

Resolutions 1373 and 1540 follow the model of what has come to be called the thematic resolution. They address broad themes not tethered to particular conflicts (even if 1373 proved a response to the 11 September 2001 terrorist attacks in the United States), they manifest the Council's more expansive interpretation of its primary responsibility to maintain international peace and security as prescribed by Article 24,[4] and they "lack any explicit or implicit time limitation" (Szasz 2002, 902). Yet each of these two resolutions breaks the mold of the thematic resolution by obliging (not recommending) that states take specific programmatic and legislative action and by creating "binding new rules of international law" (Szasz 2002, 902; see also Rosand, Millar, and Ipe 2007, 5, 10).

The work of the Council has generated voluminous literature,[5] much of it concentrated on its primary responsibility to maintain international peace and security and thus on material issues including dispute resolution, sanctions, peacekeeping, enforcement, and (newfound) "legislative authority." Certain thematic resolutions (e.g., the Council's landmark Resolution 1325 of 2000, on women, peace, and security) have spawned particular literatures, but the general phenomenon of thematic resolutions has elicited scant attention (see True-Frost 2007). While this chapter does not endeavor to examine in detail the thematic resolution, it explores another facet of the UNSC's work that the thematic resolutions disclose.

In particular, thematic resolutions illustrate a metamorphosis in the

Council's views on what constitutes international friction (Article 34), international peace and security (Article 24), and threats to the peace (Article 39). The change is not at all surprising given the complexity of conflicts that come before the Council. But its evolving understandings have increasingly, if inconsistently, situated the human being and human welfare at the forefront of its work—a sort of "first image" turn that complements the emergence and slow maturation of what Ruti Teitel (2011) dubs humanity's law. Pertinent questions thus arise. At what point did the Council begin to consider the human dimensions of threats to and breaches of international peace and security? Why did the Council engage in such a move? Does this shift deepen cosmopolitan dispositions in international relations and, if so, to what effect? To what degree does the Council's protective and empowerment work blunt the state-prerogative edges of a state-based international order with an attempt to effectuate the post-Holocaust humanitarian-based world order? Or is the Council's work merely a version of a Lockean conception of trusteeship, or an institutionalized form of assistance and rule on behalf of the other (Wight 1992, 76)? What can we learn from UNSC practices with respect to the problematic of being human in a dehumanizing world? The Security Council, this chapter argues, has proven to be a central institution in making human.

This chapter first outlines the Council's functions as set forth in the UN Charter. This seemingly tangential angle is designed to underscore how unique (and unexpected) the Council's work is with respect to making human. The bulk of the chapter then constructs a framework for understanding UNSC approaches to making human, based on a calculus of international peace and security. I identify "three Councils" by function—the cautionary Council, the protective Council, and the empowering Council—to classify responses to humanitarian crises throughout the Council's nearly seventy-year history. Whereas the cautionary Council captures reluctance to engage the human dimension of conflict and thus only modestly advances my argument, the protective Council refers to the UNSC's more active role to protect individuals from violence and harm perpetrated on them during times of conflict—sometimes as a secondary concern but sometimes, especially in recent years, as primary justification for action (e.g., in Somalia and Libya). The empowering Council denotes concern with enhancing human capacities through democratic, participative activities (e.g., elections and plebiscites), strengthening human rights, promoting the self-development of peoples, and, though the Council fails to use the terminology, employing the logic of human security (the subject of chapter 4) and addressing root causes of insecurity.

Before I proceed, four caveats are in order. First, my classificatory scheme stems from an interpretation of Council resolutions, not from deep engagements with the positions of member states or the bargaining that precedes Council decisions. I examine only that which came to be and do not delve deep into minutes of Council meetings (in instances for which such minutes are available). Here, it may be useful to refer to Ian Johnstone's work on interpretive communities. Such communities, he notes, "emerge from discursive interaction . . . and help to define the rules and norms that become embedded in institutions" (2005, 186). Johnstone specifically examines the UN Security Council and its role with respect to the Kosovo crisis. Despite failure of Council members to come to agreement on Kosovo, the case, in Johnstone's view, illustrates "the power of interpretive communities" in shaping prevailing understandings and practices of diverse agents.

Methodologically, Johnstone does not engage in exhaustive research regarding the interests and positions of individual Council members but, rather, interprets the output of Council deliberations as a kind of collective weight or product that assumes a discrete power of influence (on interpretive analysis, see also Lynch 1999, 10–18). This chapter replicates his method, which should not be construed as suggesting that the Council is merely an entity that simply acts, as if its individual members, each with its private national interests, prejudices, and preferences, do not matter. They do, as we well know in the case of the ongoing Syrian crisis, to take but one example. Rather, the point is that despite the positions of individual members, the collective determinations of the Council come to exert, as a form of knowledge, a reality independent of its producers in ways that shape the actions of others. Here, I demonstrate that the Council has come to craft a position on the meaning of being human; no research has previously addressed this issue in the way I do. Hence, second, I do not provide an exhaustive account of the Council's history or even of the selected situations discussed in this chapter, since the specifics germane to each conflict or dispute do not concern the argument advanced in this book.

Third, I recognize that Council responses to crises have been highly selective; the typology I develop is based only on resolutions passed. Nevertheless, the reader may find the account here too rosy, cursory, and fractured, as it does not treat Council failures to act (e.g., in Cambodia, Rwanda, Sri Lanka, and, for nearly three years at the time of this writing, Syria). My point is not to provide a detailed exegesis of the positions of UNSC member states or to investigate the Council's inability to craft common positions in certain instances. Rather, my goal is to examine how the Council has, over time, come to understand and respond to the human dimensions of threats to and breaches of international peace and security. That the Council has not always done this well or even consistently does not make what the Council has done and what understandings it has produced any less real or valuable.

Fourth, the temporal reach of the chapter is limited primarily to the Council's early years. My initial plan was to focus on the human element in thematic resolutions. But references to human dignity and welfare and to protection and, increasingly, empowerment of civilians compelled me to search backward for earlier evidence of such concerns. I found that the Council's responses to racist minority rule in Southern Rhodesia (1965) and to apartheid in South Africa (beginning in 1960) offer rich, compelling cases notable precisely for their intrusions in domestic affairs and express concern for infringements on human dignity. The Council grounded its reaction in "global public opinion" as deduced from previous General Assembly resolutions and debates, as well as principles enshrined in the Universal Declaration of Human Rights (UDHR). These justifications urged me to move further backward in time: were there any indications that Council members reflected on human dignity and human welfare prior to the passage of the UDHR on 19 December 1948?

## Functions of the UNSC

Article 24 of the UN Charter confers on the Security Council the "primary responsibility for the maintenance of international peace and security." Chapters VI (on the pacific settlement of disputes), VII (on threats to the peace, breaches of the peace, and acts of aggression), VIII (on regional organizations), and XII (on the International Trusteeship System) outline a variety of functions and duties granted to and mechanisms at the disposal of the Council for the fulfillment of this most solemn of missions.

Arguably, the Council's most prominent function is that of *enforcement*, which may involve "measures not involving the use of armed force," such as the imposition of sanctions (Article 41) or the creation of ad hoc international criminal tribunals that the Council thought might prove a deterrent to ongoing hostilities in the former Yugoslavia (Robertson 2006, 378–79). But "should the Security Council consider that [Article 41] measures . . . would be inadequate or have proved to be inadequate," it may authorize "action by air, sea, or land forces as may be necessary to maintain or restore international peace and security" (Article 42). The Charter's approach to enforcement is graduated. Chapter VI's pacific modes of dispute settlement are followed by the more robust and arguably more obligatory Chapter VII modes of enforcement. The 1950 action in Korea is perhaps the exception that proves the rule that rarely, if ever, has the Council circumvented the sanctions provision and directly authorized force. In that case, a mere twelve days intervened between the North Korean invasion on 25 June and the passage of Resolution 84 (7 July 1950) that established a unified command under the United States to evict the invading forces; no sanctions had been authorized.

Enforcement action and dispute settlement generally prove more newsworthy, but the Council possesses a number of other responsibilities that are perhaps lesser known or are at least less publicized. The *elective function* refers to Council responsibilities to recommend to the General Assembly the admission of new member states (Article 4(2)) and the election of the secretary-general (Article 97). In conjunction with the Assembly, the Council undertakes the appointment of judges to the International Court of Justice (ICJ Statute Article 4(1)). Article 26 outlines the *armament function*, meaning the development of "a system for the regulation of armaments." What I call the *umpire function* is found in Article 94, which permits the Council to "make recommendations or decide upon measures to be taken to give effect to the judgment" in the event a state "fails to perform the obligations incumbent upon it under a judgment rendered by the [International] Court [of Justice]."

Two additional functions prove more pertinent to our inquiry. The *investigative function*, outlined in Article 34, permits the Council to "investigate any dispute, or any situation which might lead to international friction or give rise to a dispute, in order to determine whether the continuance of the dispute or situation is likely to endanger the maintenance of international peace and security." When read in the context of Chapter VI of the Charter, on the pacific settlement of disputes, Article 34 appears an extraordinary addition. The chapter's overall agentic focus—that is, its repeated invocation of states and, as noted in several articles, "parties" (to a dispute)—is relaxed by or punctuated with Article 34's focus on situations, which provides a legal basis for the Council's thematic turn.

The investigative function is a wide-ranging, if contingent, power tethered to the likelihood that a dispute or situation will endanger the maintenance of international peace and security. In its first year of operation, the Council authorized investigations in two instances. The first, the Spanish Question, concerned whether the Security Council should oblige UN member states to terminate diplomatic relations with the dictatorial Franco regime because it constituted an international menace and potential threat to international peace and security. The second, the Greek Question, stemmed from allegations that Albania, Bulgaria, and Yugoslavia supported guerilla warfare in Greece. Nonpermanent Council members soon expressed concern over the discretion afforded by Article 34. Extensive discussions with respect to Spain and Greece clarified the Council's position: it would not curtail its interpretive license with respect to Article 34. Leland Goodrich and Edvard Hambro (1949, 245–46) maintain that members expressed impatience with legal technicalities and were inclined to rely on "common sense, practical necessities, and the spirit of the Charter" to guide interpretation. Even the USSR, which vetoed an initial resolution regarding the Greek Question, agreed during discussions that the Council

> considers itself empowered, apart from the political exigencies of a particular case, to conduct a broad investigation of the facts of any dispute or situation *brought before it*, not only with a view to determining the seriousness of the dispute or situation, but also with a view to establishing the factual bases for its recommendations under Articles 33, 36 and 37, that in conducting such an investigation the Council may authorize its subsidiary [investigative] organ to take the steps necessary to its completion, and that the decisions taken in this connection are binding upon Members under Article 25, even though the Security Council under Articles 36 and 37 can only recommend procedures, means and terms of settlement or adjustment. (emphasis added)

Article 34, Goodrich and Hambro concluded, "assumes in practice a most important place in the Charter system for pacific settlement" (247).

Others have backed the Soviet position and, in doing so, underscored the necessity of referral by member states or action by the General Assembly to activate Council interest, as happened with respect to apartheid South Africa and white racist rule in Southern Rhodesia. Thus, while, as a matter of principle, the Council discounted legalistic arguments about presumed limitations on its right or authority to launch investigative measures, it exercised restraint in practice—at least until its thematic turn in the late 1990s, which manifest a change in the Council's relationship with and treatment of Article 34. First, thematic resolutions signal the Council's growing ease with elastic applications of the article, though such elasticity is abridged by the situation's presumed effects on international peace and security.

Consequently, second, thematic resolutions evince the Council's expanding interpretation of the meaning of international peace and security and its growing sensitivity to varied and variable components that comprise and affect it. Gender-based violence and exclusions of women from political and economic life and decision making, violence perpetrated against children and the long-term destabilizing effects such brutality has on and within societies, environmental pressures and degradations, and persistent underdevelopment, poverty, and disease have all factored in the Council's increasingly complex calculus of international peace and security and thus of what is required to maintain it.

Third, Article 34's focus on situations offers the Council broad discretionary powers. Due to information uncertainty or incompleteness, the Council has often only ascertained that a situation will likely endanger international peace and security if continued unabated. Consequently, the Council mandates temporally, spatially, and agentically far-reaching action to mitigate or resolve situations in ways that may strike some observers as "broad and ambiguous," as a report written for the Swiss Mission to the United Nations on certain UNSC thematic resolutions notes (Mahony and Nash 2008, 10). But precisely this breadth and ambiguity give many of the thematic resolutions "their strategic power," for they permit "good field leadership" to "exercise flexibility," encourage the proactive pursuit of "efficient protection strategies," and invite a wide variety of participants (e.g., local community groups, think tanks, nongovernmental organizations, other international organizations, advocacy groups, and the like) to interpret and apply Council mandates. Because of the various formal and informal networks of diverse agents that materialize around thematic resolutions, Council recommendations may have exponential effects by engendering normative and epistemic innovations and shifts and finding interpretation in a range of programmatic actions and policy development framed, developed, and monitored by diverse actors.

Fourth, as ascertained in the ambiguity of "is likely" in Article 34, thematic resolutions introduce a preventive dimension into the Council's work. The existence of a working group on energy, security, and climate change suggests that the Council has become more receptive to considering probable correlations in its calculations of international peace and security.

Finally, the *determinative function* embedded in Article 39 authorizes the Council to "determine the existence of any threat to the peace, breach of the peace, or act of aggression" and to "make recommendations, or decide what measures shall be taken . . . to maintain or restore international peace and security." Like Article 34, this one also affords the Council considerable latitude—a power that was vehemently opposed at the San Francisco conference (Goodrich and Hambro 1949, 263). Yet the United States convincingly argued that a precise accounting of what constitutes a threat, breach, or act of aggression was impractical; no one could exhaustively envision, in its specificity, every possible kind of act that might constitute such. Eventually the great powers agreed to the stipulation that "no definition of aggression should be attempted other than that found in Article 2(4)" (Goodrich and Hambro 1949, 264).[6] Further, an argument could be made that Article 39 restricts Council responses to provisional measures and recommendations (Article 40) and to the enforcement measures outlined in Articles 41 and 42.[7]

Yet as early as 1964, the Council indicated that it would not circumscribe its reactions to threats to or uses of force against the territorial integrity or political independence of states, as indicated in Article 2(4). Rather, Council members looked to that article's concluding clause as vindicating its inclination to address any actions "inconsistent with the Purposes of the United Nations." Resolution 191 (18 June 1964) determined "race conflict in South Africa resulting from the policies of apartheid"—being "contrary to the Principles and Purposes of the Charter of the United Nations and inconsistent with the provisions of the Universal Declaration of Human Rights,"—to "seriously disturb international peace and security." Slightly over a year later, the Council decreed the "unilateral declaration of independence . . . by a racist minority in Southern Rhodesia" (Resolution 216 [1965]) to be "a threat to international peace and security" (Resolution 217 [1965]). Insofar as fifty-eight of the fifty-nine UN member states brought to the attention of the Council South Africa's apartheid policy, a clear normative consensus regarding the illegitimacy of racist rule emboldened it to take action in the Southern Rhodesia case.

The elastic application of Article 39's determinative function may be seen more recently in Resolutions 1308 (2000) and 1983 (2011), adopted unanimously under Article 24, which commit the Council to addressing "the HIV/AIDS pandemic as a threat to international peace and security."[8] Specific passages of Resolution 1983 (7 June 2011) are worth noting precisely for their retrospective and prospective understanding of the issue. The Council

> *Recogniz[ed]* that HIV poses one of the most formidable challenges to the development, progress and stability of societies and requires an exceptional and comprehensive global response, and not[ed] with satisfaction the unprecedented global response of Member States, public and private partnerships, non-governmental organizations and the important roles of civil society, communities, and persons living with and affected by HIV in shaping the response, . . .
>
> *Recogniz[ed]* that the spread of HIV can have a uniquely devastating impact on all sectors and levels of society, and that in conflict and post-conflict situations, these impacts may be felt more profoundly,

[*And*] *Further recognize*[*ed*] that conditions of violence and instability in conflict and post-conflict situations can exacerbate the HIV epidemic, inter alia, through large movements of people, widespread uncertainty over conditions, conflict-related sexual violence and reduced access to medical care.

Some might be alarmed at the immensurability of Council action here (akin to unease surrounding Resolutions 1373 and 1540), even if Resolution 1983 elicited celebration, not criticism. Yet Council intrusion in what presumably constitutes the domestic affairs or states is rare without some kind of provocation; much of the Council's work responds to referrals, reports, inquiries, and investigations submitted by member states, the secretary-general, and other UN organs and agencies. This is not to suggest that the Council's work is derivative. Rather, it is to underscore that the UNSC is as much a norm consumer as it is a norm developer and enforcer (on this point, see True-Frost 2007). Yet even as a norm consumer, the Council engenders new understandings and encourages, whether indirectly or directly, the construction of new networks and constellations of actors—or "webs of influence," as Mahony and Nash call them (2008, 6)—that work toward actualizing Council recommendations.

## Making Human in the UNSC

In this section, I document what I call the Council's "first image turn," which I categorize as cautionary, protective, or empowering. Rather than stemming from a deep-seated humanitarian impulse, the Council's inroads with respect to humanization precipitate from a morphing calculus of what constitutes and maintains international peace and security. For much of its history, South Africa and Southern Rhodesia notwithstanding, the Council restricted its conception of international peace and security to interstate disturbances and, gradually, civil wars (e.g., in the Congo in 1960), but it eventually broadened its notion. Given the inclusion of distinctive humanitarian elements in its later work, we might understand Council actions as designed to counter dehumanizing realities by correcting the injustices of misrecognition; exercising responsibility on behalf of others—and encouraging forms of responsibility that deliver on promises of protection, development, and peace; recognizing the self-determinative capacities of others as means of conflict resolution; resisting egregious forms of oppression and violence; and reproducing and enforcing normative frameworks and rules enshrined in international humanitarian and human rights law. I remind the reader, as indicated in the introduction to this book, that the ensuing narrative focuses not on each process as discrete, but rather on their interplay and configuration in several cases that came before the Council.

## The Cautionary Council

Given increasing polarization between the Soviet and Western camps and inability to agree on much soon after the creation of the UN, one could hardly expect the Security Council to entertain considerations of international peace and security incompatible with a particular interstate understanding of "international." A survey of the Council's early years confirms this: resolutions pertained to border disputes (e.g., the Greek Question) and transgressions (e.g., the Iranian Question), interstate violence (e.g., the Indonesia, Palestine, India-Pakistan, and Korea Questions), and the mining of important waterways (e.g., the Corfu Channel incidents).

Yet the Council, even in its early engagements with the exigencies of international politics, took some rather visionary, if ultimately cautious and noncommittal, positions with respect to human welfare. In the period before the passage of the UDHR, the Council attended in varying degrees to the safety of peoples caught up in conflict (e.g., in Indonesia and, post-UDHR adoption, Palestine and India-Pakistan) and affirmed the will of the people as expressed through elections/plebiscites as viable and preferable means of conflict resolution (in Indonesia and India-Pakistan). In this subsection, I briefly outline Council responses to the Spanish, Greek, and Indonesia Questions—chronologically the second, third, and fifth substantive issues the Council entertained[9]—to illustrate an emerging consciousness within the Council on issues of making human. The first relates to regime type and to the (international) weight that should be accorded to the will of the people; the second to reflections on the worth of individuals caught up in violence and thus to self-imposed limitations on the Council's interpretation of its functions; and the third to responsibilities associated with decolonization.

Invoking Articles 34 and 35 of the Charter, Poland brought before the Council on 9 April 1946 a motion to declare that the "existence and activities of the Franco regime . . . have led to international friction and endangered international peace and security."[10] The move intended to follow up on the "unanimous moral condemnation of the Franco regime . . . and the resolutions . . . which were adopted at the United Nations Conference on International Organization at San Francisco and at the first General Assembly of the United Nations" (Resolution 4 [29 April 1946]).

Poland framed its draft resolution in human rights language: the illegal manner by which the regime came to power, the egregious acts of violence perpetrated against civilian populations by Franco's forces during the Spanish Civil War, and the rights-oppressive nature of fascistic rule. Mindful of the domestic affairs provision of Article 2(7), the Polish ambassador, in a letter dated 8 April 1946 to the secretary-general, underscored the international nature of the matter: Franco's de facto alliance with the Axis Powers during World War II, the "massing of troops on the border with France," and the fact that Spain had become "a refuge for German personnel" (Wellens 1990, 12). Such activities, Poland maintained, violated the "peace-loving" requirement for UN membership stipulated in Article 4(1) of the Charter.[11] Coincident with punitive measures stipulated in Article 41, the draft resolution called on "all Members of the United Nations who maintain diplomatic relations with the Franco Government to sever such relations."[12] The measure was soundly defeated by a vote of 7 to 4 (Hiscocks 1973, 132).

The issue, however, raised serious questions for Council members. Did the activities of the Franco regime cause or might they produce international friction? Were they of such magnitude as to endanger international peace and security? Could the mere existence of a fascistic regime constitute grounds to trump the insulating effects of Article 2(7)? Were sanctions under Article 41 an appropriate response? On 29 April 1946, the Council resolved to "determine whether the situation in Spain has led to international friction and . . . endanger[s] international peace and security," and it established an investigative subcommittee to answer those questions (Resolution 4 [1946]).

With respect to the sanctions issue, the subcommittee rejected Poland's interpretation. In its seventh report to the Council, dated 31 May 1946, the subcommittee stipulated that "'before direct action under Article 41 or 42 can be ordered, the *Charter* requires that the Security Council must determine, under Article 39, the existence of and threat to the peace or a breach of the peace, or an act of aggression.' The Sub-Committee further stated that, in its opinion, 'the Security Council cannot, on the present evidence, make the determination required by Article 39,' and that 'therefore, none of the series of enforcement measures set out in Articles 41 and 42 can at the present time be directed by the Security Council.'"[13]

The report prompted a spirited debate in the Council, with at least one (unidentified) representative taking umbrage at the apparent restriction of the Council's powers by declaring that the subcommittee arrived at an "incorrect conclusion." Four Council members held that the very existence and activities of the Franco regime constituted "a threat to the peace within the meaning of Article 39," which therefore permitted authorization of sanctions according to Article 41.[14] Bowing to prevailing sentiment, Poland amended its draft resolution by striking references to Articles 39 and 41, yet the new draft still failed by a vote of 7 to 4, deemed a subterfuge "to have the Council take action under Chapter VII of the Charter, whereas the Sub-Committee had reported that the conditions for acting under Chapter VII did not exist in the Spanish situation."[15] The Council voted on 26 June 1946 to remain seized of the matter, perhaps to appease those irritated with the Franco regime or perhaps as notice to Spain not to engage its troops stationed along the border with France. On 4 November, absent any questionable actions that piqued the interest of the Council, member states voted to remove the matter from its agenda. Yet the Council did something unusual: it placed "all records and documents" at the Assembly's disposal (UNSC Resolution 7 [1946]).

The Assembly acted with alacrity, and its response on 12 December 1946 echoed, in many respects, the original Polish draft resolution. Its Resolution 39(I) read:

> *Convinced* that the Franco Fascist Government of Spain, which was imposed by force upon the Spanish people with the aid of the Axis Powers and which gave material assistance to the Axis Powers in the war, does not represent the Spanish people, and by its continued control of Spain is making impossible the participation of the Spanish people with the peoples of the United Nations in international affairs;
>
> [the Assembly] *Recommends* that if, within a reasonable time, there is not established a government which derives its authority from the consent of the governed, committed to respect freedom of speech, religion and assembly and to the prompt holding of an election in which the Spanish people, free from force and intimidation and regardless of party, may express their will, the Security Council consider the adequate measures to be taken in order to remedy the situation.[16]

The Assembly resolution revealed one of two important developments in the case and its relevance to making human: an emerging consensus in the Assembly regarding the salience of self-determinative, democratic forms of government. If the Security Council, under guise of a strict interpretation of its primary responsibility, glossed over the human rights concerns as expressed by Poland, the General Assembly honed in on them.

Second, on the matter of regime type and its relationship to international friction and endangerment of international peace and security, the subcommittee proved to be more forward-thinking than the Council. While the subcommittee concluded that the Franco regime and its actions specifically did not constitute international friction or represent a threat to or breach of international peace and security in the meaning of Article 39, the general matter of regime type was not insulated from international consideration by Article 2(7)—thus rejecting the sovereigntist view proffered by the Netherlands. The subcommittee's rapporteur rebuffed the Dutch representative.

> When you look at the internal affairs of a country, you start off with the postulate that it is no business of any other nation to concern itself with how the people of that country govern themselves. That is, *prima facie*, primarily a matter of domestic concern, but if the facts indicate that the regime, by its nature, by its conduct, by its operations, is likely to interfere with international peace and likely to be a menace to its neighbors, then the existence of that regime is no longer a matter of essentially domestic concern. The Charter is built on that basis. (quoted in Kim and Howell 1972, 46–47)[17]

The subcommittee thus "blurred the already hazy distinction between a dispute the continuance of which is likely to endanger international peace and security (Article 33–38 in Chapter VI, to which the domestic jurisdiction reservation applies) and a threat to [or breach of] the peace (Articles 39–50, in Chapter VII, to which it does not apply if enforcement action is ordered)" (Kim and Howell 1972, 47). If that distinction was muddled in the Spanish case, it regained its clarity in the Greek Question.

After two attempts in 1946 by the Soviet Union and the Ukraine to secure passage of a resolution condemning the presence of British troops in Greece and declaring such troops to "cause extraordinary tension fraught with grave consequences for the maintenance of international peace and security," including, according to the Ukrainian draft resolution, "border violations and the persecution of minorities" (Goodrich and Hambro 1949, 59–60), Greece charged Albania, Bulgaria, and Yugoslavia on 3 December with border incursions and with active support of the Communist insurgency. On 19 December 1946, the Council established a commission of investigation comprised of a representative from each member of the Security Council to study the allegations (Resolution 15).[18] In the course of its investigations, the commission requested "the appropriate authorities of Greece, Albania, and Yugoslavia to postpone the execution of any persons sentenced to death . . .

for political offenses" (Resolution 17 [10 February 1947]). Uncertain whether the request fell within its purview, the commission sought Council advice. Armed with a Greek protest against what it thought to be an interference in its domestic affairs in contravention of Article 2(7), the Council determined that the commission lacked such authority "unless [it] has reason to believe that the examination of any such person as a witness would assist the Commission in its work, and makes its request on this ground."

Arguably, the Greek case does little to advance the case of making human, recognizing only the contingent, instrumental value of human beings to the Council's mission. The Council clearly deferred to a powerful sovereigntist logic of prerogative at a point when an injunction against employment of the death penalty for political prisoners might have affected the course of the civil war. Yet at the same time, the Council created a functionally conditional exception to sovereign prerogative based on expected utility to the commission and, by implication, the larger Council's work. With a Soviet veto looming—the Council found unacceptable all of the recommendations of the commission—the Council voted to remove the issue from its agenda on 15 September 1947 (Goodrich and Hambro 1949, 61). Nevertheless, the Greek Question evidenced a cautionary Council ultimately erring on the side of sovereignty even though its subsidiary body, the commission, comprised of representatives from UNSC member states, ultimately proved more visionary than the Council itself.

Whereas the Security Council gingerly approached the Greek Question, ongoing Indonesian-Dutch hostilities forced members to address the loss of life, however tepid its expression of concern. The matter stemmed from Dutch colonial resistance to the Indonesian declaration of independence proclaimed on 17 August 1945, two days after the Japanese emperor surrendered to Allied forces. Dutch authorities hoped to reestablish control of the East Indies after Japan's occupation for three and a half years during World War II, during which time the Japanese encouraged nationalist movements and dismantled Dutch economic, administrative, and political infrastructure (Vickers 2005, 85). Itself occupied by the Nazis, the weakened Netherlands was unable to return to the islands with any significant presence until early 1946; the United Kingdom was therefore assigned the task of supervising Japanese troop withdrawal. But therein were sown the seeds of conflict: while the Indonesians interpreted British presence as a transition to independence, the Dutch viewed it as an interim, place-holding measure until the restoration of its colonial administration. Hostilities soon erupted between Japanese forces and the Indonesians, since the Japanese were, according to the terms of surrender, to reoccupy certain Javanese towns and villages previously relinquished to local populations. British forces aided the Japanese in their fight against the Indonesian armed militias, only to be replaced by Dutch troops during the winter of 1945–46.

The issue came before the Security Council in July 1947, after the collapse of the November 1946 Linggadjati Agreement brokered by the British, which secured Dutch recognition of the Republic of Indonesia's de facto control over certain islands and agreement by both sides to establish a United States of Indonesia by 1 January 1949. On 20 July 1947, the Dutch launched Operation Product, a military offensive designed to regain control over the republic. The Council initially called for the cessation of hostilities and demanded arbitration between the Netherlands and the Republic of Indonesia (Resolution 27 9[1 August 1947]). Satisfied with responses to and actions undertaken by both parties, the Council approved a resolution on 25 August detailing further steps to be taken (Resolution 30). Yet violence broke out again, and the Council passed three additional resolutions pertaining to ceasefires and monitoring and reporting duties; not until Resolution 36 (1 November 1947)—slightly over two years since the conflict began—did the Council call on parties, in paragraph 1, "to take appropriate measures for safeguarding life and property."

The call was desultory; the Council rarely strayed from its central preoccupation of negotiating a pacific settlement to the dispute. Resolution 63 (24 December 1948) broke from its overt focus on mediation and demanded that the Netherlands release the president of the Republic of Indonesia and other political prisoners from detention. But the resolution went further by calling on the UN Commission for Indonesia, previously known as the Committee of Good Offices, to make recommendations "for such economic measures as are required for the proper functioning of the administration and for the economic well-being of the population of the areas involved in such transfers" from the Netherlands to Indonesia (¶4(f)).

Resolution 67 of 28 January 1949, however, proved significant: exerting a humanitarian impulse, the Council appealed for the "effective maintenance of law and order and of essential services, particularly those relating to transportation, communications, health, and food and water supplies." The Council began to apprehend civilians not simply as objects of protection but as potential agents of change: it called for "free and democratic elections . . . to establish a constituent Assembly" to be supervised by "an appropriate agency of the United Nations." This was monumental, for it represented the Council's first requisition for UN supervised elections, even if we may hypothesize that the position was a consequence of its previous action on 21 April 1948 with respect to the India-Pakistan dispute. In that situation,

Resolution 47 (1948) noted "with satisfaction that both India and Pakistan desire that the question of the accession of Jammu and Kashmir to India or Pakistan should be decided through the democratic method of a free and impartial plebiscite."[19]

By concentrating on the economic well-being and development of the Indonesian people and calling for an election,[20] the Council championed not simply the allocation of sovereignty to formerly dependent peoples but self-responsibility and self-determination. The Council came to that position accidentally; it was not its express purpose or goal. If the earliest mention of the safeguarding of life and property signaled an emerging, if perfunctory, sense of the responsibilities incumbent on all parties in the arduous process of decolonization, then the democratic pull of the Council only gradually came to appear in sharper relief.

Though the reader might be inclined to dismiss as negligible the contributions of the cautionary Council to making human, several important lessons emerge from these early engagements. First, whereas the Spanish Question revealed the Council as hesitant to push forward with the democratic narrative, the Indonesia conflict showed the Council as much more willing to champion elections as a mode of conflict resolution and the restoration of order. While the stance likely stemmed from the Indo-Pakistani agreement to settle the matters of Jammu and Kashmir "through the democratic method of a free and impartial plebiscite" (Resolution 47 [21 April 1948]), we cannot entirely dismiss the Assembly's prior position with respect to Spain. Second, the Council's advocacy of safeguarding life and property with respect to the Indonesia Question signaled an emerging consensus within the Council of the responsibilities incumbent on all parties involved in the decolonization process. The position was enshrined in the foundational 1960 Declaration on the Granting of Independence to Colonial Countries and Peoples, in which the UN General Assembly (UNGA) stated that "all armed action or repressive measures of all kinds directed against dependent peoples shall cease in order to enable them to exercise peacefully and freely their right to complete independence" (UNGA 1960a).

But even with these judicious moves, the Council signaled an important movement in making human: for, to quote Hannah Arendt, "human dignity implies the recognition of [our] fellow-[human beings] or fellow-nationals as subjects, as builders of worlds or co-builders of a common world" (1973, 458). In this respect, the cautionary Council appears an analogue to a statist conception of international relations, one firmly rooted in the principles of sovereign equality and territorial integrity. If interpreted with Wight's theory of the barbarian (1992), the cautionary Council is rather a restatement of the Realist position, which demands some contemporization: the issue is not that, as he stated, barbarians have no rights but, rather, that the international community has no right to insure or protect whatever rights they have *unless* the acts of violence are so beyond the pale as to constitute a threat to or breach of the peace. In these early instances, the Council took a halting, admonitory approach, content to focus on the larger political and diplomatic issues—but the groundwork the Council laid opened the door to more robust forms of action, to which I now turn.

### The Protective Council

The protective Council has called for, authorized, or undertaken action with respect to shielding and rescuing individuals from violence and harm perpetrated on them during times of conflict. It has done so through *indirect, exhortative measures* by which the Council calls on others to protect civilians or cease their deliberate targeting, and it has engaged in *direct policing action* through imposition of sanctions or via agents of peacekeeping or peace enforcement.

Indirect, exhortative action should be construed not, perforce, as a ruse to mask an unwillingness to act (though it may in some instances) but as an elevation of international concern and the exercise of the Council's investigative and determinative functions. Thematic resolutions on the protection of children[21] or civilians[22] in armed conflict and on women, peace, and security[23] illustrate the point. By calling on diverse actors to launch investigations, submit reports, monitor behaviors, and formulate programs to achieve ostensibly nebulous objectives, by exerting "diplomatic pressure on abusers' reputations (naming non-compliers . . . , calling attention to non-compliance in floor debates, Presidential statements, [and] talking about a country in a UNSC debate)," and by establishing commissions, benchmarks, and quotas, the Council can exercise "its influence at a distance, through transmission by other actors" (Mahony and Nash 2008, 8). By detaching themes from specific theaters and conflicts, the Council can elevate humanitarian concerns to the forefront of its agenda in ways that recognize and promote a core element of contemporary understandings of human dignity: the right to be free from physical violation.

Justification for direct policing action usually relates to breaches of the peace, as with the Council's response to the North Korean invasion of South Korea. In such cases, concern for human well-being often appears as auxiliary to the primary purpose of conflict cessation. In the Korea conflict, the

Council passed three resolutions—82 (25 June 1950), 83 (27 June 1950), and 84 (7 July 1950)—that, respectively, determined the North Korean attack to be a breach of the peace, called on UN members to assist South Korea in repelling the act of aggression, and established a unified command under authority of the United States, before it recognized "the hardships and privations to which the people of Korea are being subjected as a result of the continued prosecution by the North Korean forces of their unlawful attack" and requested the unified command "to exercise responsibility for determining the requirements of the relief and support of the civilian population of Korea and for establishing in the field the procedures for providing such relief and support (Resolution 85 [31 July 1950], ¶2). The military action was not justified or framed in terms of the humanitarian crisis that resulted from the attack, nor was the Council completely immune to considerations of human welfare, as Resolution 85 demonstrated.

Justification for direct policing action may also place the protection of human beings at the forefront of consideration. Here, the unprecedented Council-authorized humanitarian intervention in Somalia via Resolution 794 (3 December 1992) illustrates. Even the initial resolution pertaining to the crisis, Resolution 733 (23 January 1992), framed the matter in terms of the Council's grave alarm "at the rapid deterioration of the situation in Somalia and the heavy loss of human life."

Yet my concern here is with laying groundwork: might the Council have engaged in earlier instances of protective action? While Somalia is certainly monumental given the Council's authorization of "the use of all necessary means"—diplomatic code for the use of force—to secure the delivery of humanitarian aid, the placement of humanitarian motivations at the forefront of Council work finds useful precedents in the South Africa and Southern Rhodesia cases, the first instances in which the Council unequivocally expanded the parameters of the meaning of international peace and security by including in its calculus systematic violations of human rights based on racist rule.

The matter of racism in South Africa first attracted the attention of the General Assembly in 1946. India requested "that the discriminatory treatment of Indians in the Union of South Africa be included on the agenda of the very first session of the General Assembly,"[24] which resulted in adoption of Resolution A/44(I) of 8 December 1946.[25] Yet the broader policy of apartheid, or racial segregation, was not entertained by the Assembly until 1950, nearly two years after adoption of the UDHR. Resolution 395(V), approved on 2 December 1950, maintained that "a policy of 'racial segregation' (*Apartheid*) is necessarily based on doctrines of racial discrimination" in contravention of the Charter and the Universal Declaration of Human Rights. In 1953, at the request of thirteen UN member states that solicited the secretary-general to study "the question of race conflict in South Africa resulting from the policies of *apartheid*," the Assembly, via Resolution 616(VIII), established a commission to that end and moved forward on the issue.

The Security Council, however, remained disengaged until 1 April 1960, when twenty-nine member states lodged a formal complaint against South Africa for the Sharpeville massacre, in which sixty-nine "unarmed and peaceful demonstrators against racial discrimination and segregation in the Union of South Africa" were murdered (Resolution 134). Ascertaining that the situation had "led to international friction and if continued might endanger international peace and security," the Council condemned the violence and called on South Africa "to initiate measures aimed at bringing about racial harmony based on equality." But it was South Africa's export of apartheid to South-West Africa that elicited a more forceful response: the Council called on states to "cease forthwith the sale and shipment of arms, ammunition of all types and military vehicles to South Africa" (Resolution 181 [7 August 1963]), which the Assembly supported but extended to include a recommendation to states to refrain from exporting oil to South Africa (A/1899(XVIII) [13 November 1963]). Only in 1977, via Resolution 418 (4 November 1977), did the Council make mandatory the embargo on arms, though not on oil.

The Southern Rhodesia case further illustrates the Council's concern with human welfare and dignity. Ian Smith, head of the white minority colonial administration, unilaterally declared independence from Great Britain. Oddly, we might have expected London to push for Council action; on the contrary, the Foreign Office wanted the Council out of its business. At the Council's 1064th meeting (9 September 1963), during which members voted on inclusion of the matter on its agenda, and again at the 1066th meeting, the British ambassador framed the issue as a matter of domestic jurisdiction covered by Article 2(7). The Council, he argued, "had no ground . . . to take action either under Chapter VI or Chapter VII of the Charter."[26] The representative of Ghana, however, successfully rebuffed London, by explaining that General Assembly resolutions, in addition to "deliberations of the Special Committee on the Situation with regard to the Implementation of the Declaration on the Granting of Independence to Colonial Countries and Peoples," indicated that matters of decolonization, especially those concerning the subjugation of one race by another, fell within the purview of the UN.[27] The draft resolution offered jointly by the representatives of Ghana, Mali, the United Arab Republic, Uganda, Tanganyika, and Morocco expressed concern that "'the most powerful air force at present existing on the African continent' and a 'small but highly efficient army recruited on a racial basis' would be transferred to the exclusive control of the Southern Rhodesian Government . . . [which is] representative of only 6 percent of the European population and totally unrepresentative of the 94 percent African population." The result, the representatives concluded, "could only result in a conflict on the African continent."[28] Though the draft resolution to request that the United Kingdom not transfer to Southern Rhodesia "any powers or attributes of sovereignty and armed forces which would aggravate the already explosive situation" garnered eight affirmative votes and two abstentions, the United Kingdom's veto torpedoed Council action.

As Ian Smith inched close to declaring independence, however, the UNSC held additional meetings despite Britain's repeated questioning of the Council's competence to discuss the matter. On 6 May 1965, it passed Resolution 202, which requested states not to recognize "a unilateral declaration of independence for Southern Rhodesia by the minority government" and called on Britain to "promote the country's attainment of independence by a democratic system of government in accordance with the aspirations of the majority of the population." Once Smith broke from Britain, however, London altered its position, presumably because its fundamental interests and, one surmises, its international reputation were then affronted by a regime that was arguably much weaker. In eight days, the Council moved from a position of condemnation of "the racist minority" (Resolution 216 [12 November 1965]) to a more intrusive and commanding one by calling on states to not recognize the illegal regime, to "desist from providing it with arms, equipment and military material, and to do their utmost in order to break all economic relations with Southern Rhodesia, including an embargo on oil and petroleum products" (Resolution 217 [20 November 1965]). On 9 April 1966, the Council, determining that the situation constituted "a threat to the peace," imposed mandatory sanctions—the first time in its history (Resolution 221)—and authorized a naval blockade against the Mozambican port of Beira, then held by Portugal, the main port through which supplies were funneled to landlocked Southern Rhodesia.

The South Africa and Southern Rhodesia cases illustrate a Council beginning to grapple with the complexities of making human given the residue of colonial legacies that persisted in denying racially based majorities particular rights and privileges. Put in the language of chapter 1, the Security Council's actions with respect to South Africa and Southern Rhodesia reflect a precarious balancing of the rationalist and revolutionist positions in Martin Wight's theory of humankind. Under the rationalist, international society perspective, "barbarians have appropriate rights" secured by trusteeship arrangements (in this case, the Council was acting as trustee); in the revolutionist, world society position, barbarians "have equal rights" even if the content of those rights is contested (Wight 1992, 82–83). At minimum, we have in the South Africa and Southern Rhodesia cases an incarnation of rationalist trusteeship in which an institution of international society acted on behalf of a people by imposing sanctions; at maximum, we have a doctrine of full and equal rights posited by the Council and hence an embrace of elements affiliated with revolutionism or world society. Equal rights, according to the Council, demanded democratic, participative forms of rule reflective of the will of the majority—a principle the Council began to express in its early years. But with respect to South Africa and Southern Rhodesia, the Council was unwilling to move into deeper protective territory as it would later do in unprecedented fashion in relation to Somalia. Still, however, imposition of sanctions—even voluntary ones at first—represent a distinct move toward advancing a conception of human dignity predicated on self-worth, self-determination, and full recognition as legal equals.

## The Empowering Council

The Council's work on empowerment, which resonates, as was discussed in chapter 2, with the Charter's aspirational preamble, might be interpreted as recovering particular meanings and promoting new understandings of to whom the Charter's prefatory phrase "we the peoples of the United Nations" refers. In this vein, the Council has promoted democratic, participative schemes of governance (e.g., elections and plebiscites), expressed concern with advancing and protecting human rights, encouraged the self-development of peoples, and—though the Council fails to use the terminology—advanced the logic of human security (the subject of chapter 4) by turning attention to the root causes of insecurity.

First, early Council forays into empowerment came in the form of supporting or promoting democratic procedures as conflict resolution. Two particular instances stand out. On 21 April 1948, the Council endorsed an Indian-Pakistani agreement to settle the question of Jammu and Kashmir's accession to either country "through the democratic method of a free and impartial plebiscite" (Resolution 47). Less than one year later, the Council proposed a resolution of the Indonesia conflict through "free and democratic elections" and even offered the assistance of an appropriate UN agency to supervise the elections (Resolution 67 [28 January 1949]). This support for elections proved to be forward-thinking. At the end of the Cold War, parties to the Nicaragua conflict called on the UN to assist with election organization and monitoring; this quickly became a core activity affiliated not only with Council-approved UN peacekeeping missions (e.g., in Namibia, Cambodia, Haiti, East Timor, and Liberia) but also with general electoral organization and supervisory assistance (over one hundred countries have requested UN election support since 1991). In the 2000s, as an increasing number of private agencies and nongovernmental organizations began to provide election-monitoring services, the UN moved away from election observation and toward technical assistance.[29]

Second, the Council outlined a fairly robust and comprehensive blueprint for empowerment with respect to the self-development of peoples in UN-administered trusteeships and non-self-governing territories. On 2 April 1947, the Security Council appointed the United States as administering authority over the Pacific Islands formerly held by Japan as League mandates (Resolution 21). As chief administrator, the United States was obligated to manage the islands "in conjunction with . . . Charter provisions" in Chapter XI; the resolution specified with great precision obligations (Resolution 21[1947], ¶6) vis-à-vis the care of the peoples of the Pacific Islands and their eventual movement toward self-government. The language was not entirely new, however.

If Article 55 represents the crescendo in the Charter's overture to human rights, human dignity, and human welfare that was first enunciated in Article 1, then obligations outlined in Chapters XI and XII to ensure the political, economic, social, and educational advancement of nonindependent peoples in preparation for independence are its denouement. In contrast to Article 1, which paints a very broad-brush picture of defense and advancement of equal rights, self-determination, human rights, and the resolution of international problems of an "economic, social, cultural or humanitarian character," Article 55 articulates with somewhat greater specificity the responsibilities that the UN shall undertake and that its members, via Article 56, pledge to work toward. Such obligations encompass the promotion of "higher standards of living, full employment, and conditions of economic and social progress and development; solutions of international economic, social, health, and related problems; . . . and universal respect for, and observance of, human rights and fundamental freedoms."

The thematic that renders "we the peoples" central to the organization's mission culminates in Chapters XI and XII, on non-self-governing territories and trusteeships. Article 73, Chapter XI's anchor, obligates administering authorities, UN-appointed trustees, and all member states to "recognize the principle that the interests of the inhabitants . . . are paramount, and accept as sacred trust the obligation to promote to the utmost, within the system of international peace and security established by the present Charter, the well-being of the inhabitants," which includes empowering them politically, economically, socially, educationally, and scientifically; assisting peoples "in the progressive development" of their free political institutions; and encouraging research toward "constructive measures of development." The General Assembly embossed its interpretation of Chapter XI: far from outlining a static relationship of dependency, the provisions point to a "dynamic state of evolution and progress towards a 'full measure of self-government.'"[30] This self-determinative frame provides the optic through which I view the third empowering initiative of the Security Council: the thematic resolution. Adoption of the thematic resolution represents a fairly new and robust exercise of Council functions that disentangles issues from discrete contexts and cycles of violence and thus evidences its appreciation of the broader dimensions of violence as not merely physical or criminal but social, political, and economic—a perspective that one can plausibly argue is rooted in Article 55's calculus.

Most thematic resolutions properly constitute indirect, exhortative protection measures, though a compelling case can be made for classifying several of them as directly intrusive, quasi-policing initiatives. Resolutions such as 1612 (on children and armed conflict), 1674 (on the protection of civilians), and 1820 (on women, peace, and security) are notable precisely because they represent the Security Council's latest, most deeply penetrating measures into domestic jurisdictions, with respect to their subject matters (Mahony and Nash 2008, 19). Each imposes on states and nonstate actors regular robust reporting procedures on the implementation of recommendations; outlines prohibited activities and reminds actors of their criminal liability for the planning, commission, and assistance of such acts; and proposes frameworks for achieving the multiple objectives identified to protect civilians and prevent armed conflict. Yet those resolutions also distinctly advance a logic of empowerment.

For instance, the Council has affirmed the "important role that education can play in supporting efforts to halt and prevent abuses committed against civilians" (Resolution 1674 [28 April 2006]) and in "empowering vulnerable civilians" (Resolution 1894 [11 November 2009]).[31] The Council has proven to be particularly concerned with children and has attended to the role of education as a tool in the arsenal of preventing conflict—a position that echoes Arendt's understanding of educational institutions as salient institutions for socializing individuals and preparing them to be active, responsible citizens.[32] Resolution 1379 (20 November 2001) asked "agencies, funds and programmes of the United Nations" to "devote particular attention and adequate resources to the rehabilitation of children affected by armed conflict, particularly their counseling, education and appropriate vocational opportunities, as a preventive measure and as a means of reintegrating them into society," as well as to "promote a culture of peace, including through support for peace education programmes." Resolutions 1460 (30 January 2003) and 1674 (28 April 2004) reiterated the need for states and international organizations to ensure proper, long-term education for children and civilians in the service of sustainable peace.

Resolutions evince the Council's considerable reflection on and grappling with the issue of women, peace, and security. They repeatedly reaffirm the central role of women "in the prevention and resolution of conflicts and peace-building, and stress the importance of their equal participation and full involvement in all efforts for the maintenance and promotion of peace and security, and the need to increase their role in decision-making." To that end, the UNSC has proposed and encouraged development of a variety of programmatic and policy endeavors (Resolution 1325 [31 October 2000]). In Resolution 1625 (14 September 2005, ¶4(c)), Council members called for the "strengthening [of] the capacities of civil society groups, including women's groups . . . to promote a culture of peace."

The Council's emphasis on empowerment is cast instrumentally as a form of responsibility, that is, as a technique to end and prevent conflict. This is not to suggest that initiatives to make human need entirely be altruistic. But it is to highlight the connection between thematic resolutions, the objectives outlined in Article 55 of the Charter, and humanization. Moreover, it underscores the salience of making human to the Council's work vis-à-vis international peace and security: recognizing the claims of the marginalized, abused others; taking responsibility for their plight; and encouraging initiatives to empower them. Verbiage in resolutions confirms the view: the Council expressed its "grave concern at the harmful and widespread impact of armed conflict on children" because of the "long-term consequences this has for durable peace, security and development" (Resolution 1261 [30 August 1999]). Some may deign to criticize the Council for instrumentally framing human welfare and thus failing to be concerned with violence perpetrated against children for their sake. That interpretation is, to a degree, unfair. As the world's premier body for managing international peace and security, the Council must justify its interventions and, moreover, its disentanglement of themes from distinct conflicts; even its permanent members recognize that there are limits to its extraordinary powers.

More broadly, the Council has urged UN agencies and organs and other international organizations, states, and nongovernmental organizations to address "root causes of armed conflict and political and social crises in a comprehensive manner, including by promoting sustainable development, poverty eradication, national reconciliation, good governance, democracy, gender equality, the rule of law and respect for and protection of human rights" (Resolution 1625 [14 September 2005]; see also the preambles of Resolutions 1265 [17 September 1999] and 1366 [30 August 2001]). Such emphases reveal a changing appraisal of international peace and security to include the protection of children, which Resolution 1311 (11 August 2000) locates in "the purposes and principles of the Charter . . . and the primary responsibility of the Security Council for the maintenance of international peace and security" (something the earlier Resolution 1261 did not do); embargoes on the trade of natural resources implicated in conflict (e.g., Resolution 1459 [28 January 2003]); and civilizational dialogue, the promotion of tolerance, and the mutually implicative roles of the "media, civil and religious society, the business community and educational institutions" toward constructing and maintaining peace and security (Resolution 1624 [14 September 2005]).

Expanding the parameters of international peace and security in human-centric, not necessarily state-centric, terms raises the specter that the Council increasingly acts as a primary institution or site of making human. Specifically, I wish to return now to an argument introduced in chapter 2. As I noted there, Meilaender (2009, 103) writes that "we know persons only as bodies and when we encounter a living human body our moral task is to seek to recognize the person who is there." The encounter is, essentially, a two-level game. On the first level, the spectacle of human bodies gives rise, in Meilaender's view, to awareness of the human species (as distinct from animals) and thus to a conception of human dignity meaning "the integrity and flourishing of the human species" (118). But human dignity is but a "placeholder for what is thought to be characteristically human" (1); hence we need a conception of "personal dignity . . . to make clear that, however different we may be in the degree to which we possess some of the characteristically human capacities, we are equal persons whose comparative 'worth' cannot and ought not be assessed." That is the second level: to discern a person in his or her specificity as an individual.

The Security Council is confronted by bodies of multiple sorts, as pummeled, battered, bruised, maimed and mutilated—victims, as it were, of armed conflict, criminal activity, and terrorism. We expect to find, therefore, references to victimhood, even if some (Carpenter 2005) criticize them for reproducing gendered essentialisms and causing blindness to gender-based sexual violence against men. The Council has come to identify particular types of victims: women, children, civilians writ large, humanitarian relief workers,[33] journalists,[34] and the sexually exploited[35] (refugees, peacekeepers, international organization personnel, and diplomats are also variously mentioned in a slew of post–Cold War resolutions). By distinguishing particular groups, the Council presents us with a puzzle. Surely the Council can recognize not the person (i.e., the specificity of an individual) but only the body (or, rather, a mass of bodies) defined as a consequence of victimization. But confrontation with victimized bodies could hardly give rise to a conception of human dignity. As Daly (2013, 54) notes, "[T]o reduce one to one's body—whether by torture, extreme poverty, or other degradation—is to compel a person to focus only on fulfilling his or her bodily need . . . Because we are more similar in our bodies (all having like needs for food, water, medical care, shelter, etc.) than in our minds, reducing one to one's body erodes the value of individuation that dignity seeks to protect." Surely the Council has taken great care in identifying certain groups based on their victimization. Victimhood resides at the heart of the Council's justificatory framework—and the protective dimension of its work, at least rhetorically, is fully at play. But any presumed vulnerability of peoples—indeed, their victimhood—is but a superficial rendering of what is at stake in the Council's classificatory scheme. So why does the Council articulate a grammar of protection and empowerment in the particularistic language of identifications? Is it because of the peoples' presumed "weakness"? Beyond victimhood, what do these groups of people have in common?

The answer lies not in Council determinations but, rather, I believe, in understanding why these groups are targeted in the first place. Their targeting owes to social identity, status, and role. Put differently, it seems that the Council views some*thing* between personal and human dignity that relates to the *social signification* or status (Waldron 2012a) of each category, both as central to the fabric of social existence and as derivative from the context in which those particular groups are situated. The Council, in other words, affirms the human being as a social being. On this view, women procreate and are often the transmitters of culture (to their children); thus, to murder or rape them destroys or disrupts not only bloodlines but the transmission of community values, narratives, and traditions. Journalists inform. Humanitarian relief workers care and tend to those in need. All these groups of people represent continuity: a continuity that violence aims to interrupt, if not eradicate. The dignity of the species is defined and preserved by defense of these chains of continuity; the dignity of individual persons is affirmed by responding to their victimhood.

On that reading, we may understand why children, as representatives of a bloodline, are frequently targeted: they represent (especially in the context of ethnic, racial, and nationalistic violence) the continuation of a hated group. Enemies of a group may consider it more expedient to kill the children in that group along with the adults (e.g., as in Rwanda and Bosnia), or the enemies may deem it more "profitable" to forcibly enlist the children of a group and compel their loyalty by encouraging them to murder their families and terrorize surrounding villages (as in Uganda). In still other societies, combatants may forcibly transfer children from one group to another. It thus might appear remarkable that Article 2 of the 1948 Genocide Convention (1948) and Article 6(e) of the 1998 Rome Statute for the International Criminal Court determine that the transference of children from one group to another constitutes an act of genocide. This legal move unequivocally substantiates the interpretation offered here: transference interrupts the continuous transmission of culture from adults to children. Two critical observations follow: first, the law admits a relaxation of the presumed immutability of the groups against whom genocide may be committed (racial, ethnical, national, religious), since they suggest that forcibly transferred children may be socialized into new modes of cultural and social being. This implies, second, that "culture"—comprised, as it were, of traditions, group narratives, collective practices, and hence identity—is socially constructed. Any conception of dignity must, then, be invariably attuned to this existential dimension (see Kateb 2011).

Acts of violence perpetrated on groups, no matter how defined, are ultimately "injustices of misrecognition," to use Nancy Fraser's terminology. As a matter of social justice, not individual psychology, misrecognition entails denial "of the status of a full partner in social interaction and prevent[ion] from participati[on] as a peer in social life" (Fraser quoted in Tétreault and Lipschutz 2009, 152; see also Fraser 2000, 1995). The German Federal Court of Justice held in a 1999 case that "the perpetrators of genocide do not target a person 'in his capacity as an individual'; they do not see the victim as a human being but only as a member of the persecuted group'" (quoted in Cassese 2008, 137). One can argue that the Council, by virtue of identifying discrete groups requiring special protections, attempts to correct such an injustice of misrecognition; in doing so, the Council elevates victims' key claims to and roles in social life and verifies the necessity of insuring continuities that otherwise would be lost. In this way, the Council, a state-based institution of international society illustrative of the management of international affairs by great powers, has come to appreciate the significance of the individual in international affairs. Put differently, world society claims of a post-Holocaust world order occasionally occupy a seat at the table of that high political body charged with maintaining that most fundamental of international society's elementary goals: order.

## Conclusion

Jeremy Greenstock, former British ambassador to the UN, observed that the "threat of nuclear annihilation" and "the spread of freedom and democracy and the rejection of colonialism, in both moral and political terms," played strong roles in the "remarkable reduction in the number of wars between states to settle a clash of interests or to enlarge territory since 1945" (Greenstock 2008, 249). The UN, in its capacities as framework and actor, also contributed to this reduction: "The existence of a forum for the discussion and resolution of problems between states, within which flowed a gradually strengthening current of condemnation in relation to the use of force against collective interest, made it increasingly more difficult for individual states to resort to military action to promote national interests without incurring real penalties."

While arguably all work of the UN is oriented toward cultivating conditions for order and peace, the Security Council is charged with the primary responsibility of maintaining international peace and security. This chapter has argued that such work has unexpectedly, if not consistently and perhaps even unconsciously, extended beyond the interstate mechanics of international peace and security to consider its humanitarian dimensions, hence deepening the notion of collective interest. In sociological terms, the "gradual strengthening current of condemnation of the use of force" and the discursive framework within which to entertain a panoply of issues that come, in many cases, to constitute collective interest manifest what Norbert Elias called a "'civilizing process' in which individuals learn how to control aggressive inclinations and adjust their thoughts and actions in response to the legitimate needs of other members of society" (Linklater and Suganami 2006, 121–22). The notion of civility is, in Linklater and Suganami's estimation, a "useful tool for thinking further about . . . the transformation of international systems into international societies and about the evolution of global ethical standards in the modern states-system" (122). On this point, they take note of Adam Watson's thoughts on diplomacy (1982, 20; quoted in Linklater and Suganami 2006, 122n9): "The diplomatic dialogue is . . . a civilized process based on awareness and respect for other people's point of view; and a civilizing one also, because the continuous exchange of ideas, and the attempts to find mutually acceptable solutions to conflicts of interest, increase that awareness and respect."

The Security Council has proven, perhaps unexpectedly, to be an engine or source of defending and promoting respect for human dignity—of, in short, making human. In some cases, the Council's characterization of victims has perpetuated gendered essentialisms (e.g., the vulnerability and weakness of women and children) and caused blindness to certain forms of gender-based violence (e.g., the raping of men by men; on these points, see Carpenter 2005). But via the expansion of its mission and focus, albeit not always consistently, the Council has countered the appearance of scorned ethnic or racial minorities, abused women, traumatized children, and emasculated men with the sheer fact that they are human beings. It has found a cornerstone of peace in the self-determinative capacities of individuals, argued for the empowerment of people so that they may achieve the fullest levels of their polity's development, and predicated international peace and stability on common responsibilities, especially with respect to decolonization, the equality of races, and the full rights of individual human beings.

The Security Council has thus come to humanize the dehumanized by recognizing (and attempting to reverse) injustices of misrecognition; distinguishing certain categories of peoples by virtue of victimizations that attack their social status; linking the protection and empowerment of peoples not simply with international peace and security but, more conceptually, with the continuity required for the perpetuation of the human species and with appreciation of diversity in ways of human flourishing; iterating degrees and types of responsibility (e.g., criminal liability of perpetrators of abuse and violence, the legal obligations of states); altering the terrain of legitimate forms of resistance (through the exercise of rights, empowering peoples, enhancing capabilities, and addressing the root causes of insecurity); reflecting on how violations of human livelihood and annihilations of the human person impinge on international peace and security; repeatedly insisting that certain norms and rights and liberties and practices are inviolable; and establishing parameters of action that diverse actors are recommended to undertake to ameliorate degrading conditions and empower civilians. The Security Council does not always perform these tasks, perform them consistently, or perform them well. But the work of the Council illustrates an awareness and a willingness to sometimes situate the most primordial building block of international relations—the individual—at the forefront of its work and its calculations of how best to maintain international peace and security.

CHAPTER 4

# Human Security

## *Making Human through Protection and Empowerment*

It is my personal view that we need a new culture of international relations—with the precept of human security at its core. Such a culture, though intrinsically embedded in the UN's ideals, was never truly enacted in practice. In our ever-more interdependent world it's more important than ever before that we embrace and enact principles of human security, international law and multilateral cooperation, human rights, responsibility to protect as well as protection of the environment and sustainable development. When in January 1941 Franklin D. Roosevelt addressed the United States Congress, he spoke of freedoms that the world should be founded upon. He spoke of freedom of speech and expression, freedom from want and freedom from fear—everywhere and anywhere in the world. He saw these freedoms not as "vision of a distant millennium," but rather as a "definite basis for a kind of world attainable" in his own time and generation. They became the very foundation of the United Nations.

—Srgjan Kerim[1]

On 1 February 2008, Simon Romero of the *New York Times* reported on a nonviolent separatist movement in San Andrés, a Caribbean archipelago owned by Colombia but claimed by Nicaragua. The province's thirty-five-thousand Raizals, English-speaking descendants of African slaves who comprise approximately one-third of the population, "symbolically declared independence" in June 2007 by removing the Colombian flag from public buildings (Romero 2008). If deposition of the flag was largely ignored, a diplomatic row several months later provided the Raizals with an opportunity to publicize the province's plight, which one independence advocate equated with "a subtle kind of apartheid, but more cruel than the colonialism Colombia threw off from Spain."

> Many . . . say state spending here focuses on the needs of tourists, like a recently completed beachfront walkway. A short drive away, past mansions owned by mainlanders, is a large garbage dump with the unlikely name Magic Garden where recently a dozen Raizals searched for scrap metal and discarded food . . . "I don't see how Nicaragua or Colombia would give me more to eat," said Janice Bent, 43, who scavenges through trash to feed her four children. "If I can survive doing this, I can survive under independence."

Minority Rights Group International (MRG), a nongovernmental organization devoted to promoting indigenous and minority peoples' rights, found that though the Raizals represent slightly less than one-third of the population and "have educational performance levels that are equal to or greater than other ethnic groups," they account for three-quarters of the province's poor and earn five hundred dollars per year compared to the fifteen-hundred-dollar average annual income of whites and mestizos (MRG 2008). Unemployment hovers at 70 percent according to the UN high commissioner for human rights. As Colombia encourages greater immigration to the province from the mainland and finalizes deals for megaprojects to develop the archipelago into a resort, all the while excluding the Raizals from employment and other economic enhancing opportunities, charges of subtle apartheid may be increasingly difficult to deny.

The situation reveals several important clues that help us unpack the relationship between state and human security. First, though people may survive despite the state, the state still matters; the symbolic declaration of independence affirms the idea of (self-determinative) statehood. Second, human security matters more, especially in conditions of persistent, systematic, and deliberate deprivations. Whereas the previously quoted Ms. Bent determined that neither Colombia nor Nicaragua can be relied on to make available basic provisions—hence raising, for her, the attractiveness of an independent San Andrés—"Aldin Leon Robinson, a retired house painter who lives on social security payments of about $200 a month" gives Colombia his fealty because Bogotá ensures the basic condition of his livelihood (Romero 2008). These individuals' respective circumstances underscore citizen expectations of the state to perform at least minimal functions, that is, to guarantee a modicum of conditions conducive for self-development and hence for dignity. Persistent neglect or failure to ensure those conditions may result in, at minimum, talk of independence and, at maximum, sustained (perhaps violent) secessionist movements.

Read together, those points yield a third: human security depends not simply or even primarily on human ingenuity and individual action. Rather, as Ms. Bent and Mr. Robinson suggest, human security presupposes an institutional framework designed to stabilize conditions within which human beings may develop their skills and talents and thus flourish—a point underscored by what I referred to, in the previous chapter, as the "empowering" UN Security Council and its revised calculus of international peace and security. But institutions need not always be understood in bureaucratic terms. We may think of relations of care—operative at household, community, municipal, state, regional, and transnational levels—as an institutionalized, or routinized, practice. Though practices or relations of care have long been regarded as private, relegated to the home, and usually classified as women's work, Fiona Robinson (2011) has demonstrated that entitlements to, responsibilities for, and remunerations of care determine and govern a myriad of decisions at all levels, with potentially grave repercussions for the otherized. Relations of care are thus very much central to public life. On this reading, the care framework—one that situates responsiveness to the needs of others and hence is constructed on a relational ontology (Robinson 2011, 4; see also Held 2006, 29–43)—becomes a useful tool to evaluate the performance of institutions. As Held notes, "relations between persons"—and, we might add, relations between persons and the institutions that are designed to serve and assist them—"can be criticized when they become dominating, exploitative, mistrustful, or hostile," while relations that are attuned to "the effectiveness of . . . efforts to meet needs" of others in responsible and responsive ways are "encouraged and maintained" (2006, 37, 36). On this view, societies construct

> institutions to provide safety and security for weaker members— those who are less able to protect themselves from the rigor and cruelties of the savage world [*responsibility*] . . . Institutions also establish norms of behavior that enforce solidarity and mechanisms of group preservation [*normative reproduction*]. Whether these security institutions emerged out of altruism, self-interest, biological imperatives, or social contract is less important than the fact that key social institutions are built on identifiable human security elements internalized and carried by each individual [*self-responsibility*], and they reflect the

efficacy of those elements in the general protection and enhancement of human life. (Bedeski 2007, 5)

But garbage dumps, even improbably named ones, do not constitute institutions in any caring, protective or empowerment sense. Foragers of food in them, along with recipients of social security payments, do, however, illustrate security's multidimensionality, as well as the extent to which human security and state security, perception and policy, and institutions and individual ingenuity are intertwined. The human security concept, defined in broad brushstrokes as freedom from want, freedom from fear, and freedom to live in dignity—or, phrased differently, the survival, welfare, well-being, and wellness of a person and peoples—combines objective elements of protection and empowerment with subjective perceptions of security. Human security aims at a comprehensive and holistic conception of security rooted, as Heidi Hudson explains, "in terms of the real-life, everyday experiences of human beings and their complex social and economic relations as these are embedded within global structures." Hudson notes that it "therefore becomes imperative to view security in terms of patterns of systemic inclusion and exclusion of people" (2005, 163; see also Thomas 2004) at multiple levels (e.g., local, national, regional, international, transnational).

On that reading, human security becomes a useful analytical tool to gauge effects of political, social, and economic processes—whether local, national, or transnational—on human welfare and livelihood. Security, von Tigerstrom (2007, 3) maintains, "is an important human value"; hence, defining it "amounts to making a normative claim about when we should consider ourselves to be secure." Defined as a *human* value, security bridges the divide between its individual and collective referents. Whereas the scholarship and practice of international relations have long tended toward a statist rendering of security and its collective referent (to the exclusion of its individual referent),[2] human security broadens the notion of the collective to include multiple kinds of human communities—whether at the village, regional, national, or transnational level—and how different types of relationships between people and communities affect perceived and experienced (in)security. In doing so, it necessarily tends to the individual.

Tadjbakhsh and Chenoy (2009, 18–19) characterize the shift as altering the status of the individual

from that of a simple citizen of his state into that of an actor involved in international relations. The individual becomes an "agent" who can be actively engaged in defining potential security threats, and who can participate in efforts to mitigate them. The survival, well-being and dignity of the individual become the ultimate goal, and constructs such as the state, the institutions of political democracy, and the market are relegated to secondary status as simply means to achieve that goal.

But as Fiona Robinson (2011, 9–10) warns, we must not define the "human" of human security as autonomous and atomistic. We are relational, embodied, interdependent selves whose survival, well-being, and dignity are inherently tethered to, defined, and produced by "relations of responsibility and care" that are "subject to change and . . . saturated with different forms and levels of power" (55). The relational/care approach to human security alerts relevant stakeholders, policy analysts, and policy makers to the myriad of complex, situational factors that affect the "distribution, nature, and amount of care work undertaken" and required to produce securer peoples and communities.

This chapter unfolds as follows. The first section outlines the human security concept, which I limit to its conceptual development within the UN system for two principal reasons. First, human security first appeared under UN auspices in 1994; member states have since been engaged in its definition, clarification, and operationalization. Second, focusing on developments within the policy world rather than on academic debates, which have too often been disconnected from practical developments and, further, sidelined by definitional contestation, speaks more to this book's concerns: the internationalization of humanizing practices. The second, major section of this chapter explores the value that the concept of human security adds to analyzing security through the prism of making human: succinctly stated, human security humanizes marginalized or "forgotten" peoples by elevating their lived conditions to the center of security analysis. It thus substantiates the argument of chapter 2 by being centrally concerned with dignity's corporeal and sociopolitical dimensions, including concern with the social status of human beings.

## Human Security: Outline of a Concept

By now, the story of human security is a familiar one. Its appearance in the 1994 *Human Development Report* embodied both the optimism and the anxieties associated with the end of the Cold War. But if the concept initially capitalized on anticipations of a peace dividend, then egregious intrastate conflicts and wide-scale deprivations informed its development. Dr. Mahbub al-Huq and his team in the United Nations Development Programme (UNDP) came to understand persistent deprivations experienced by peoples (e.g., identity-based repression, endemic poverty, persistent hunger and malnutrition, disease, and resource misallocation or scarcity) as destabilizing to states. Because insecurities emanate from multiple sources, al-Huq and the compilers of the *Human Development Report* maintained that our conception of security must be broadened from an "exclusive stress on territorial security to a much greater stress on people's security" (UNDP 1994, 24); hence they framed human security as "safety from such chronic threats as hunger, disease and repression . . . and . . . protection from sudden and hurtful disruptions in the patterns of daily life" in economic, food, health, environmental, personal, community, and political security domains (23–25).

The sheer breadth of the concept as initially articulated engendered diverse interpretations and applications—not to mention contestations and resistances. Canada and Japan, among others, championed human security and eventually proclaimed it "as the guiding principle of their foreign policies" (Tadjbakhsh and Chenoy 2009, 1–2). But whereas Ottawa preferred a narrower approach that focused on "freedom from fear" or the protection of peoples from violent conflict and the traditional understandings of security threats, Tokyo underscored human security's "freedom from want" or developmental dimension. Keen on obtaining greater conceptual clarity, the Japanese government, in cooperation with the UN Secretariat, established the Commission on Human Security (CHS) in 2001. Sadako Ogata, one of the CHS's cochairs, sharpened the concept's focus—or, at the very least, made a robust case on behalf of a broader, context-oriented view focused on what Taylor Owen (2004, 284) refers to as a threshold-based conceptualization of human security, which attaches our understanding of "threats" to their "severity rather than their cause." While peoples usually adapt to scarcities and exclusions, severe, persistent and deliberate deprivations invariably alter perceptions, which may lead to demonizations of others, as happened in Bosnia, Kosovo, Chechnya, Georgia, Sierra Leone, Burundi, and Rwanda. Consequently, "[t]hose who feel marginalized, deprived or angered by what they perceive as injustices caused by poverty and inequity" may resort to violence (Ogata 2002, 2).[3] The question, then, is how to manage such conflicts.

The human security concept responds to that question by analytically disassembling the state into its smallest components—individuals and the communities in which they live—in order to put it back together again. How this ought to be done was outlined in the CHS's 2003 final report,

*Human Security Now,* in terms of a protective/empowerment framework. Human security, the CHS (2003b, 1) maintained,

> means protecting vital freedoms. It means protecting people from critical and pervasive threats and situations, building on their strengths and aspirations. It also means creating systems that give people the building blocks of survival, dignity and livelihood. Human security connects different types of freedoms—freedom from want, freedom from fear and freedom to take action on one's own behalf. To do this, it offers two general strategies: *protection* and *empowerment.*

Protection means the development of "norms, processes and institutions that systematically address insecurities."[4] Examples of domestic protection initiatives include strengthening and training civilian police and military, promoting human rights education, and demobilizing combatants, as well as "meeting immediate needs of displaced people; launching reconstruction and development programs; promoting reconciliation and coexistence; and advancing effective governance" (CHS 2003b, 2). International protection initiatives include the 1997 Ottawa Convention, banning antipersonnel landmines; the creation of the International Criminal Court in 1998; agreement on and work toward the 2000 Millennium Development Goals; and the creation in 2003 of the Kimberley Process Certification Scheme to interdict the sale of diamonds mined in regions mired in conflict. Even human security's critics have lauded these successes as "impressive" (Paris 2004, 370).

As further evidence of the concept's policy and practical reach, collaborations such as the Human Security Network and the African Human Security Initiative (a voluntary network of seven African states that permits key African nongovernmental organizations to monitor the performance of governments with respect to human security issues) have emerged to coordinate ideas about and craft human security programs. The European Union,[5] the African Union (see Tieku 2007), the Organization of American States, the Association of Southeast Asian Nations, and the Pacific Islands Forum have devised human security platforms and polices.[6] In May 2004, the UN Secretariat opened the Human Security Unit (HSU) to integrate human security in all of the institution's activities and to manage programs financed by the UN Trust Fund for Human Security (UNTFHS).[7]

The protective component of human security is complemented by its empowerment dimension, which is geared toward helping and enabling people "to develop their potential and become full participants in decision-making"

(CHS 2003a, 1), as well as toward cultivating multistakeholder partnerships that should help communities mitigate the impact of and, where possible, prevent the recurrence of insecurities. Initiatives might include ensuring access to health care, education, skills development programs, and microfinance; carefully crafting "affirmative action programmes . . . so that all sections of society gain" (UNDP 1994, 39); and cultivating the formation of public spaces built on principles of toleration and dialogue that, in the end, encourage local leadership (CHS 2003b, 11). Work of this sort may be seen in projects funded by the UNTFHS, which was established through the initiative and generous contributions of Greece, Japan, Slovenia, and Thailand. The UNTFHS finances programs in partnership with UNDP and other actors in five focus areas, including democratic governance, poverty reduction, crisis prevention and recovery, energy and environment, and HIV/AIDS.[8]

Yet the tension between the broad developmental and the narrower protective interpretations of human security stymied political agreement on the concept, and the issue of intervention haunted it. After the 1994 Rwandan genocide and 1999 NATO air campaign in defense of Kosovo, the International Commission on Intervention and State Sovereignty (ICISS 2001) reframed humanitarian intervention as a "responsibility to protect" (R2P) populations from egregious harm and suffering when the state is unwilling or unable to do so under it. Human security and R2P seemed inextricably linked. However, in the wake of the US-led invasions of Afghanistan and Iraq, states distinctly and emphatically separated R2P from human security at the 2005 World Summit (UNGA 2005, ¶¶138–40, p. 30 [on R2P], and ¶143, p. 31 [on human security]; UNGA 2012, ¶3). The official UN Secretariat position and the repeated mantra of the UN General Assembly is that "the use of force is not envisaged in the application of the human security concept" (United Nations Secretary-General 2010, ¶23, pp. 6–7). Human security, the UN has held, must be implemented in ways that respect state sovereignty.

That the human security concept prompted a wide array of projects and programs and yet remained terminologically imprecise impelled the UNGA to host a thematic debate on 22 May 2008 to garner clarity. Three points emerged. The first reiterated the very problem that prompted the debate: while member states lauded the "contribution that human security brings to addressing current global challenges from achieving the Millennium Development Goals to advancing peace-building efforts and responding to climate change, among others" (UN PGA 2008, ¶6, p. 2), some also warned of the risk of "conceptual overstretch" that could "drain it of any real operational applicability" (¶7, p. 2). A second, definitional point stipulated the need to differentiate human security from R2P (¶11, p. 3). The final point celebrated human security "as a *people centered and multi-sectoral approach*" that "provides a significant opportunity for the United Nations to better integrate the three pillars of the organization's work (i.e., security, development and human rights) and offer coordinated responses that can more efficiently address current challenges facing the world . . . In this regard, Member States emphasized the contribution of human security in the UN's effort to implement the 'One UN' reform programme" (¶12, pp. 3–4).

What might be the most memorable element of the debate came from the then-president of the General Assembly, Srgjan Kerim of Slovenia. He advocated the construction of a "new culture of international relations" with the human security concept at its "core" (Kerim 2008).[9] Such a culture must move "beyond fragmented responses" by approaching interconnected security problems with a "comprehensive, integrated and people-centred" perspective. If the protective/empowerment framework suggests anything about this new culture, it is that it encourages "complex and extensive forms of coordination and centralization" in the guise of "a comprehensive international infrastructure that shields self-reliance from menacing threats" (Duffield 2006, 24). To assist practitioners (and states) in developing and implementing human security projects, the Human Security Unit issued a "handbook" in 2009 aimed at operationalizing human security's five central principles: people-centered, multisectoral, comprehensive, context-specific, and prevention-oriented. Table 1 summarizes the principles and the relevant approaches.

In view of the multidimensionality of threats and insecurities, the UN Secretariat remained wed to a broad view of human security.[10] The secretary-general's much-anticipated report of 8 March 2010 on human security underscored that broad view. The report lauded human security as

> an invaluable tool for assisting Governments in identifying critical and pervasive threats to the welfare of their people and the stability of their sovereignty. It advances programmes and policies that counter and address emerging threats in a manner that is contextually relevant and prioritized. This helps Governments and the international community to better utilize their resources and to develop strategies that strengthen the protection and empowerment framework needed for the assurance of human security and the promotion of peace and stability at every level—local, national, regional and international. (United Nations Secretary-General 2010, 1)

TABLE 1. Human Security Principles and Approaches

| Human Security Principle | Human Security Approach |
|---|---|
| People-centered | • Inclusive and participatory<br>• Consider individuals and communities in defining their needs/vulnerabilities and in acting as agents of change<br>• Collectively determine which insecurities to address and identify available resources including indigenous coping mechanisms |
| Multi-sectoral | • Promote dialogue among key actors from different sectors<br>• Ensure coherence and coordination across traditionally separate sectors/fields<br>• Assess positive and negative externalities of each response on the overall human security situation of the affected community(ies) |
| Comprehensive | • Holistic analysis including the seven areas of human security [personal, food, health, economic, community, political, and environmental]<br>• Address the wide spectrum of threats, vulnerabilities, and capacities<br>• Consider actors and sectors not previously considered relevant to security |
| Context-specific | • Requires in-depth analysis of the targeted situation<br>• Focuses on core freedoms and rights under threat<br>• Identifies the concrete needs of affected community(ies) and enables the development of appropriate solutions embedded in local realities, capacities and coping mechanisms<br>• Takes into account local, national, regional, and global dimensions and their impact on the targeted situation |
| Prevention-oriented | • Identify risks, threats, and hazards, and address their root causes |

*Source:* HSU 2009, 12.

Despite the clear programmatic manifestations of human security and its advances toward countering and addressing emerging threats, some member states remained troubled by its definitional ambiguity, as evidenced during the UNGA follow-up debate of 20–21 May 2010 on the secretary-general's report (see UNGA 2010a, 2010b). While two states, Iran and Venezuela, rejected the concept, Bolivia, Russia, and China thought the concept "too abstract and imprecise for international application" (UNGA 2010b). A majority of states, still concerned about the need for greater clarity, nevertheless found promise in the many practical applications of the concept at international, regional, and country levels, while a few states (e.g., Austria, Gabon, and South Korea) hailed human security as "forward-thinking, synergistic and adaptable to the work of the UN." Notwithstanding the predominantly favorable reception to human security, a new divide seemed to have emerged during the debate, between member states focused on confronting broad structural and systemic causes of human insecurities (e.g., the global financial crisis, climate change) and those focused on addressing country-specific problems. Indicative of the depth of the divide, the representative from the Solomon Islands indicted the latter as a symptoms-based approach that only creates a "false sense of security."

An informal thematic debate hosted by the UNGA president was held in April 2011 to help bridge the abyss, which, in turn, instigated a series of consultations between member states and Mr. Yukio Takasu, the special adviser to the secretary-general on human security, starting in November 2011. A synthesis of positions led to publication of the secretary-general's second report on human security on 5 April 2012, which outlined the parameters of an emerging state consensus centered on two points. First, states agreed that, far from threatening member states' sovereignty with international governance or, worse, intervention, human security "enhances the coping capacity of societies." Second, states came to appreciate the need for the generation of "political strategies" to appropriately address the various insecurities and threats people face.[11]

The consultative strategy worked. On 10 September 2012, the UNGA adopted by consensus Resolution 66/290, which expressed a common understanding of human security. It thus caps a long, painstaking process by which key advocates of human security struggled to forge state support and during which states defused any potential challenge that they thought human security posed to them and their sovereignty. Given the importance of the resolution, I here quote at length from the main section:

> 3. [The General Assembly] *Agrees* that human security is an approach to assist Member States in identifying and addressing widespread

and cross-cutting challenges to the survival, livelihood and dignity of their people. Based on this, a common understanding of the notion of human security includes the following:

(a) The right of people to live in freedom and dignity, free from poverty and despair. All individuals, in particular vulnerable people, are entitled to freedom from fear and freedom from want, with an equal opportunity to enjoy all their rights and fully develop their human potential;

(b) Human security calls for people-centred, comprehensive, context-specific and prevention-oriented responses that strengthen the protection and empowerment of all people and all communities;

(c) Human security recognizes the interlinkages between peace, development and human rights, and equally considers civil, political, economic, social and cultural rights;

(d) The notion of human security is distinct from the responsibility to protect and its implementation;

(e) Human security does not entail the threat or the use of force or coercive measures. Human security does not replace State security;

(f) Human security is based on national ownership. Since the political, economic, social and cultural conditions for human security vary significantly across and within countries, and at different points in time, human security strengthens national solutions which are compatible with local realities;

(g) Governments retain the primary role and responsibility for ensuring the survival, livelihood and dignity of their citizens. The role of the international community is to complement and provide the necessary support to Governments, upon their request, so as to strengthen their capacity to respond to current and emerging threats. Human security requires greater collaboration and partnership among Governments, international and regional organizations and civil society;

(h) Human security must be implemented with full respect for the purposes and principles enshrined in the Charter of the United Nations, including full respect for the sovereignty of States, territorial integrity and non-interference in matters that are essentially within the domestic jurisdiction of States. Human security does not entail additional legal obligations on the part of States. (UNGA 2012)

If we were to parse this common understanding—to draw a road map, as it were, to lay out where we have been and to chart where we are going, diplomatically and programmatically—several landmarks are worth noting.

First, the resolution poses an elastic conception of security, since, as noted in ¶3(f), "conditions for human security vary significantly." Second, the resolution reads into human security a state-centrism in several forms: as an instrument in the toolbox of state authority and sovereignty, as a program of "national ownership", and as state prerogative, as indicated by the notation at ¶3(h) that human security "does not entail additional legal obligations on the part of States." This second point is tempered, however, by a third, major one: the qualification of a state-centric logic of prerogative by normative logics of responsiveness and responsibility to people. Human security is then framed as an optic or tool to help states identify and address "widespread and cross-cutting challenges to the survival, livelihood and dignity of their people" (¶3(g)). Fourth, to help states meet such an obligation, the resolution evinces a networked, collaborative, and heterarchic understanding of global politics by calling for greater thematic interlinkages between "peace, development, and human rights" (¶3(c)) and for "greater collaboration and partnership among Governments, international and regional organizations, and civil society" (¶3(g)). Yet nonstate actors and the international community writ large are secondary to states; they merely "complement and provide the necessary support to Governments upon their request."

## Making Human: The Added Value of Human Security

Though supporters and detractors of human security continue to spar over definitional matters, programs indicate some confluence of understanding around what human security means practically and existentially. Human security apprehends and aims to defend, promote, and sustain the human status of marginalized or "forgotten" peoples: ethnic minorities such as the Raizals, the under- and unemployed, the impoverished, the diseased, the hungry and malnourished, the trafficked, the sexualized objects, the under- or uneducated, the illiterate, and inner-city and rural dwellers alike. Such is the import of the UN Human Security Unit's 2006 booklet *Human Security for All—Integrated Responses to Protect and Empower People and Their Communities: A Look at Nine Promising Efforts* (*HSFA*), which both illustrates "practical applications of human security" and, in the process, "give[s] the concept a human face" (HSU 2006). Featured projects include reducing the demand for illicit drugs in Afghanistan, empowering women and girls in Central America, supplying energy to West African villages, protecting women and children from human trafficking in Cambodia and Vietnam, expanding quality access to education in Kosovo, attending to the needs of the displaced in Colombia, giving voice to the silenced in Africa and Afghanistan, mobilizing rural communities in East Timor, and stabilizing refugee communities in Tanzania.

The rhetorical appeal of *HSFA* hinges on its tracing strategy. Via biographical vignettes, the report personalizes the effects of various threats and insecurities (e.g., unemployment, food scarcity, crime syndicate operations), which are themselves manifestations of broader transnational maladies (e.g., food insecurity, drug or human trafficking). In that view, human security translates globalizing processes and their ill effects into manageable chunks by reterritorializing and reading them as impingements on human capability and livelihood and, in turn, on community and state capacity.

The pragmatic appeal of *HSFA* stems from its operational strategy: demonstrating an integrated, comprehensive, contextualized, "beyond-the-box" approach to problem solving. For instance, learning animal husbandry, establishing communal rice banks, and accessing microcredit have ostensibly tangential connection to human trafficking, yet *HSFA* shows that in rural Cambodian communities targeted by human traffickers, alleviating income and food insecurities through those efforts—which empower women—have eradicated the problem. Employed, educated, and food-secure women engaged in community life through practices of care and responsibility are not susceptible to the financial promises of traffickers and do not become enmeshed in gendered dynamics of patriarchal control and violence (HSU 2006, 13–15).

Even as critics applaud such results, they also impugn perceived implications. No matter their positive outcomes within at-risk communities, the efforts outlined in the report—for example, community counseling, (sex, antidrug, health, food/nutritional) educational initiatives, media campaigns to promote awareness of disease transmission, low-technology energy-producing generators, seed banks, and construction of (commercial plant) nurseries—illustrate well human security's strong welfare orientation (Carafano and Smith 1996), breadth (since human security conceivably incorporates virtually "anything that presents a critical threat to life and livelihood . . . whatever the source" [Newman 2004, 358; see also Buzan 2004b; MacFarlane and Khong 2006; Paris 2001]), and, in extreme cases, seeming endorsement of forms of intervention (Hoge 2008). How are policy makers to respond to diversified threats and their sometimes uncertain source? What value does human security really add to security discourse and analysis?

Responses to that question consistently underscore a particular set of features that differentiate human security from conventional notions of state security: its people-centered focus; situational and hence nongeneralizable nature; multidimensionality; demand for multisectoral, integrated, and comprehensive responses; prevention orientation that focuses on root causes of violence, threats, and insecurities; and utility in serving both as a "benchmark for impact evaluation" and a tool to identify "institutional gaps in security infrastructure" (HSU 2009, 7–11; see also Owen 2004; Hudson 2005; Tadjbakhsh and Chenoy 2007, 105–6). Far from endearing critics to human security, such responses have tended to distance them from the concept even further, precisely because of human security's differentiation from, not its complementarities to, state or conventional security analyses and concerns.

Therein lies part of the problem. Human security does not subtract the state out of security analysis; rather, it adds the human being. In doing so, human security seeks to augment state capacity and sustainability—which critics seem to miss—by admitting a variety of elements that factor into perceptions of insecurities and experiences of threat. Further, by calling for coordinated multisectoral activity, human security lessens burdens on states insofar as it draws on a range of actors (and their unique strengths) to substantiate and stabilize states and the communities within them. By ignoring those points, as well as practical (or, at the very least, discursive) developments and concurrences among states, critics talk past human security's advocates.

Rather than focus on points that have already been raised in the literature, I wish to consider another added value of the human security concept: because it situates the real-life, everyday experiences of peoples at the forefront of analysis, the ways in which it operationalizes the processes of making human, reconfigure state institutions to make them more responsive and attentive to people. In the remaining pages of this chapter, I explore the idea from the standpoint of four of the five processes of making human: reflection, replication/reproduction, responsibility, and recognition.

## Reflection

In chapter 1, I employed the language of *zoē* and *bios* to get at the issue of making human. Whereas *zoē* refers to biological life common to animals and humans, *bios* pertains to a distinctly human life lived in community (if not always in communion) with others. To use spatial imagery, *bios* inhabits a public realm characterized by intersubjective recognition, acceptance, and inclusion, while *zoē* inhabits a private, segregated realm defined not by biological sameness but by difference; the dignity that is supposedly ours by virtue of being categorized, scientifically, as human, is stripped, and the dignity that is ours by virtue of being an individual person endowed with specific skills, capacities, and potentialities is ultimately denied. By ignoring, displacing, or marginalizing the insecurities and threats experienced and perceived by ordinary peoples, conventional security analysis contributed to a blindness (especially during the Cold War) to how politics affected ordinary peoples.

Human security may be read as dismantling the barriers that entrap *zoē* and transforming it (back) to *bios*, which demands a degree of reflection regarding "our most basic notions of what it means to be human" (Smith 2007, 243). In this regard, human security encourages reflection on the status of others and the situations in which they live, which broadens the horizons of security analysis. As such, it concomitantly demands that we interrogate the boundaries between public and private life that perpetuate and even exacerbate human suffering and insecurity, especially ones (re)produced by hegemonic masculinities, racisms, or classist prejudices.

For Robinson, human security "must [therefore] recognize the importance of relations and networks of responsibility and care in determining people's everyday experiences of security and insecurity" (2011, 10). As a form of maintenance of selves, relations, and communities, care "is a foundation of the human condition that makes the 'continuity of life and social institutions possible'" (15). Yet Robinson cautions that when care is ascertained in terms of "benevolence, charity, or attention to 'victims' or the 'vulnerable,'" it "could serve to reinforce existing patterns of domination and dependency within and among societies and at the global level" (165). She therefore urges us "to read care ethics [and human security] through the prism of historical and contemporary relations of colonialism . . . as well as within the context of contemporary relations of race and geopolitics." Thus one might respond to the sexual trafficking of girls and young women from rural Cambodian villages (HSU 2009, 13–14) by simply arresting perpetrators and, perhaps, providing necessary health care to the "victims." This does little to remedy their plight or to forestall deeper, more enduring maladies that have befallen Cambodian society and state: sex trafficking has emptied rural villages of young women, forced young men in search of wives to depart for urban environments (where they often do not find jobs or wives), robbed villages of youthful ingenuity and productive labor power, led to further economic degradation in rural areas and to potential food collapse as less land is farmed, and contributed to urban overcrowding, unsanitary conditions, unemployment, and petty crime. A more reflective, sensitive approach encourages consideration of means to empower young women and girls and the communities in which they live through skills training, establishment of communal rice banks, and providing access to microcredit, as human security programs have done.

If human security stretches the ontological subject of security to include diverse types of people, it likewise broadens our perspective of what may constitute a security threat. Indeed, the 1994 UNDP *Human Development Report* listed seven broad "areas" of security, including personal, food, health, economic, community, political, and environmental. As I noted earlier, the sheer breadth of the accounting invited criticism. To remedy this, Taylor Owen, following, it seems, Sadako Ogata, proposed a threshold-based reading of human security, attuned not so much to the proximate cause of a threat or insecurity but to its severity. This leaves unmolested human security's context orientation, permitting us to perceive substantial variation in security threats and insecurities among and within states: for instance, Vanuatu's chief security threat might be experienced as rising ocean levels that displace populations and contaminate drinking water, while East Timor's might be food insecurity. Further, a threshold- or severity-based approach provides policy makers the rationale to differentiate between and rank insecurities and threats and determine which demand or require more immediate attention—an especially useful provision for societies with limited resources.

Elastic conceptions of subject and situation presupposed by the human security framework owes to what has become a truism in international relations: the end of the Cold War liberated thinking and policy from the straightjacket of bipolar rivalry. Yet that straightjacket's untying was a process, not a singular event. In his second inaugural address, Ronald Reagan (1985) boldly announced, "There is only one way safely and legitimately to reduce the cost of national security, and that is to reduce the need for it." For him, the calculus of cost and need reduction hinged on nuclear disarmament. But the underlining idea, as many countries long understood, resonated beyond denuclearization; indeed, one can plausibly argue that it was anticipated in the 1976 Declaration of Concord of the Association of Southeast Asian Nations (ASEAN). National and regional stability and "resilience," the declaration maintained, precipitate from social and economic development. By "improving the living conditions of local populations," ASEAN leaders "expected to check subversive influences" and stabilize their societies (Emmers 2004, 11; ASEAN 1976; MacFarlane and Khong 2006, 128).

The emphasis on checking subversive influences may strike some as morally objectionable, especially given Indonesia's suppression of minorities at the time in East Timor and Banda Aceh. Such actions do not, obviously, cohere with human security. But I raise this antecedent precisely because of the logic shared by the ASEAN declaration, the Reagan inaugural, and human security: they link the individual with the community and translate the stability, resilience, and security of each in terms of the other. Put differently, though people are human security's *immediate* referents and beneficiaries, the state is its *ultimate* referent and beneficiary. Even so, calculations of state and international order, stability, and security are extricated from purely statist confines. Human security analysis forces the humanitarian element to percolate to strategic and tactical importance.

On that reading, human security is a means—that is, an "ongoing process of minimizing obstacles and threats to the protection and promotion of human life and its potential for becoming more fully human" (Kim 1984, 186)—to the end of state viability, since violence "destroys or diminishes life-sustaining and life-enhancing processes, [and] hence [is] the principal source of human insecurity."[12] The logic defends the sovereign state "on the grounds that the state is of authentic value to its population" (Wheeler and Morris 1996, 151). States, after all, "can be powerful custodians of human welfare, and thus worthy of contingent loyalty" (Harbour 1999, 80; see also UNDP 1994, 31). Whether and how well states fulfill these roles is an empirical matter on which we may reasonably evaluate state performance. I call this logic *pragmatic cosmopolitanism*; attachment of the adjective *pragmatic* qualifies the noun *cosmopolitanism*. The move is not merely grammatical. It focuses attention on the specificity of deprivations, insecurities, or threats—no matter from which level (transnational, international, regional, national, municipal)—and their effects on human livelihood and practices of care and responsibility (on many of these issues, see Robinson 2011).

Care and responsibility demand attentiveness to the specific demands associated with particular contexts. Such an orientation is supposed to aid in the development of more situationally appropriate methods to obtain security and promote subjective experiences of feeling secure; human security aims to do this through empowerment. "[E]mpowering individuals and communities to develop the capabilities for making informed choices and acting on their own behalf" (Oberlietner 2005, 187) is key to the concept's implementation. Empowerment, though, depends on the presence of "abundance of possibilities," which, as the Spanish philosopher José Ortega y Gasset put it, "is a symptom of thriving life . . . Success in life depends on amplitude of possibilities" (1961, 19–20). Success also hinges on the protection of those possibilities, which is the point of the human security concept—and why the state remains central to it.

Objection may be levied from at least two directions. On the one hand, the protective/empowerment framework may be read maximally as a welfare entitlement scheme and may be criticized on that basis (see Carafano and Smith 1996). Yet one may relax interpretation of the point and construe amplitude of possibilities as self-generated: I, as an empowered individual, utilize available resources in conjunction with my specific interests and skill sets in ways that magnify my potential and expand my life possibilities as dictated by my interests and vision for my future. We might identify this as human security's chief existential, humanizing import and its contribution to dignity. On this personal level, human security may only require an analytic assessment and mapping of insecurities and threats and the framing of policies and programs undertaken at the substate level to counter those, which do not perforce entail welfarist redistributive schemes. While some threats (e.g., drug and human trafficking) may require more robust, intrusive police actions, others (e.g., food insecurity) may simply require training in irrigation and food storage techniques, not handouts by the state or an international agent.

On the other hand, some may criticize human security as not sufficiently distinguished from development. Being mutually implicative, these concepts do blur. But whereas human development is a broad "process of widening the range of people's choices," human security more narrowly focuses on protecting or enhancing the conditions within which "people can exercise these choices safely and freely" (UNDP 1994, 23). Notably, UNDP linked the perennial pathological condition of international relations—violence—to severe, persistent, preventable, deliberate deprivations in human life. Framed in this manner, human security, being centrally (though not solely) focused on contexts within which people are denied access to vital resources, directs attention to remedying both the deliberateness of such practices and their longer-term repercussions, which is precisely what makes human security a security—and not simply a developmental—problem.

### Replication/Reproduction

Human security might be an unlikely candidate to make human through replication or reproduction of prevailing norms, given its contextual orientation (UNGA 2012, ¶3(b)) and equal regard for all people. Yet in the policy world, emphasis on building the capacities of states and peoples, coupled with donor demands for fiscal accountability, have encouraged formulations of "lessons learned" that, in turn, feed into the identification and cultivation of "best practices." In 2009, the HSU provided a blueprint for applying the

TABLE 2. Human Security Program Phases

| Phase | Goals and Tasks |
| --- | --- |
| **Phase 1: Analysis, Mapping, and Planning** | • Establish participatory processes and collectively identify needs/vulnerabilities and capacities of the affected community(ies)<br>• Map insecurities based on actual vulnerabilities and capacities with less focus on what is feasible and more emphasis on what is needed<br>• Establish priorities through needs/vulnerabilities and capacity analysis in consultation with the affected community(ies)<br>• Identify root causes of insecurities and their inter-linkages<br>• Cluster insecurities based on comprehensive and multi-sectoral mapping<br>• Establish strategies/responses that incorporate empowerment and protection measures<br>• Outline short, medium, and long-term strategies/outcomes even if they will not be implemented in the particular program (Outlining strategies at different stages with the community is an important foundation for sustainability)<br>• Establish multi-actor planning to ensure coherence on goals and the allocation of responsibilities and tasks |
| **Phase 2: Implementation** | • Collaborate with local partners, ensuring that actions do not unintentionally undermine any other human security component/principles and that they respect the local norms and practices of the affected community(ies)<br>• Consider the changing dynamics of risks and threats; adjust to changes as necessary for the protection and empowerment of the affected community(ies)<br>• Build capacity of the affected community(ies) and local institutions<br>• Monitor the program and use findings for learning and adaptation |
| **Phase 3: Impact Assessment** | • Are we doing the right thing as opposed to whether or not we are doing things right?<br>• Does the program alleviate identified human insecurities while at the same time avoiding negative externalities?<br>• Deriving lessons learned from failures and successes |

*Source:* HSU 2009, 13.

human security concept and integrating it into policy. Table 2 summarizes goals and tasks associated with each of three phases of human security program development: analysis, mapping, and planning; implementation; and impact assessment.

For my limited purposes here, I wish to focus on impact assessment, which the HSU defines expansively: impact assessment looks beyond the evaluation of programs "against indicators of efficiency" (e.g., temporal, functional, financial) and is framed around "the longer term consequences of the programme," including questions related to the program's legitimacy (HSU 2009, 22), which, in turn, is hinged on responsiveness to the needs of people as ascertained through careful listening to and inclusion of them in planning and implementation phases. Human security impact assessments calculate the ratio of programmatic costs to benefits, specify changes required at the policy and institutional levels, make recommendations for similar future projects, and address how human security initiatives might be best institutionalized at local and national levels and "owned" by communities to promote self-development and encourage self-initiative (25). At each phase, "valuable information on a host of insecurities" may be collected and "if shared appropriately can contribute to the advancement of human security" (26). All information, the HSU handbook recommends, should be compiled in the form of databanks from which lessons may be learned and best practices may be gleaned.

The logic underpinning a best practice relates to the probability that particular techniques, methods, or procedures will efficiently produce desired outcomes. In 2006, the UN Economic and Social Council (ECOSOC) included "best practices" in its *Definition of Basic Concepts and Terminologies in Governance and Public Administration* (UN ECOSOC 2006, 12–13), thereby illustrating the extent to which the best practices approach has proliferated within the UN system. The logic has infiltrated the world of human security project management, as evidenced by the publication in December 2010 of a joint United Nations–Bhutan report that outlines best practices with respect to promoting income and health security for vulnerable people, including women and children (United Nations–Bhutan 2010).

King and Murray (2001–2) have attempted to devise a composite index of human security similar to the UNDP's Human Development Index, which measures longevity of life, educational levels, and standard of living to derive an aggregate score of human development. But the danger of such an index, as pointed out by others (e.g., Mack quoted in Tadjbakhsh and Chenoy 2007, 241), is that it inevitably invites comparative analysis and hence the ranking of states. Developing countries, which would fall lower on any such scale, resist such a move because it would likely be construed as an avenue for greater Western interference and intrusion.

Development of even a hypothetical index reveals some of the tensions between human security's normative aspiration and its operational engagements that a "best practices" approach might engender. One of human security's most often touted values to security analysis is its orientation around "the micro impact of international policies and agreements" (McRae 2001, 17). In that regard, human security demands a high degree of coordination between international and domestic agents, policy makers, and academic analysts who are called on to use local-level, not national-level data, since "significant variance occurs not just between countries, but [also] within them" (Nhema 2006, 197). It is difficult to deny that the benefits of coordination and data collection across contexts may be substantial, especially when the lived experiences of peoples under threat may be quite similar. Specific information (about disease mitigation, poverty reduction, landmine detection and eradication techniques, agricultural productivity, etc.) can be gleaned from programs and activities that have successfully mitigated or ameliorated a problem; it can then be applied in other contexts to enhance research and policy effectiveness, reduce duplication of effort and therefore improve efficient utilization of limited resources, and increase transparency of local, regional, national, and international action and policy. Improving programs to directly benefit and empower at-risk people is the clear attraction of best practices.

The danger inevitably lies not necessarily in imposing a uniformity of technique that would necessarily undermine human security's contextual, needs-based approach to the lived experiences of real peoples—which a best practice, as a normalizing force, might encourage. Rather, the danger of employing best practices with respect to human security is the tacit assumption that comes with it: the superiority of the practice itself, which, because of the certitude of its deployment and the effectuation of desired results, is deemed *best*. What has been deemed best is usually synonymous with "the preferred," "the acceptable," and quite possibly "the only." In a field wholly dependent on international donors and commitments with finite resources, only the preferred and acceptable would presumably attract resources, while alternative, locally generated or sensitive methods may not. Those who fail to adopt best practices might therefore be perceived as irresponsible and hence unworthy of assistance.

Feminist theorists alert us to another potential danger of human security best practices, which, if adequately addressed, would further expand the positive impact of the human security approach. Bernedette Muthien

(2000), Viviene Taylor (2004), Charli Carpenter (2005), Jacqui True (2011), and Fiona Robinson (2011) have examined gender-based exclusions and essentialisms. In the human security framework, these might appear as blindness to gender-based violence against men (e.g., Carpenter 2005), identifying women as either agents of peace or as victims (e.g., True 2011), replicating patriarchal ideas and programs currently embedded in states and their organs (e.g., Taylor 2004), or treating the human subject of human security as isolated from the communities and power dynamics within which they are actually located (Robinson 2011). In other words, the human security framework has been deployed in some instances in ways that normatively and practically reproduce forms of gender-based (not to mention race- or class-based) violence.

The challenge, therefore, is to mainstream gender in transformative ways into decision making about and implementation of international public policy (True 2011). Muthien and Robinson, among others, maintain that the human security approach needs to discount the public/private divide especially when actions undertaken in private reproduce violence, exploitation, domination, and insecurity. One way of the doing this, Robinson argues, is to link human security with a distinct focus on practices and relations of care and responsibility. To avoid the potential that care enacted through an international human security approach might degenerate into a paternalism of the sort that characterized North-South imperial relations, Robinson (2011, 104–5) cautions against the essentialization of women's roles as caregivers and demands that we "interrogate the norms and structures that construct care as 'feminine.'" Likewise, we must attend to "relations and practices of care that have become broken, exploitative, or inadequate," no matter their location. Thus "a fully feminist ethics of care must be democratic," which demands not only hearing all voices but consciously assigning responsibilities for care among a diversity of actors. This requires, in turn, a sensitivity to and awareness of "historical and contemporary relations of colonialism and neocolonialism." The point is to replace normative strictures long reproductive of violence and exploitation with ones that inculcate and cultivate normative and practical commitments to inclusion, equality, attentiveness, and responsibility.

## Responsibility

National or state security has its own imperatives, logics, economy, and technologies that evidence a state's responsibility to itself (as an independent entity) and to its citizens. Ronald Reagan aimed to alter its calculus by reducing national security's costs and necessity in the field of nuclear weaponry. But the national security equation, especially when read in terms of necessity, cannot be predeterminedly narrowed, for necessity is subject to multiple variables, including perception, fear, and the development of new technologies and misuse of existing ones for sinister purposes. New discourses, economies, and technologies emerge to counter the unforeseen. Human security is one such technology based on a logic of state responsibility toward its citizens; but it also reveals layered sets of international responsibilities if one takes seriously two claims: first, that insecurities and threats are "interrelated or mutually dependent" in our globalizing world and, second, that human security has equal moral regard for all peoples (von Tigerstrom 2007, 54; see also 54–58, 72–88).

At the level of the state, antecedents of human security may be found from the ancient Greeks onward (see MacFarlane and Khong 2006, 23–60). But an unlikely source of human security as responsibility is worth identifying. Thomas Hobbes maintained that

> among so many dangers therefore, as the natural lusts of men do daily threaten each other withal, to have a care of one's self is not a matter so scornfully to be looked upon, as if so be there had not been a power and will left in one to have done otherwise. For every man is desirous of what is good for him, and shuns what is evil . . . It is therefore neither absurd, nor reprehensible, neither against the dictates of true reason, for a man to use all his endeavors to preserve and defend his body and the members thereof from death and sorrows. (Hobbes 1949, 26–27)

The passage underscores the salience of self-interest and the individual right of self-defense as facets of self-responsibility. Yet Hobbes's conception of care of the self captures human security in its most rudimentary, minimal sense: as security of subjects against other subjects and a degree of liberty ensured and protected by the state to permit people to achieve "what is good" for them. The state, on this view, facilitates human security primarily by policing relations between individuals, not necessarily by offering entitlement packages. Yet the function of protection is not borne by the state only; Hobbes leaves a residual right of self-defense with subjects—a sort of exit clause, as it were, from the social contract that creates the state. Individuals consent to civil authority so that such authority will *preserve* and *protect* their lives; that is the foundation of the social contract. Preservation and protection become the Leviathan's chief ends; "covenants not to defend a man's own body are void" (Hobbes [1668] 1994, II.xxi[11], 141). Thus, if the sovereign loses the means or the willingness to protect subjects and, likewise, if the subject's life is threatened under conditions of captivity, the subject "cannot be understood to be bound by covenant to subjection, and therefore may, if he can, make his escape by any means whatsoever" (II.xxi[20–22], 144–45).

The extent to which the state polices, preserves, and protects is a matter of both interpretation and context. Hobbes's minimal reading is not, on second glance, so minimal after all. The sovereign, he maintains, is likewise obligated "to secure" subjects "in such sort as that . . . they may nourish themselves and live contentedly" (II.xvii[13], 109). Though, prima facie, the emphasis remains squarely on individual responsibility and empowerment, Hobbes admits that

> the end for which [the Leviathan] was trusted . . . [is] the procuration of *the safety of the people*, to which [sovereignty] is obliged by the law of nature . . . But by safety here is *not* meant a bare preservation, but also all other contentments of life, which [all individuals] by lawful industry, without danger or hurt to the commonwealth, shall acquire. (II.xxx[1], 219)

Protection and empowerment do not necessarily end with the relationship between state and citizen, however. Advocates of human security recognize that it "seeks to harness other institutions alongside the state" (McCormack 2007, 81; see also CHS 2003b; HSU 2006, 2009; UNGA 2012, ¶3(g)) in ways that constitute and cultivate relations of responsibility and care. This view is echoed by Foucault, who described care of the self as "not an exercise in solitude, but a true social practice" (1986, 51–52). Care of the self, "or the attention one devotes to the care that others should take of themselves, appears then as the intensification of social relations" (53), which returns us to the earlier discussion on best practices.[13]

The implication is Janus-faced: on the one hand, failure to exercise rights responsibly or to manage "properly" one's life invites increased surveillance and policing, whether directly or indirectly, and, with that, a conclusion that any failure owes not to others but to an irresponsible self; on the other hand, protected subjects with rights are empowered and humanized, enabled to take responsibility for their self-development. To wit, food insecurity is mitigated not by endless provisions of food supplies but by establishing exchanges and seed banks and instructing others on sustainable irrigation, the benefits of crop rotation and proper storage techniques, and animal husbandry (see Benedict 2009, ¶27). While such types of human security initiatives may evince a logic of best practices, their local success ultimately hinges on "patient listening" to others to ascertain experienced insecurities and conditions and on working in solidarity with them to build the life projects that they are unable to complete (see Simmons 2011). To resist paternalistic, imposing frames of reference and operation, successful responsible human security projects must inculcate these basic elements of practices of care (see Robinson 2011).

### Recognition

The sixty-second president of the UN General Assembly hosted the first thematic debate on human security and envisioned a new culture of international relations with human security at its core. Tadjbakhsh and Chenoy (2007, 13) give shape to that vision by stressing human security's ontological presupposition and normative vision—its promises to focus "on individuals and peoples" and "on values and goals such as dignity, equity and solidarity." They continue, "[B]ut this new paradigm involves more than just setting the individual up as the centre of a constellation of threats, actors and programmes. *It changes the very status of the individual*, who is no longer consubstantial to the state—an infinitesimal part of an organic whole—but an equal subject and actor in international politics."[14]

As noted earlier, Robinson warns that we must not define the "human" of human security as autonomous and atomistic to the detriment of recognizing our relational, embodied, interdependent selves. In a similar vein, equality must not be read in absolute, predetermined ways that ignore or underplay differences in capacities, capabilities, and circumstance. To wit, many marginalized peoples—for example, women, indigenous peoples, LGBT persons, ethnic and racial minorities, and non-Western communities—have criticized human rights for reproducing (and imposing) an undifferentiated conception of the human and construing humanity as a "homogeneous totality" (Festa 2010, 13; for a feminist critique of human rights universalisms, see Reilly 2007). Succinctly, a dominant perception is that human rights discourse often tends to erase or minimize the very things that make us human: our identities, histories, and affiliations (see Rajagopal 2003, 171–232).

This point may elicit protest from the human rights community, who take seriously their commitment to the equal rights of all. Nevertheless, we must heed the criticisms. Contrary to its promise, there are many instances in which human rights has been "blind to the tremendous variety that human-rights struggles take in the form of social movement resistance in the Third World," especially with respect to gender, development, and democracy (Rajagopal 2003, 12)—and, I would add, sexuality. The human rights frame provides important leverage and has been the basis for profound advances, but it is not, as Simmons (2011), Rajagopal, and others aver, without limitations. Governments may be and often are resistant or unresponsive to reminders of their human rights obligations. Even modern democracies under guise of majority rule may justify the denial or restriction of rights to minorities, especially when those minorities are declared nonpersons (e.g., women or refugees), undeserving of a full scheme of equal rights (e.g., African Americans, blacks in apartheid South Africa, Muslims in Myanmar), morally indecent (e.g., LGBT persons), or threats to national livelihood and security (e.g., Japanese Americans during World War II, suspected terrorists in a post-9/11 world).

When such groups advocate for their rights, those who deny them may retort that articulations of human rights as pertaining to specific communities dilute the universality of human rights. While this "special rights" argument has strikingly lost much traction with respect to women, indigenous peoples, and ethnic and religious minorities, it has been resurrected within the UN General Assembly's Afro-Asian bloc with respect to LGBT rights (see Gennarini 2012; IGLHRC 2012). Despite the hollowness and clear political underpinnings of the argument, it nevertheless exemplifies the extent to which the human rights frame may actually fail to help resist discrimination, violence, and legislative action directed against abhorred groups.

Consequently, those who have been denied rights consider the language and logic of human rights too legalistic and constraining (Mertus 2007). Even some courts have been reluctant to adjudicate discrimination claims on grounds of equality-based rights violations and have instead relied on liberty-based arguments (Yoshino 2007, 187–96). This shift to liberty over rights emboldens some in the LGBT community as many denounce the acronym (and hence calls for LGBT rights) as too narrow and hegemonic. In those views, assertions of LGBT rights come to reflect racialized (white), Western, gay male, middle- and upper-class, able-bodied, and monogamy biases (see Seidman 1993).[15] Alternatively, as an echo of Simmons's argument about self-ascription of identity (2011), they campaign for recognition of the multiplicity of identities and diversity of ways of expressing and practicing one's sexuality (see Gross 2007).[16] Subgroups share a core belief not in the presumed universality or automaticity of rights but in the multidimensionality of being human. Put differently, these perspectives emphasize less the *rights* and more the *human* of human rights.

By taking the relational, socially embedded, intersubjective self as its subject, human security likewise takes the very signifiers that have served as perverse justification of rights deprivations and exploitations as its starting point (at least in instances of deliberate and imposed deprivations; this is Ogata's argument [2002]). When deprivations, insecurities, or threats are nondeliberate and systemic in nature (e.g., natural disasters), human security takes the specificity of lived human experience, not human identity, as its starting point. Human security thus adds to, rather than subtracts from, the conception of the human being and the myriad of being human.

Finally, to return to this section's opening theme, by situating the individual at the center of security analysis, human security, in its boldest formulation, aims to engender a "new paradigm of security" that shifts attention from "external aggression to protecting people from a range of menaces" and stimulates new and reinvigorates existing multisectoral, multistakeholder initiatives (CHS 2003b, 2–3). Consequently, supporters think that human security expands normative boundaries in ways that require "a rethinking of state sovereignty" (Hubert 2004, 351). Critics (perhaps unwittingly) reproduce this transformative view: insofar as the human security concept resides at the interface of the state and the individual, it exposes a rift between, on the one hand, sovereignty construed as prerogative and autonomy and, on the other, sovereignty framed as relational and in terms of responsibility.[17]

## Human Security and a Humanitarian Post-Holocaust World Politics

In the introduction to this book, I referred to the aforementioned rift between understandings of sovereignty more obliquely, in terms of a postwar state-based international relations and a humanitarian post-Holocaust world politics. I do not suggest that these two approaches are mutually exclusive; as this book hopefully demonstrates, they clearly are not. But each entails a certain set of priorities and commitments that help make the distinction possible. Over time, however, the humanitarian commitments of a post-Holocaust world politics—human rights, human development, and criminal accountability being a few—have come to intrude, in varying degrees, on the prerogatives of state. In my view, one commitment in particular underlines all of them: making human. To practice the slogan "Never again!" means that we need to strive to recognize the human in the brutalized body, the rights-deprived, the impoverished and diseased, and the abhorred other. Making human is, in short, the recognition that the human being is not merely a biological designation but a constructed social status.

In the arsenal of post-Holocaust weaponry to combat dehumanization, human security proved a late development. Given early successes, notwithstanding coetaneous definitional debates, Canadian foreign minister Lloyd Axworthy (2001, 10) lauded human security as a "central organizing principle of international relations and a major catalyst for finding a new approach to conducting diplomacy." This may seem hyperbole in retrospect, but Axworthy captured two important dimensions of the human security concept. First, human security increasingly has served as a center of gravity—"a catalytic concept," as the CHS (2003b) called it—around which a particular set of global governance initiatives have been organized, many of which were summarized earlier in this chapter. Second, human security has been utilized as an evaluative tool. In terms of project management, impact assessments address project rationale, development, implementation, and response/effect in ways that help improve future projects (see also McRae 2001). Externally, human security has been used by communities, states, and international agents to assess perceived and experienced insecurities and to prioritize needs that demand the most urgent attention.[18] MacFarlane and Khong (2006, 228) put a different gloss on the added value of human security: it opens up the state and security to alternative analyses that cohere with the messy realities of violence in a post–Cold War era, provides "a vocabulary for describing and understanding the human consequences of internal and civil wars," increases the likelihood of UN response to egregious threats to human security, and reframes human development concerns with respect to economics, the environment, health, and gender in ways that have won these traditionally conceived low-politics issues policy priority and institutional resource allocation (230).

Such assessments emphasize programmatic shifts and developments. Human security was the outgrowth of an attempt to capture and respond to the challenges and complexities of a post–Cold War globalizing world and to reconfigure international relations with a more humane face. Its subjectivization of security has proven not to be as radical as critics have claimed. It does not subtract states from equations of security but only adds another, key variable to security analysis: human persons and their well-being. While systemic threats—or negative solidarities, as Arendt called them, remain (e.g., world war, nuclear holocaust, terrorism, environmental collapse, market-based exacerbations of poverty), the human security concept contextualizes, rather than absolutizing, the notion of security and opens it to a range of locally experienced maladies (drought and conflict over scarce food and water resources, human trafficking, environmental degradation, etc.) that reveal varying degrees of exposure to dislocations, risks, and disparities produced or exacerbated by globalization. Disquiet with the concept might, then, come from at least two directions.

First, attentiveness to the vast range of human insecurities and the multiplication of crises and emergencies might very well deflect scrutiny of international (global?) economic and political structures thought to produce and exacerbate exclusions, marginalizations, and oppressions (see Teitel 2011, 146). Fragmented responses merely remedy (temporarily and episodically) symptoms of deeper and persistent structural maladies. This is, as mentioned earlier, the new divide among states with respect to human security. But we might think through the rift by comprehending the human security concept as helping us understand what is required to protect and empower human beings. Equipped with (micro) identification of "minimums" (to engender perceptions and experiences of security) and understandings of how best to articulate them, we might then approach the macro problem of reforming embedded political and economic structures to achieve such minimums.

Second, a concern with minimums leads to angst over human security's presumed welfarist and even interventionist tactics. On my reading, those are effects of a deeper logic: apprehension that human security's humane face (presumably) undercuts state sovereignty. In one significant sense, it does. Sovereignty increasingly denotes or is associated with responsibility (in this case, to citizens); it no longer means primarily prerogative. But this idea is not new; states have long recognized limits on their behaviors (the laws of war, diplomatic immunity, etc.), even if they have occasionally ignored those limitations. In another sense, the humane face of human security does not undercut sovereignty, for human security very well may be construed as a means to the end of state security and stability.

The issue of state sovereignty, while related to this study, is decidedly beyond it. It is sufficient to note here that the disquiet contains truth and relates to a more fundamental unease with putting a humane face on an often inhumane world. For an example of that unease, we can appeal to an earlier instance in which the citadel of sovereignty was breached in the name of humanity: the prosecution of individuals at the international military tribunals for the Far East and in Nuremberg for crimes committed during the course of World War II, to which I now turn.

## CHAPTER 5

# International Criminal Law

## *Making Human through Retribution, Restitution, and Responsibility*

In Germany today [1963], this notion of "prominent Jews" has not yet
been forgotten. While the veterans and other privileged groups are
no longer mentioned, the fate of the "famous" Jews is still deplored at
the expense of all others. There are more than a few people, especially
among the culture elite, who still publicly regret the fact that
Germany sent Einstein packing, without realizing that it was a much
greater crime to kill little Hans Cohn from around the corner, even
though he was no genius.

—Hannah Arendt[1]

Crimes against humanity are serious acts of violence which harm
human beings by striking what is most essential to them: their life,
liberty, physical welfare, health, or dignity. They are inhumane
acts that by their extent and gravity go beyond the limits tolerable
to the international community, which must perforce demand
their punishment. But crimes against humanity also transcend the
individual because when the individual is assaulted, humanity comes
under attack and is negated. It is therefore the concept of humanity
as victim which essentially characterises crimes against humanity.

—International Criminal Tribunal for Yugoslavia[2]

International criminal law (hereinafter abbreviated as ICL) may be variously
praised for perforating sovereign immunity and combating the culture of impunity that has dominated international affairs, disentangling the criminal
actions of individuals from what were previously construed as irreproachable
acts of states, affirming the notion that certain acts exceed particular (normative, legal) standards of behavior, bestowing legal weight and reality to

the notion of humankind, and thus constituting a significant (if not always consistently deployed) ethical advance in international relations. Read from that perspective, Arendt's striking remark, in the preceding epigraph, about little Hans Cohn—in my estimation, the moral apex of her narrative of the Eichmann trial (1963a)—is of particular relevance for this chapter. By juxtaposing the fate of the ordinary, anonymous, isolate Jew to the fate of privileged Jews, she underscores why the isolated, atomic individual, as well as community-based theories of selves, ultimately lack defense.

Ordinary, anonymous, isolated life is expendable, even if its extermination may elicit initial outrage; in the deindividualized aggregate, such lives, as history repeatedly demonstrates, are even more so.[3] Once we are defined out of social existence (whether as individual beings or as members of a group) and are forced to rely on our biological status as *Homo sapiens* for social, political, and legal standing, the matter of our future becomes a straightforward empirical problem: what are the most efficient means for managing "us" and reducing the managerial burden on "them"?[4] By recognizing the "social" of the social individual, international criminal law responds to injuries inflicted and suffered and attempts to remedy the injury sustained by the community of humankind (see Simpson 2007, 60; Cassese 2008; Teitel 2011, 75). This move—one that replicates the logic of domestic criminal law—surely represents one of the most concrete ways of attributing to humanity an existence and substance it otherwise lacked. Thus our reading of ICL should not only emphasize its retributive function (see, e.g., Haque 2005) but examine its restorative and reparative roles.

This chapter takes a slightly different approach toward "restorative justice" by focusing on the restoration of human status and hence dignity. By individualizing responsibility, ICL divorces the commission of crimes from perceived national dispositions and gives humanity actionable content and socio-politico-juridical reality. By locating guilt, delivering judgment, and clarifying the content and parameters of an otherwise slippery concept of human dignity, ICL transforms victims—hapless, helpless, and brutalized objects—into human beings whose lives matter(ed). By situating individual perpetrators in contexts that reveal not inexorable outcomes but calculated decisions and by exploring their intentions, decisions, and actions, ICL reveals perpetrators to be human, not incarnations of evil or blindly obedient automatons. International criminal law, in short, makes victims and perpetrators human and humanizes the societies in which they live. As with other empirical chapters in this book, my aim in this chapter is not to provide an exhaustive history of ICL. Rather, I here employ broad brushstrokes to explore and expose its humanizing elements.

## Humanizing Humanity

> The privilege of opening the first trial in history for crimes against the peace of the world imposes a grave responsibility. The wrongs which we seek to condemn and punish have been so calculated, so malignant, and so devastating, that civilization cannot tolerate their being ignored, because it cannot survive their being repeated. That four great nations, flushed with victory and stung with injury stay the hand of vengeance and voluntarily submit their captive enemies to the judgment of the law is one of the most significant tributes that Power has ever paid to Reason.
>
> —Robert Jackson[5]

Accounts of ICL's origins variously begin with the 1474 trial of Peter von Hagenbach for what we today would call crimes against humanity and war crimes committed against the resident civilians of Breisach (see Gordon 2012); the 1649 trial of Charles I, the "first war crimes trial of a head of state" (Robertson 2006, 4); piracy (see Bassiouni 1996); the mixed slaving tribunals of the nineteenth century (see Bethell 1966; Kontorovitch 2009); the aborted prosecution of the German authors of World War I and the "'Young Turks' responsible for the massacres of the Armenians in 1915–16" (Cassese 2008, 317–19); or, more generally, the just war tradition and various national statutes and international customs regarding permissible acts in times of war (see Meron 2000a; Teitel 2011). Yet most agree that the birth of contemporary ICL can be dated to the promulgation of the London Charter on 8 August 1945 that created the International Military Tribunal for trying captured Nazis and to the issuance of the Tokyo Charter on 26 April 1946 that established the International Military Tribunal for the Far East for trying Japanese officials for atrocities. The United Nations enthusiastically pursued the Nuremberg precedent. It charged its newly minted subsidiary organ, the International Law Commission (ILC), with the task of preparing a draft code of international crimes. Also appointing a special rapporteur to formulate a draft statute for a permanent international criminal court (which the League of Nations shelved in 1937), the General Assembly appeared poised to deliver on the promise of international criminal justice—until the Cold War halted those efforts by 1954.

The thawing of US-Soviet relations fueled optimism about the possibilities of international cooperation. At the 1989 UN General Assembly General Debate, Soviet Premier Mikhail Gorbachev and the representative from Trinidad and Tobago called on the UN to draft a statute for a permanent International Criminal Court. While the ICC Statute was being formulated, waning superpower support for former client states helped contribute to disintegration of states, both violent (e.g., in Yugoslavia and Ethiopia) and nonviolent (e.g., in Czechoslovakia and the USSR). Ethnic tensions, long stabilized during the Cold War, began to fester, providing an impetus for the international community to act. Unable and unwilling to halt atrocities in two of the most egregious post–Cold War conflicts, the UN Security Council, in the absence of a permanent international criminal court, took the unprecedented step of establishing under its authority two ad hoc criminal tribunals to try those suspected of committing genocide, ethnic cleansing, and other crimes in the former Yugoslavia and Rwanda. Following the 1993 constitution of the International Criminal Tribunal for the former Yugoslavia (ICTY) and the 1994 creation of the International Criminal Tribunal for Rwanda (ICTR), the ILC produced a draft statute in 1994 for the International Criminal Court (ICC), which was approved by 120 states at a 1998 conference in Rome. Boasting 122 state members as of 15 January 2014, the ICC was then entertaining twenty-one cases in eight situations—two (concerning Sudan and Libya) referred by the Security Council, five (concerning Uganda, the Central African Republic, the Democratic Republic of Congo, the Ivory Coast, and Mali) self-referred, and one (concerning Kenya) launched by the prosecutor with approval of a pretrial chamber.

A series of other atrocities occurred in the 1990s over which the ICC could not obtain jurisdiction precisely because they occurred before the court came into existence on 1 July 2002. Since the international community generally and the UN Security Council specifically were experiencing tribunal fatigue precipitated by the exorbitantly expensive ad hoc tribunals, innovative methods were favored. The hybrid tribunal—a blend of national and international staff and law—was born (see Mundis 2001; Dickinson 2003; Nouwen 2006). In 2000, the UNSC authorized the UN secretary-general to create the Special Court for Sierra Leone (SCSL). Coming into existence in January 2002, the SCSL adjudicates alleged crimes against humanity, violations of Common Article 3 of the Geneva Conventions, serious violations of international humanitarian law, and certain criminal offenses under Sierra Leonese law that were allegedly committed during the 1990s civil war (see Mundis 2001, 935–38). In 2001, the UN Transitional Authority of East Timor, charged with the task of administering East Timor after its 1999 vote for independence and the subsequent brutal Indonesian assault on and eventual withdrawal from the territory, issued Regulation 2000/11, which created the Special Panels for Serious Crimes in the District Court of Dili. These panels, which concluded their work in 2006, had jurisdiction over genocide, war crimes, crimes against humanity, murder, and sexual offenses (see Mundis 2001, 942–45; Stahn 2001). As with East Timor, the UN administered Kosovo after the 1999 NATO air campaign against Serbia and Milošević's forced withdrawal. In 2001, the UN Mission in Kosovo (UN-MIK) created a mechanism to try those suspected of committing breaches of international humanitarian law and ethnically related crimes, including "incitement to commit hate crimes" (UNMIK Regulation 2000/4 quoted in Mundis 2001, 948). In 2005, the UN General Assembly, after years of painstaking negotiations, finally came to an agreement with the Hun Sen regime to establish the Extraordinary Chambers in the Courts of Cambodia to try former Khmer Rouge leaders of crimes that occurred during its genocidal reign from 1975 to 1979 (see Mundis 2001, 939–42). In May 2007, the UN Security Council created the Special Tribunal for Lebanon to try those suspected of committing terrorist attacks in Lebanon since 14 February 2005, the day on which a massive car bomb assassinated former prime minister Rafiq Hariri and twenty-two others.

State leaders are not immune. Most famously, in 1998, the UK House of Lords rejected former Chilean leader Augusto Pinochet's claims of immunity, thereby clearing the way for his extradition to Spain to face charges of torture and crimes against humanity. While Pinochet never faced trial in Spain (presumably owing to ill health), the case severely impinged on the principle of sovereign immunity. Liberia's Charles Taylor was convicted by the SCSL in April 2012 for various crimes, including terror, sexual violence, and crimes against humanity. Chad's Hissène Habré will now face trial given the ruling by the International Court of Justice that Senegal, where Habré resides, is in breach of its obligations to extradite or prosecute (ICJ 2012b; see Knutsen 2013). Former Ivory Coast prime minister Laurent Gbagbo was arrested and sent to the ICC in November 2011 to face crimes against humanity charges, the first head of state to be turned over to the ICC. Sudan's Omar al-Bashir earned the dubious distinction of being the first sitting head of state to be indicted by the court, while Libya's Muammar Gadaffi, now dead, was the second to be indicted. Rwanda's Jean Kambanda pled guilty to genocide at the ICTR in 1997, and Serbia's Slobodan Milošević died in prison while on trial at the ICTY.

These factual developments, which I have quite superficially summarized, reflect "the cumulative presence" of certain elements that have come to define ICL (Cassese 2008, 11–13). First, particular acts have been designated in various international treaties as criminal acts for which individuals can be held legally liable. Though the list of what are called treaty crimes (e.g., drug trafficking, money laundering, and hijackings) is relatively long, only a few crimes have been elevated to the status of core crimes: war crimes, crimes against humanity, and genocide, which voluminous case law has defined and clarified, often in excruciating detail. Though prosecutable at Nuremberg, crimes against the peace (or crimes of aggression) proved too contentious to include in the ICC Statute. At a 2010 ICC review conference in Kampala, Uganda, states agreed to a definition of aggression based on UNGA Resolution 3314(XXIX); a vote will be scheduled after January 2017 to determine whether to append the crime of aggression to the ICC's jurisdictional purview for ratifying states only. Torture and sexual violence (whether as a crime against humanity, an act of genocide, an element of torture, or an outrage on human dignity as envisaged in Common Article 3 of the Geneva Convention) have ascended to core crime status, while terrorism, as evidenced by its jurisdictional inclusion in the work of the Special Tribunal for Lebanon and with respect to near-universal condemnations of it within the UN, might very well be advancing to such status.

Second, a pragmatic-moral imperative for prosecution and preventive action arises from the recognition that "civilization cannot tolerate" ignoring the commission of core crimes, "because it cannot survive their being repeated" (Jackson 1945). Thus, third, prohibitions against such acts "are intended to protect values considered important by the whole international community," which, fourth, "may in principle be prosecuted and punished by any state" (Cassese 2008, 11). This point was the subject of the 2012 International Court of Justice case *Belgium v. Senegal*. In oral hearings on 21 March, Belgium maintained that Senegal was in breach of the Convention against Torture and Other Cruel, Inhuman, or Degrading Treatment or Punishment (Torture Convention) because it had failed to prosecute or extradite Habré. Moreover, Belgium maintained that Senegal had failed "to incorporate in due time in its domestic law the provisions necessary to enable the Senegalese judicial authorities to exercise the universal jurisdiction provided for in Article 5, paragraph 2" of the Torture Convention (ICJ 2012a, 2). On 20 July, judges determined that Senegal was indeed obligated to prosecute or extradite, which led to the convening of a court by Senegal in February 2013 to try Habré (Knutsen 2013).

That International Court of Justice ruling is significant on many levels: it offers a clear defense of human rights against the prerogatives of sovereignty; affirms the notion that international agreements cannot be conveniently ignored; indicates that the Torture Convention clarifies enduring "common interests" and "shared values" (ICJ 2012b, ¶68, p. 26); and confirms that the prohibition of torture is both a customary rule of international law to which all states are now presumably subject and a peremptory norm from which, according to the Vienna Convention on the Law of Treaties, no derogation is permitted—even if the United States has successfully evaded action taken against its practices of torturing suspects in the War on Terror (¶99, p. 33).[6] *Belgium v. Senegal* also underscores the logic on which ICL is premised: it is the community that is injured by the criminal act and in whose name charges are levied. The assumption that obligations arise from communal interests and values is the basis on which the Torture Convention was constructed (¶68, p. 26), and that assumption has been reflected in a range of "international instruments of universal application" and in the "domestic law of almost all States." On this logic, humanity is not only the protectorate (or subject) of the community of states—on which it remains dependent for its preservation, protection, and advancement—but a legal entity (an object) possessive of a right to existence that cannot be forsaken. In this instance, both reflection on the status of others and articulations of levels and techniques of responsibility by states toward their citizens appear salient in the legal discourse of humanization and in strategies by activists to hold those states to their obligations.

Embedded in the logic of the International Court of Justice lies a conception of an "international community," which Gerry Simpson (2007, 60) traces to emerging "self-consciousness . . . of a moral community" at the signing of the Treaty of Versailles, when great powers conceived "serious violations of that community's dominant mores" not as matters of bilateral relations (the conventional international law model) but as "a breach of the rights of all states or of international society." But whereas the Treaty of Versailles rather tenuously symbolized that transformation in consciousness— the Leipzig trials were rather an ersatz attempt, and the renegotiation of peace with Turkey at Lausanne omitted culpability for what was dubbed the Armenian "business"—Nuremberg effectuated it. Judges in one of the successor trials to Nuremberg, the Einsatzgruppen Case (formally *The United States v. Ohlendorf*), underscored what the International Military Tribunal accomplished.

> Nuremberg has only demonstrated how humanity can be defended in court, and it is inconceivable that with this precedent extant, the law of humanity should ever lack for a tribunal. Where law exists a court will rise. Thus, the court of humanity, if it may be so termed, will never adjourn. (quoted in Teitel 2011, 77)

While humanity was embodied and corporatized to juridical effect, the state, that other dominant corporate entity, was being disaggregated—necessarily so, given the failings of the Versailles model of state responsibility and the punitive reparations levied against Germany. In his opening statement at Nuremberg, Robert Jackson (1945) attacked the thesis of state responsibility.

> [T]hat a state, any more than a corporation commits crimes, is a fiction. Crimes always are committed only by persons. While it is quite proper to employ the fiction of responsibility of a state or corporation for the purpose of imposing a collective liability, it is quite intolerable to let such a legalism become the basis of personal immunity.

Simpson (2007, 62) takes issue with the prevailing narrative that the Versailles model of the criminal state fell into disrepute and was replaced by a model of individual criminal responsibility (aka the Nuremberg model) after World War II. Notions of collective or state responsibility informed the Allied response to the vanquished: Germany was divided into four Allied military sectors; the Americans introduced a "highly intrusive programme of economic control, decentralization of indigenous political power and complete military and 'industrial' disarmament" in Germany; Germany and Japan were designated as enemy states, which barred them from membership in the UN (a reference that remains in the Charter to this day); and at Nuremberg, US officials insisted to no avail on trying German institutions and organizations (the banking system, the industrialized sector, the media, etc.). The model remains alive today, Simpson avers: the UN Security Council has acted to deprive states (e.g., Iraq, Syria, Iran, Libya, and North Korea) of their sovereign prerogatives, and great powers in the 1990s and 2000s "began to deploy the image of the criminal state in their rhetoric" (65). Simpson also cites the ILC's Draft Articles on State Responsibility, which envisions "acts that would give rise to criminal liability on the part of states" (64). The reference is, however, dated. Simpson refers to the first, 1996 Draft Articles, which listed, in Article 19, specific crimes that may be collectively ascribed to the state: aggression, maintenance by force of colonial domination, slavery, genocide, apartheid, and serious environmental offenses that may spark reparations and other claims for recompense. The 2001 version omits any such references and replaces the language of "crime" with "breaches of international obligations" (Articles 2, 12) "in force for a State" (Article 13) and breaches of obligations arising under peremptory norms (Articles 40–41),[7] which, as a matter of customary international law, include that which was originally stipulated in the 1996 Draft Articles.

Simpson maintains that the conventional narrative is only partially correct; collective forms of responsibility very much exist. But political/collective and criminal forms of responsibility are not synonymous; the substantial revision of the Draft Articles between 1996 and 2001 reflects the distinction. Some of the remedies envisioned in the Draft Articles are compensatory in nature (reflective of tort law and civil law more generally, not criminal law) and hence speak to collective forms of political responsibility. Still, Simpson has a point: international criminal law cannot rely "on the fiction of detachability"; the state cannot always be construed "as an entity distinct from its bad apples and rogue statesmen" (2007, 63). Yet in my estimation, Simpson misses a critical contribution of ICL with respect to its relationship to political responsibility: ICL subtracts assessments of national character from the equation of collective responsibility and substitutes in its place delicts planned, ordered, and committed by individuals. Stated slightly differently, international criminal law rationalizes the notion of responsibility by differentiating between corporate and natural persons. Breaches of legal obligations are determined by measuring behavior against objective, if interpreted and occasionally contested, rules, not on the basis of the presumed attributes of (elusive, generalized) character "types." As Arendt (1994, 128) caustically noted in 1945, even "those who knew Germany most intimately had not the slightest idea fifteen years ago" of the potentialities of "German history and the so-called German national character." Robert Jackson (1945), too, iterated that kind of argument.

> We would also make clear that we have no purpose to incriminate the whole German people. We know that the Party was not put in power by a majority of the German vote. We know it came to power by an evil alliance between the most extreme of the Nazi revolutionists, the most unrestrained of the German reactionaries and the most aggressive of the German militarists. If the German populace had willingly accepted the Nazi program, no Storm-troopers would have been needed in the early days of the Party and there would have been no need for concentration camps or the Gestapo, both of which institutions were inaugurated as soon as the Nazis gained control of the German State. Only after these lawless innovations proved successful at home were they taken abroad.

Yet Jackson slips, for he immediately proceeds to attribute to "the masses of the German people" a "sober, industrious, and self-disciplined character" that translated into "German fortitude and proficiency in war." A more judicious reading might interpret his identification of German national characteristics (which is itself a supreme act of deindividuation) not as causal (e.g., he does not assert that national character led directly to the Holocaust) but as correlative, that is, as a contributing factor to the rise of the Nazi regime. But prosecutorial opening statements are, by nature, designed to compel; dramatic license and flourish are to be expected. Jackson had to remain focused on the Nazi leadership slated for punishment, not populations, despite the varied forms of collective or political responsibility imposed on the Germans (and, for that matter, on the Japanese).

Of course, conflicts are messy, and the attempt to disambiguate through individualizing responsibility should not be interpreted as an attempt to deemphasize or ignore the roles of ordinary people in the commission (and enabling) of crimes. Transitional justice efforts centered on reconciliation and restoration are thus critical in helping societies combat tendencies toward collective attribution and revenge. Individualizing responsibility at the highest levels (crimes of such magnitude are usually planned and organized) has the effect of humanizing the collective and ought to be read as working in tandem with reconciliation and restoration measures. First, individualizing responsibility helps eradicate cultures of impunity (where all are guilty, no one is), which often generates calls for revenge (see Minow 1998; Akhavan 2001). Second, through trial proceedings and carefully crafted judgments, ICL generates new cognitive scripts framed around chronicling, in exhaustive, corroborated detail, facts, chains of command, and causal links of the crimes that occurred. Narrating or rendering crimes in all of their specificity disarticulates, if it does not erase, cognitive scripts informed by collective (national) self-righteousness (e.g., the myth of a "Greater Serbia" or the Hamitic hypothesis that affirmed Tutsi superiority over Hutu incompetence and, conversely, "Hutu fears of Tutsi perfidy" [Berkeley 2002, 104]), as well as mythologies of victims to be avenged or of expendable peoples (whether *Ostjuden* or Hutu, bourgeois or Bantu). Finally, such processes help deflate or undermine attributions of crimes to radical, demonic evil or national characters, which, in the past, have substituted for *mens rea* and thus served as midwives for impunity. Real human beings, not devils incarnate, commit crimes; to explain all such atrocities as evil only explains them away.

To the extent that crimes have generally occurred under cover of sovereign prerogative, national interests, and acts of state, it is necessary to distinguish between (legitimate and hence immune) acts of state and criminal offenses and, further, to differentiate levels of complicity—to rethink, as it were, the notions of complicity, responsibility, and the commission of crimes given that ICL considers most responsible not the actual perpetrators of the crimes but those who plan, organize, order, and finance such crimes. Nuremberg (and the *Eichmann* case discussed later in this chapter) certainly helped us articulate such a measure, since the Holocaust was clearly extraneous to the war effort and, indeed, hampered it. A clear expression of such a measure is found in a 1950 judgment issued by the Supreme Military Tribunal in Italy. Quoted by the ICTY appeals chamber in its 1995 response to Duško Tadić's challenge to the tribunal's legality and authority,[8] the chamber argued that the crimes for which the accused were charged

> cannot be considered political offences, as they do not harm a political interest of a particular State, nor a political right of a particular citizen. They are, instead, crimes of *lèse-humanité* . . . and, as previously demonstrated, the norms prohibiting them have a universal character, not simply a territorial one. Such crimes, therefore, due to their very subject matter and particular nature are precisely of a different and opposite kind from political offences. The latter generally concern only the States against whom they are committed; the former concern all civilised States, and are to be opposed and punished, in the same way as the crimes of piracy, trade of women and minors, and enslavement are to be opposed and punished, wherever they may have been committed. (*Prosecutor v. Duško Tadić* 1995, ¶57)

One particular presupposition on which the ruling is based deserves attention: that a distinction can (and must) be made between legitimate and illegitimate political interests of a state. To substantiate the distinction, judges of the appeals chamber cited the Israeli Supreme Court's decision regarding Adolf Eichmann's appeal: illegitimate interests that constitute core crimes are those that

> impair the foundations and security of the international community . . . [and] violate the universal moral values and humanitarian principles that lie hidden in the criminal law systems adopted by civilised nations. The underlying principle in international law regarding such crimes is that the individual who has committed any of them and who, when doing so, may be presumed to have fully comprehended the heinous nature of his act, must account for his conduct . . . Those crimes entail individual criminal responsibility because they challenge the foundations of international society and affront the conscience of civilised nations.

Despite the formulation of a yardstick by which to distinguish between legitimate and illegitimate interests and actions, execution of the obligations inherent in ICL—to prosecute or extradite—are not systematically respected. Politics intrudes. Many situations are ignored, and many alleged criminals are not prosecuted, leading to charges of selection biases and favoritism at work.[9] Trials may be excessively lengthy and hence costly. International courts and tribunals only try those most responsible (e.g., those who order or finance crimes), leaving unpunished the many who murder and maim. Yet where all are guilty (the corporate model of guilt), no one is; even if "the idea of humanity . . . implies the obligation of a general responsibility . . . for all crimes committed" (Arendt 1994, 131), it may prove too burdensome to enact.

As argued in my treatment of Arendt in chapter 1, people "recoiled" from the evils and savageries committed by others and hence rejected a conception of common humanity in favor of discrete notions of race and nationality—each with its idiosyncratic notions of good and evil, civilized and barbarian. Yet in political and pragmatic senses, Arendt concludes, "the idea of humanity, excluding no people and assigning a monopoly of guilt to no one, is the only guarantee that one 'superior race' after another may not feel obligated to follow the 'natural law' of the right of the powerful, and exterminate 'inferior races unworthy of survival.'" Individual responsibility for the planning, organizing, financing, training, aiding and abetting, and committing of harms on others necessarily follows as an effective, if not always consistently applied, manner of responding to the dehumanization of others. Characterizing certain acts as violations of humanity is, as Teitel notes (2011, 81), "one of the ways the humanity law framework is defining the subject and impact of globalization in terms of its affected personality, and its ability to transcend borders to protect diverse peoples, and persons."

## Humanizing the Victim

To be a victim presupposes the sufferance of harm. On this broad formulation, one might be a victim of an agentless act (e.g., a tornado or tsunami) or of an act by which a perpetrator causes harm to another willfully, knowingly, or with awareness of the possible effects. For the limited purposes of this chapter, I shall not dissect the concept of victim, as Bouris (2007) has expertly done; rather, I herein adopt the definition of a victim as found in international criminal law. According to Rule 85 of the International Criminal Court's *Rules of Procedure and Evidence*, victims are "natural persons who have suffered harm as a result of the commission of any crime within the jurisdiction of the Court [war crimes, crimes against humanity, and genocide]." However, victims may also include "organizations or institutions that have sustained direct harm to any of their property which is dedicated to religion, education, art or science or charitable purposes, and to their historic monuments, hospitals and other places and objects for humanitarian purposes" (ICC 2002, 31).

The ICC's definition leaves certain questions unanswered. First, it does not instruct on the type of harm suffered. Must it be primarily physical in nature, or might it be construed in emotional/psychological terms, such as the effects precipitant from watching one's family brutalized and murdered? Second, must harm be experienced directly, as in a perpetration of an act against the body? Or might it be indirect, as in the case of survivor's guilt suffered after a massacre? These are empirical questions that can only be answered with respect to the context in which harm has allegedly been caused. For instance, the Extraordinary Chambers in the Courts of Cambodia (ECCC) Internal Rules (Rev. 8) of the provides for an expansive conception of victimhood, in ostensible keeping with the Khmer Rouge's nationwide purge from 1975 to 1979, during which roughly one-quarter (1.7 million) of the population was exterminated. Without defining the term, the document stipulates that those declaring the "status of Victim [must] specify the alleged crime and attach any evidence of the injury suffered, or tending to show the guilt of the alleged perpetrator" (ECCC 2011, Rule 23 bis (4)). Conversely, the Special Tribunal for Lebanon, established to convict those responsible for the assassination of former prime minister Rafiq Hariri and twenty-two others, offers greater contextual precision given the singular incident that informs the tribunal's jurisdiction: a victim is "[a]nyone who has suffered harm—be it physical, material or mental—as a direct result of an attack within the tribunal's jurisdiction."[10]

ICL can transform victims from objects used by others into human subjects with rights, in three ways: first, by recognizing the losses and harms suffered and restoring the voice of victims through their inclusion in ICL processes; second, upon reflection of harms and losses suffered, by ordering reparations and promoting other community-based restorative measures as other-regarding acts of care and responsibility; and third, by grappling with and attempting to clarify the sometimes maddeningly ambiguous concept of dignity. More has already been written by others about the first two ways, so, in the interest of space, I here devote more attention to the third.

A variety of transitional justice mechanisms, including trials, truth and reconciliation commissions, and reparations, enhance the visibility of victims and end the silence imposed on them, by recognizing their losses and harms suffered and allowing them to recover their dignity and worth as human beings (on these issues, see Minow 1998; David and Choi 2005;

Simpson 2007, chap. 4; SáCouto 2012). Put in Booth's idiom (1993), the story lines that constitute our selves are not entirely self-determined in any absolute, pure sense; that is the price we pay for living in society. But even the dignity of those from whom it has been presumably stripped may be at least partially restored by allowing them to tell their story. Like the Security Council, institutions of ICL confront victimized bodies and attempt to recognize in them and transform them back into human persons. Their stories of suffering in turn contribute to the construction of comprehensive, official narratives to help societies come to terms with atrocities. Martha Minow (1998, 13) reasons that "avenging the self can be too costly emotionally, by stroking consuming fires of hatred." In that view, the development of fora—whether criminal trials or truth commissions—in which victims relay their experiences and confront their alleged tormentors might encourage the redirection of hatred and revenge toward more constructive forms of engagement, especially when accompanied by political and social reform and rehabilitative initiatives (see Nino 1996; David and Choi 2005). The aggregate of such stories as told in courts and tribunals, subject to rules and regulations that demand corroboration, helps judges produce "credible documents . . . that acknowledge and condemn horrors" and, in doing so, helps "articulate both norms and a commitment to work to realize them" (Minow 1998, 50; see also Hirsh 2003).

Victims and witnesses were not always included in international criminal legal proceedings, however. Nuremberg excluded them (the case was easily constructed on voluminous extant documentary evidence). The ICTY and ICTR, in contrast, permitted victim testimony as deemed necessary by the prosecutor. Further, per their shared Rules of Procedure and Evidence, victims were treated as objects of protection, counseling, and support (see Corrie 2007, 2–5). The ICC breaks away somewhat from that model by allowing, per Article 68(3) of the ICC Statute, victim participation when their "personal interests are affected"; the court determines the extent of how and when "their views and concerns" shall be "presented and considered at stages of the proceedings determined to be appropriate . . . and in a manner which is not prejudicial to or inconsistent with the rights of the accused." SáCouto lauds the ICC and ECCC for allowing "victims to participate in criminal proceedings independent of their role as witnesses for either the prosecution or defense" (2012, 5).

Whether or not victim and witness participation provides victims adequate space and time to tell their stories or promotes healing is highly debatable (see SáCouto 2012). Ten minutes of testimony may be cathartic for one victim, while the same temporal limitation may frustrate another. Yet limiting victim participation might be construed as a necessary corrective to two particular hazards. First, by allowing victims to tell their stories, trials may be choked by testimony—some of it negligibly, tangentially, or, worse, not related to the case at hand, as happened during the Eichmann trial (see Arendt 1963a; Mulisch 2005). Second, as the ICTY learned during the *Tadić* case, granting anonymity and special protections to witnesses must be reserved only for clearly documented instances in which the witness faces credible and corroborated threats of violence as retaliation for testimony. Robertson (2006, 398–99) recounts the incident of "Witness L," the ICTY prosecutor's star witness. For three days, the witness was granted special dispensation by the court to testify in secret. He offered a trove of information; he even led prosecutors to mass graves. One day, Witness L "swore he had been present when Tadić killed his father." Robertson reports, "'But isn't your father still alive?' the defense asked on day three." The witness insisted he watched his father die. Robertson continues, "'But this man is your father,' said the cross examiner, calling to court an old man who rushed to embrace the witness."

Given its specific jurisdiction based on subject matter, the Special Tribunal for Lebanon carefully reviews applications submitted by alleged victims. An applicant must specify "the circumstances under which [he or she] became a victim of the attack on 14 February 2005"; detail damages, loss, or harm sustained (including "physical injuries, psychological harm, loss or damage of possessions, etc."); and document the nature of medical or psychological treatment received (for which receipts, X-rays, prescriptions, invoices, and other forms of documentation must be provided), as well as material losses suffered, proven by attachment of receipts or invoices.[11] Applicants may also request legal representation and nondisclosure of certain information if the applicant has "any reason to believe that the fact of revealing [one's] identity to the public attending the proceedings might endanger" the applicant or the applicant's family. To avoid the type of perjury committed by Witness L in the *Tadić* case, the Special Tribunal for Lebanon requires that the identities of witnesses be disclosed to all parties in the proceedings, except under exceptional circumstances.

SáCouto suggests that despite the problems and limitations victims face (and the problems they cause), ICL proceedings—even if not the most appropriate site for doing to the work of visibility, storytelling, and healing—open up space "for the emergence of other mechanisms that offer a unique opportunity" to further the goal of visibility (2012, 7). That brings me to a second manner in which ICL humanizes victims: through reparative and restorative justice. The ICC established the first Trust Fund for Victims in international criminal justice history, the basis of which may be read as effectuation of the UNGA's 1985 *Declaration on Basic Principles of Justice for Victims of Crimes and Abuse of Power*, which affirmed that crime victims are entitled to access to judicial mechanisms in order to obtain redress for their injuries (UNGA 1985, Annex articles 5–7). The trust fund is charged with fulfilling two mandates: "implementing Court-ordered reparations" and "using voluntary contributions . . . to provide victims and their families . . . with physical rehabilitation, material support, and/or psychological rehabilitation."[12] With respect to the second, general assistance objective, the trust fund offers (as of January 2014) "vocational training, counseling, reconciliation workshops, reconstructive surgery and more to an estimated 80,000 victims of crimes under the ICC's jurisdiction."[13] The aim coheres with the logic of human security addressed in chapter 4: to enhance the well-being of communities and their citizens through reconciliation and empowerment initiatives. Put differently, the trust fund's diverse activities aim to (re)create persons out of victimized bodies by helping them rebuild their lives and regain their dignity through tangible effectuations of an other-regarding responsibility (see ReliefWeb 2012).

But dignity as an objective of ICL mechanisms is not limited to reparative justice. Judges have endeavored to attribute specific, actionable content to it, to which I now turn. As discussed in chapter 2, national constitutions variously treat dignity either as a first-order, foundational principle or as simply one right among other rights, a division that ICL, in its development, seems to repudiate. In 1998, the trial chamber in the *Furundžija* judgment (*Prosecutor v. Anto Furundžija* 1998, ¶183, p. 72) replicated the position that dignity was a foundational principle.

> The essence of the whole corpus of international humanitarian law as well as human rights law lies in the protection of the human dignity of every person, whatever his or her gender. The general principle of respect for human dignity is the basic underpinning and indeed the very *raison d'être* of international humanitarian law and human rights law; indeed in modern times it has become of such paramount importance as to permeate the whole body of international law. This principle is intended to shield human beings from outrages upon their personal dignity, *whether such outrages are carried out by unlawfully attacking the body or by humiliating and debasing the honour, the self-respect or the mental well being of a person.*[14]

Yet as a legal matter, the foundational view has proven insufficient to convict peoples charged with violating dignity; the *actus reus*, or objective element of the crime, must be distinct. Put in the logic of chapter 2, violations of dignity are, in this view, simply crimes among crimes; analogously, dignity is one right among many.

To illustrate, in the ICTR's landmark *Akayesu* judgment (1998), the former mayor of the Taba commune was found guilty of counts related to genocide (the first ever such conviction) and sexual violence but was exonerated for committing outrages on personal dignity as articulated in Common Article 3 of the Geneva Conventions. A commonsense reading would surely protest: rape is an outrage on personal dignity. The judges did not dismiss that position. But the *Akayesu* judges found relevant the decision of the appeals chamber in *Kunarac et al.* (2002, ¶191): an outrage on dignity must be a discrete crime. In both the *Kunarac* and *Akayesu* cases, prosecutors charged the defendants with rape as outrages on personal dignity under Common Article 3 of the Geneva Conventions. Yet nowhere in the subsection in Common Article 3 is rape mentioned; the "general proscription . . . is against inhuman treatment . . . 'An outrage against personal dignity within Article 3 of the Statute is a *species* of inhuman treatment that is deplorable, occasioning more serious suffering than most prohibited acts falling within the *genus*'" (*Prosecutor v. Zlatko Aleksovski* 1999, ¶54, p. 19, quoted in *Kunarac et al.* 2001, ¶150, pp. 171–72).[15] The genus of prohibited acts—inhuman treatment— had previously been defined in the 1998 *Delalic* case as "an intentional act or omission, that is, an act that, judged objectively, is deliberate and not accidental, which causes *serious mental or physical suffering or injury or constitutes a serious attack on human dignity*'" (quoted in *Kunarac et al.* 2001, ¶502, p. 172). Thus the trial chamber concluded that

> the offence of outrages on personal dignity requires:
> (i) that the accused intentionally committed or participated in an act or omission which would be generally considered to cause serious humiliation, degradation or otherwise be a serious attack on human dignity, and
> (ii) that he knew that the act or omission could have that effect. (¶514, pp. 176–77)

Succinctly stated, a charge or conviction cannot result simply because dignity has been affronted by the commission of another crime; "each offence must be hanged, as it were, on its own statutory hook" (*Kunarac et al.* 2002, ¶191). The appeals chamber reasoned that "rape [in the particular case before it] is only evidence of the outrage; the substantial crime is not rape but the outrage occasioned by the rape. This leaves open the argument that . . . convictions for both may not be possible" (¶190, p. 58). It also leaves open the question of whether, at least in international criminal law, the social content of dignity, or dignity as social status, becomes the more salient element of its conceptualization and our understanding of it.

The *Kunarac* appeals chamber agreed with the judgment of the trial chamber that the sale of several girls by Kovac, one of the defendants in the case, "constituted a particularly degrading attack on their dignity" (2002, ¶17, p. 5). Further, that they were "made to dance naked on a table, . . . were 'lent' and sold to other men and that FWS-75 and FWS-87 [tribunal aliases assigned to the victims] were raped by Kovac while he was playing 'Swan Lake' were all correctly characterised by the Trial Chamber as outrages upon personal dignity" (¶159, p. 49). The appeals chamber reasoned that

> [i]n explaining that outrages upon personal dignity are constituted by "any act or omission which would be *generally* considered to cause serious humiliation, degradation or otherwise be a serious attack on human dignity," the Trial Chamber correctly defined the objective threshold for an act to constitute an outrage upon personal dignity. It was not obliged to list the acts which constitute outrages upon personal dignity. (*Kunarac et al.*, ¶163, p. 50)

If an accounting of acts is not required, how, then, are we to recognize when an outrage on dignity occurs? The *Aleksovski* Trial Chamber (1999, ¶56, p. 20, quoted in *Kunarac et al.* 2001, ¶500, p. 172) opined that "[a]n outrage against personal dignity is an act which is animated by contempt for the human dignity of another person." We may wish to recall Meilaender's distinction between personal and human dignity as treated in chapter 2. In his view, the spectacle of human bodies fosters an awareness of the human species and thus the species' "integrity and flourishing" (2009, 103). If human dignity relates to human capacities as distinct from the capacities of other species, personal dignity refers to the equal moral worth of individual persons who, in varying degrees, develop and express the capacities that distinguish us as *Homo sapiens*. On this reading, violations of human dignity are acts that deny our human status and hence our autonomy to create, invent, construct, remodel, renovate, communicate (to write and speak freely), act, group, associate, cooperate, and the like—that is, acts that deny us the ability to act like human beings. On the *Aleksovski* reasoning, an outrage against human dignity denies the victim's *status* as fully human (see Waldron 2012a) and thus their ability to partake in communion and community with others in any meaningful sense.

An outrage against personal dignity is one that, following from the objectification of the victim (as property, chattel, object of abuse, etc.), denies the victim's place in the human family to develop in his or her specific capacities those elements that both make us human in a socially constructed sense and constitute us as individuals. The ICL approach does not simply rest a conception of dignity on presumed equal moral worth—though prosecution of those who impinge, affront, assail, or otherwise deny the dignity of others does, in the end, affirm it. Rather, by recognizing, for instance, that the rape of Tutsi or Bosnian Muslim women engendered their stigmatization, humiliation, marginalization, and, often, exclusion from their communities, ICL has substantiated the notion that dignity (in its human and personal variants) not only rests on the inviolability of the body but relates to an individual's psychoemotional health. The effects of these outrages are, crucially, measured in terms of their corrosive effects on status and standing in community.

In part, ICL construes an assault on status and standing as rooted in "serious humiliation or degradation to the victim. It is not necessary for the act to directly harm the physical or mental well-being of the victim. It is enough that the act causes real and lasting suffering to the individual arising from the humiliation or ridicule." We find the clearest articulation of this position in the ICTR case *Nahimana et al.* (2003, ¶115), which drew on the Nuremberg conviction of Julius Streicher for persecution of Jews as effected through anti-Semitic writings.

> The Chamber considers it evident that hate speech targeting a population on the basis of ethnicity, or other discriminatory grounds, reaches this level of gravity and constitutes persecution. Hate speech is a discriminatory form of aggression that destroys the dignity of those in the group under attack. It creates a lesser status not only in the eyes of the group members themselves but also in the eyes of others who perceive and treat them as less than human. The denigration of a person on the basis of his or her ethnic identity or other group membership in and of itself, as well as in its other consequences, can be an irreversible harm. (¶114)

However, suffering and the sense that one's dignity is affronted are subjective.

> [I]t obviously depend[s] on [the victim's] temperament. Sensitive individuals tend to be more prone to perceive their treatment by others

to be humiliating and, in addition, they tend to suffer from the effects thereof more grievously. On the other hand, the perpetrator would be hard-pressed to cause serious distress to individuals with nonchalant dispositions because such persons are not as preoccupied with their treatment by others and, even should they find that treatment to be humiliating, they tend to be able to cope better by shrugging it off. Thus, the same act by a perpetrator may cause intense suffering to the former, but inconsequential discomfort to the latter. This difference in result is occasioned by the subjective element. In the prosecution of an accused for a criminal offence, the subjective element must be tempered by objective factors; otherwise, unfairness to the accused would result because his/her culpability would depend not on the gravity of the act but wholly on the sensitivity of the victim. Consequently, an objective component to the *actus reus* is apposite: the humiliation to the victim must be so intense that the reasonable person would be outraged . . . While the perpetrator need not have had the specific intent to humiliate or degrade the victim, he must have been able to perceive this to be the foreseeable and reasonable consequence of his actions. (*Aleksovski* 1999, ¶56, pp. 20–22)

Two years later, the *Kunarac* trial chamber rejected the notion that humiliation or degradation must cause "lasting suffering," as long as the harm caused is "real and serious" (*Kunarac et al.* 2001, ¶501, p. 172). Judges opined that "it is not open to regard the fact that a victim has recovered or is overcoming the effects of such an offence as indicating of itself that the relevant acts did not constitute an outrage upon personal dignity. Obviously, if the humiliation and suffering caused is only fleeting in nature, it may be difficult to accept that it is real and serious. However this does not suggest that any sort of minimum temporal requirement of the effects of an outrage upon personal dignity is an *element* of the offence." The position was reproduced in the *Krstić* judgment of 2 August 2001 (¶513, p. 181) in a way that suggests the matter is settled in a manner congruent with the argument outlined in chapter 2 based on Waldron (2012a) and Daly (2013).

Serious harm need not cause permanent and irremediable harm, but it must involve harm that goes beyond temporary unhappiness, embarrassment or humiliation. It must be harm that results in a grave and long term disadvantage to a person's ability to lead a normal and constructive life.

If an outrage on dignity entails the impingement on, diminishment, degradation, or erasure of being *human* in ways that result in a lasting diminishment of the meaning of human *being*, it follows that dignity refers to the self-determinative capacities of individual persons within communities and hence to the meaning of being human itself.

## Humanizing the Perpetrator: The Case of Adolf Eichmann

If ICL humanizes communities and victims, it likewise humanizes those accused of perpetrating crimes, in part by affirming their dignity. From the standpoint of dignity's corporeal dimension, ICL affirms "minimum principles of humanity and dignity which constitute the inspiration for the international standards governing the protection of the rights of convicted persons" (*Erdemovic* 1996, ¶74). Such principles build on a 1990 UN General Assembly resolution on the treatment of prisoners that evidences a "long-standing concern . . . for the humanization of criminal justice and the protection of human rights" (UNGA 1990). While the measure indicates, as a generic statement, that all prisoners retain their rights as enumerated in the Universal Declaration of Human Rights and relevant international covenants, the resolution's annex on basic principles for the treatment of prisoners specifically calls on states to abolish or strictly curtail the use of solitary confinement as punishment and to ensure access to health care.

The annex also affirms rights consonant with what I call the "interior dimension of dignity," or the integrity of our psychological, emotional, and intellectual capacities and development. Discrimination on any grounds— "race, color, sex, language, religion, political or other opinion, national or social origin, property, birth, or other social status"—is banned, though "it is desirable to respect the religious beliefs and cultural precepts of the group to which prisoners belong." Further, prisoners retain the right "to take part in cultural activities and education aimed at the full development of the human personality."

Finally, from the standpoint of dignity's sociopolitical dimension, the act of prosecution (no matter how provisional or inconsistent) resists the temptation to rationalize egregious crimes as sovereign prerogative (especially when relevant actors lack political will to prosecute), attribute them to a presumed national character predisposed to dehumanizing other, or explain them away as acts of evil. Rather, the perpetrator is not to be explained away as demonic but should be regarded as a context-bound individual who has, in the course of events and in the company of others, made particular decisions about the status and fate of others, for which the perpetrator must be held accountable. Status in community entails responsibility.

This point applies an argument in chapter 3 that concerned why the UN Security Council identified categories of peoples in need of protection. Why, I there asked, does the Council speak in the language of protection and empowerment structured by the grammar of particular identifications that stemmed beyond national, ethnic, racial, religious, and gender identities? While victimhood resides at the heart of the Council's discursive and justificatory framework, it is a limited optic through which to view Council action. Rather, I argued, the answer lies not in Council considerations but in the answer to the question of why these groups are targeted in the first place, which I attributed to social identity and status in human community and continuity. The Council, in other words, affirms the human being as a social, relational being. To murder or rape women ensures destruction—in whole or in part—or disruption of the continuous transmission of blood, community value, culture, and tradition. To target journalists is to disrupt the transmission of information. To target humanitarian relief workers is to disrupt systems and structures of care for those in need. To target children is to foil the bloodline of a despised group and may involve murder, forcible enlistment, or abduction and transfer to another group. Such abductions, to reiterate, are construed as acts of genocide according to the Genocide Convention and the International Criminal Court. Tellingly, the equation admits a relaxation of the presumed immutability of the groups against whom genocide may be committed (racial, ethnical, national, religious), but it also underscores why the forcible transference of children constitutes a core crime: transference interrupts the continuous transmission of culture from adults to children. By implication, the equation likewise indicates that culture and identity, as social constructions, are fundamental to our understanding of dignity, since our associations and affiliations give individual lives meaning. Prosecution of those who attempt to or in fact do eradicate lines of social continuity upholds the notion that the dignity of the species is intimately related to such contiguous and sustained social bonds (Waldron 2012a; Daly 2013).

Nancy Fraser captures this point by describing acts of violence perpetrated on groups as beginning with "injustices of misrecognition," or denying them "the status of a full partner in social interaction" and preventing them from "participating as a peer in social life" (Fraser quoted in Tétreault and Lipschutz 2009, 152; see also Fraser 2000, 1995). The German Federal Court of Justice iterated the point in a 1999 case: "perpetrators of genocide do not target a person 'in his capacity as an individual'; 'they do not see the

victim as a human being but only as a member of the persecuted group'"
(quoted in Cassese 2008, 137). While this argument affirms the dignity of
victims, it may be interpreted as affirming the dignity of perpetrators. Injustices of misrecognition abstract the subject from social relations. To fail to
prosecute or to explain away the acts of perpetrators as transcendent (e.g.,
evil) or sovereign is to commit another kind of injustice of misrecognition,
for it exonerates the accused from the myriad of obligations that living in
community with others entails. Institutions of ICL advance the notion but
also recognize and respect the dignity of the perpetrator through the conferral of procedural rights, ensuring conformity with basic standards of treatment and providing for opportunities for defense in ways that, ultimately,
reveal the egoistic, thoughtless, and other motivations of fallible human beings. A belated development with respect to the rights of the accused appears
in the Special Tribunal for Lebanon, which, for the first time in ICL history,
has created the fully independent Defence Office, with equal procedural
rights to the prosecutor. The Defence Office does not represent the accused;
that is the job of defense counsel. Rather, the office acts as an oversight body
charged with ensuring "the protection of the rights of the accused" through
active monitoring of defense representation and proceedings, training defense counsel, and representing the rights of the accused at the institutional
level (Special Tribunal for Lebanon 2014).

The remainder of this section illustrates the preceding arguments by considering the Adolf Eichmann case and, in particular, two narratives of the
trial crafted by Harry Mulisch and Hannah Arendt. The reader may be struck
by the datedness of the case. However, I select this example because today's
"humanistic" approach to the treatment of the accused has a history. Notwithstanding a recent revival of criticism of Arendt (Lipstadt 2011; Lilla 2013a,
2013b), some of which is based on evidence not known to Arendt at the time,
I argue that we find the seeds of the humanizing approach in their work.

British and Soviet resistance to the American plan to try Nazis at the end
of World War II is well known. While the British advocated summary executions, Moscow preferred show trials followed by preordained execution.
Similar kinds of responses can be found in all post-Holocaust atrocities,
and the kidnapping of Adolf Eichmann and transport to Israel to face trial
was no exception. Israeli public opinion clearly viewed him as more devilish
than human and demanded his execution. Even the judges had to resist such
propensities. But Arendt and Mulisch swam against the punitive tide and
resisted attempts to magnify Eichmann's role in the Holocaust as transcendent evil or reduce him to an unwitting cog forced to participate against his
will. Thus their accounts merit special attention. While Arendt is perhaps

most (in)famously known for her series in the *New Yorker* that was reworked into *Eichmann in Jerusalem: A Report on the Banality of Evil* (1963a), a similar, if lesser-known, venture was underway in the Netherlands. *Criminal Case 40/61, the Trial of Adolf Eichmann* (2005) reproduces in nearly exact form, albeit for the first time in English, Mulisch's weekly reports for the Dutch weekly *Elseviers Weekblad*.[16] Each author sought to understand how a seemingly ordinary individual, certified as sane by a team of psychiatrists and adjudged to lack the virulent anti-Semitism that drove Julius Streicher or the ideological zealotry of Himmler, could participate in such heinous crimes. Each taught us, above all, the necessity to resist explaining away seemingly incomprehensible acts by appealing to the imagery and rhetoric of evil, a national character or type, or predestined fate.[17]

During his trial, Eichmann was "turned into a myth" (Mulisch 2005, 142), and the media became a willing accomplice. The news daily *France Soir* described his "snake eyes," while *Libération* saw in each of his eyes "a gas chamber" (37). A Dutch newspaper quoted a popular minister at the time: "'Eichmann . . . has become a non-man, a phenomenon of absolute godlessness and non-humanness'" (43). If the trial judges resisted as much as possible the mythology surrounding Eichmann, the appeals chamber and the state qua prosecution cultivated the myth. But at the center of the myth-making endeavor stood the Israeli attorney general and chief prosecutor in the case, Gideon Hausner. Though Eichmann was *Obersturmbannführer*, head of section IV (Gestapo) B-4 (Jews) of the Head Office for Reich Security (Mulisch 2005, xii; Arendt 1963a, 31), the state presented him as the chief "organizer and executioner" of the Holocaust. More bombastically, Hausner proclaimed that while "it is no longer possible to believe in God[,] now let it at least be possible to believe in the Devil" (Mulisch 2005, 50). Knowing the Devil was beyond the reach of the prosecution, Hausner retreated somewhat; at the very least, he wanted "to prove that Eichmann was 'worse than Hitler'" (142).

That statement is surely peculiar, for Hitler—the mastermind of Nazi horror—was presumably the worst. But the statement aimed, first, "to satisfy the need for mankind to have a clear, simple, and horrible picture" of the Holocaust and its agents and, second, to rouse, influence, and even, in some sense, conform to public opinion (Arendt 1963a, 10). It was Hausner's third point—to prove Israeli fortitude and thus to overcome the image of diasporic meekness—that informed his proposition. Put differently (if unkindly), the prosecutorial strategy required the presence of an otherworldly, nearly omnipotent foe, for if the Israeli prosecution could vanquish this enemy, the state could prove its mettle. Nationalist narratives thus trumped cosmopolitan ones, even if the cosmopolitan promise at the heart of the trial—genocidaires need to be held responsible for their crimes—was realized. More damningly, Hausner's comment unwittingly suggested something more profound, and Mulisch and Arendt seemed to intuit as much.

They, like the trial judges, found material a series of events that Eichmann experienced during the summer of 1941 when he was sent to various sites to study responses to the Jewish Question. What he observed at Chelmno (the killing of Jews in mobile gas vans), Minsk (the killing of Jews by shooting), Lwów ("a spring of blood like a fountain," gushing from the earth where Jews, both dead and alive, had been buried [Arendt 1963a, 89]), and Treblinka (the gas chambers and crematorium [Mulisch 2005, 13–14; Arendt 1963a, 87–89]) disgusted him to the point of making him physically ill. Shortly after those visits, Eichmann "'*for the first and last time*', took an initiative contrary to orders." Instead of sending a shipment of twenty thousand Jews from the Rhineland and five thousand Gypsies to Riga or Minsk, "where they would have been immediately shot by the *Einsatzgruppen*," he "directed the transport to the ghetto of Lódz, where he knew that no preparations for extermination had yet been made" (Arendt 1963a, 94–95).

His initiative raised the specter that "the Devil" had a conscience (at least temporarily), and that argument earned Mulisch and Arendt considerable enmity, even among their friends.[18] It was heresy to humanize the perpetrator. When confronted with horrifying violence, many invariably appeal to the image of the monster, the demonic, the demented, to explain (usually away) the acts. Surely, only the abnormal or the Satanic are capable of committing such atrocities. Yet Arendt and Mulisch's critics failed to realize at the time that their reflections helped illuminate the importance of Hausner's assertion that Eichmann was worse than Hitler.

Both Mulisch (2005, 14) and Arendt (1963a, 95) determine, based on Eichmann's testimony, that he had a conscience, which Arendt felicitously described as having functioned normally (or the way we would expect it to function) for about four weeks, "whereupon it began to function the other way around." The obvious question is why it "reversed itself." The answer lies in the "considerable trouble" in which Eichmann found himself after the Lódz incident, which, unfortunately, was not explored by Arendt, Mulisch, or the court (Arendt 1963a, 95). We can only imagine that the anger of his superiors provoked a radical shift in Eichmann's approach; three weeks later, at a meeting in Prague called by Reinhardt Heydrich, head of the Sicherheitsdienst des Reichsführers-SS (SD),[19] Eichmann, perhaps to ingratiate himself with party leadership, proposed that "the camps used for the detention of [Russian] Communists [a category to be liquidated on the spot by the

*Einsatzgruppen*] can also include Jews." Heydrich upped the proverbial ante; as a test of Eichmann's loyalty in light of the Lódz ghetto incident, Eichmann was ordered to send fifty thousand Jews from the Reich "to the centers of the *Einsatzgruppen* operations at Riga and Minsk." Eichmann complied.

On one reading, Eichmann displayed a basic human tendency to respond to sanction by acquiescing in the preferred outcome of superiors. In doing so, he revealed himself to be not demonic but exceedingly normal—no more mythical or larger than life than a rock, which was Dr. Dieter Wechtenbruch's conclusion after extensive psychiatric evaluation (Mulisch 2005, 43).[20] Indeed, some even went so far as to opine that had the Israelis "put an empty SS uniform in the cage, with an SS hat hovering above it, they would have had a defendant of greater reality" (41). Ironically, however, the very attempt to humanize Eichmann was tinged with dehumanizing grit. If he could not be larger than life, transcendent and demonic, he was reduced to a pathetically simple, abject creature—"a somewhat grubby man with a cold, wearing glasses" (37). He became, virtually, a nonbeing.

Yet Eichmann's response to reprimand revealed his extraordinary capacity for ignoring the humanity of others. This was the prosecution's interpretation, fueled, as it were, by the four objectives that Israeli prime minister David Ben Gurion associated with the trial: (1) "to establish before the nations of the world how millions of people . . . were murdered by the Nazis"; (2) to demonstrate that the Jews "had always faced 'a hostile world,' . . . degenerated until they went to their death like sheep, and how only the establishment of a Jewish state had enabled Jews to hit back"; (3) to educate young Jews inside Israel who "were in danger of losing their ties with the Jewish people and, by implication, with their own history"; and (4) "to ferret out other Nazis—for example, the connection between the Nazis and some Arab rulers" (Arendt 1963a, 9–10). The man in the glass booth simply had to be larger than life; anything less would have compromised the project of Israeli nation building.

The myth became central to the purpose of the trial, which was needed to generate a conclusive narrative of what happened, how, when, and why. But the questions of what, how, and who had already been answered at Nuremberg. The question of why demanded deeper analysis—and it is with respect to this question that government objectives informed and shaped the prosecution's strategy. Anti-Semitism, theories of collective guilt, and attributions of national character, the latest manifestation of which is Daniel Goldhagen's *Hitler's Willing Executioners*, rounded out what conceptions of individualized responsibility could not explain: how the mass of society acquiesced in the attempted annihilation of European Jewry. The Eichmann trial had to go beyond Nuremberg to provide a fuller portrait of this most devastating and heinous of crimes. In doing so, the trial became a spectacle. For example, witnesses were allowed to testify even as it became clear in cross-examination that they lacked or had only tangential connection to Eichmann and that they offered poor testimony:

> Sick children, thrown out of the children's ward on the fifth floor (witness Ross). Babies, ripped apart like a rag in front of their mothers' eyes (witness Buzminsky). Neighborhoods, chosen at random, closed off, starved, and then burned. The inhabitants, jumping out of their windows and attempting to crawl with their broken limbs; the soldiers, first laughing at them for a while, and then throwing them into the fire. Churches filled with believers set ablaze (witness Masia). Old priests forced to play horseback-riding matches on each others' backs (photograph). Old women made to scrub a square clean with toothbrushes (photograph). Orchestras playing dance music, while thousands of naked families are being executed (witness Wells) . . . Dogs being given sugar cubes for having bitten flesh out of a girl (witness Buzminsky) . . . Meadows covered with skulls and bones (witness Berman). Naked people in winter, covered with water and frozen (witness Neumann) . . . A man who has to choose between his wife and his mother; if not, both will be executed (witness Dworzecki). (Mulisch 2005, 88–89)

Repeatedly, the trial judges resisted such testimony yet found it difficult to silence the voices of those who had suffered. Against the wisdom of the district court judges who opposed mythologizing Eichmann and explicitly or implicitly attributing the Holocaust to Eichmann exclusively, such testimony only enabled acceptance of the myth; indeed, the appeals court bought it. If Hausner wanted Eichmann to be worse than Hitler, the appellate judgment declared it so: "'the appellant had received no superior orders at all. He was his own superior, and he gave all orders in matters that concerned Jewish affairs'; he had, moreover, 'eclipsed in importance all his superiors, including Müller'" (Arendt 1963a, 249). In rejecting Eichmann's appeal and sealing his fate, the judges concluded that "the idea of the Final Solution would never have assumed the infernal forms of the flayed skin and tortured flesh of millions of Jews without the fanatical zeal and the unquenchable blood thirst of the appellant and his accomplices."

This conclusion does not, on the face of it, prove Hausner's claim, but he does get at something fundamental. Mulisch (2005, 128) intuits that the "great lesson of National Socialism" or the "true origin of the horror" concerns "the order as fate" (104). Arendt framed it as the banality of evil, by which she meant that evil did not have Satanic dimensions in this particular case. Neither was Eichmann driven by ideology (as was Himmler) or by virulent anti-Semitism (as was Streicher).[21] Indeed, Eichmann admitted that he "had never read the official party literature" and that he read *Mein Kampf* "only superficially and not in its entirety" (Mulisch 2005, 93; cf. Arendt 1963a, 33). He was simply the "calm, dutiful civil servant" about whom no one thinks. Eichmann was, as Mulisch importuned, in all of the artistic and literary imagery of mass horror that predated Nazism, in all of the studies of Hitler and Nazi leadership,[22] the one missing person—not a mere cog, for surely he knew what he was doing, but a follower who abandoned the project of asking hard questions. By his own admission, the bored salesman of the Austrian Vacuum Oil Company joined the Nazi Party out of sheer ennui. "'Why not join the S.S.?'" asked Ernst Kaltenbrunner, "a young lawyer in Linz who later became chief of the Head Office for Reich Security," and Eichmann replied, "Why not?" (Arendt 1963a, 31–33; Mulisch 2005, 93).

Eichmann's blasé "Why not?"—designed to forestall inquiry—replaced the interrogatory, reflective "Why?" that one would normally ask. The troubling extent to which this was true unfolded during testimony surrounding the Lódz ghetto incident in which the judges pressed Eichmann after he shockingly announced that "as a norm I have adhered to the Kantian imperative, and for a long time already" (Mulisch 2005, 113). Judge Yitzhak Raveh, incredulous, observed that if one takes that statement at face value, we are left with the unfathomable claim that "the death trains were rattling to Poland in the name of the categorical imperative, that the crematoriums were roaring in the name of morality." But Eichmann persisted and, to everyone's surprise, "came up with an approximately correct definition of the categorical imperative: 'I meant by my remark about Kant that the principle of my will must always be such that it can become the principle of general laws'" (Arendt 1963a, 136).[23] He explained that "from the moment he was charged with carrying out the Final Solution he had ceased to live according to Kantian principles." We assume that moment came during the Prague meeting.

Arendt concluded that Eichmann only gave part of the story. Rather, during this "period of crimes legalized by the state," Eichmann

had not simply dismissed the Kantian formula . . . [but] had distorted it to read: Act as if the principle of your actions were the same as that of the legislator or of the law of the land—or, in Hans Frank's formulation of "the categorical imperative in the Third Reich," which

Eichmann might have known: "Act in such a way that the Führer, if he knew your actions, would approve it."

In Eichmann's world, Hitler's orders emerged "as something larger than the one giving it and the one receiving it—again as something mystical—as a superhuman power that has to be obeyed" (Mulisch 2005, 111). Rudolf Höss, Auschwitz camp commander, testified at Nuremberg in a manner that substantiates that opinion: Eichmann "was not obsessed with the extermination of the Jews . . . but he was obsessed with 'orders.'"

The obsession was indeed consuming—and damning. In March 1944, facing defeat at the hands of the Soviet army, Himmler ordered that the exterminations at Auschwitz and the evacuation of Hungarian Jews from Budapest, the last major continental European urban center from which the Jews had not yet been liquidated, be terminated immediately. Eichmann, charged with deporting all Jews in Hungary, disobeyed Himmler and even threatened "'to seek a new decision from the Führer'" (Arendt 1963a, 147; Mulisch 2005, 111–12).[24] In Eichmann's view, Himmler betrayed the Führer's order and had become "a renegade" (Mulisch 2005, 111); the evacuation and extermination orders could only be rescinded by Hitler himself, and as we know, no such order was issued. In fact, in his testimony, Eichmann mused that Hitler betrayed his own commandment, for he "let certain Jews escape" (112). Disturbed, Eichmann determined that if the initial order was to retain validity and meaning, he had to act consistently, and thus he rejected Himmler's directives. At the end of the war, "when no more orders came, he immediately changed into a 'peaceable citizen,' as Servatius so rightly remarked" (93). In this episode, we ascertain why Eichmann was worse than Hitler, for he "is less a criminal than he is someone who is capable of anything" (112) because he unquestionably follows orders.

Arendt arrived at a similar conclusion. Following orders is, simply stated, banal—that is, ordinary and lacking originality. It requires no thought. In Eichmann's words, "one is to click one's heels together and say 'Yes, sir'" (Mulisch 2005, 110). This absence of thinking intrigued Arendt[25] and prompted her to investigate the faculties of thinking, willing, and judgment that would preoccupy her for the remainder of her life. Certainly, in her report on the trial, she did not fully explore the matter in any conclusive sense, which likely contributed to the invective against her. Thoughtlessness is not evil, though it may be a contributing factor to or a feature of evildoing in particular contexts; international criminal law appreciates this. Individual criminal responsibility evolves not only from the *actus reus*, the act classified as a crime, but also from *mens rea*, the mental or subjective element that requires the crime be committed with intent and knowledge. The Rome Statute of the ICC defines intent in relation to conduct as the will to engage in the conduct; in relation to consequences, the "person means to cause that consequence or is aware that it will occur in the ordinary course of events" (Article 30(2)). Knowledge "means awareness that a circumstance exists or a consequence will occur in the ordinary course of events" (Article 30(3)). Eichmann's thoughtlessness manifested not only as speaking predominantly in clichés but also, for Arendt, as an inability or reluctance to concentrate on the implications of what he was doing, to reflect, as it were, on his actions, even though he was completely aware of the effects of his actions (e.g., that the train shipments of Jews that he meticulously organized ended at the labor camps and gas chambers). The execution of the order—in this case, the commission of a crime—substituted for thinking and became routine, "implemented without moral revulsion and political indignation and resistance" (Butler 2011). Eichmann acted without intention, if we mean by "intention" the ability "to think reflectively about one's own action as a political being, whose own life and thinking is bound up with the life and thinking of others."

Thoughtlessness serves as an appropriate, if uncomfortable, optic through which to view the commission of mass atrocities. While such atrocities require architects—hence ICL's pursuit of only those most responsible—their execution hinges on laborers willing and able to translate the blueprints into reality and not to question the convictions underlying the vision. The specter disturbs. Mulisch wonders, "[h]ow will we be protected against ourselves . . . ?" (2005, 149), especially given that

> neither the family nor the school nor any other institution is capable of building a dam of sufficient height against the barbarism. An education as rigorous as that of the Germans, one-sidedly geared toward knowledge and obedience, seemed even to boost it . . . The intellect does not offer any guarantee against the revelation . . . [I]t is perhaps not the responsibility of education to form dams against bloody revelations. That is more the job of another revelation. Which one? A moral one such as the Christian revelation . . . turned out to be worthless . . . [for, i]n the final analysis, Christians are happy with their deaths, even when it comes to them in the shape of the Nazis. (150–52)

Yet Mulisch tempers his pessimism by praising English pedagogy, which he adjudges as more "trustworthy than the German or Dutch," since it "is not primarily focused on obedience, knowledge, or intellect, but on cultivating all sorts of small rules of life, manners, habits, and faces, granted, resulting in English people, but at least not barbarians" (151). We must ignore his sarcasm. But the deeper point—cultivation of social graces, grooming a proclivity to critically investigate, self-examine, and question in the presence of others—is relevant. In the previous two chapters, education appeared as an antidote to dehumanization, as a tool in the arsenal to empower marginalized peoples and to resist our human tendencies to ghettoize our mentalities and, consequently, others. Education as consciousness raising impels us to reimagine forms of life (Cornell 1995, 78); to reflect on and interrogate social structures, systems, and beliefs; and to abandon thoughtless trust in the directive "as something larger than the one giving it and the one receiving it . . . as a superhuman power that has to be obeyed" (Mulisch 2005, 111).

James Waller (2002) offers a four-pronged model to help us understand the allure of that superhuman power that has so often inoculated people against thoughtful interdiction of evildoing. The first prong, our ancestral shadow, "focuses on three tendencies of human nature . . . that are particularly relevant in shaping our responses to authority," including *ethnocentrism* ("the tendency to focus on one's own group as the 'right' one"), *xenophobia* ("the tendency to fear outsiders or strangers"), and the *desire for social dominance.* The second prong includes forces that mold the identities of the perpetrators, such as *cultural belief systems* ("about external, controlling influences on one's life; authority orientation; ideological commitment"), *moral disengagement* "of the perpetrator from the victim, (facilitated by moral justification, euphemistic labeling of evil actions, and exonerating comparison)," and *rational self-interest,* "professional and personal" (19–20). The third prong, what Waller calls a "culture of cruelty," considers the immediate social context within which evildoing occurs; it concerns such matters as *professional socialization* ("built on escalating commitments, ritual conduct, and the repression of conscience"), *binding factors of the group* "that cement one's adherence to the group and its activities (including diffusion of responsibility, deindividuation, and conformity to peer pressure)," and the *merger of the role and person.* The fourth prong "analyzes three features of the social death of the victims: *us-them thinking, dehumanization of the victims* (for example, the use of language in defining the victims as less than human), and *blaming the victims* (a legitimization of the victim as the enemy and, thus, deserving of their victimization." While his account is laudably comprehensive, I append to it one additional factor: impoverishment of opportunity and capability. As we saw in the previous chapter, the human security concept was developed in response to serious, persistent deprivations that, no matter their cause, have contributed to violence in many instances, especially when those deprivations are perceived to be experienced unevenly across racial, ethnic, national, or religious lines.[26]

Waller's model returns us to the topic at beginning of this chapter: humanizing the collective by attempting to understand the context within which egregious crimes have occurred. Whole cultures or peoples or religions or ethnic groups and the like are not evil in and of themselves. No discernible collective "character" can or should substitute for individual responsibility. Far from mindlessly reproducing the Manichean dichotomy of good versus evil and distancing ourselves from grappling with the ugly features of human life, we must, Mulisch exhorts, "get in *contact* with the domains below the belt, with the darkness, with the 'myth'" (2005, 153). In this regard, both Mulisch and Arendt anticipated Judith Shklar's brand of liberalism (1982), which "put cruelty first" and, in doing so, urged political thought not to ignore human propensity toward cruelty but to engage and understand it as undeniably *human* and *political*. While we can never erase the existential uncertainty that comes with living with others, humanization of the collective, the victim, and the perpetrator offers a kind of existentially optimistic rebuttal. By exploring the terrain of negative solidarity, we may stake out room for constructing forms of positive solidarity and countering our bleakest proclivities.

## Conclusion

In 1982, Oscar Schachter, president of the International Studies Association, called on the discipline to attend "the status of individuals and the extent to which they are accorded human dignity and justice" (1982, 315). Drawing on developments in postwar international relations, Schachter tethered his understanding of human dignity and justice to "the right to security of person, . . . access to and the provision of basic human needs, . . . and the right to constitute a political community based on a sense of shared identity" (323). Chapter 3 of the present study treated the security of the person as it has factored into the maintenance of international peace and security by the world's foremost institutional agent charged with that task, the UN Security Council, while chapter 4 used the prism of human security to consider human protection and empowerment in contexts of insecurities. Notably absent in Schachter's formulation was what Karl Jaspers called the "barely perceptible dawn" of cosmopolitan justice at Nuremberg (see Fine 2007, 98), that is, the radical attempt to extricate responsibility qua sovereign prerogative and to revitalize it with cosmopolitan vigor. This chapter demonstrated how ICL has played a vital role in the project of making human, by recognizing injustices of misrecognition; reflecting on the status of victims and perpetrators; resisting cultures of impunity and attributions of crimes to sovereign prerogative or to "'streak[s] of satanic greatness'" (Jaspers quoted in Fine 2007, 98); individualizing crimes, which disaggregates them from presumed national characters; iterating degrees and types of responsibility (e.g., criminal liability of perpetrators of abuse and violence, the legal obligations of states); prosecuting the accused; and, finally, lending the notion of humanity itself a substance worthy of legal defense.

But as we have seen in the three cases explored thus far, while the aggregate of humanity is increasingly treated as having existence in ways that translate into varying international political obligations of protection, empowerment, restitution, and reparation, membership in humanity is not, as a result of human choice, automatic. Deliberate exclusions characterize development of the concept and apprehension of its content; humanity as an idea and a reality unfolds through an ongoing struggle of who is or is not a member and who has status—and to what degree. These themes come into sharp relief with respect to the matter of self-determination, to which I now turn.

## CHAPTER 6

# The International Court of Justice

## *Making Human through Self-Determination*

> The advent of international organizations not only heralded the growing expansion of international legal personality (no longer a monopoly of States), but also shifted attention to the importance of fulfilling the needs and aspirations of people. In this sense, international organizations have contributed to a return to the *droit des gens,* in the framework of the new times, and to a revival of its humanist vision, faithful to the teachings of the "founding fathers" of the law of nations . . . Yet, the considerable development of international law in our times, assists us, in current-day rethinking of those juridical institutions, to identify an element, in my view, of greater transcendence in those juridical institutions: that of the care with the conditions of living of the "people" or the "population."
>
> —Judge Antonio Cançado Trindade[1]

On 22 July 2010, the International Court of Justice (ICJ) concluded that Kosovo's declaration of independence, which "representatives of the people of Kosovo" unilaterally proclaimed from Serbia on 17 February 2008, did not violate any applicable rule of international law. Between 9 and 15 January 2011, after decades of civil war, the southern region of Sudan held a referendum on whether it should remain a part of the Republic of Sudan or secede. Of the votes cast, 98.83 percent favored independence (Results 2011), which was officially proclaimed on 9 July 2011. Two months later, the Palestinian Authority formally applied for UN membership (Associated Press 2011). Lacking support in the UN Security Council, it solicited the General Assembly for an upgrade to nonmember status, which was granted in November 2012 by a vote of 138 to 9, with 41 abstentions. Seven months earlier, Mali's desert Tuareg people, led by the National Movement for the Liberation of Azawad (MNLA), proclaimed an independent state of Azawad, which it had desired since Mali's independence from France in 1960. Initially backed by Islamist groups, the MNLA soon found itself at odds with its more powerful and extremist partners. After weeks of armed struggle, the Islamists took control of key northern cities and imposed strict Sharia law. In December 2012, the UN Security Council authorized a French-led intervention force comprised of African Union and MNLA troops to oust the extremists, which it had accomplished two months later.

These cases underscore the extent to which peoples have attempted to reconcile international law's statist discourse of sovereign equality with its contrasting language of self-determination, the subjects of which are not states but peoples, their communities, and even cultures. Politically, self-determination may serve as the conceptual midwife for new states, as with South Sudan and East Timor. Alternatively, it may be deployed to leverage reforms within states to increase minority peoples' participation in and access to political processes or to accrue greater degrees of autonomy and internal self-governance, as with Quebec and Scotland.[2] On this reading, self-determination plays an important role in the realization of human dignity as status, for it seeks to actualize a peoples' recognition as autonomous and free. Yet while the concept of self-determination "introduces a diversity and particularity into international law," its use and interpretation also "internationalizes assumptions about identity that perpetuate and justify inequalities of culture and gender." These, in turn, neuter self-determination's emancipatory potential (Knop 2002, 6).[3] Simply stated, some groups (e.g., the Tuaregs, South Ossetians, and Chechnyans) are denied self-determinative rights and freedoms, while others (e.g., South Sudanese, East Timorese, Quebecois, Scots) obtain them in varying degrees. Dignity through self-determination appears an unreliable vehicle.

In part, the utility of the vehicle hinges on questions of how the "self" of self-determination is defined and what methods are employed to effectuate it. With respect to the former, Milena Sterio (2013, 16) and Hurst Hannum (2002, 231) consider objective and subjective elements to help determine who constitutes the subject of self-determination. At minimum, members of the group need to consciously perceive themselves as separate and distinct. Objectively, delineation of a group's distinctiveness may include reference to common ethnicity, language, history, religion, and culture. This "self" has thus been variously defined as colonized peoples and inhabitants of non-self-governing territories, mandates, and trusteeships, as well in terms of race, color, creed, ethnicity, nationality, language, and religion. With respect to the question of method, referenda and negotiated settlements such as those that produced East Timor and South Sudan are deemed acceptable, while irredentism and armed resistance, as with Biafra (1967–70) and Azawad, are not. Actions such as Kosovo's unilateral declaration of independence and Palestine's application for UN membership, which sought, respectively, to conclusively settle and to revitalize stalled peace talks, exacerbate confusion regarding the conditions in which self-determination is permitted to override the international community *Grundnorm* of territorial integrity, or, in international legal parlance, *uti possidetis*.[4]

Long affiliated with nationalist movements and bound up with decolonization, self-determination has been attached to the corporate ideal of the state. Recently, however, scholars have attempted to extricate it from those moorings. Karen Knop (2002) adds indigenous peoples and women to the list of self-determination's selves, while Omar Dahbour (2013) and Jan Klabbers (2006) enlarge the pool of relevant actors to include all those who demand greater voice and participation in political processes. In determining this self, Knop urges us to tend to how and by whom boundaries around the self are drawn and thus to consider who *within* them is excluded (e.g., women and indigenous peoples and minority groups, such as the Hmong in Southeast Asia or the Kurds in the Middle East, who might become entangled in larger self-determination movements to the sacrifice of their own claims and rights). Dahbour criticizes the nationalist appropriation of self-determination for its fixation on "getting right" the connection between states and nations, rather than "protecting the political freedoms of citizens as such" (2013, 8).[5] Under the rubric of self-determination, he thus includes populist movements for more responsive government (e.g., the Arab Spring), protests against corporate excess (e.g., by indigenous peoples in Amazonia against logging and farming and by Bolivian villagers against the privatization of water), acts of sabotage (e.g., against oil pipelines in Nigeria, to protest increased pollution, and against fast-food restaurants in France and Italy), and electoral expressions of peoples' will (e.g., the defeat of the European Constitution in France and the Netherlands). Each requires that we reconceptualize self-determination to capture "the struggle to assert sovereignty over peoples' lands, resources, governments, and countries against the agencies of 'globalization'—whether transnational corporations or hegemonic states."

Knop's earlier examination of the ways in which "groups affected by the right of self-determination of peoples may be included in or excluded from its interpretation" (2002, 4) tends more toward leveraging the international right to self-determination domestically to obtain more democratic responsiveness or self-governance. In particular, she considers seven interwar European plebiscites during which women were permitted "for the first time . . . to participate in an international expression of popular sovereignty" (12); the use by women in UN trust territories of the right to petition the Trusteeship Council in ways that "mark a place in the history of self-determination for colonial women as participants in its interpretation" (328) by intertwining self-determination and women's equality in many areas of social, economic, and political life; and a 1981 UN Human Rights Committee case in which Sandra Lovelace, an indigenous woman, successfully challenged Canada's Indian Act, which placed an undue burden on indigenous women but not on indigenous men (358).

Milena Sterio (2013) adopts a more conventional, statist approach to self-determination. However, she moves beyond decolonization and proposes a "great power theory" of self-determination to explain why East Timor and South Sudan became sovereign whereas Chechnya, South Ossetia, and Abkhazia have not. Mining cases for principles and guidelines, she formulates a set of criteria to assess the validity of self-determination claims by minority peoples in existing states: systematic oppression, a weak central government, international administration, and support by the great powers for independence claims (57). Compared to the ICJ's restrained advisory opinion on Kosovo,[6] Sterio's substantive rendering offers sound guidance to adjudge self-determination claims and when those amount to a right to remedial secession.

Together, Dahbour, Knop, and Sterio anticipate this chapter's concerns. Self-determination foregrounds a people's claims to a political future, both internally and externally.[7] As such, by offering the promise of being recognized, self-determination relates to and enhances a peoples' sense of self and what it means to be human. While much of the existing literature on self-determination considers debates pertaining to territoriality, governance structures, legality, analysis of successful and unsuccessful claims and movements, decolonization, nationalism, and the like, I here bracket those issues as much as possible and aim, instead, to explore the humanizing dimensions of self-determination as concept and practice. Congruent with previous cases, this chapter does not aim to provide an exhaustive history of self-determination or of the Kosovo case on which it predominantly focuses; rather, it offers a preliminary investigation into how self-determination illustrates the operation of processes of making human in world politics. Likewise, coincident with this book's focus, I here largely limit my focus to ways in which the United Nations and its agents and organs have been at the forefront of humanization. The ICJ, being one of the six principal organs of the United Nations, has, in the guise of the Kosovo question, for the first time provided sustained treatment of what I call making human, as it considered something more foundational and primordial than the recognition of a state—that is, recognition of people, their suffering, and their needs. Several of the separate but concurring opinions alert us to the complexity of conditions that influence self-determination, and they thus reveal the extent to which the ICJ is slowly but perceptibly altering its calculus on such matters. I begin the present discussion by outlining the concept of self-determination. Then I proceed to assess the advisory opinion.

## Self-Determination: A Brief Overview

The idea of self-determination was born in the wake of World War I, to manage the disintegration and dismantling of the multiethnic, multinational Austro-Hungarian Empire and Ottoman Empire. While Woodrow Wilson and Vladimir Lenin enthusiastically endorsed the principle, Wilson's secretary of state, Robert Lansing, warned at the Paris Peace Conference that the concept was "'simply loaded with dynamite'" (quoted in Klabbers 2006, 187). Even if states eventually rejected its inclusion in the Covenant of the League of Nations, it nevertheless proved useful in reconfiguring the territories and minority peoples of the fallen empires. As Sterio (2013, 27) observes, only a fairly restrictive conception and application of self-determination, one that did not "pose any threats to the norm of territorial integrity of states," proved acceptable to the international community at the time. On her view, this explains why new states such as Czechoslovakia, Austria, Hungary, and Yugoslavia were created—carved, as they were, more or less from the footprint of the former Austro-Hungarian Empire—whereas the attempted secession in 1920 of the Åaland Islands from Finland and reunion with Sweden was rejected by the League of Nations' International Committee of Jurists (27–30). While the committee averred that international law did not "recognize the right of national groups . . . to separate themselves from the State of which they form a part by the simple expression of a wish," it did recognize or suggest exceptions to this prohibition. Crucially, it left open the question "as to whether a manifest and continued abuse of sovereign power, to the detriment of a section of the population of a State, would . . . give to an international dispute, arising therefrom, such a character that its object should be considered as one which is not confined to the domestic jurisdiction of the State concerned, but comes within the sphere of action of the League of Nations" (quoted on 28). This case did not satisfy the condition of oppression. In fact, the Finnish government expressed willingness "to grant the Åalanders 'satisfactory guarantees' that their language and culture would be preserved" (30). Had Helsinki refused to respect and protect their Swedish identity and cultural heritage however, the commission would have advised "the separation of the islands from Finland, based on the wishes of the inhabitants which would be freely expressed by means of a plebiscite."

Ascertaining that it had jurisdiction in the matter, the committee appointed a commission of rapporteurs to recommend a political solution. The commission vehemently rejected any notion giving to minority peoples, "either of language or religion, or to any fractions of a population the right of withdrawing from the community to which they belong, because it is their wish or their good pleasure," as it would "destroy order and stability within States and to inaugurate anarchy in international life." The commission accepted this logic and stipulated that separation should be "an exceptional solution, a last resort when the State lacks either the will or the power to enact and apply just and effective guarantees" of the rights of peoples (29). Several of the separate opinions in the Kosovo case would pick up on this theme.

For many scholars, 1945 marks a turning point in the concept of self-determination, since it was twice incorporated into the UN Charter: first, in Article 1, to buttress "friendly relations among nations" predicated on "respect for the principles of equal rights and self-determination of peoples"; second, in Article 55, to help create "conditions of stability and well-being" that were conceived of as "necessary for peaceful and friendly relations among nations." Vague as the invocations were, decolonization provided the context that gave substance to self-determination, contributing to its morphing from a principle to an internationally recognized legal right within fifteen years. In December 1960, the UNGA approved Resolution 1514, the "Declaration on the Granting of Independence to Colonial Countries and Peoples," and its follow-up resolution, 1541, to which was appended an annex that specified "the modalities of self-determination for colonized peoples" (Sterio 2013, 11; Hannum 2002, 220–21), including "emergence as a sovereign state," "free association with an independent state," or "integration with an independent state" (UNGA 1960b, Principle VI). While neither resolution explicitly defined self-determination, Resolution 1514 identified adjuncts—the free determination of peoples of their political status and their economic, social, and cultural development—associated with the right (UNGA 1960a, ¶2).

Though the term was expressly omitted from the 1948 Universal Declaration of Human Rights, it appeared in the two 1966 international covenants on human rights. Though the covenants do little to explicate the concept or define peoples, they are lauded for making two contributions. First, the covenants conferred "an obligation on . . . states to respect a people's right to some form of democratic self-governance" (Sterio 2013, 11).[8] Second, they affirmed the universality of the right to self-determination, which is declared by their common first article to extend to "all peoples." As many international legal scholars conclude, the formulation suggests "a scope beyond that of decolonization" (Hannum 2002, 225). Yet at the time of drafting the covenants, that suggestion was quickly neutered. Hannum quotes the director of the United Nations Division of Human Rights, who was intimately involved in the drafting process: "despite the broad formulation of article 1 . . . , self-determination 'would be understood in United Nations doctrine as a right belonging only to colonial peoples, which once it had been successfully exercised could not be invoked again, and it would not include a right of secession except for colonies.'"[9]

By 1970, however, that view appeared more relaxed. While the territorial integrity and political unity of states was upheld, the "Declaration on Principles of International Law concerning Friendly Relations and Co-operation among States in Accordance with the Charter of the United Nations" allowed for the exercise of self-determination outside decolonization in the event that states fail to represent "the whole people belonging to the territory without distinction as to race, creed, or color" (UNGA 1970). Hannum and Sterio concur that the widely accepted interpretation of the provision determines that a state is not representative "if it formally excludes a particular group from participation in the political process" (Hannum 2002, 224), such as apartheid South Africa and the white racist regime of Ian Smith in South Rhodesia. Sterio, however, admits that the provision "potentially" confers the right of secession "on racial or religious groups" living in unrepresentative societies in limited and exceptional circumstances (2013, 12, 16).

That self-determination may entail a right to secede as a last resort— even if it revives a suggestion made in the 1920 Åaland Islands case—is, of course, highly contentious. Failure to fully and conclusively address it in the Kosovo case constitutes a substantial deficiency of the advisory opinion. To be fair, however, one could hardly imagine the ICJ—or any court for that matter—ordering for all intents and purposes the disintegration of a state. In this regard, self-determination may appeal to innate senses of democracy and justice, but it generates considerable unease practically speaking, for it "can only be used to undermine perceived internal and external stability" (Cassese 1995, 6).

Whether we construe self-determination in political or individual terms or as adding to justice or subtracting from stability, we might think of it as a natalist concept, as discussed in chapter 1. Its performative dimensions are obvious enough, whether manifested as claims to independence by colonized or oppressed peoples or as rights to autonomy within existing states. Self-determination entails the exercise of self-responsibility and the enunciation of an identity to carve out separate space to Be. From such claims follow its necessary intersubjectivity: for example, agreement on who constitutes its subject, negotiations pertaining to its actualization, and resolutions specifying shared understandings of rights that ensue from self-determination claims. Conceptually, self-determination diametrically opposes and corrects what Arendt identified as the cardinal offense against humanity: expulsion of some of its members. On that reading, self-determination's anchoring to decolonization and statehood permitted excluded, marginalized peoples standing or status in the political organization of the world; recognized their autonomy, independence, and theoretical (at least) capacity to govern themselves; conferred on them expectations of self-responsibility and obligations to act according to community norms—to reproduce, as it were, prevailing conceptions about what it means to be an independent, sovereign people; and hence stretched the boundaries of European willingness to share the world with others. Yet in self-determination's actualization in a postcolonial world inheres disruptive and adverse potentialities: disintegration of states, violence to thwart or realize self-determinative objectives, alteration of internal governance and hence impingement on domestic stability, and exclusionary (i.e., potentially racist, xenophobic, oppressive) practices. Given the burden that self-determination represents—recall Arendt's musing that positive solidarity might, by virtue of the responsibilities it imposes, prove to be an "intolerable situation" (1968a, 83)—we need a new understanding of the concept.

Here, I draw on the interpretation of Jan Klabbers (2006, 189), who reconstitutes self-determination "as a procedural right," that is, as a right of peoples "to see their position taken into account whenever their futures are being decided," which Klabbers claims "may not amount to a right to secede or even to a right to autonomy or self-government" but "does amount to a right to be taken seriously." Such an interpretation accords with judicial and quasi-judicial practice, Klabbers maintains. Whereas self-determination during the era of decolonization was virtually synonymous with independence from colonial rule, its subject being a colonized people living within clearly defined imperially drawn boundaries that were, as a condition of recognition, to remain unaltered, its postcolonial meaning is "too indeterminate" (190). While the ICJ has repeatedly affirmed the right to self-determination, it also repeatedly failed to apply it (192). Such failure owes partly to the formulation of the questions submitted to it and partly to findings that the court lacked jurisdiction in particular cases in which issues pertaining to self-determination were broached.

In the two 1966 South-West Africa cases (*Ethiopia v. South Africa* and *Liberia v. South Africa*), the ICJ found that Ethiopia and Liberia lacked standing and thus could not bring suit against apartheid South Africa for violating its obligations as a mandatory power over South-West Africa. The 1971 advisory opinion on the legal consequences of the continued presence of South Africa in Namibia concerned only the legal consequences of a Security Council resolution and thus did not permit an expansive explication of self-determination. The 1975 advisory opinion on the *Western Sahara* case ultimately concerned not the self-determinative rights of the peoples of Western Sahara but the territory's status at the time of colonization by Spain and hence its legal relationship to Morocco and Mauritania, both of which claimed the territory. Finally, in the 1995 case concerning East Timor (*Portugal v. Australia*) in which Portugal, East Timor's former colonial ruler, argued that Australia violated the self-determinative rights of the East Timorese with respect to natural resource exploitation, the ICJ found it lacked jurisdiction.

According to the view of Klabbers, in only one of those cases did the ICJ say something substantive about self-determination: the *Western Sahara* opinion defined it as "the need to pay regard to the freely expressed will of peoples" (ICJ 1975, ¶59, p. 33). For Klabbers, this formulation trumps the judges' later, surprising acceptance of Portugal's "assertion [in the *East Timor* case] that the right of peoples to self-determination, as it evolved from the Charter and from United Nations practice, has an *erga omnes* character, [and] is irreproachable" (ICJ 1995, ¶29, p. 16). While an *erga omnes* obligation, referring to an obligation owed to the world community as a whole (in contradistinction to obligations owed to one's treaty partners), could be construed as an obligation to pay regard to the will of peoples, it was not at all clear what is owed to whom and why in the *East Timor* case; the ICJ remained disappointingly silent on the broader issue.

In 2004, the ICJ provided valuable insight into its understanding of a right to self-determination in a case Klabbers does not discuss. In its advisory opinion regarding the legal consequences of the Israeli construction of a wall surrounding the Palestinian territories, the ICJ found that by encroaching on lands considered Palestinian, "settling parts of its own population and new immigrants in [the occupied] territories" (ICJ 2004, ¶120, p. 184) and displacing Palestinian peoples, Israel was in breach of its obligation to respect the Palestinian's right to self-determination, which the ICJ reaffirmed was an *erga omnes* obligation (¶122, p. 184; ¶155–56, p. 199). On this reading, the *erga omnes* character of the obligation to respect the right to self-determination is a negative one: it is simply an obligation to inaction, that is, an obligation *not to impede* the actualization of the right itself. In this instance, it was clear how the obligation should be translated practically: enjoining the Israelis from building additional settlements (which the Security Council had denounced), transferring populations, and even constructing the wall in such a way as to sever additional land from Palestinian ownership and use. However, the negative construction of the obligation could not stand as a general principle. Certainly it could not be read as an injunction to states to remain silent in the face of self-determinative, potentially secessionist claims of restive peoples. But that is precisely the nagging conclusion one is left with in the Kosovo advisory opinion. By casting the obligation to respect the right to self-determination in largely negative terms, the ICJ has repeatedly avoided messy issues that it found were (rightly) best left to relevant political actors. Any direct articulation of what a right to self-determination meant in practical terms would likely have been condemned by states as inappropriate interference in peace processes or in the affairs of domestic governance, regardless of the international legal issues at stake.

Klabbers' procedural reconstruction of the right, contrariwise, demands something more: that is, a positive obligation to, at minimum, take into account the claims of the other and, at maximum, formulate policy around such claims. The minimal and maximal versions fulfill two of William Paul Simmons's (2011) three modalities for reversing the marginalization of the other, as recounted in this book's introduction: listening to the voice of the other and working in solidarity with others to help them realize their self-determinative, self-creative potentials. Read in that vein, self-determination proved a potent emancipatory tool in the UN arsenal to manage decolonization. Klabbers merely picks up on the underlying, if never fully expressed, democratizing logic and asserts it as a less fully loaded conception to subtract self-determination from its more radical variant, secession.

So what, in the end, may we ascertain about self-determination? First, at the very least, self-determination entails having one's voice recognized. Klabbers's framing of self-determination as a procedural right "to be taken seriously" underlines the concept's participative dimension and hence may be construed as a vehicle for or buttress of democratic governance within and between states. Second, how this right is exercised is a contingent matter, the details of which are to be worked out given the exigencies of circumstance. Thus self-determination is one of those general concepts that will remain, for better or for worse, ambiguous. Third, self-determination, even in more restrictive understanding of Klabbers, demands (or involves) recognition of another's humanity and status as political agent. Sometimes recognition is freely or unproblematically granted, as between the English and the Scots or between the French-speaking Quebecois and the English-speaking Canadians; at other times, recognition must be forced, as with Kosovo. Yet even in extreme circumstances, such as the persistent, systematic, and deliberate exclusion of certain peoples from political processes, as well as their repeated oppression, self-determination does not necessarily entail the right to secede. Thus, fourth, self-determination and secession need to be decoupled, as they have been in the declaratory enunciations of the General Assembly. However, fifth, exceptional, extreme circumstances may be grounds for claims to remedial secession if several conditions are met, as Sterio maintains.

Even so, questions remain. How are self-determination claims resolved if a peoples' voice is recognized and "taken seriously" to the point of being involved in internationally sponsored settlement discussions, such as with Kosovo, but ultimately stymied by intransigent local actors and their sponsoring great powers? How are claims to being recognized as partners in negotiation, let alone as autonomous or independent, secured in the absence of a willingness to share the world with different, sometimes despised others? Admittedly, while the general aspects of these questions are beyond the scope of this study, they emerge in specific ways in the Kosovo case, to which I now turn.

## Kosovo, Recognition, and Making Human

Though recounting the long and troubled history of Kosovo is beyond the scope of this chapter, a brief primer here is warranted. During World War II, Axis forces occupied Yugoslavia. While Italy controlled Kosovo as part of its grip on Greater Albania, the Nazis, Hungarians, and Bulgarians carved up the remainder of Yugoslavia. The pan-Yugoslav Partisans, led by Josip Broz Tito, initiated a guerilla campaign to oust Axis forces; it would eventually become the largest resistance army in occupied Western and Central Europe. To recruit Kosovar Albanians in the liberation struggle, Tito, astutely and disingenuously, as it were, allegedly promised them "the right to unite with Albania after the war" (Judah 1999). Once it became clear in 1945 that the promise would not be kept, ethnic Albanians engaged in protests, which Tito, leader of the newly independent Communist state of Yugoslavia, quickly quashed. As added insult to injury, he assigned Kosovo the status of "autonomous province" under the aegis of the Socialist Republic of Serbia.

Organization of Yugoslavia into republics helped quell the problem of nationalist rivalries, as each republic was granted equal status and rights; provinces, however, were lesser in political status and hence were denied the scheme of rights available to the republics. By 1974, Tito granted Kosovo full autonomy, which de facto, though not de jure, placed it on the level of republic status. Unsatisfied, Kosovo demanded full de jure republic status. Tensions with Serbia escalated and became more visceral following Tito's death in 1980. Taking advantage of Serbian complaints of harassment by Albanians in Kosovo, Slobodan Milošević, who assumed power in 1989, stripped Kosovo of its autonomy.

The disintegration of Yugoslavia in the 1990s proved an impetus for Kosovar Albanians to seek separation from Serbia. Kosovo's leader, Ibrahim Rugova, "opted for peaceful resistance to Serbian rule under Milošević," but by 1997, the Kosovo Liberation Army indicted Rugova's pacifism as ineffectual and unleashed a violent guerilla campaign to wrestle Kosovo from Serbia's grip (Judah 1999). In 1998, "open conflict between Serbian military and police forces and Kosovar Albanian forces resulted in the deaths of over 1,500 Kosovar Albanians and forced 400,000 people from their homes" (NATO 1999). Following failed diplomatic initiatives to resolve the conflict, the North Atlantic Council of the North Atlantic Treaty Organization (NATO) issued "Activation Orders for air strikes." Last-minute negotiations convinced Milošević to comply with NATO's demands to end violence and facilitate the return of refugees, and the air strike orders were cancelled.

In early 1999, however, violence flared "following a number of acts of provocation on both sides," and on 23 March 1999, NATO commenced a seventy-seven-day aerial bombardment of Serbia and Serbian targets inside Kosovo, after several failed rounds of talks and Milošević's refusal to capitulate. The humanitarian effects of Serbian and Kosovar acts of aggression and the NATO campaign were astonishing. On 12 July 1999, UN secretary-general Kofi Annan reported that of a 1998 population of 1.7 million, eight hundred thousand people sought refuge in neighboring countries, and five hundred thousand persons "may have been internally displaced" (UN secretary-general's report quoted in Cançado Trindade 2010, ¶119, pp. 571–72).[10] The ending of the air strikes precipitated a major international commitment to Kosovo as outlined in UN Security Council Resolution 1244 of 10 June 1999, which authorized Annan to establish an "international civil presence in Kosovo in order to provide 'an interim administration . . . while establishing and overseeing the development of provisional democratic self-governing institutions'" (Resolution 1244 quoted in ICJ 2010, ¶58, p. 426).

By 2006, international negotiations led by UN special envoy Martti

Ahtisaari began to determine the final status of Kosovo. Though Ahtisaari delivered a draft settlement in February 2007 to the relevant parties, neither Serbia nor Russia, which backed Belgrade and holds a veto power in the Security Council, accepted the plan's envisioned "international supervision" of Kosovo. Frustrated with delays, Pristina unilaterally declared independence on 17 February 2008. Cognizant of the unsettled nature of international law on this question, the UN General Assembly voted on 8 October 2008 to request an advisory opinion from the ICJ on whether the declaration "by the Provisional Institutions of Self-Government of Kosovo [was] in accordance international law." On 22 July 2010, the court answered in the affirmative, by a vote of 10 to 4.[11]

The majority opinion rested on two premises. The first concerned the absence of a general prohibition on unilateral declarations of independence in international law (ICJ 2010, ¶¶78–84, pp. 436–39) and, more specifically, the lack of an explicit prohibition in UNSC Resolution 1244 (1999), the *lex specialis*, or controlling law, in Kosovo at the time. The majority determined that Resolution 1244 established "an interim regime . . . [not] a permanent institutional framework" (ICJ 2010, ¶¶85–100 at ¶100, p. 443; see also ¶114, p. 449) and only enjoined a settlement procured through violence. Second, the majority found that Resolution 1244 only bound the Provisional Institutions of Self-Government of Kosovo, the Republic of Serbia, and UN member states and UN organs. Textual analysis confirmed for the majority that, contrary to the assertion contained in the UNGA request, the authors of the declaration acted as representatives of the people of Kosovo and not as representatives of the Provisional Assembly of Kosovo (ICJ 2010, ¶105, pp. 445–46). As such, being omitted from the text, they were not expressly bound by the terms of the resolution (ICJ 2010, ¶¶116–18, pp. 450–52).

Four of the ten judges in the majority, thinking that the issue demanded more than the narrow and somewhat cursory examination given to it by their peers, issued separate opinions or declarations.[12] Judge Bruno Simma criticized the ICJ for reproducing the "anachronistic, extremely consensualist" view of international law embodied by the *Lotus* principle, which equates "the absence of a prohibition with the existence of a permissive rule" (Simma 2010, ¶3, p. 479). In his view, the court could have considered

whether international law can be deliberately neutral or silent on a certain issue, and whether it allows for the concept of toleration, something which breaks from the binary understanding of permission/prohibition and which allows for a range of non-prohibited options . . . In this sense, I am concerned that the narrowness of the

Court's approach might constitute a weakness, going forward, in its ability to deal with the great shades of nuance that permeate international law. (¶9, pp. 480–81)

Judge Bernardo Sepúlveda-Amor (2010, 491) likewise preferred to look at "the larger picture." Consideration of "the scope of self-determination, the question of 'remedial secession,' the extent of the Security Council's powers with regard to the principle of territorial integrity, the continuation or derogation of an international civil and military administration . . . , and . . . the effect of the recognition or non-recognition of a State" would have, on his view, ensured that the court "remain faithful to the requirements of its judicial character in the exercise of its advisory jurisdiction . . . [by] ascertain[ing] . . . the legal questions really in issue in questions formulated in a request" (at ¶34–35, pp. 498–99).

Judges Abdulqawi Ahmed Yusef and Antonio Cançado Trindade maintained that self-determination in its "post-colonial" formulation admits limitations on internal autonomy stemming from "prolonged adversity of systematic oppression" (Cançado Trindade 2010, ¶¶173–76, pp. 592–93; Yusef 2010, ¶¶7–9, pp. 620–21). Yusef adjudged that though "international law disfavors the fragmentation of existing States and seeks to protect their boundaries," it nevertheless "pays close attention to acts involving atrocities, persecution, discrimination and crimes against humanity inside the State" (Yusef 2010, ¶7, pp. 620–21). Drawing on international treaties and case law, he asserted that when certain criteria have been met—for example, "egregious violations of human rights or humanitarian law" (¶11, p. 622), "discrimination against a people, its persecution due to its racial or ethnic characteristics, and the denial of autonomous political structures and access to government" (¶16, p. 624)—either claims of external self-determination or unilateral declarations of independence may be permissible. Further, Yusef opined that the court should have analyzed the question delivered to it in light of

> the violent break-up of Yugoslavia, the removal of the autonomy of Kosovo by the Serbian authorities, the history of ethnic cleansing and crimes against humanity . . . , and the extended period of [UN] administration of Kosovo which *de facto* separated it from Serbia to protect its population and provide it with institutions of self-government. (¶13, p. 623; see also Sterio 2013)

These were the specific situations that made Kosovo unique, on Yusef's view, thereby mitigating the potential that any ruling explicitly in favor of the declaration could be used as a precedent to encourage secessionist movements everywhere, that is, as a spark to ignite the dynamite Robert Lansing thought self-determination to be.

International law—and domestic law—had already carved out a space for remedial forms of secession when exceptional circumstances "may transform an entitlement to internal self-determination into a right to claim separate statehood from the parent State." For instance, in the *Katangese Peoples' Congress v. Zaire*, a case before the African Commission of Human and Peoples' Rights, the commission maintained that, "in the absence of concrete evidence of violations of human rights," the territorial integrity of Zaire needed to be respected, though Katanga was permitted to exercise internal self-determination coincident with its rights as stipulated in the African Charter of Human and Peoples' Rights (quoted in Yusef 2010, ¶14, p. 623). Likewise, with respect to Quebec, the Canadian Supreme Court admitted that there "may be a right to external self-determination where a people is denied any meaningful exercise of its right to self-determination internally" (¶15, pp. 623–24). In other words, at minimum, self-determination demands "the right to be taken seriously," or procedural rights pertaining to participation in political processes (Klabbers 2006).

Cançado Trindade extended Judge Yusef's logic in a comprehensive, ninety-two-page exegesis that focused predominantly on the humanitarian tragedy in Kosovo as the principal factual background against which the independence claim must be judged. For him, the conceptual and legal background is found in

> the emergence and evolution of the International Law of Human Rights[, which] came to concentrate further attention in the treatment dispensed by the State to all human beings under its jurisdiction, in the conditions of living of the population, in sum, in the function of the State as promoter of the common good. (Cançado Trindade 2010, ¶185, p. 597)

If the events in Kosovo established a particular claim, Cançado Trindade situated it within a broader narrative in international relations and international law that has been sensitive to "the recurring and growing attention dispensed to the needs and aspirations of the 'people' or the 'population' (in the mandates system under the League of Nations, in the trusteeship system under the United Nations, and in contemporary U.N. experiments of international territorial administration)" (¶2, p. 525; cf. Cronin 2003). Kosovo's declaration, he concluded, was legal not primarily because of the absence of a general prohibition on such declarations or because its authors were not expressly prohibited by Resolution 1244 from issuing such a declaration. Rather, it was legal because it effectuated the UN primary objective of settling the conflict, cohered with the humanitarian thrust of UN activity with respect to Kosovo, and reflected international legal strictures that, on his interpretation, have clearly tended toward the protection and advancement of people from systematic oppression (¶184, pp. 596–97).

The ICJ's decision was comprised of a majority opinion, four separate concurring and three dissenting opinions, and two declarations (one concurring, one dissenting). It raises distinct issues surrounding, for example, clarification of the rules governing state recognition, the extent of the Security Council's powers, the contours of a postcolonial conception of self-determination, and politico-legal explication of the concept of "peoples." Given thematic linkages between the issues, I address them in pairs in the discussion that follows.

### Recognition and a Postcolonial Concept of Self-Determination

While recognition of states is undoubtedly a matter to be settled through political and diplomatic means, international law provides two competing frameworks within which to couch such decisions. The declaratory theory maintains that an entity becomes sovereign when it has fulfilled the requisite conditions identified in the 1933 Montevideo Convention on the Rights and Duties of States (permanent population, territory, defined borders, and a government capable of engaging in relations with other like units). Alternatively, the constitutive theory maintains that an entity becomes sovereign when others recognize it as such (see Carter et al. 2007, 448). Neither framework is employed in any pure sense. Contrary to the declaratory theory, entities such as Taiwan may possess the objective criteria outlined in the Montevideo Convention but are not recognized as sovereign (even if they possess special status in international society). Consistent with the constitutive theory, though contrary to its conclusion, entities such as Kosovo may declare independence and may be recognized by some (even dominant) states but are not accepted by a majority of states and thus not considered sovereign. So we must look to the actual practices of states to determine what, if anything, figures prominently and frequently in international community acts of recognition.

Hurst Hannum observes that conditions attached to recognition of new states—such as those articulated by the European Union and the United

States with regard to the newly independent states of the former Yugoslavia and the Soviet Union and pertaining to human rights, international security, and democracy—are always political, never legal, criteria and thus subject to change (2002, 237; see also Gong 1984). But accounting for a longer time horizon might reveal, as Cançado Trindade attempted to do, that the criteria we construe as political and contingent could very well morph into customary international law, especially given consistency in practice. Customary international law emerges not merely from behavioral repetition but also from the subjective belief (*opinio juris*) that the practice is binding or obligatory. Cançado Trindade makes the point that given the prevalence of human rights concerns in practices of recognition and in international community activity, we might very well contend that strict adherence to the most fundamental human rights, especially vis-à-vis the core crimes as identified in international criminal law, appears increasingly as settled criteria for determining the legality of claims of secession, self-determination, or independence. Hannum (2002, 235) appreciates and anticipates this claim, though he frames it in different language.

> [T]he right of secession is seen as a variant of the right of self-defense— you defend yourself by seceding from an oppressive system . . . There can be compelling reasons for secession such as if the physical survival or the cultural autonomy of a nation is threatened, or if a population would feel economically excluded and permanently deprived.

Even the 1948 Universal Declaration of Human Rights, albeit in the preamble, invokes "rebellion against tyranny and oppression" as a "last resort." Hannum strongly infers that the hurdle for outright secession and independence must be high; mere economic exclusion and human rights infringements cannot be permitted as grounds for rebellion, secession, and independence claims. On this point, Cançado Trindade agrees. His lengthy opinion hones in on the fact that the hurdle, set exceedingly high, had been surpassed in the case of Kosovo, subject, as it were, to oppression and ethnic cleansing. Indeed, one might conclude that customary international law prohibitions against genocide, ethnic cleansing, and gross violations of human rights intimate that "international law should recognize a right to secession only in the rare circumstance when the physical existence of a territorially concentrated group is threatened by gross violations of fundamental human rights" (Hannum 2002, 236).

To the traditional frameworks for recognition under international law, Yusef and Cançado Trindade append the additional criterion of considering the extent to which basic human rights have been egregiously, systematically, and persistently violated, which gives much greater weight to this kind of reasoning.[13] In this vein, Cançado Trindade characterized his opinion as emanating from "an essentially humanist outlook of the treatment of peoples under the law of nations, from a historical as well as a deontological perspective" (Cançado Trindade 2010, ¶2, p. 525). He situates the human person at the center not simply of legal analysis but also of international relations. Critically, for him and Judge Yusef, there are certain conditions in which being human trumps the principle of *uti possidetis*, meaning "as you possess," which has been the determinative principle of international law governing independence/secessionist claims. In 1986, the ICJ affirmed the validity of the principle in the frontier dispute case *Burkina Faso/Mali*.

> [*Uti possidetis*] . . . is logically connected with the phenomenon of obtaining independence, wherever it occurs. Its obvious purpose is to prevent the independence and stability of new states being endangered by fratricidal struggles provoked by the changing of frontiers following the withdrawal of the administering power. (ICJ 1986, ¶20, p. 565)

In *Burkina Faso/Mali*, *uti possidetis* retained its conventional international law usage. But a careful reading suggests that fratricidal conflicts may also demand reverse application: permitting the fracturing of existing states and demanding the rigorous protection of new territorial and political divisions in order to stop fratricidal struggles from hurtling inexorably out of control (such as happened in Rwanda and as is happening at the time of this writing, in mid-2014, in the Central African Republic and South Sudan). While the justification may be humanitarian and oriented toward world society, the result is a robust defense of statehood and international society.

Yusef and Cançado Trindade approach that reverse reading of *uti possidetis*. While it is true that their separate, concurring opinions were not entirely accepted by the five judges in the majority, that fact alone does not obscure their potential contributions to the development of international law—chief among which concerns the clarification of conditions that satisfy a postcolonial conception of self-determination. Their opinions provide an optic through which to revise a standing principle that dictates against the fragmentation of existing states and through which we may read it as, in the end, achieving the same objective as conventional usage: preservation of states. But any reverse reading of *uti possidetis* must apply only in the specific instance of persistent, systematic, and egregious human rights abuses.

The Yusef and Cançado Trindade opinions, moreover, underscore the evolutionary character of a doctrine of self-determination or self-government. Throughout the nineteenth-century, self-government (at least on the European continent) was read in terms of, if not dominated by, the monarchical principle demanding that only peoples governed by a recognized European royal would be welcomed into the sovereign family of nations. Woodrow Wilson decoupled self-determination from a particular form of government in the early twentieth century and championed it in populist, national terms. But self-determination's exclusion from the Covenant of the League of Nations and its 1921 rejection by a League-established international commission on the Åaland Islands further robbed the concept of its practical vigor. As mentioned earlier, the term appears in the UN Charter and thus occupies a space in the UN-based postwar system, but it remains plagued by definitional ambiguities. Its firm tethering during decolonization to a doctrine of *uti possidetis* may now be entering its postcolonial incarnation, increasingly and almost inextricably bound to exceptional (and intentional) humanitarian crises (on the evolution of the concept, see Halperin and Scheffer 1992). By situating the suffering of the people of Kosovo at the center of analysis, either implicitly (in the majority opinion) or explicitly (particularly in the Yusef and Cançado Trindade opinions), the case elevates the human person in international legal and political discourse. Moreover, precisely by affirming their claims to recognition that stemmed from their experience of suffering, it makes human those who were dehumanized.

Suffering, though, is a moral minefield. Does the egregious suffering of some impose duties on others to act? Does not halting or mitigating the suffering of others constitute additional harm? These questions are fairly obvious and often recited; the responses to them vary depending on the ethical and theoretical commitments of the observer. At minimum, Linklater suggests that societies may promulgate cosmopolitan harm conventions that require neither abandonment of national attachments nor "that loyalty to the whole of humankind should come before duties to particular communities" (2001, 264). All such conventions require are "friendship towards the rest of the human race, support for the Kantian notion of respect for persons or some equivalent notion of the equality of all human beings, and the conviction that there ought to be harm conventions which are . . . not . . . 'restricted to any one country or its inhabitants.'"

On Linklater's view, making human would simply require recognition of the other and minimal moral reflection predicated on two essential points. First, processes of making human demand willingness to believe that "the differences between insiders and outsiders are not always relevant reasons for treating outsiders less well than insiders." In other words, to use Arendtian language I have already used at the beginning of chapter 2 of this book, Linklater's position requires that we be willing to share the world with others as cobuilders of a common world. Second, making human demands a willingness to believe that human beings do not deserve to be oppressed and violated because of the type of human being they are (keeping in mind, of course, that understandings of what constitutes oppression and violation change across time and space). But the cosmopolitanism of Yusef and Cançado Trindade—supported, as it were, in rather important, if limited, case law—might be construed as pushing the boundaries of that moral minimum a little further: egregious, systematic suffering might constitute grounds for permitting unilateral declarations of independence, precisely because the bounds of being human in particular societies may be no more than the claims of *zoē*, or basic biological life. In certain instances, it may take international organizations to mediate between the conflicting demands of a statist international society and the more cosmopolitan pretensions of world society.

## On the Powers of the UN Security Council and the Meaning of "Peoples"

Nathaniel Berman identifies an "international law of nationalism," which he defines as "a historically contingent array of doctrinal and policy options for development by a contingent embodiment of international authority of nationalist conflicts whose protagonists are designated by a contingent set of legal categories" (2002, 107). But "rather than a smooth process of customary law 'ripening,' [the] history [of an international law of nationalism] has been one of construction, denunciation, rupture, and resumption." If what Berman claims is true—that there is such a law of nationalism—the UNGA's request and the ICJ's response could be read as signifying a rationalization and clarification of that law. Summarily, the case aims to establish clear parameters for nationalist interventions in the realm of interstate law.

While Berman concentrates on discontinuities of an international law of nationalism subject to the political preferences and interests of states, the Kosovo case underscores another source of discontinuity that may prove salient in the future. The advisory opinion directs our attention to the fact that the state is contingent on the definition of "a people"—itself an unsettled matter in international law and international politics. This may seem counterintuitive, but it reflects what Berman (108) calls the international legal projection onto protagonists of "a set of historically contingent categories—

states, nations, peoples, minorities, religions, races, indigenous peoples, individuals, and so on—a set whose elements and valorizations have changed over time." While there may be international documents regarding colonized, occupied, or indigenous peoples, there is no single definition of who or what constitutes a people (see also Hannum 2002, 231–33). Indeed, the construction of a people varies. In situations of occupation by another people, all those under occupied rule become a people by virtue of international legal designation. In situations of underrepresentation or nonrepresentation in government, all those underrepresented or nonrepresented become a people. Their status as a people is essentially a rhetorical construction by others, tied to a particular fact or set of facts that constitute a kind of midwife for their political recognition. Critically, the lack of a definition—or, more appropriately stated, the contingency of multiple definitions—permits the international community to deny peoples (usually self-defined) their presumed rights in international law, as Knop (2002) has illustrated.

But in the Kosovo case, we see that an unnamed, undefined, unofficial, amorphous "people" can subvert an entire international legal order—and Sepúlveda-Amor's contention that the ICJ needed to consider "the extent of the Security Council's powers with regard to the principle of territorial integrity" can be read in this vein (2010, ¶35, p. 499). That clause, coupled with the majority opinion, strongly suggests that the powers of the Security Council are limited when confronted by the will of the people. It seems that the authors of Kosovo's declaration of independence understood this, for they identified themselves not as agents of the Provisional Institutions of Self-Government, which were bound by UNSC Resolution 1244, but as "representatives of the people of Kosovo," not expressly bound by the terms of the resolution. Felicitously stated, their self-signification as *somebody* in a world in which they were, legally, *nobody*, subverted the post–World War II international legal order.

This legal order is predicated on a conditional hierarchy of obligations. Article 103 of the UN Charter declares that obligations under the Charter prevail over all other international obligations. Yet this hierarchy is conditional precisely because such obligations supersede all others, as Article 103 notes, "in the event of a conflict between the obligations of the Members of the United Nations under the present Charter and their obligations under any other international agreement." At the tip of the apex of this international legal order resides the UN Security Council. By virtue of Articles 25 and 49 of the Charter, the Council is granted binding powers over all UN member states to ensure that the principles and purposes of the Charter are upheld and to enable it to fulfill its primary responsibility vis-à-vis the maintenance of international peace and security.[14] In the event of a conflict between obligations arising from Security Council resolutions and other obligations in international law, the ICJ has ruled (in the *Lockerbie* case) that Council-imposed obligations, even if temporary, always prevail (ICJ 1992).

The Kosovo advisory opinion, though, inadvertently delineates how this order may be circumvented; the eye of the proverbial needle may indeed be large enough for a camel the size of Kosovo to fit through. On the one hand, the majority found that both international law and UNSC Resolution 1244 do not expressly prohibit a unilateral declaration of independence. On the other, the majority determined that the resolution bound to its terms only particular actors: the Provisional Institutions of Self-Government of Kosovo, UN member States, and the UN and its organs. In other words, the language of the resolution was deemed to be particularly determinative, not exhaustively determinative.

The majority arrived at this conclusion after review of two distinct sets of Council resolutions (and hence of prior Council practices). This first set involved resolutions focused on comparable situations (e.g., UNSC Resolution 1251 [1999], on Cyprus, and Resolution 787 [1992], on the Republic of Srpska), which expressly and unequivocally established conditions with regard to the final statuses of political communities and thereby precluded unilateral action by any actor to determine a final settlement (ICJ 2010, ¶¶ 112 and 114, pp. 448, 449). Resolution 1244, by contrast, omitted similar provisions.

The second set of resolutions involved those related to Kosovo. Resolutions prior to Resolution 1244 made clear "demands on actors other than United Nations Member States and intergovernmental organizations," including "the Kosovo Albanian leadership" and "all other elements of the Kosovo Albanian community" (¶116, p. 450). Resolution 1244 lacked such language (¶117, pp. 450–51). The absence might be found in the contexts in which the resolutions were passed. Whereas the earlier resolutions concerned ongoing violence in which diverse actors from the Kosovar and Serbian communities participated, Resolution 1244 attended to the political settlement and thus was selectively directed toward pertinent politico-legal actors—and therein lay the key to the court's judgment. "When interpreting Security Council resolutions," the majority opinion held, "the Court must establish, on a case by case basis, considering all relevant circumstances, for whom the Security Council intended to create binding legal obligations." Yet the selectivity of approach taken by the Council eventually unraveled what was intended to be a tightly controlled international process of determining Kosovo's final status.

While the ICJ reaffirmed the hierarchy of international law and the legal and political preeminence of the UNSC, it left open the possibility that, in the absence of any exhaustive accounting in Security Council resolutions, excluded actors could conceivably and legally make declarations free of Council restraints—perhaps in ways that circumvent or even subvert the Council's will or its carefully crafted compromise of discordant permanent Council member positions. Put differently, the majority sought in Kosovo's declaration of independence linguistic clues as to the identity of the authors. Concluding that the authors were *nobody* in any official politico-legal sense, the judges ascertained that relevant law and restrictions vis-à-vis actions affecting the final status of Kosovo did not apply to them. Hence the legality of the declaration rested precisely on its *alegality*, or its emergence from outside the legal order—which strikes one as affirming Agamben's view (1998) of the extralegal character of sovereignty.[15] To offer this reading is not to suggest that any self-proclaimed group of individuals may collectively announce secession from an existing state or subvert the international legal order. Rather, it is to emphasize the precarious, contingent definition of "a people"; the rarity of (successful) secessionist declarations; the evolving set of rules that constitute sovereignty; and the importance of considering the self-constitutive, self-assertive acts of ordinary peoples vis-à-vis the making of sovereignty.

## Conclusion

While the Kosovo advisory opinion lacks in significant respects and was even criticized by Judge Simma for reproducing an anachronistic legal principle that equates the absence of a prohibition with legality, it nevertheless offers three key insights into an unsettled, evolving right to self-determination in a postcolonial era, in ways that pertain to the argument of this book. First, oppression matters, as Judges Cançado Trindade and Yusef maintain. But nothing in their opinions dictates that this fact alone is sufficient to justify a claim to remedial secession, even if it is of significant probative value. Milena Sterio (2013, 60–61) makes a convincing supporting argument.

> Typically, a people attracts global attention only when it can show how horrifically it is being treated and how abusive its central government is. Instances of mild human rights violations typically do not attract the same level of international political and media scrutiny . . . For example, the world was appalled at the harsh treatment inflicted on the Kosovar Albanians . . . Similarly, the East Timorese were able to depict decades of unfavorable treatment and human rights

abuses . . . , and the South Sudanese were equally able to highlight the suffering inflicted against them . . . Other separatist movements have faced more minor forms of repression, insufficient to persuade the world community that some form of action may be needed to help the separatist movement. Such groups include the Basque in Spain, the Quebecois in Canada, the Kurds in Turkey, the Turkish Cypriots in Cyprus, the Zanzibaris in Tanzania, the Saharawis in Morocco, and the Biafrans in Nigeria.

Second, territorial integrity overrides claims to external self-determination, unless the evidence amassed related to egregious, systematic oppression is of sufficient gravity to convince key actors in the international community that a secessionist self-determinative claim warrants support. Yet, third, parent-state consent is a necessary condition. After the advisory opinion was issued, the Serbian minister of foreign affairs remarked that "never in the history of the United Nations has a territory achieved statehood by seceding from a parent state that did not give its consent at the end of the process" (Hannum 2011, 159). Bangladesh, for instance, may have "won its physical battle for independence from Pakistan in 1971," but it "was not recognized by most states or admitted as a member of the United Nations until 1974—after Pakistan itself had accepted the partition." In the case of Kosovo, the advisory opinion did not settle the matter, thereby making imperative a deal between Belgrade and Pristina. In April 2013, the two finally concluded a historic agreement to normalize relations (Gvosdev 2013). While it falls short of recognizing Kosovo's independence, Belgrade did acknowledge "that the government in Pristina exercises administrative authority over the territory"; further, it dropped its objection to Kosovo applying for membership in international organizations.[16] In return, Pristina accepted a substantial degree of Serbian self-rule in the four northern Serb-dominated municipalities in Kosovo "so long as they acknowledge that they are nominally part of Kosovo."

The April 2013 agreement illustrates the degree to which key international claims are attached to or stem from dignity as status. Kosovar Albanians, long affronted by their diminished status within the Yugoslav Republic and harsh treatment by Serbian authorities, insisted on recognition as a people with full political standing. Serbian minorities in a self-declared independent Kosovo demanded protection from assault, as well as freedom from Kosovar institutions of which they are suspicious (European Forum 2014). Settlement of the issue demanded that both parties set aside crucial, likely paralyzing disagreements pertaining to Serbian recognition of Kosovo's independence and Belgrade's insistence that the Serb communities in northern Kosovo be granted separate status. For Belgrade, Kosovo's autonomy and status as ward of the international community was an irreversible fait accompli. For Pristina, failure to compromise on minority Serbs might very well have eroded whatever international support it had. For both, the carrot of European Union membership proved the magic wand to compel them to sidestep contentious matters.

The Kosovo case and the larger grappling with the issue of self-determination strongly suggest that sovereignty is not simply a razor-sharp divide between state-based international society and world society but a fulcrum on which their differences may be reconciled. Nonstate actors can and do "fundamentally alter the basic principles and dynamics of the society of sovereign states" (Reus Smit 2005, 91). In that regard, the chief importance of the Kosovo advisory opinion lies with its focus on oppression, which, in at least two of the opinions on the case, is used as leverage to counter the effects of dehumanization. The emphasis in this instance—egregious, systematic human rights abuses—may be read as a complement to the case of the Palestinian wall: if respecting the right to self-determination is an *erga omnes* obligation largely interpreted in the negative terms of inaction, this opinion suggests that the obligation needs to be interpreted positively—that is, as requiring action—in extreme conditions.

To return to earlier language, the question of how *bios* and *zoē* relate in the modern polity must necessarily occupy political thought. Though dehumanization may command greater attention because it exposes us to the brazen mechanics of power as enacted on and against the human body and (re)produces discourses of inclusion/exclusion and subjects and subjectivities bound up with various structures of domination, humanization likewise demands attention since the same structures of domination, the same technologies of power, and the same discourses are at work. The ICJ's grappling with the Kosovo case and the larger issue of self-determination illustrates. In relation to this case, the people of Kosovo did not engage in entirely self-responsible and morally reflective acts or adhere strictly to human rights norms, though they used such norms in their defense (considering that segments of the Kosovo population also inflicted harm and egregious suffering on the Serbian people). But through self-assertive acts of resistance, a self-creative act of constituting a political self (a *nobody* that, by virtue of its placement outside and freed from the constraints of the particular legal order, eventually became grounds for the legality of its distinct sovereign status and thus its status as *somebody*), and moral and legal reflection on the part of a set of international judges, the Kosovo people metamorphosed from an object on and against whom power was deployed (*zoē*) to a subject (*bios*) worthy of claiming and living a full and distinctly political life in a broader community of sovereign states.

CHAPTER 7

# Conclusion

## *World Society of Our Making*

Human beings, with whatever equipment nature and/or society
provides, construct society, and society is indispensable to the
actualization of whatever human beings may "naturally" be; society
constructs human beings out of the raw materials of nature, whether
inner nature or, less problematically, the outer nature of their material
circumstances.

—Nicholas Onuf[1]

Today, as we take to heart the lessons of the current economic crisis,
which sees the State's public authorities directly involved in correcting
errors and malfunctions, it seems more realistic to re-evaluate their
role and their powers, which need to be prudently reviewed and
remodeled so as to enable them, perhaps through new forms of
engagement, to address the challenges of today's world. Once the role
of public authorities has been more clearly defined, one could foresee
an increase in the new forms of political participation, nationally
and internationally, that have come about through the activity of
organizations operating in civil society; in this way it is to be hoped
that the citizens' interest and participation in the res publica will
become more deeply rooted.

—Pope Benedict XVI[2]

In June 2012, the US Senate Judiciary Subcommittee on the Constitution, Civil Rights, and Human Rights convened its first hearing on solitary
confinement—a practice that apparently is more widespread in the United
States than some might imagine; 81,622 prisoners were placed in "restricted
housing" in 2005, according to a Bureau of Justice report (Guenther 2012).
A range of social workers, psychologists, and former prisoners testified, but
I surmise that the testimony tendered by a Vanderbilt University associ-

ate professor proved unusual for a congressional hearing. Lisa Guenther approached the issue through the optic of phenomenology, which is

> a philosophical method for uncovering the structure of lived experience . . . Rather than attempting to prove a set of objective facts, phenomenology tracks the way that a *meaningful* experience of the world emerges for someone in the total situation of their Being-in-the-world. It's not that facts are unimportant, but rather that they are not meaningful in themselves; they become meaningful when they are experienced *by* someone in relation to a wider context or horizon.

The details of her argument are worth recounting, even if the case is removed from the kind of international instances examined thus far. "What happens," she asks, "when that horizon shrinks to the space of a 6-by-9 cell?" Confinement "violates the very structure of our being" in society because it robs the inmate of "the critical challenges that others pose to our own interpretation of the world." The presence of others offers "a chance and an obligation" to explain ourselves to others; isolation "asks too little of prisoners."

In light of the previous chapters' findings, we may reconstruct her argument: the presence of the unprotected, disempowered, brutalized, oppressed, marginalized, and excluded lends an opportunity to and imposes an obligation on various institutions of international society, let alone other human beings, to rebut our dehumanizing proclivities and to explain ourselves to the violated *and to each other*. Isolation from implacable assaults on the human condition asks too little of ourselves and our politics. Engagement with them yields a broader question, no less imperative because of its breadth: what kind of world society are we willing to make? This question does not presuppose solidarity among human beings; the divisions we perceive and fabricate, magnify and exploit, insure against simple presumption. Rather, the matter hinges on understanding the parameters that define the human *being*, which, in turn, shape and constrain the multiple ways of being *human*. In these final pages of this study, I examine making human as a central incident in the construction of a wider world order and the global governance of human dignity.

## Making Human in a Post-Holocaust Humanitarian World Order

Throughout this book, I have occasionally referred to a post-Holocaust humanitarian world order to capture a way of thinking about and enacting a "different kind" of international relations or world politics, one that situates at the center of analysis not the state or the atomistic, autonomous individual but the relational, social self. By distinguishing between that order and a postwar interstate order, I do not intend to suggest their incommensurability; indeed, the cases have demonstrated their overlap. The point is to underscore different logics and mentalities that license distinct kinds of activities. The narrative I offer posits the former as a subterranean undercurrent in and less a geographic moment of international relations history, even if the moniker "post-Holocaust" signifies a temporal designation. I reference one of, if not the, most egregious crimes of the twentieth century because, while humanitarian logics clearly predate the Holocaust, Nazi crimes compelled the architects of a postwar interstate order to include, however curbed by the imperatives of interstate politics, defense of the human being as a central pillar of the new world order. Lending this humanitarian precept of order political gravitas are the concern with people and peoples as expressed in the UN Charter, the Universal Declaration of Human Rights, and the Genocide Convention; the prosecution of war criminals and genocidaires by the Nuremberg and Tokyo tribunals; and the drafting of a code of international crimes in the immediate aftermath of World War II. These developments signaled, even if sometimes superficially and inconsistently, commitment to "never again" permit such an egregious assault on the human condition to occur.

Over time and especially in the post–Cold War era, principles of this post-Holocaust humanitarian world order found expression in a range of policy and programmatic initiatives, including, among others, human development, human dignity, human rights, human security, individual criminal responsibility in international law, the expansion of international humanitarian law, the responsibility to protect doctrine, the prohibition on the use of child soldiers, the convention on antipersonnel landmines, the Kimberley Process Certification Scheme, decolonization and self-determination, microfinance, programs of community development, the UN Millennium Development Goals, public health initiatives, and vaccination programs such as the Advance Market Commitment. As indicative of the progress made in the area of international humanitarian law, Theodor Meron, noted jurist and president of the International Criminal Tribunal for the Former Yugoslavia, reflected on the humanization of that subfield of international law—an idea on which Ruti Teitel (2011) would later expand. The law of war, Meron argued,

has been changing and acquiring a more humane face: the inroads made on the dominant role of reciprocity; the fostering of accountability; and innovations in the formation, formulation, and interpretation of rules. These trends are manifested in both the substance and the language of the law. Indeed, the increasing substitution of "international humanitarian law" for terms such as "law of war" and "law of armed conflict" reflects the influence of the human rights movement. Although the term "international humanitarian law" initially referred to the four 1949 Geneva Conventions, it is now increasingly used to signify the entire law of armed conflict. (2000a, 239)

Teitel affixes the label "humanity's law" to such developments. This human-centric shift in international relations appears all the more remarkable given that in 1964, Ian Brownlie, one of the leading scholars of international law in the mid-twentieth century, characterized the status of the individual in international law as limited, ill-defined, and tenuous at best. But evidence for a world order that prioritizes human being and human welfare does not end there. In some regional integration projects (e.g., the European Union) individuals have been granted actionable rights to bring claims against states for breaches of obligations in areas such as human rights and the environment (see Alvarez 2006, part III). Even the high political body charged with the solemn task of maintaining international peace and security—the UN Security Council—has not remained immune from considerations of human welfare, as chapter 3 of this study explored. Since the end of the Cold War, the Council has used its interpretive and declaratory powers (Alvarez 2006, 189–98) to broaden the scope of what it considers to constitute a threat to or breach of international peace and security (by adopting resolutions on issues that are not country-specific, such as HIV/AIDS,[3] international crimes,[4] terrorism,[5] and the trade in illicit (conflict) diamonds)[6] and to recognize issues that are not country- or conflict-specific but are germane to international peace and security (e.g., the protection of civilians in armed conflict; the plight of children in armed conflict and their future rehabilitation; diverse linkages between women, peace, and security; and human security).

Read in the aggregate, such developments appear to abrade—in some cases, quite significantly—the edifice of a state-centric conception of international relations, by appealing to a more primordial, more fundamental unit of analysis: the individual. While it may be hyperbole to claim that these developments signify the decline of the state, it is reasonable to maintain that, owing to evolving conceptions of state responsibility and legitimacy, these developments shape a post-Holocaust humanitarian world order by effectuating certain principles or elements. Here, I treat four of these principles as derived from the aforementioned initiatives and as a way of summarizing this book.

First, a post-Holocaust humanitarian world order is buttressed by a critical ethics of care. Phenomenology demands attentiveness to the way a meaningful experience of the world emerges for particular selves. To a degree, it thus shares with a critical ethics of care an attunement to human experiences and the relations that shape such. A critical ethics of care enlarges that demand with a reformist, ameliorative orientation. Meaning, in short, may stem from positive, empowering experiences but also from exploitative socioeconomic and political arrangements that inhibit self-development. Therefore, as Robinson explains, a critical ethics of care obligates us to "identify and change social institutions that make individuals needy and dependent in the first place" (1999, 110). According to Robinson, this emphatically does not entail

> that the powerful must learn to "care about" the suffering and the destitute in what could possibly—although not necessarily—become a paternalistic act which preserves existing power relations. It means that those who are powerful have a responsibility to approach moral problems by looking carefully at where, why, and how the structures of existing social and personal relations have led to exclusion and marginalization, as well as how attachments may have degenerated or broken down so as to cause suffering. (46)

In this study, the reformist mentality of a critical ethics of care appears as the introduction of new concepts or the generation of new procedures in partnership with diverse actors to respond more effectively to the precariousness of the human condition. For instance, we have the Security Council's alteration of its calculus of international peace and security to frame the protection and empowerment of people as a key objective of sustainable peace, the development of the human security agenda as a response to persistent deprivations and insecurities, formulation of core crimes in international law and the systematization of prosecution of individuals for their commission, and the grappling with the parameters and dimensions of self-determination. In Arendtian terms, each appears as a natalist moment in the "normal" course of events: insertions into the world by word and deed that, through spontaneity, innovation, and the cultivation of intersubjective agreement, (re)constitute that world.

The examples I explored are, to state the obvious, a few in a world of many; Robinson (1999, 2011), Held (2006), and Engster (2007), among others, have explored diverse ways that practices of care have pervaded international relations. In 2009, a distinctive expression of care appeared in the form of a papal encyclical, *Caritas in Veritate*, or *Charity in Truth*. Though Vatican officials insisted that it was not a response to the global economic crisis, its release on the eve of the July 2009 G8 summit in L'Aquila, Italy, and its explicit critical and ultimately reformist message belied that claim (Donadio and Goodstein 2009). If Benedict XVI praised the productive power of capitalism, he also criticized its tendency to elevate short-term interests above longer-term concerns related to worker rights, the good of community, and environmental sustainability. While the pope celebrated economic advances that both alleviated the plight of billions of people and permitted some developing states to take "their place among the great powers . . . to play important roles in the future" (Benedict 2009, ¶23), he also censured the "'super-development' of a wasteful and consumerist kind which forms an unacceptable contrast with the ongoing situations of dehumanizing deprivation" (¶22). While he saw viable forms of transformative political participation made possible by multiple channels of connectedness in a globalized world, he also condemned corruption and illegality, the "downsizing of social security systems as the price to be paid for seeking greater competitive advantage in the global market" (¶25), and "cultural models and social norms of behaviour . . . which hinder the process of development" by contributing to contexts that permit the exploitation and oppression of the poor in many underdeveloped countries (¶22). To rectify unbridled capitalism's wrongs, he proposed a range of institutional reforms and structural adjustments, all eventually predicated on *caritas*—translated variously as "love," "care," and "charity."

*Caritas*, the pope exhorted, "can be recognized as an authentic expression of humanity and as an element of fundamental importance in human relations" (¶3). *Caritas* is "the principle not only of micro-relationships (with friends, with family members or within small groups) but also of macro-relationships (social, economic and political ones)" (¶2). Further, *caritas* aims to "promote a person-based and community-oriented culture of world-wide integration . . . [and] to steer the globalization of humanity in relational terms, in terms of communion and the sharing of goods" (¶42). Care, in short, requires an active partnering with others that is predicated on listening to and working in solidarity with them to self-develop, not, as Robinson averred, a potentially paternalistic, welfarist system of handouts that inculcates dependency. To take but one example in the encyclical, Benedict maintained that food insecurity cannot be tackled simply by distributing existing stocks of foodstuffs. Rather, it

> needs to be addressed within a long-term perspective, eliminating the structural causes that give rise to it and promoting the agricultural development of poorer countries. This can be done by investing in rural infrastructures, irrigation systems, transport, organization of markets, and in the development and dissemination of agricultural technology that can make the best use of the human, natural and socio-economic resources that are more readily available at the local level, while guaranteeing their sustainability over the long term as well. All this needs to be accomplished with the involvement of local communities in choices and decisions that affect the use of agricultural land. (¶27)

The encyclical reads like a theologized version of the United Nations Development Programme's *Human Development Report*, which situates people and their communities at the center of economic debate, policy, and advocacy in ways that look beyond macroeconomic growth to consider investments in education, nutrition, health, and employment skills as salient means to long-term, sustainable development and growth. This foundational commitment to the development, security, and well-being of the human person marks a second major component of a post-Holocaust humanitarian world order: prioritization of the human being in ways that give "persons and peoples a legal and ethical status that is not entirely dependent on their membership in a particular political community" (Teitel 2011, 195). As discussed in chapter 1, Hannah Arendt anticipated Teitel's point by celebrating the generation of a crime against humanity in the wake of World War II as a historic shift that altered interstate relations in two ways. First, it conferred legal and political substance on the concept of humanity, which hitherto existed only as a figment of a clerical or philosophical imagination. A crime against humanity affronted the natural condition of human diversity. In Arendt's view, this positive form of solidarity—a taking of responsibility for the human condition—signaled the ability of human communities and human persons to move beyond the negative solidarity born from threats of annihilation and to realize the power of acting in concert to reframe our common world. Second, a crime against humanity disentangled human beings from statist trappings, even if perpetrators often act in the name of the state. But invention of a crime against and in the name of humanity did not simply entail restrictions on individual action; it constrained the state, the logic of which would be replicated in diverse ways in the postwar order.

The cases explored in this book demonstrate variability of prioritization, the effects of which disrupt stabilized meanings and practices of sovereignty as prerogative. In its more moderate forms, prioritization appears in the guise of the human security framework that has been interpreted and formulated by states as a program of national ownership to enhance their coping capacities, as well as the coping capacities of the communities within them, or as a self-determinative right procedurally interpreted as a right to be heard in domestic governance arrangements and decision making. Prioritization likewise appears in moderate forms as the initiatives of an empowering Security Council that partners with a variety of actors to implement and report on the execution of recommendations, promote educational and skills training programs in the service of long-term sustainable peace, rehabilitate children affected by violence through counseling, and encourage the inclusion and participation of women in political processes and economic development. In its more robust forms, prioritization entails protective initiatives authorized by the Security Council (e.g., sanctions, interventions, peacekeeping); the individualization and systematization of accountability for the commission of core crimes in international law notwithstanding ICL institutional reliance on states to apprehend suspects; and possibly, in certain circumstances, remedial secession given conditions of egregious, systematic human rights abuses.

The second principle shaping the post-Holocaust humanitarian world order, prioritization, is intimately linked with a third: recognition and defense of the notion that all *Homo sapiens* are human beings with equable claims to human dignity. In the introduction, I criticized the cosmopolitan thesis of equal moral status, not because it is inherently wrong, but because, as a foundational premise, it blinds us to the social manufacture of the idea of being human and the myriad of ways to be human. Theoretically speaking, our human history of truculent practices demands that we start from the maldistribution of the status of "human being." The point, as Arendt importuned, is not to try in vain to "escape from the grimness of the present into a nostalgia for a still intact past, or into the anticipated oblivion of a better future" (1973, ix) but to work in the shadow of and against existing destructive and distintegrative processes (1968a, 82).[7] Thus I opted to reframe the cosmopolitan declarative "We *are* morally equal" as the interrogatory "*How* do we *become* morally equal and, moreover, *effectuate* such equality?"

We might construe the emphasis on equality as echoing Waldron's thesis

(2012a) of the leveling of dignity. Yet this is and will remain an unfinished project, as our understandings of the human being, of socially acceptable ways of being human, and of dignity itself change over time. The cases do not automatically posit all *Homo sapiens* as human beings, but they illustrate how the *Homo sapiens* who were its subjects (*zoē*) were transformed into *bios*. For instance, a Security Council that defines international peace and security in statist terms might necessarily disregard the plight of collateral damage (*zoē*), as the cautionary Council was wont to do. But a Council that apprehends cycles of violence based on systematic patterns of exclusion, marginalization, and deprivation, as evidenced by the Council's thematic turn in the 1990s and 2000s, renegotiates the meaning of the human being in international relations as central to the objective of maintaining international peace and security. The human security concept likewise attaches equal moral worth to all human beings and their communities and aims to remake exploited, marginalized, oppressed, deprived *zoē* into *bios* through various protective and empowering activities. In the case of self-determination, however, the claims of *zoē* (a subjected people) to become *bios* (whether an independent state or a people granted substantial rights of internal self-rule) are always curtailed by the demands of interstate order: border stabilization and the peaceful resolution of disagreement impinge on the exercise of the right.

Finally, a post-Holocaust humanitarian world order is emancipatory in orientation insofar as "all social arrangements [are ultimately judged] by their capacity to embrace open dialogue with all others" (Linklater 1996, 280). In an extreme form, failure to persistently do so may entail rupture from an existing state and creation of a new one, such as we saw with Kosovo, East Timor, and South Sudan. In more moderate forms, emancipation may entail a substantial set of institutional, procedural, and policy reforms as intimated by the human security concept; internal governance arrangements to realize the self-determinative claims of indigenous or minority peoples; or shifts in mentality to sensitize actors to gendered, racialized, sexualized, and economized forms of exploitation.

Emancipatory actions are anticipated by the "how" of the interrogatory "*How* do we *become* morally equal and, moreover, *effectuate* such equality?" For Iver Neuman (2001, 504), such emancipatory "practices and arrangements of world society" (as he calls them) include the discourse of human rights, interventions launched with the imprimatur of the international community to protect humans from violence, the displacement or erosion of the division between domestic and foreign policy as evidenced by the migration to international actors of functions once solely associated with the state, the "growth of the number and density" of international advocacy networks and NGOs, and knowledge production and dissemination by and through journalists and the scholarly community. These practices not only reflect certain socially significant meanings attached to the terms *world society* or *common world*—meanings that lend actions the status of a practice—but logically entail a prior understanding of world society or the common world.

World society, as I have maintained, is not something to be found but, rather, a construction hinged on willingness to share the world with others and accord them dignity. Hence Neuman's practices of world society, while they perform some of the work required by willingness, are necessarily practices of a different, second-order sort; that is, they rest on more primordial, first-order practices. Let us return for a moment to an earlier argument. For Arendt (1958, 53), the common world is both physical (a space of fabricated things) and ideational (a space of action, appearance, interaction, and speech). Its singular importance owes not to fabricated, manufactured things but to the intersubjective web of assumptions, understandings, meanings, values, norms, principles, and rules derived from engagement with others. These ideational elements prove the binding elements that permit us to speak of a common world, and they lend it an ontological and determinative reality.[8] But these intersubjective elements do not automatically bind this world as a unitary whole. Rather, this world, as a space in-between human beings, relates *and* separates them. As such, the world, this in-between, operates as both a descriptor and "an evaluative category" (Janover 2011, 26). In its most extreme cosmopolitan formulation, a common world (or world society) rests on the premise that all members of the biological species *Homo sapiens* are human, and thus world society is ontologically equable with the human population. As a descriptor, such a formulation tells us everything and therefore nothing. Membership is often parsed along lines of race, ethnicity, nationality, religion, gender, sexuality, and sundry other signifiers. As an evaluative category that problematizes, not assumes, membership, however, a common world or world society admits of multiple, overlapping, and sometimes conflicting conceptions, degrees, and categories. Through this concept enter processes of making human as a set of first-order practices.

Recognition (of others, which implies acceptance) may be the most obvious mode of effectuating membership. But intersubjective recognition does not stop at the simple fact that another recognizes me as a human being, for intersubjectivity implies a process of negotiation or reconciliation of differing views. Recognition theoretically demands that no matter what type of human being I am, my membership in this common world is not adjudged inferior or extraneous. Yet recognition is not always automatic; in many instances, it unfolds over time, bound up as it were with the contingencies of context and with other processes: reflection on the status and worth of others; the reproduction of prevailing behavioral norms; resistance against forms of oppression, marginalization, and dehumanization; and the taking of responsibility for self and/or others. I summarize each below.

Reflection on what it means to be human does not offer presuppositions about human nature, for

> it is not possible to state what human nature is and be done with it; not least, the words "human" and "nature" have a history, and any empirical claim has meaning in the light of that history . . . The sciences of being human are open-ended: to utter a description, let alone to claim a truth, potentially re-creates the subject. "Self-reflection is at the same time self-formation, self-creation." Past, present, and future debate about the subject—man or woman, being human or human nature, culture or nature—gives the field its subject matter. Our being, as well as our understanding of it, is historical . . . Historical narratives are basic to identity and to human self-knowledge, collectively and individually. (Smith 2007, 243)

Previous chapters assayed narratives in diverse settings that, through phenomenological reflection on the lived experiences of marginalized peoples, clarified parameters for recognition and the nature of responses/resistances to oppression and, further, indicated appropriate roles that specified and affirmed community responsibilities toward others and responsibilities toward oneself.

As argued in chapter 3, the UN Security Council advances the project of making human by responding to injustices of misrecognition in contexts of violence and iterating various degrees and types of responsibility. In doing so, the Council has confirmed a reading of dignity hinged on the social status of the human being; institutions of international criminal law develop the theme, as chapter 5 explored. Violations of dignity, various tribunals maintain, are rooted in the diminishment of the social status of the individual in ways that substantially undermine one's ability to craft a meaningful life, not merely in violations of the body and in subsequent psychological and emotive harm. The International Court of Justice further grounded the argument with respect to Kosovo, while the human security agenda, the subject of chapter 4, reindividualizes it by taking as central to its project of protection and empowerment the very signifiers—our identities, our histories, our affiliations—that give us meaning.

Each of the cases discussed in this book evinces definitive tendencies in world politics toward a logic of order that, at heart, demands the reproduction of particular mores, norms, and behaviors to ensure a modicum of social stability. While the Security Council may be prone to discursively examining the parameters of acceptable behaviors in contexts of violence, it may be less consistently oriented toward enforcing them in any coercive interventionist sense. Both the ICJ and institutions of ICL have reiterated basic conceptions of human dignity as a constraint on political life, all the while underscoring the centrality of human status in world politics. Human security contains its own logic of replication in the form of best practices. While best practices harbor clear attractions—proven methods that have successfully mitigated or ameliorated insecurities or threats in multiple contexts, the reduction of duplication of efforts, and the more effective mobilization of limited resources—they also contain potential negative ramifications. Failure to adopt a best practice, which functions as a force of normalization, might discourage investment and transform "subjects with rights" back into "objects of regulation" (Neumann and Sending 2010, 115) or, worse, might let insecure peoples fend for themselves.

Finally, in all the cases discussed in this book, exposure to human suffering activated among relevant actors recognition of a need to respond. Resistance thus plays a salient role in reconstituting human beings qua human beings in the face of oppression. On this point, we find various institutions counteracting, though not always consistently, dehumanizing logics, practices, and contexts: they do so through the deployment of force; admission that egregious human rights abuses may open legal space for the consideration of claims of external self-determination; empowering human beings to substantiate their coping capacities; or opening up prevailing, silencing discourses to consideration of diverse forms of marginalization and dehumanization.

## Making Human and International Relations

The problem of making human pervades social life at all levels. Though we may be accustomed to thinking about extreme, obvious forms of dehumanization—e.g., enslavement, genocide, ethnic cleansing—other pertinent forms shape sociopolitical relations. "Don't ask, don't tell" and "Separate but equal" policies pithily capture the dilemmas of being human in a world subsequent to particularistic narratives of the human being. Yet they also capture the dilemmas of a world grappling with others who do not measure up to the socially sanctioned yardstick of the human being.

This book sought to gain traction on the slippery concept of the human being and, in doing so, to explore, in limited ways, how elements of world society, or what I have called a "post-Holocaust humanitarian world order," blend with the state institutions of international relations. I began with the work of Gerritt Gong (1984) and Martin Wight (1992, 49–98), each of whom examined historical practices and arrangements that attached membership in the international society of states coincident with particularistic (European) notions of civility and legitimacy. Their arguments strongly suggest that fragmented visions of world society cohabit the same analytical space as unitary (cosmopolitan) notions of humanity, which became the basis for my claim that we ought to begin not with cosmopolitanism but with cruelty. As ethically appealing as the thesis that all *Homo sapiens* are human may be, we must recognize that varying conceptualizations of what it means to be human have been the source of a whole lot of world (dis)order, especially if we think that colonial and imperial systems were fortified with logics of superiority bred from the depravity of racially constructed notions of civilization. From various chauvin*isms* (e.g., racism, sexism, nationalism, ethnocentrism) and sundry other psychologically (and socially) embedded frames of reference have precipitated a range of dehumanizing, exclusionary, and oppressive practices. Laundering through the states system magnifies their effects.

But human history involves not just truculent practices but conciliatory, cooperative, even complaisant connections between diverse peoples (see Linklater 2010). We should not valorize such relations in ways that serve as the definitional foundation of world society or provide us with traction on a post-Holocaust humanitarian conception of world order. Neither should we uncritically and automatically universalize membership in world society (see Vincent 1986) or even so neatly distinguish world society from international society by virtue of any presumed moral cosmopolitanism (see Wheeler 2000). By putting cruelty first, we are theoretically compelled to destabilize the very notion of what it means to be human and our constructs of world society. Superimposed on the macro vision of humankind are various modes of organizing an otherwise undifferentiated and largely meaningless mass of human beings: class, ethnicity, gender, ideology, interests, nationality and nationalisms, occupation, race, religion, and sexualities are a few of many schemes by which human beings make sense of the diversity of being human.

I might have arranged this book around chapters devoted to each of those schematics and to understanding how processes of making human reconcile antagonisms produced by them, yet I eschewed singular examination of any of those logics or lenses. Given the extent and multiplicity of dehumanizing practices, their justifications, and oftentimes their mutual imbrication (e.g., animosities that combine economic, ethnic, religious, and gender prejudices, as with rapes of Tutsi women in the Rwandan genocide), I opted to examine the broader issue of the social construction of the human being and its associated practice of clarifying the notion of dignity that has been accorded a privileged place in late twentieth-century discourses on international law and world order (see Kelman 1977; Jacobson 1982; Meron 2000a; Teitel 2011; Daly 2013). Stated differently, by starting with exploitation and oppression, we may consider methods of defusing our reactions to and the implications of difference.

Of course, much of the work of making human occurs at the micro level of the individual. On that reading, empathy and the hard work of introspection and moral reflection deliver us from solipsistic fear and disgust of difference (see Nussbaum 2010 for an application). Yet we do not (or cannot) always disentangle ourselves from socially and doctrinally sanctioned prejudices that become an inherent part of our psychosocial makeup; when imported into and sanctioned by political institutions, (de)humanizing practices have exponential effects. Thus, by investigating the processes of making human through institutions of international society, I sought to give traction, in another kind of way, to Mayall's claim that the task of diplomacy is to translate human interests and values into reality: this investigation shows that not only human diversity, livelihood, and dignity but also the meaning of human being and being human have become integral subjects of international relations.

By defining what is human, by clarifying the bounds of appropriate human conduct and ways of being, and by allocating the status of human and, with it, dignity, our (de)humanizing proclivities contribute to the structuring of social, economic, and political relations domestically and internationally. Because of their ramifications, I understand making human to be a primary institution in international relations, that is, a first-order practice. A primary institution (as mentioned in this book's introduction) is defined by "durable and recognized patterns of shared practices rooted in values commonly held" that in the end "play a constitutive role in relation to both the pieces/players and the rules of the game" (Buzan 2004a, 181), even if the content of those presumably commonly held values, in this case "humanity," is contestable. Though processes of making human as matters of interpersonal relations obviously predate the 1945 UN Charter, the scale of brutality during World War II ushered in something qualitatively different: a prioritization of the human being in international relations. Decades of programmatic and policy initiatives led Harold Jacobson, in his 1982 presidential address to the International Studies Association's annual convention, to characterize postwar developments as "adding up to a historic consensus on the meaning of human dignity and justice . . . and thus on the broad outlines of world order" (320). The post–Cold War era offers further proof of his thesis. I here take two examples. The Rome Statute for the International Criminal Court (1998) proclaims that "all peoples are united by common bonds, their cultures pieced together in a shared heritage"; the concern is "that this delicate mosaic may be shattered at any time" since "millions of children, women and men have been victims of unimaginable atrocities that deeply shock the conscience of humanity." Instrumental reasons for action conjoin ethical ones: since "such grave crimes threaten the peace, security and well-being of the world," the goal is "to put an end to impunity for the perpetrators of these crimes and thus to contribute to the prevention of such crimes." A similar logic is found in the 1997 Ottawa Convention, on antipersonnel landmines: ethical considerations (preventing the maiming and killing of civilians) there abut instrumental (if also somewhat normative) considerations—confidence-building measures that might plausibly substantiate cooperation oriented toward future security.[9]

Jacobson and Teitel (2011), among many others referenced throughout this book, perceive a qualitative change in international relations, from overt orientation toward the state—its material security, well-being, and interests—to a broadening of the horizon of the "stuff" that matters in international political life. In policy and practical terms, the four cases examined in this book demonstrate the utility and added value that an approach concerned with making human can have toward remedying injustices and dehumanizations, as it encourages policy makers, scholars, and activists, among others, to reflect on how best to respond to dehumanization in meaningful, caring, inclusive, sustainable ways. The cases illustrate a diversity of approaches to making human: awareness campaigns,[10] educational initiatives, skills training, community counseling, dialogic forums, interpersonal exchanges, expansion of access to microfinance, construction of seed banks, and the conclusion of harm conventions and treaties for minority protection.

To be sure, the state remains supreme in many of those activities. Likewise, parochial state interests often trump considerations of justice and dignity. While interstate violence has diminished considerably, rampant intrastate violence (much of it along ethnic and racial lines) casts a pall on the many ethical commitments and advances in international affairs. Yet stories are rarely one-dimensional, and while some may prefer to focus on violence as the perennial condition of international relations and on the state as the primary actor, other elements of the human condition, even if obscured in troubled times, must necessarily occupy at least a chapter. For Jacobson, cumulative developments associated with justice and dignity signaled a new kind of world order and world society. Processes of making human construct human beings not only intrinsically but also by virtue of their impact on social, political, and economic relations, world order and world society writ large.

Yet the point is to distance ourselves from formulations that equate world society with "all parts of the human community" (Bull 1995, 269), which James Mayall (2000, 14) replicates with the "view that humanity is one." In the introduction, I invoked Buzan's reconstruction of world society as comprised partly of an interhuman domain, meaning the aggregate of interactions between human persons. The implication is that patterned, persistent forms of interaction, whether collaborative or combative, shape sociopolitical relations across state borders and sometimes in ways that affect state policy. While Buzan's reformulation helps clarify an otherwise ambiguous concept, we cannot assume the "human" of the interhuman, since interactions among dominant groups may curtail the status and rights claims of certain types of human beings. If we start from cruelty and recognize our propensity to diminish the other, our perception of world society admits less conciliatory, more exclusive, hierarchic, and marginalizing practices on which it is constructed and refined. The upshot is that it then permits inquiry into the manufacture of the human being as a central building block in the construction of wider notions of humanity, humankind, or world society. *Making Human*'s contribution to the literature must be read in that regard.

As deeply constitutive, primordial forms of interaction, processes of making human generate and structure a range of social relations and thus provide greater traction for understanding the myriad forms world society may assume (imperial, hierarchic models built on standards of civilization; democratic forms built on dialogic inclusiveness and participation; civilizational models that partition the globe; etc.). Attentiveness to matters of membership and belonging—how they are decided, who is a member and to what degree, and so on—may have ramifications for various theoretical approaches to the study of international relations and, in practical terms, for international peace and security, human rights, and the like. Different kinds of (interstate, interhuman, transnational, world) societies may, based on their conceptions of human being and membership, license different behaviors; different behaviors might then be forecasted in terms of the likelihood of conflict and violence.

Of course, the preceding is but a preliminary sketch of how incorporating a perspective concerned with making human into the study of international relations may alter our theoretical constructs. More sustained and engaged research is necessary; I briefly identify five additional avenues of engagement. First, future research may examine the interrelationships between making human and other primary institutions (e.g., sovereignty, statehood, diplomacy, international law, balance of power or management of international relations by great powers, the market) and how those both alter and redefine relations between diverse actors as well as their identities and interests. This study, for instance, has raised questions regarding adjustments in meanings and practices of sovereignty; how power shapes and is shaped by the machinations of making human; the deployment of certain institutions (management by great powers, the market, international law, diplomacy) to counter dehumanization; and how, in particular, management of international affairs by great powers has expanded to consider the plight and meaning of being human.

Second, packaging diverse humanitarian and dignitary initiatives under the rubric of making human not only highlights conceptual continuities between them but raises questions regarding the conditions under which moral progress in international relations and world politics is possible. Third and relatedly, the making human perspective might be explored from the sociological standpoint of the notion of civility and the "civilizing process in which individuals learn how to control aggressive inclinations and adjust their thoughts and actions in response to the legitimate needs of other members of society" (Linklater and Suganami 2006, 121–22).[11] But that story is more complex than appears and encompasses more than simply restraining one's aggressive impulses. Threats to human beings may be and have been translated into threats to international order; even if the state is the primary cause for suffering, the norms of sovereignty and nonintervention have been relaxed when the wider order itself is destabilized. Force may be and has been deployed to make human. Therefore, finding ways to efficaciously implement the processes of making human may help stabilize international and world order, as indicated by many initiatives of the empowering UN Security Council, including its call for sustained intercivilizational dialogue (Resolution 1624 [14 September 2005]) and for the development of "educational programmes that will inculcate future generations with the lessons of the [Rwandan] Genocide in order to help prevent future genocides" (Resolution 2150 [16 April 2014], ¶2).[12] In short, civility and, I would add, processes of making human provide "useful tool[s] for thinking further about . . . the transformation of international systems into international societies and about the evolution of global ethical standards in the modern states-system" (Linklater and Suganami 2006, 122).

Finally, as I submitted in the conclusion of chapter 4, further attention might be devoted to understanding international relations in terms of heterarchy, not anarchy. The constellation of diverse actors working to achieve objectives related to improving human well-being—a "global governance of human dignity," as I have called it—approaches Volker Rittberger's characterization of the post–Cold War, post-Westphalian world as heterarchic. By heterarchy, he meant "a multipartite structure encompassing states, international organizations as well as private and civil societal non-state actors" (2008a, 28), marked by the "rules-based collective management of transsovereign problems through horizontal policy coordination and cooperation" (2008b, 16). In this reading, *heterarchy* appears a more ornamental term for global governance. Both capture the multiplicity of horizontal, overlapping, mutually implicative and sometimes conflicting networks and centers of power and authority that exist in contemporary international relations. But *heterarchy*, by virtue of its etymological conjoining of *heter*, meaning "other" or "different," and *archy* or *archein*, meaning "rule" or "to rule," frames a multitude of processes in terms of an organizing principle that gets us thinking about transcending anarchy, long construed as the organizing principle of international relations. In short, how many quantitative changes related to the construction of a post-Holocaust humanitarian world order produce a qualitative change in the anarchical arrangement of interstate order?

A global governance of human dignity, buttressed by principles and elements of a post-Holocaust humanitarian world order, grounds the occasional notation in international relations literature that the individual is the "ultimate member" of all political relations, including international and world societies (Wight 1978, 106; cf. Bull 1995, 21). The remark should not be construed as necessarily portending the supersession of a society of states by a nonstate polity (or polities) organized around, say, identity or class or civilizations. In its more minimal incarnation, the notation anticipates a kind of arrangement in which the objectives, capacity, sustainability, and stability of the state and the states-system are measured in terms of the well-being of their human occupants. The relationship between state and citizen is then reframed in responsible, responsive, and, ultimately, caring terms. Consequently, co-option of humanitarian concerns into domestic and international policy reduces perceived tensions between a humanitarian world order and an interstate order.

Hedley Bull (1995, 21) once mused that world order "is more fundamental and primordial than international order because the ultimate units of the great society of all mankind are not states (or nations, tribes, empires, classes or parties) but individual human beings, which are permanent and indestructible in a sense in which groupings of them of this or that sort are not." Mervyn Frost (1986, 135) questioned Bull: clearly, individuals are not permanent and indestructible "in any literal sense." Frost therefore concluded that Bull argues "against those who would see the well-being of some collectivity, for example, a class, as more important than the well-being of the individuals within it. If this interpretation of Bull is correct, then there is implicit in Bull's theory a substantive normative theory in terms of which the good of individuals is more important than the good of social wholes." Frost's point was prescient. *Making Human* pushes the logic: processes of making human, as primordial practices of interhuman interaction, act as a primary institution of international relations precisely because they serve as basic building blocks of human sociability.

Frost (1986, 178) leverages the issue in Hegel: "within the autonomous state the individual is constituted as a free citizen, but for his citizenship to be fully actualized his state needs to be recognized by other states as autonomous." We might move the argument forward, that is, beyond the state: the full actualization of one's humanity—that is, individuality and status as human with dignity—requires recognition qua human by other human beings. Recognition may sometimes be the result of other processes to make others human, which this study examined. In this fundamental, basic sense, we constitute each other. How we mutually constitute one another is, centrally, the problem not only of personhood and interpersonal relations but, ultimately, of international relations and world order.

# Notes

## Introduction

1. Ostensibly innocuous, the term *man* has enacted tremendous violence not because it shares an auditory ugliness with the other epithets but because it erases or conceals its opposite: *woman*. Of course, as Susan Sontag ([1973] 2013, 776) rightly notes, "[L]anguage is not . . . the source of the prejudice that identifies 'men' as the human race, and associates most human activities with men only. Language merely expresses the sexist order that has prevailed throughout history."

2. Confronted with the scale of calculated brutality during World War II, international community sentiment could not prevaricate. The preamble of the 1948 Universal Declaration of Human Rights, for instance, asserts that "recognition of the inherent dignity and of the equal and inalienable rights of *all members of the human family* is the foundation of freedom, justice and peace in the world" (emphasis added).

3. Some exemplary works include Bernstein 2002; Waller 2002; Mann 2005; Jeffrey 2008; Eagleton 2010; and Svendsen 2010.

4. The Universal Declaration of Human Rights begins with a dystopic awareness of the human propensity for cruelty: "Whereas disregard and contempt for human rights have resulted in barbarous acts which have outraged the conscience of mankind, and the advent of a world in which human beings shall enjoy freedom of speech and belief and freedom from fear and want has been proclaimed as the highest aspiration of the common people . . ."

5. The alliterative flourish is not designed to oversimplify the inquiry. Neither is the list intended to be exhaustive.

6. Thus, to wit, the potential to become a murderer would necessarily conflict with another's right to live and become a self and thus could not constitute grounds for equal regard in conditions of reciprocity. Living in community with others perforce entails restrictions on what we can do, legitimately and ethically, and who we may become.

7. See, for example, Honneth 1995; Mason 2000, 51–54. In their work on the injuries of class, Richard Sennett and Jonathan Cobb discovered that the 150 working-class individuals they interviewed in depth over a one-year period felt that "they have to

earn the right to communal respect [and dignity] by showing others they totally take care of themselves" (1973, 40, 56). Sennett's other work—on cooperation (2012), craft (2008), respect (2003), and character (1998)—serves as a model for the kind of work I aim to do here: to combine analyses on the individual and systems levels with an acute exploration of what it means to be human in political life.

8. On 26 July 2013, the UN Office of the High Commissioner for Human Rights launched its Free & Equal public information campaign in Cape Town, South Africa. The campaign aims "to raise awareness about violence and discrimination against . . . LGBT people . . . and focus on the need for both legal reforms and public education to counter homophobia and transphobia" (Penn 2013). The campaign's official website is www.unfe.org/.

9. The report (Human Rights Watch 2013, 3) indicates that the eighty-one estimated drone attacks carried out by the US Joint Special Operations Command, "a semi-covert arm of the military," and the CIA in Yemen—one in 2002 and the rest since 2009—have killed "at least 473 combatants and civilians."

10. My search of the ninety-seven-page report did not locate a specific instance in which farmers shielding themselves from sun were killed, but I did find references to *qat* (or *khat*) farmers who were victims in attacks on known al-Qaeda operatives in the Arabian Peninsula.

11. Giorgio Agamben (1993, 43) also iterated this point: "The fact that must constitute the point of departure for any discourse on ethics is that there is no essence, no historical or spiritual vocation, no biological destiny that humans must enact or realize. This is only why something like an ethics can exist, because it is clear that if humans were or had to be this or that substance, this or that destiny, no ethical experience would be possible—there would only be tasks to be done."

12. See True 2011, 77, for citations.

13. For example, while same-sex marriage in South Africa has effectuated constitutional provisions of equality, enhanced visibility of lesbians has contributed to the horror of corrective rape.

14. On dignity as an expressive norm, see Khaitan 2012. Of course, what "nonharmful" means in practice is highly contestable. For instance, certain governments and societies find great moral and social harm in the very existence of LGBT persons (e.g., Cameroon, Russia, Zimbabwe, Nigeria, Uganda). Others may take a more narrow (and tolerable) approach to harm by hinging it on age of consent, forcible sexual encounter, child pornography, various specified modes of exploitation, and the like. The frame of making human offers guidance on these points. By switching to a prism that underlines the sheer diversity of human living and by resting a conception of antidiscrimination on a notion of liberty—that is, a degree of freedom accorded to a person's construction of a meaningful life—the humanization frame ties action and policy to their material effects on others.

15. See Reilly 2007 for a feminist critique of human rights universalisms as masking certain biases.

16. Consider also the criminalization of homosexuality, which, as of 28 October 2013, seventy-six countries enact, according to the UN Office of the High Commission for Human Rights (2013). Five of those countries—Iran, Saudi Arabia, Yemen, Sudan, and Mauritania—impose the death penalty for being homosexual.

17. Suspect classes have been defined as a function of a history of purposeful dis-

crimination, political powerlessness, immutable traits, and grossly unfair treatment. In 1976, the United States Supreme Court articulated that a suspect class is one "'saddled with such disabilities, or subjected to such a history of purposeful unequal treatment, or relegated to such a position of political powerlessness as to command extraordinary protection from the majoritarian political process.' While the treatment of the aged in this Nation has not been wholly free of discrimination, such persons, unlike, say, those who have been discriminated against on the basis of race or national origin, have not experienced a 'history of purposeful unequal treatment' or been subjected to unique disabilities on the basis of stereotyped characteristics not truly indicative of their abilities" (*Massachusetts Board of Retirement v. Murgia* [1976]).

18. In international relations history, I think of Japan, which had been excluded by European international society. Japan internalized European norms (in the Meiji Restoration), but the Japanese defeat of Russia during the war of 1904–5 (a formidable act of resistance) marked Japan's entry into international society and thus, arguably, signified the point at which the Japanese were accepted as fully human.

19. Biopolitics is variously defined as the "disciplinary training of the human body in institutions" or the "regulation of the population at the level of state" (Jaeger 2010, 55).

20. John Burton's (1972) cobweb model of international relations may be the exception that proved Isaak's point at the time. Jacobson (1982, 317–20) offers possible explanations for the neglect of individuals, human dignity, and justice in international relations.

21. On world society, see Bull 1995; Linklater 1998; Williams 2005. For a broad overview of English School theory, see Linklater and Suganami 2006.

22. Cf. Linklater's assertion (1998, 24) that "an elementary universalism" centered on individual rights "underpins the society of states."

23. Conceptions of world society that precede the English School share this preoccupation (see Burton 1972; Luard 1976, 1990; for a summary of world society conceptions, Buzan 2004a, 63–89).

24. Patrick Hayden's *Political Evil in a Global Age* (2009) is a notable cosmopolitan exception that also begins from this premise.

25. At the 2013 general debate of the UN General Assembly, 72 of 192 heads of state, foreign ministers, and other dignitaries invoked "dignity" 115 times, most often in conjunction with dire poverty, development, and the use of chemical weapons in Syria.

26. For example, see Sylvester 1994, 1996; Tickner and Sjoberg 2011. On feminism and international law, see, for example, Charlesworth, Chinkin, and Wright 1991; Nijman 2004, 428–45.

27. For a superb summary of the contributions of critical theory to international relations, see Linklater 1996.

28. For a concise overview of the English School as theory, see Buzan 2004a, 24–26.

29. On the distinction between problem-solving theory and critical theory, see Cox 1986, 208.

## Chapter 1

1. Arendt 1973, 298.
2. Booth 1993, 91.

3. Enloe summarized the work of socialist scholars in Britain's History Workshop as "committed to a democratic sort of scholarly practice that presumes value in human experience for its own sake: if a person has dwelt on this planet, they are worthy of being recorded; to be recorded assigns dignity; all humans, because of their humanity, possess dignity, or should" (1996, 187).

4. We might add that the world does not always find sacred the condition of belonging to a social group that usually becomes the cause for one's targeting.

5. Tétreault and Lipschutz use this term to capture "the free will and agency of the individual and the social structures that set limits to human thought and action" (2009, 1). Differently stated, "the social individual [is] capable of acting on her own volition, but with the proviso that no one acts in a vacuum" (3).

6. I thus seek to add to a burgeoning literature that finds fruitful conversation between Arendt and international relations. See, for example, Lang and Williams 2005; Birmingham 2006; Owens 2007; Burke 2008; Parekh 2008; Hayden 2009.

7. The Greeks included the gods in this listing, but I shall be more secular in my formulation.

8. In important respects, Hannah Arendt's thinking parallels the insights of Gong and Wight, but she would object to individual acts of mimicry, since they have historically raised red flags of suspicion. Writing about nineteenth-century German Jews who, in their zeal to be accepted as "normal" in bourgeois German society, converted to Christianity, Arendt underscored society's suspicion of the parvenu: if they renounced what was central to their identity and betrayed their own people, what else would they renounce or betray in their quest for individual advancement ([1957] 1997)?

9. Salter (2002, 4) writes that "the trope of the barbarian is familiar: lacking in manners, language and morals."

10. See Salter 2002 on "old" and "new" barbarians.

11. In March 2012, the leading Tunisian Islamist party, Ennahdha, "declared itself against any mention of Shariah law in the constitution," for many reasons, including Salafi militants who "preach the most radical versions of political Islam" and "multiply their [acts of] violence and provocations. On some campuses, they aggress non-veiled women. They prevent cultural events. They hold giant prayers in the beautiful center of the capital, where one of their rallying cries: 'Death to the Jews!'" (http://www.islamopediaonline.org/editorials-and-analysis/these-tunisian-islamists-say-no-shariah, accessed 6 June 2012).

12. Arendt ignores two facts: first, the imperial experience that negated the protective effects of belonging to some kind of organized community; second, the fact that states are often the chief perpetrators of rights denial or abuses. One might maintain that she argued for an absolute or pure concept of national self-determination, which rests on the assumption that a nationally or ethnically homogeneous state would not sacrifice its citizens. Cambodia under the Khmer Rouge either refutes that notion or is the exception that proves the rule.

13. Consider the claims of Norbert Elias and Jayan Nayar presented as epigraphs at the beginning of this book.

14. Indeed, a blueprint for Auschwitz adorns the cover of Agamben's *Homo Sacer* (1998).

15. To illustrate, piracy long remained an intractable problem off the Horn of Africa

despite military patrols by navies from around the world, precisely because of the sheer enormity of geographic space within which the pirates operate: patrols simply cannot be everywhere all of the time.

16. Momigliano (1980) unpacks Weber's conception of guest, which we might reframe as the conditionally, precariously tolerated presence of the Other. I reframe the matter as one of quasi toleration, because of injunctions (e.g., on movement, intermarriage, choice of residence, etc.) placed on such "guests." One might think, for example, of the Jews in many countries of pre-Holocaust Europe who were forced to pay "Jew taxes" or of Asians in Uganda prior to their 1971 expulsion by Idi Amin.

17. The Jewish Museum of New York hosted an exhibition, *The Power of Conversation: Jewish Women and Their Salons* (4 March—10 July 2005), that featured artifacts from Rahel's salon.

18. The *New York Times* reported on 25 January 2010 that "new rules of hunger etiquette" emerged in the aftermath of the 12 January 2010 Haiti earthquake: "Stealing food, it is widely known, might get you killed. Children are most likely to return with something to eat, but no matter what is found, or how hungry the forager, everything must be shared" (Cave 2010).

19. Anthony Lang and John Williams maintain that Arendt conceived of "individuals as political agents, acting within specific circumstances, but always retaining a unique character and capable of unpredictable and surprising acts of great political significance" (2005, 2).

20. On these questions, see Booth et al. 2001.

21. Arendt writes that "the crimes against human rights, which have become a specialty of totalitarian regimes, can always be justified by the pretext that right is equivalent to being good or useful for the whole in distinction to its parts" (1973, 298–99). The very corruptibility of the universal could suggest either that all claims to universality are weak and easily manipulated or, given the trenchant logic of human rights in international relations, in need of grounding by a moral minimum. For Arendt, that was the right to have rights, or the right to belong to a community. Andrew Linklater (2001, 274) proposes that the concept of harm acts as one such moral minimum, as it "is present in all moral codes [and] . . . is universal without being foundational (the keystone of all moralities) or exhaustive (encompassing the full range of moral duties and responsibilities)." Hayden 2009 might be read as proposing that actions and policies that make humans superfluous (a form of harm) be construed as another such moral minimum.

22. Robert Fine's chapter on cosmopolitanism and punishment (2007, 96–114) provides a superb defense of Arendt against charges that she trivialized the destruction of European Jewry by using the phrase "banality of evil." He maintains that the spirit of Arendt's response to her critics was that "because we can find no rational explanation for such phenomena, we are tempted to declare them beyond human understanding. However, the cosmopolitan institution is to resist this temptation and through judgment and understanding to reconstruct the idea of humanity in the face of its eradication" (113–14).

23. The capture of Eichmann by Israeli agents in 1960 and his trial in 1961, which Arendt attended as a reporter for the *New Yorker*, provided her the opportunity to explore the omnipresent tension between the claims of humanity and the claims of

the state. Those reports were collected and republished under the title *Eichmann in Jerusalem* (1963a) and are partially the subject of chapter 5.

24. See Owens 2007 (37–43, 75–80) for an excellent summary of how the Greeks and Romans conceived of the relationship between law and war.

25. Arendt locates this "refounding and reconstitution" in the "inherent capacity" of the American Constitution "to be amended and augmented" (1963b, 202).

26. Parallels in international relations scholarship may be located in literature on global civil society (e.g., Lipschutz 1992), transnational movements (e.g., Keck and Sikkink 1998), popular dissent (e.g., Bleiker 2000), and democratic internationalism (e.g., Falk 1999; Gilbert 1999). While Arendt had no such conceptual language at her disposal during her lifetime, she approximated those developments in her ruminations on civic activism.

27. Keene (2002, 123) maintains that Gong tells only half the story; he omits from consideration "the entry of some civilized states—notably Germany, Russia and Japan—into the uncivilized world." Dehumanization is not always the result of an external action directed against or perception of certain people but may be the result of actions one perpetrates as measured against some normative ideal. This perspective parallels my own and some of what Wight and Arendt maintained: that humanization is not always a process external to the self but may also result from self-directed action. Some processes I have identified (e.g., reflection and responsibility) capture that.

28. See, for example, McCarthy 2009 for an exegesis of race, empire, and the idea of human development.

29. Recall Wight's observation that international society absorbed but did not digest different peoples.

30. Serena Parekh (2008, 42–66) phrases it slightly differently: "[W]hy did human dignity all of a sudden require a defense? Why was it no longer something that could be taken for granted? A significant part of the answer has to do with the *ethos* of modernity, . . . [which "reduces everything, including human life, to a means to an end"]." Consequently, Arendt concluded that the ethos of modernity "ultimately undermined the concept of human dignity, and thus made the assertion of human rights necessary" (43–44).

31. Edward Keene's *Beyond the Anarchical Society* (2002, 124), which builds on the insight that "nineteenth-century structures of imperial and confederal governance might have a relevance to the growth of international organization in the twentieth century," appears as an apt analogue to Arendt's argument that encounters with presumably less-capable others spawned construction of (racialized) hierarchies and managerial schemes to govern them. See also McCarthy 2009.

## Chapter 2

1. Address at Johns Hopkins University, 14 June 1955 (Hammarksjöld 2005, 151).

2. Arendt 1973, 458.

3. Arendt's fear of "legally imposed equality in social and private life" as leading "to some form of tyranny" (Cornell 2010, 223) likely stemmed from her experiences with the Nazis.

4. Emphasis added.

5. I thank my research assistant, Kelly Ehrenreich, for extraordinary care in sifting through the constitutions of all 193 members of the UN—and more—to locate every possible invocation of the term *dignity*. Her count includes constitutions valid up to December 2011. The 142 countries include Afghanistan, Albania, Andorra, Angola, Antigua and Barbuda, Armenia, Azerbaijan, Bahrain, Barbados, Belarus, Belgium, Belize, Benin, Bosnia Herzegovina, Brazil, Bulgaria, Burkina Faso, Cambodia, Cameroon, Cape Verde, Central African Republic, Chad, Chile, China, Colombia, Comoros, Congo (Republic of), Costa Rica, Croatia, Cuba, Czech Republic, Dominica, East Timor, Ecuador, Egypt, El Salvador, Equatorial Guinea, Eritrea, Estonia, Ethiopia, Fiji, Finland, Gabon, Gambia, Georgia, Germany, Greece, Grenada, Guatemala, Guinea-Bissau, Guyana, Haiti, Honduras, Hungary, India, Indonesia, Iran, Iraq, Ireland, Israel, Italy, Ivory Coast, Jamaica, Japan, Kazakhstan, Kenya, Kosovo, Kuwait, Kyrgyz Republic, Latvia, Lebanon, Lesotho, Libya, Liechtenstein, Lithuania, Macedonia, Madagascar, Malawi, Maldives, Mali, Mauritania, Mexico, Moldova, Mongolia, Montenegro, Mozambique, Myanmar, Namibia, Nepal, Nicaragua, Nigeria, North Korea, Oman, Pakistan, Panama, Papua New Guinea, Paraguay, Peru, Philippines, Poland, Portugal, Romania, Russia, Rwanda, Sao Tome and Principe, Saudi Arabia, Serbia, Seychelles, Sierra Leone, Slovakia, Slovenia, Solomon Islands, Somalia, South Africa, South Korea, South Sudan, Spain, Sri Lanka, St. Kitts and Nevis, St. Lucia, St. Vincent and the Grenadines, Sudan, Suriname, Swaziland, Switzerland, Syria, Tajikistan, Tanzania, Thailand, Togo, Trinidad and Tobago, Tunisia, Turkey, Turkmenistan, Tuvalu, Uganda, Ukraine, Uzbekistan, Venezuela, Vietnam, Yemen, and Zambia.

6. The 1993 Peruvian Constitution affirms that respecting dignity is the "supreme purpose" of the state, while the Colombian Constitution determines that the Republic of Colombia was established to protect all persons and their dignity.

7. Jacobson understands the consensus to include the right to the security of the person; access to basic human needs; the right to constitute a political community; and the full range of civil rights (1982, 323).

8. Address to the American Association for the United Nations, New York, 14 September 1953.

9. Address at Williamsburg, Virginia, 14 May 1956.

10. Herbert Kelman's 1977 presidential address to the International Studies Association annual convention outlined conditions (including international peace, social justice, and individual freedom), criteria, and dialectics of human dignity, which anticipate, in certain fundamental respects, the formulations of Schachter and Hicks.

11. Cf. Smith 2010, 439; Smith articulates that human dignity has something to do with "reflexivity, rationality, self-causality, creativity, and freedom."

12. Emphasis added. Violations of human dignity include acts that significantly impede or outright deny our human abilities and impulses to create, invent, construct, remodel, renovate, communicate, act, group, cooperate, and the like. As Kateb (2011, 14) pithily remarks, violations of human dignity mirror the old Nazi phrase "life unworthy of life."

13. Critical theorists such as Horkheimer (1974) and Marcuse (1955) indicted positivism and scientific rationality as tools of domination (over nature and fellow human beings).

14. See Feinberg 2005, in which Kenneth Feinberg recounts his experiences administering the 9/11 Victims Compensation Fund.

15. Cf. E. H. Carr's formulation (1961, 42) that the "individual human being . . . is a social phenomenon, both the product and the conscious or unconscious spokesman of the society to which [s/]he belongs."

16. *Prosecutor v. Radislav Krstić* 2001, ¶513, p. 181.

17. Judges at the International Criminal Tribunal for Rwanda (ICTR) and the International Criminal Tribunal for the former Yugoslavia (ICTY) have been instrumental in advancing international criminal jurisprudence with respect to sexual violence. The ICTR's *Prosecutor v. Jean-Paul Akayesu* (1998) and the ICTY's *Prosecutor v. Anto Furundžija* (1998) and *Prosecutor v. Dragoljub Kunarac* (2001) judgments have provided uncomfortable, nearly pornographic detail about what "instruments" (including bodily appendages, tools such as broomsticks, and the like) must be inserted into which human orifices to constitute rape, as well as how other forms of sexual oppression and exploitation constitute violations of human dignity.

18. At the time of Hammarskjöld's appointment as secretary-general in April 1953, there were 60 UN members. By the time of his death in September 1961, there were 104 state members.

19. For a decent summary of negotiations and positions on UN Security Council reform, see *Center for UN Reform Education*, http://www.centerforunreform.org/node/23, accessed 18 June 2012.

20. As of 1 December 2013, thirty-nine hundred nongovernmental organizations enjoy consultative status with ECOSOC. See *NGO Branch, Department of Economic and Social Affairs*, http://csonet.org/index.php?menu=17.

21. A/Res/1541(XV) 1960, Principle II, "Principles Which Should Guide Members in Determining Whether or Not an Obligation Exists to Transmit the Information Called For under Article 73(e) of the Charter," http://www.un.org/peace/etimor99/a1541xv.pdf, accessed 30 January 2012.

22. United Nations Global Compact, http://www.unglobalcompact.org/, accessed 21 June 2012.

23. Juxtaposed to this "virtuous triangle" is the "sinister triangle" of drugs, crime, and terrorism (see Costa 2005).

## Chapter 3

1. All UN Security Council resolutions can be found online at http://www.un.org/en/sc/documents/resolutions/index.shtml. All resolutions were accessed during the month of January 2012, unless otherwise noted.

2. Per Article 25, member states pledge "to accept and carry out the decisions" of the Council. Article 49 not only reiterates those binding obligations with respect to threats to and breaches of the peace and acts of aggression (Chapter VII decisions) but also affords the Council discretion in determining the particular actions states shall undertake.

3. See   http://www.securitycouncilreport.org/site/c.glKWLeMTIsG/b.2400809/

k.2E0A/Publications_on_Thematic__General_Issues.htm, accessed 16 January 2012.

4. Resolution 1540 may be interpreted as stemming from the Council's responsibility to establish "a system for the regulation of armaments" as articulated in Article 26.

5. For more recent book-length treatments of the Council's history and work, see Hurd 2007; Lowe et al. 2008; Bosco 2009.

6. Under this compromise position, an act of aggression would encompass threats or uses of force "against the territorial integrity or political independence of any state, or in any other manner inconsistent with the Purposes of the United Nations."

7. This is precisely what makes resolutions 1373 and 1540 monumental: they obligate states to make changes in law and policy. One could, however, make a strong legal argument that mandating changes in law and policy falls under the ambit of Article 41 by virtue of its emphasis on "measures not involving the use of armed force." That matter, though, is beyond the scope of this chapter.

8. SC/10272, Security Council 65476547th meeting (a.m.), "Unanimously Adopting 1983 (2011), Security Council Encourages Inclusion of HIV Prevention, Treatment, Care Support in Implementing Peacekeeping Mandates," Department of Public Information, News and Media Division, New York, http://www.un.org/News/Press/docs/2011/sc10272.doc.htm, accessed 3 January 2012.

9. Substantive issues that came before the Council in the period 1946–48 include, in chronological order, the Iranian Question, the Spanish Question, the Greek Question, the Corfu Channel incidents, and the Indonesia Question. As the Iranian situation concerned the stationing of Soviet troops inside the border with Iran and as the Corfu Channel incidents had been framed as the obstruction of navigation through an important waterway, I omit them from consideration. I also omit from consideration the election of both new members to the UN and ICJ judges, matters of UNSC procedure, armaments regulations, and the like.

10. Draft resolution, *Repertoire of the Practice of the Security Council*, http://untreaty.un.org/cod/repertory/art41/english/rep_orig_vol2-art41_e.pdf, accessed 23 December 2011. The *Repertoire* was first created in 1952 to fulfill a mandate issued by the General Assembly in Resolution 686(VII) to document "the Council's interpretation and application of the Charter" and report on its activities. "The material presented in the *Repertoire* is exclusively based on official documents," including Council resolutions and decisions, verbatim records of Council meetings, the secretary-general's reports to and correspondence with the Council, and other official documents from member states. Each volume of the print version covers two to six years. Page numbers between the online and print versions differ. In this instance, for example, the report cited appears on page 182 of the print version but page 4 of the online edition. The online edition has disaggregated volumes into chapters and often chapters into particular subsections and saved them as a series of distinct PDF files. The website offers a comprehensive menu to facilitate research. Though I use the online edition, available at http://www.un.org/en/sc/repertoire/ (accessed 6 January 2012), I also provide print page numbers when available.

11. One Spanish human rights nongovernmental organization, Equipo Nizkor, used the UN identification of the Franco regime as aligned with the Axis Powers as grounds for equating that regime's actions as equable with the crimes outlined in

the Nuremberg Charter, which would make it ineligible for UN membership as a peace-loving state (Spain was admitted to the UN in December 1955). See http://www.derechos.org/nizkor/espana/doc/impuspa.html, accessed 16 January 2012.

12. Draft resolution, http://www.un.org/en/sc/repertoire/46-51/Chapter%208/46-51_08-7-The%20Spanish%20question.pdf, accessed 3 June 2014.

13. Ibid., p. 306 (where the subcommittee report is referenced).

14. http://untreaty.un.org/cod/repertory/art41/english/rep_orig_vol2-art41_e.pdf, ¶5, p. 4 (accessed 23 December 2011, URL is no longer accessible).

15. Ibid., ¶6, p. 5.

16. UNGA Resolution 39(I) (12 December 1946), http://www.derechos.org/nizkor/espana/doc/impuspa.html, accessed 8 December 2011.

17. To the argument, one can append the fact that the monarchical principle was upheld at the 1815 Congress of Vienna as the only legitimate form of government. Regime type very much mattered for the purposes of international peace and stability and thus could not be construed as a purely domestic matter. On the monarchical principle, see Reus-Smit 1999, 87–121.

18. On the creation of the commission, see also "Case 1: Commission of Investigation concerning Greek Frontier Incidents," in "Chapter V: Subsidiary Organs of the Security Council," *Repertoire*, http://www.un.org/en/sc/repertoire/46-51/46-51_05.pdf#page=4, p. 182, accessed 2 June 2014.

19. The UN Commission for India and Pakistan twice called for a plebiscite (on 13 August 1948 and 5 January 1949). In the 1950s, India distanced itself from its commitment to host elections, because Pakistan failed to withdraw its forces from the areas as required and because domestic elections in India had affirmed Kashmir's status "as part of India" (http://news.bbc.co.uk/2/hi/south_asia/1766582.stm, accessed 6 January 2012).

20. Elections were never held. The Council's active diplomatic engagement with the parties and threats from the US Congress to cancel all Marshall Plan funds allocated to the Netherlands for reconstruction and development effectively forced the Dutch hand. Negotiations led by the United States, not the UN, resulted in the formal transfer of sovereignty from the Netherlands to Indonesia on 27 December 1949.

21. For example, Resolutions 1261 (30 August 1999), 1314 (11 August 2000), 1379 (20 November 2001), 1460 (30 January 2003), 1539 (22 April 2004), 1612 (26 July 2005), 1882 (4 August 2009), 1998 (12 July 2011), 2068 (19 September 2012), and 2143 (7 March 2014).

22. For example, Resolutions 1265 (17 September 1999), 1296 (19 April 2000), 1674 (28 April 2006), 1738 (23 December 2006), and 1894 (11 November 2009).

23. For example, Resolutions 1325 (31 October 2000), 1612 (26 July 2005), 1674 (28 April 2006), 1820 (19 June 2008), 1888 (30 September 2009), 1889 (5 October 2009), 1894 (11 November 2009), 1960 (16 December 2010), 2106 (24 June 2013), and 2122 (18 October 2013).

24. "The United Nations: Partner in the Struggle against Apartheid," http://www.un.org/en/events/mandeladay/apartheid.shtml, accessed 7 January 2012.

25. All UN General Assembly resolutions are accessible at http://www.un.org/documents/resga.htm.

26. "Case 18: Situation in Southern Rhodesia," in "Chapter XII: Consideration of

the Provisions of Other Articles of the Charter," *Repertoire*, http://legal.un.org/reper
tory/art39/english/rep_supp3_vol2-art39_e.pdf, ¶35, p. 202, accessed 4 June 2014.

27. See   http://legal.un.org/repertory/art39/english/rep_supp3_vol2-art39_e.pdf,
¶30, p. 201, accessed 4 June 2014.

28. Decision of 13 September 1963 (1069th meeting), "Chapter VIII: Maintenance
of International Peace and Security," *Repertoire*, http://www.un.org/en/sc/reper
toire/59-63/Chapter%208/59-63_08-24-Situation%20in%20Southern%20Rhode
sia.pdf, print p. 218, accessed 6 January 2012.

29. http://www.un.org/wcm/content/site/undpa/main/issues/elections/, accessed 30
January 2012.

30. A/Res/1541(XV) 1960, Principle II, "Principles Which Should Guide Members
in Determining Whether or Not an Obligation Exists to Transmit the Information
Called For under Article 73(e) of the Charter," http://daccess-dds-ny.un.org/doc/
RESOLUTION/GEN/NR0/153/15/IMG/NR015315.pdf?OpenElement,   accessed
4 June 2014.

31. On 16 April 2014, the Council underscored the central role of education in the
prevention of genocide, and urged member states to "develop educational programmes
that will inculcate future generations with the lessons" of the Rwandan genocide (Resolution 2150).

32. With a description oddly reminiscent of the salon, which I treated in chapter 1 as
a nonspace existing between private and public, Arendt characterized schools as a primary institution interposed "between the private domain of home and the world . . .
[which] make the transition from the family to the world possible at all" (1993, 188–
89). Education responds to the needs of developing, individual selves; nourishes "the
free development of characteristic qualities and talents" (189); reflects the educator's
"responsibility for the world" by preparing youths "in advance for the task of renewing
a common world" (189, 196); and, toward that end, cultivates skills to enable youth to
learn how to speak and (re)present themselves in public.

33. Resolution 1502 (26 August 2003). For a history of Security Council meetings
and work related to the protection of humanitarian relief workers, see "Protection
of United Nations Personnel, Associated Personnel, and Humanitarian Personnel in
Conflict Zones," *Repertoire*, http://www.un.org/en/sc/repertoire/2000-2003/Chap
ter%208/Thematic/00-03_8_44%20Protection%20of%20United%20Nations%20
personnel.pdf, print pp. 793–95, accessed 3 June 2014.

34. Resolution 1738 (23 December 2006), on the protection of civilians in armed
conflict, specifically focuses on journalists.

35. For instance, five UNSC resolutions deal with sexual exploitation during the
period 28 March 2002—24 March 2005: Resolutions 1400 (28 March 2002), which
renewed the mandate in Sierra Leone and expressed concern "about allegations of
sexual abuse"; 1463 (24 September 2002), which included a "reference to the need
for the prevention of sexual abuse and exploitation as part of the mandate renewal
for peacekeeping in Sierra Leone"; 1460 (30 January 2003), "on children in armed
conflict," which "noted with concern the exploitation of children by peacekeepers";
1565 (1 October 2004), which renewed the UN mission in the Congo and "requested
the Secretary-General [to] investigate allegations of sexual exploitation by UN peacekeeping personnel and to take preventive measures"; and 1590 (24 March 2005), the

"first resolution to affirm zero tolerance of sexual exploitation in all UN peacekeeping operations" This is obviously a small sampling; much work has been done since the adoption of Resolution 1590. Many UNSC resolutions make mention of the victims of armed conflict, the subjects of criminal activity, and the like.

## Chapter 4

1. Kerim 2008.

2. See Muthien 2000 for an excellent feminist critique of such concepts as security, harm, and protection and for their reconstruction from a feminist understanding of human security.

3. For a similar argument that links poverty and terrorism, see Bush 2002. Consider also the spring 2009 riots that occurred in thirty-two countries because, owing to sudden and drastic increases in global food prices, people could no longer afford basic food staples.

4. See also, for specific issue targets, the UNGA Millennium Declaration, A/55/2, 8 September 2000, http://www.un.org/millennium/declaration/ares552e.htm, accessed 18 June 2010.

5. See the so-called Barcelona Report, *A Human Security Doctrine for Europe*, http://www.lse.ac.uk/internationalDevelopment/research/CSHS/humanSecurity/barcelonaReport.pdf, accessed 4 June 2014.

6. "Informal Thematic Debate on Human Security," 14 April 2011, http://www.un.org/en/ga/president/65/initiatives/HumanSecurity.html, accessed 26 March 2013.

7. Human Security Unit, http://unocha.org/humansecurity/, accessed 4 June 2014.

8. United Nations Development Programme, "UNDP Partnerships: United Nations Trust Fund for Human Security," www.undp.org/partners/humansecurity.shtml, accessed 9 September 2008. Between 1999 and 2008, the UNTFHS financed over 170 different projects in over seventy-seven states. See http://www.unocha.org/humansecurity/trust-fund/un-trust-fund-human-security, accessed 25 August 2014.

9. Documents, video proceedings, and statements of all United Nations General Assembly actions may be accessed through http://www.unocha.org/humansecurity/humansecurity/resources/publications-and-products/Human-Security-At-The-General-Assembly, accessed 4 June 2014.

10. This insight has given rise to a host of case studies that explore human security in practice. See Glasius and Kaldor 2006; MacLean et al. 2006; McRae and Hubert 2001.

11. See http://unocha.org/humansecurity/about-human-security/human-security-un, accessed 7 May 2013.

12. The point is iterated in the 2012 UNGA resolution framing human security as a tool.

13. Foucault (2007, 46) would also argue that care of the self is a tool of normalization, as it takes "the view of disorder and analyz[es] it with increasing subtly, that is to say, order is what remains . . . when everything that is prohibited has in fact been prevented."

14. Emphasis added.

15. Seidman found that for black men and lesbians, "'gay' signifies the experience

of a white, middle-class, urban culture organized around sex, consumerism, and civil rights" (120).

16. These subgroups maintain that their diversities may be captured by appending additional letters to the acronym LGBT or by generating new acronyms (which has the unfortunate consequence of proliferating silo mentalities). A more extreme position posits that we ought to abandon the LGBT designation altogether, on the grounds that sexual practice is not a "master category of . . . self-identity" (Seidman 1993, 121).

17. A vast and rich historically informed literature on sovereignty exists. See, for example, Thomson and Krasner 1989; Barkin and Cronin 1994; Chayes and Chayes 1995; Krasner 1999; Weinert 2007.

18. King and Murray (2001–2, 585), for instance, propose a "measurable definition of human security: the number of years of future life spent outside a state of 'generalized poverty.' . . . [meaning] when an individual falls below the threshold of any key domain of human well-being."

## Chapter 5

1. Arendt 1963a.

2. *Prosecutor v. Drazen Erdemovic* 1996, ¶28.

3. Robertson (2006, 372) recounts a Sarajevo joke, circa 1994: "When someone kills a man, he is put in prison. When someone kills twenty people, he is declared mentally insane. But when someone kills 200,000 people, he is invited to Geneva for peace negotiations." Robert Jackson (1945), chief prosecutor at Nuremberg, noted, in a similar vein, that "while it is quite proper to employ the fiction of responsibility of a state or corporation for the purpose of imposing a collective liability, it is quite intolerable to let such a legalism become the basis of personal immunity," which is precisely what mass murder has historically entailed.

4. Historical experiences of the stateless, especially during the interwar period, gave Hannah Arendt (1973, 296–97) fodder for her claim that the most fundamental human right is "the right to have rights."

5. Jackson 1945.

6. On the matter of Senegal's alleged violation of Article 5(2) of the Torture Convention—that Senegal did not amend its domestic law that would permit it to exercise universal jurisdiction in alleged torture cases—the ICJ ruled that it had no jurisdiction (ICJ 2012b, 28).

7. See http://legal.un.org/ilc/texts/instruments/english/commentaries/9_6_2001.pdf, accessed 4 June 2014. The 1996 version can be found at http://shodhganga.inflibnet.ac.in/bitstream/10603/11130/17/17_appendix.pdf, accessed 4 June 2014.

8. Tadić also assailed the legality of the tribunal, claiming that its establishment by the UNSC was an ultra vires act. The appeals chamber—perhaps not surprisingly, though not uncritically—affirmed the legality of the tribunal as established under the obligatory powers granted to the Security Council by the UN Charter. On the matter of the ICTY's jurisdictional primacy over national courts, appeals chamber judges maintained that in international (and domestic) law, only states, not individuals, have

the right to plead a violation of sovereignty (*Prosecutor v. Dusko Tadic* 1995, ¶55). In this instance, no state challenged Council decisions or brought forth a motion to this effect.

9. An article on international justice in the August 2012 *Christian Science Monitor* illustrates: "If you're a protectorate or client state of a Security Council member, chances are that the ICC prosecutor isn't going to be jumping out of his or her chair to open a full-blown criminal investigation. Why Libya and not Bashar al-Assad and Syria's bloody maelstrom? Ask Moscow. Why Cote d'Ivoire but not Mahinda Rajapaksa and the brutal ending to Sri Lanka's civil war? Ask Beijing. Why Kenya but not the violent suppression of protests in Yemen or Bahrain by those governments? Ask Washington" (Eckel 2012).

10. "Victims' Participation," Registry, Special Tribunal for Lebanon, http://www.stl-tsl.org/en/about-the-stl/structure-of-the-stl/registry/victim-participation, accessed 11 February 2012.

11. "Victim Participation Application Form," Registry, Special Tribunal for Lebanon, http://www.stl-tsl.org/en/about-the-stl/structure-of-the-stl/registry/victim-participation/application-form-for-participating-to-the-proceedings, accessed 11 February 2012.

12. http://www.trustfundforvictims.org/two-roles-tfv, accessed 22 December 2013.

13. http://www.trustfundforvictims.org/, accessed 22 December 2013.

14. Emphasis added. For ease of reference, I occasionally use the last name of the defendant rather than the full formal case designation. Cases are listed in the bibliography under *Prosecutor v. . . .*

15. The Trial Chamber in the *Blaškić* case (2000, ¶155, p. 52) defined "inhuman treatment" as including "not only acts such as torture and intentionally causing great suffering or inflicting serious injury to body, mind or health" but also "acts contravening the fundamental principle of humane treatment, in particular those which constitute an attack on human dignity. In the final analysis, deciding whether an act constitutes inhuman treatment is a question of fact to be ruled on with all the circumstances of the case in mind."

16. Mulisch (2005, 159) offered his services to a Dutch newspaper as a matter of self-exploration: he was what the Nazis would have called a half Jew (his mother was Jewish), while his father was a Dutch collaborator, for which he served three years in prison (xiv). For better or for worse, Mulisch's account reads as a supplement to Arendt's; she even declared that he "is almost the only writer on the subject to put the person of the defendant at the center of his report and whose evaluation of Eichmann coincides with my own on some essential points" (Arendt 1963a, 282).

17. This section adapts but substantially revises my 2006 review essay of Mulisch's book for *Human Rights and Human Welfare*.

18. On the tendency to discredit those who attempt to understand the human beings who commit egregious crimes as somehow justifying such behavior, see Waller 2002, 15–18.

19. The initial task of the SD was "to spy on [Nazi] party members, and thus to give the SS [of which the SD was part] an ascendancy over the regular party apparatus." See Arendt 1963a, 94, 95, 36.

20. Wechtenbruch served as assistant for the defense attorney in the case, Robert Servatius, and spoke with Eichmann "for months, every day for at least three hours" (Mulisch 2005, 43). Multiple psychiatrists affirmed Wechtenbruch's diagnosis.

21. Deborah Lipstadt (2011) and Mark Lilla (2013a, 2013b) reject Arendt's reading and find in Eichmann's testimony evidence of an erstwhile Nazi and anti-Semite.

22. If the Nazi horror had a precursor, an image, then, Mulisch (2005, 88) writes, it was foreshadowed in art: in Dante's ninth circle of hell and Goethe's *Faust*; in E. T. A. Hoffmann's *The Sandman*, whose titular character "brings in misery, distress, and transitory, eternal destruction everywhere he enters the scene" (90); and in André Breton's superlative imagery of obeying one's "fiercest and most frequent impulses," which would mean walking "out into the streets with a gun in [one's] hands" to see what would happen (quoted on 91). On this view, then, Hitler was no agent, though one could rightly argue he put into motion a systematic slaughter only inferentially imagined. Artistically, "Hitler's world was depicted before its arrival" (92).

23. The actual imperative as Kant framed it reads, "Act only according to that maxim by which you can at the same time will that it would become a universal law." Mulisch (2005, 113, 143, 156) only tangentially refers to this high point in Eichmann's testimony.

24. Arendt reports, "In less than two months, 147 trains, carrying 434,351 people in sealed freight cars, a hundred persons to a car, left [Hungary], and the gas chambers at Auschwitz were hardly able to cope with the multitude" (1963a, 140). This figure represents more than half the Jewish population.

25. For a similar argument, see also Marcuse 1964; Waller 2002, 202–29). Arendt (1973, 307), too, anticipated the idea, but with a slightly different emphasis: "[T]he disturbing factor in the success of totalitarianism is rather the true selflessness of its adherents: it may be understandable that a Nazi or a Bolshevik will not be shaken in his conviction by crimes against people who do not belong to the movement or are even hostile to it; but the amazing fact is that neither is he likely to waver when the monster begins to devour its own children and not even if he becomes a victim of persecution himself, if he is framed and condemned, if he is purged from the party and sent to a forced-labor or a concentration camp. On the contrary, to the wonder of the whole civilized world, he may even be willing to help in his own prosecution and frame his own death sentence if only his status as a member of the movement is not touched."

26. My comments here echo Gurr's "frustration-aggression thesis" (1969).

## Chapter 6

1. Cançado Trindade 2010, ¶53, ¶65.

2. For a comprehensive review of developments with respect to internal and external self-determination, see Wheatley 2005.

3. Christine Chinkin, a leading feminist theorist of international law, argues for the reconstruction of the concept of self-determination to embrace both men and women: "One should recognize that to take the 'self' as 'a single relevant' entity is actually 'masking the fact that the most powerful identity is usually a construct of the most

powerful players in the group,' and as a result, this self is most often male" (quoted in Nijman 2004, 440).

4. Elizabeth Chadwick (2011, 8) casts a sober, somewhat pessimistic light on self-determination, arguing that "very few peoples have succeeded in acquiring rights of self-determination without the consent of their state and/or of the broader international community, and fewer still have attained complete independence, either *de facto* or *de jure*, through the use of force and/or secessionist tactics."

5. Jan Klabbers (2006), whose argument I treat later in this chapter, distances self-determination from territoriality and conceives it as a "bundle of procedural rights: a right to be heard and to be taken seriously" (202; see also Young 2000).

6. Hurst Hannum (2011, 156) provides one of the more colorful criticisms of the narrow opinion, declaring it to be "lame."

7. Indeed, a state's treatment of its minority peoples serves as an entry point for international community involvement (see Wheatley 2005).

8. The ICJ's advisory opinion regarding the legal consequences of the construction of a wall in the occupied Palestinian territory reaffirmed the covenant's conferral of an obligation on states "to promote the realization of [the right to self-determination] and to respect it, in conformity with the provisions of the Charter of the United Nations" (ICJ 2004, ¶88, p. 172).

9. Of the regional human rights documents, only the African Charter on Human and Peoples' Rights mentions self-determination, albeit in the restrictive contexts of domination (Article 19) or oppression and colonization (Article 20).

10. Hannum (2011, 157–58) questions the degree to which the humanitarian crisis provides any basis for claims to remedial secession.

11. The court's Chinese judge at the time, Shi Jiuyong, had announced his retirement and thus did not participate in the proceedings.

12. I omit from consideration Judge Kenneth Keith's separate opinion. He opined that the ICJ should have declined the General Assembly's request, as it ought, on his view, to have come from the Security Council. Nevertheless, he concurred with the majority.

13. Consider that the Clinton administration repeatedly emphasized Kosovo's right of self-determination in the months leading up to NATO's air campaign against Serbia. Also, the Rambouillet Accords, to which Milošević refused to accede, "contained a provision allowing for the 'will of the people' to determine a 'final settlement' for the province's international status" (Ambrosio 2002, 344).

14. Article 1(6), further, extends conditional governance over nonmembers, insofar as it maintains that "the Organization shall ensure that states which are not Members of the United Nations act in accordance with these Principles so far as may be necessary for the maintenance of international peace and security."

15. That conclusion very much echoes a lacunae exposed by the US Supreme Court with regard to US treatment of international law. In *Medellin v. Texas* (2007), a majority reaffirmed, by a vote of 6 to 3, that treaties in the United States cannot be assumed to be self-executing; in the absence of implementing congressional legislation, nonfederal or substate actors are not bound by international treaties even if the obligations in such treaties are clearly intended for such agents (as they were in the Vienna Convention on Consular Relations, the subject of *Medellin*).

16. Kosovo is an official member state of the World Bank (effective 29 June 2009); the International Monetary Fund (effective 29 June 2009); the International Bar Association (effective 28 May 2009); and, by late 2012, the European Bank for Reconstruction and Development (World Bank 2014). As of 8 June 2014, 108 of 193 UN member states (or 55.96 percent of membership) recognize Kosovo; 39 of them did so after the advisory opinion was issued, 8 after the Kosovo-Servia agreement of April 2013. See http://www.kosovothanksyou.com/, accessed 10 January 2014.

## Chapter 7

1. Onuf 1989, 46.
2. Benedict 2009, ¶24.
3. See S/Res/1308 (17 July 2000) and S/Res/1983 (7 June 2011).
4. Most of these resolutions pertain to the two ad hoc international criminal tribunals for the former Yugoslavia and Rwanda. However, Resolutions 1593 (31 March 2005) and 1970 (26 February 2011) referred the situations in Sudan and Libya, respectively, to the International Criminal Court.
5. The Council has passed thirty-five resolutions related to terrorism, including hostage taking and airline hijacking, from 1946 through 5 June 2014.
6. For example, S/Res/1459 (28 January 2003).
7. On this point, I read Arendt's later thoughts as explanation of her earlier ones. Her discussion of disintegrative tendencies—that is, the disposal of "traditionally accepted metaphysical and religious beliefs" that "accompanied the grandiose development of the natural sciences and the victory of the nation state over all other forms of government," which, though they took "centuries to undermine the ancient beliefs and political ways of life," in "a few decades" broke down "beliefs and ways of life in all other parts of the world" (1968a, 82–83)—illuminates her previous argument, in *Origins* (1973, ix), that "the subterranean stream of Western history has finally come to the surface and usurped the dignity of our tradition."
8. Cf. Martin Buber's conception of the "between" as "the real place and bearer of what happens between" humans. He explains that "it has received no specific attention because, in distinction from the individual souls and its context, it does not exhibit a smooth continuity, but is ever and again re-constituted in accordance with [human beings'] meetings with one another; hence what is experience has been annexed naturally to the continuous elements, the soul and its world" (1965, 203).
9. Contracting parties assert their determination "to put an end to the suffering and casualties caused by anti-personnel mines, that kill or maim hundreds of people every week, mostly innocent and defenceless civilians and especially children, obstruct economic development and reconstruction, inhibit the repatriation of refugees and internally displaced persons, and have other severe consequences for years after emplacement," and "to do their utmost in providing assistance for the care and rehabilitation, including the social and economic reintegration of mine victims." Contracting states also recognize "that a total ban of anti-personnel mines would also be an important confidence-building measure" (Ottawa Convention 1997, preamble).
10. Examples are campaigns regarding the plight of endangered species; environ-

mental degradation; transmission, detection, treatment, and prevention of infectious diseases, such as avian flu and HIV/AIDS; and the promotion of human rights.

11. See, for instance, Wheeler's work on saving strangers (2000), Meron's on the humanization of the law of war (2000a, 2000b), Linklater's on cosmopolitan harm conventions (2001), Cronin's on minority protection regimes (2003), and Teitel's on humanity's law (2011).

12. Indicative that the moral advance represented by international protection regimes and cosmopolitan harm conventions cannot and should not be overstated, Cronin and Linklater concede that ethical development in international relations remains stunted because of bias and selective application. Among many other elements we may add to that list of causes is resentment. Linklater observes "that the West has had the upper hand in defining the rights that most deserve protection is bitterly resented in many non-Western societies" (2001, 272–73). Along similar lines, Cronin reveals that some international protection regimes, such as the regime based on the interwar minority treaties, were unequally applied; in part, resulting resentment led to that regime's collapse.

# Bibliography

ACLU (American Civil Liberties Union). 2011. "Non-Discrimination Laws: State-by-State Information." Accessed 3 June 2012. http://www.aclu.org/maps/non-discrimination-laws-state-state-information-map.

Adler, Emmanuel, and Vincent Pouliot, eds. 2011. *International Practices*. Cambridge: Cambridge University Press.

Agamben, Giorgio. 1993. *The Coming Community*. Minneapolis: University of Minnesota Press.

Agamben, Giorgio. 1998. Homer Sacer: *Sovereign Power and Bare Life*. Translated by Daniel Heller-Roazen. Stanford: Stanford University Press.

Agamben, Giorgio. 2000. *Means without End: Notes on Politics*. Translated by Vincenzo Binetti and Cesare Casarino. Minneapolis: University of Minnesota Press.

Aiken, Nevin. 2010. "Learning to Live Together: Transitional Justice and Intergroup Reconciliation in Northern Ireland." *International Journal of Transitional Justice* 4 (2): 166–88.

Akhavan, Payam. 2001. "Beyond Impunity: Can International Criminal Justice Prevent Future Atrocities?" *American Journal of International Law* 95 (1): 7–31.

Alvarez, Jose. 2003. "Hegemonic International Law Revisited." *American Journal of International Law* 97 (4): 873–88.

Alvarez, Jose. 2006. *International Organizations as Law-Makers*. New York: Oxford University Press.

Ambrosio, Thomas. 2002. "The Accommodation of Nations in Inter*state* Law: Some Preliminary Conclusions." In *International Law and the Rise of Nations: The State System and the Challenge of Ethnic Groups*, edited by Robert J. Beck and Thomas Ambrosio, 341–52. New York: Chatham House Publishers of Seven Bridges Press.

Anghie, Antony. 2004. *Imperialism, Sovereignty, and the Making of International Law*. Cambridge: Cambridge University Press.

Annan, Kofi. 2000. *We the Peoples: The Role of the United Nations in the 21st Century*. New York: United Nations Department of Public Information. Accessed 22 January 2012. http://www.un.org/millennium/sg/report/ch0.pdf.

Annan, Kofi. 2005. *In Larger Freedom: Towards Development, Security, and Human*

*Rights For All.* Report of the Secretary-General. A/59/2005. 21 March. Accessed 22 January 2012. http://www.un.org/largerfreedom/contents.htm.

Arendt, Hannah. [1943] 2007. "We Refugees." In *The Jewish Writings*, edited by Jerome Kohn and Ron Feldman, 264–74. New York: Schocken.

Arendt, Hannah. [1944] 2007. "The Jew as Pariah: A Hidden Tradition." In *The Jewish Writings*, edited by Jerome Kohn and Ron Feldman, 275–97. New York: Schocken.

Arendt, Hannah. 1951. *The Burden of Our Time.* London: Secker and Warburg.

Arendt, Hannah [1957] 1997. *Rahel Varnhagen: The Life of a Jewess.* Edited by Liliane Weissberg. Translated by Richard and Clara Winston. Baltimore: Johns Hopkins University Press.

Arendt, Hannah. 1958. *The Human Condition.* Chicago: University of Chicago Press.

Arendt, Hannah. 1963a. *Eichmann in Jerusalem: A Report on the Banality of Evil.* New York: Penguin.

Arendt, Hannah. 1963b. *On Revolution.* New York: Penguin.

Arendt, Hannah. 1968a. "Karl Jaspers: Citizen of the World?" In *Men in Dark Times*, 81–94. New York: Harvest.

Arendt, Hannah. 1968b. "On Humanity in Dark Times: Thoughts about Lessing." In *Men in Dark Times*, 3–31. New York: Harvest.

Arendt, Hannah. 1972. *Crises of the Republic.* New York: Harcourt Brace Jovanovich / Harvest.

Arendt, Hannah. 1973. *The Origins of Totalitarianism.* New York: Harcourt Brace Jovanovich / Harvest.

Arendt, Hannah. 1982. *Lectures on Kant's Political Philosophy.* Edited by Ronald Beiner. Chicago: University of Chicago Press.

Arendt, Hannah. 1993. "The Crisis in Education." In *Between Past and Future*, 173–96. New York: Penguin.

Arendt, Hannah. 1994. *Essays in Understanding, 1930–1954.* Edited by Jerome Kohn. New York: Harcourt Brace.

Arendt, Hannah. 2005. "Introduction *into* Politics." In *The Promise of Politics*, 93–200. New York: Schocken.

ASEAN (Association of Southeast Asian Nations).1976. *Declaration of ASEAN Concord.* Indonesia, 24 February. Accessed 3 June 2014. http://www.asean.org/news/item/declaration-of-asean-concord-indonesia-24-february-1976.

Associated Press. 2011. "Palestinians to Seek UN Recognition for Independent State in September." Haaretz.com, 10 January. Accessed 10 January 2011. http://www.haaretz.com/news/diplomacy-defense/palestinians-to-seek-un-recognition-for-independent-state-in-september-1.336215.

Axworthy, Lloyd. 2001. Introduction to *Human Security and the New Diplomacy: Protecting People, Promoting Peace*, edited by Rob McRae and Don Hubert, 3–13. Montreal: McGill University Press.

Bain, William. 2003. *Between Anarchy and Society: Trusteeship and the Obligations of Power.* Oxford: Oxford University Press.

Ban, Ki-moon. 2013. *A Life of Dignity for All: Accelerating Progress towards the Millennium Development Goals and Advancing the United Nations Development Agenda beyond 2015.* Report of the Secretary-General. A/68/202. 26 July. Accessed 3

June 2014. http://www.un.org/millenniumgoals/pdf/A%20Life%20of%20Dig nity%20for%20All.pdf.

Barker, Ernest, trans. 1958. *The Politics of Aristotle*. London: Oxford University Press.

Barkin, J. Samuel, and Bruce Cronin. 1994. "The State and the Nation: Changing Norms and the Rules of Sovereignty in International Relations." *International Organization* 48 (1): 107–30.

Barnett, Michael, and Raymond Duvall. 2005. *Power in Global Governance*. Cambridge: Cambridge University Press.

Barry, Brian. 1999. "Statism and Nationalism: A Cosmopolitan Critique." In *Global Justice*, edited by Ian Shapiro and L. Brilmayer, 12–66. New York: New York University Press.

Bartelson, Jens. 2009. *Visions of World Community*. Cambridge: Cambridge University Press.

Bassiouni, M. Cherif. 1996. "International Crimes: *Jus Cogens* and *Obligatio Erga Omnes*." *Law and Contemporary Problems* 59 (4): 63–74.

Bawer, Bruce. 1993. *A Place at the Table: The Gay Individual in American Society*. New York: Simon and Schuster.

Bedeski, Robert. 2007. *Human Security and the Chinese State: Historical Transformations and the Modern Quest for Sovereignty*. New York: Routledge.

Beiner, Ronald. 1997. *Philosophy in a Time of Lost Spirit: Essays on Contemporary Theory*. Toronto: University of Toronto Press.

Benedict XVI. 2009. *Caritas in Veritate*. Accessed 20 May 2012. http://www.vatican. va/holy_father/benedict_xvi/encyclicals/documents/hf_ben-xvi_enc_20090629_ caritas-in-veritate_en.html.

Benhabib, Seyla. 2010. "International Law and Human Plurality in the Shadow of Totalitarianism: Hannah Arendt and Raphael Lemkin." In *Politics in Dark Times: Encounters with Hannah Arendt*, edited by Seyla Benhabib, 219–43. New York: Cambridge University Press.

Berkeley, Bill. 2002. "Road to a Genocide." In *The New Killing Fields: Massacre and the Politics of Intervention*, edited by Nicolaus Mills and Kira Brunner, 103–16. New York: Basic Books.

Berman, Nathaniel. 2002. "The International Law of Nationalism: Group Identity and Legal History." In *International Law and the Rise of Nations: The State System and the Challenge of Ethnic Groups*, edited by Robert J. Beck and Thomas Ambrosio, 106–35. New York: Chatham House Publishers of Seven Bridges Press.

Bernstein, Richard. 2002. *Radical Evil: A Philosophical Investigation*. Cambridge: Polity.

Bethell, Leslie. 1966. "The Mixed Commissions for the Suppression of the Transatlantic Slave Trade in the Nineteenth Century." *Journal of African History* 7 (1): 79–93.

Birmingham, Peg. 2006. *Hannah Arendt and Human Rights: The Predicament of Common Responsibility*. Indianapolis: Indiana University Press.

Bleiker, Roland. 2000. *Popular Dissent, Human Agency, and Global Politics*. Cambridge: Cambridge University Press.

Blum, Yehuda. 2005. "Proposals for UN Security Council Reform." *American Journal of International Law* 99 (3): 632–49.

Booth, Ken, et al., eds. 2001. *How Might We Live? Global Ethics in the New Century.* Cambridge: Cambridge University Press.

Booth, Wayne. 1993. "Individualism and the Mystery of the Social Self; or, Does Amnesty Have a Leg to Stand On?" In *Freedom and Interpretation: The Oxford Amnesty Lectures, 1992,* edited by Barbara Johnson, 69–101. New York: Basic Books.

Bosco, David. 2009. *Five to Rule Them All: The UN Security Council and the Making of the Modern World.* New York: Oxford University Press.

Bouris, Erica. 2007. *Complex Political Victims.* Bloomfield, CT: Kumarian.

Brown, Chris. 2001. "World Society and the English School: An 'International Society' Perspective on World Society." *European Journal of International Relations* 7 (4): 423–41.

Brownlie, Ian. 1964. "The Place of the Individual in International Law." *Virginia Law Review* 50 (3): 435–62.

Buber, Martin. 1950. *Paths in Utopia.* Translated by R. F. C. Hull. New York: MacMillan.

Buber, Martin. 1965. *Between Man and Man.* New York: Collier Books.

Bull, Hedley. 1966. "The Grotian Conception of International Society." In *Diplomatic Investigations: Essays in the Theory of International Relations,* edited by Herbert Butterfield and Martin Wight, 51–73. Cambridge, MA: Harvard University Press.

Bull, Hedley. 1977. "The State's Positive Role in World Affairs." *Daedalus* 108 (4): 111–23.

Bull, Hedley. 1995. *The Anarchical Society: A Study of Order in World Politics.* New York: Columbia University Press.

Bull, Hedley, and Adam Watson, eds. 1984. *The Expansion of International Society.* Oxford: Clarendon.

Burke, Anthony. 2008. "Recovering Humanity from Man: Hannah Arendt's Troubled Cosmopolitanism." *International Politics* 45 (4): 514–21.

Burton, John. 1972. *World Society.* Cambridge: Cambridge University Press.

Bush, George. 2002. "President Outlines U.S. Plan to Help World's Poor." Remarks at the United Nations Financing for Development Conference, Cintermex Convention Center, Monterrey, Mexico. Accessed 26 June 2014. http://georgewbushwhitehouse.archives.gov/news/releases/2002/03/20020322-1.html.

Butler, Judith. 2011. "Hannah Arendt's Challenge to Adolf Eichmann." *Guardian,* 29 August. Accessed 16 January 2014. http://www.theguardian.com/commentisfree/2011/aug/29/hannah-arendt-adolf-eichmann-banality-of-evil.

Butler, Judith, and Joan Scott, eds. 1992. *Feminists Theorize the Political.* New York: Routledge.

Buzan, Barry. 1993. "From International System to International Society: Structural Realism and Regime Theory Meet the English School." *International Organization* 47 (3): 327–52.

Buzan, Barry. 2001. "The English School: An Underexploited Resource in IR." *Review of International Studies* 27 (3): 471–88.

Buzan, Barry. 2004a. *From International to World Society? English School Theory and the Structure of Globalisation.* Cambridge: Cambridge University Press.

Buzan, Barry. 2004b. "A Reductionist, Idealistic Notion that Adds Little Analytical Value." *Security Dialogue* 35 (3): 369–70.

Buzan, Barry. 2005. "International Political Economy and Globalization." In *International Society and Its Critics*, edited by Alex J. Bellamy, 115–34. Oxford: Oxford University Press.

Buzan, Barry 2006. "An English School Perspective on 'What Kind of World Order?'" *Cooperation and Conflict* 41 (4): 364–69.

Cançado Trindade, Antonio. 2010. *Separate Opinion of Judge Cançado Trindade*. Accessed 25 May 2012. http://www.icj-cij.org/docket/files/141/16003.pdf.

Carafano, James Jay, and Janice Smith. 2006. "The Muddled Notion of 'Human Security' at the UN: A Guide for US Policymakers." *Backgrounder* 1966:1–14. Accessed 9 September 2008. www.heritage.org/Research/WorldwideFreedom/upload/bg_1966.pdf.

Carpenter, Charli. 2005. "'Women, Children, and Other Vulnerable Groups': Gender, Strategic Frames, and the Protection of Civilians as a Transnational Issue." *International Studies Quarterly* 49 (2): 295–334.

Carr, E. H. 1961. *What Is History?* New York: Vintage Books.

Carter, Barry, et al. 2007. *International Law*. New York. Wolters Kluwer / Aspen.

Cassese, Antonio. 1995. *Self-Determination of Peoples: A Legal Reappraisal*. Cambridge: Cambridge University Press.

Cassese, Antonio. 2008. *International Criminal Law*. Oxford: Oxford University Press.

Cave, Damien. 2010. "Fighting Starvation, Haitians Share Portions." *New York Times*, 25 January. Accessed 26 January 2010. http://www.nytimes.com/2010/01/26/world/americas/26hunger.html?hp.

Chadwick, Elizabeth. 2011. *Self-Determination in the Post-9/11 Era*. New York: Routledge.

Charlesworth, Hilary, Christine Chinkin, and Shelley Wright. 1991. "Feminist Approaches to International Law." *American Journal of International Law* 85 (4): 613–45.

*Charter of the United Nations*. 1945. New York: United Nations. http://www.un.org/en/documents/charter/. Accessed 3 June 2014.

Chayes, Abram, and Antonia Handler Chayes. 1995. *The New Sovereignty: Compliance with International Regulatory Agreements*. Cambridge, MA: Harvard University Press.

Chesterman, Simon, et al. 2008. *Law and Practice of the United Nations: Documents and Commentary*. New York: Oxford University Press.

CHS (Commission on Human Security). 2003a. *Outline of the Report of the Commission on Human Security*. Accessed 18 June 2011. http://www.humansecurity-chs.org/finalreport/index.html.

CHS. 2003b. *Human Security Now*. Accessed 18 June 2010. http://www.humansecurity-chs.org/finalreport/English/FinalReport.pdf.

Clinton, Hillary Rodham. 2011. "Remarks in Recognition of International Human Rights Day." *U.S. Department of State*, 6 December. Accessed August 23, 2013. http://www.state.gov/secretary/rm/2011/12/178368.htm.

Cohen, G. A. 1988. *History, Labour, and Freedom: Themes from Marx*. Oxford: Oxford University Press.

Confortini, Catia. 2012. *Intelligent Compassion: Feminist Critical Methodology in the Women's International League for Peace and Freedom*. New York: Oxford University Press.

Cornell, Drucilla. 1995. "What Is Ethical Feminism?" In *Feminist Contentions: A Philosophical Exchange*, 75–106. New York: Routledge.

Cornell, Drucilla. 2010. "Thinking Big in Dark Times." In *Thinking in Dark Times: Hannah Arendt on Ethics and Politics*, edited by Roger Berkowitz et al., 221–27. New York: Fordham University Press.

Corrie, Karen. 2007. "Victims' Participation and Defendants' Due Process Rights: Compatible Regimes at the International Criminal Court." American Non-Governmental Organizations Coalition for the International Criminal Court. Accessed 19 May 2012. http://www.amicc.org/docs/Corrie%20Victims.pdf.

Costa, Antonio. 2005. "Talking Points at the Meeting with Representatives of Member States." United Nations Office on Drugs and Crimes. 6 May. Accessed 28 July 2012. http://www.antoniomariacosta.com/cc/index.php?option=com_content&view=article&id=233:talking-points-at-the-meeting-with-representatives-of-member-states&catid=37:unodc-speeches&Itemid=48.

Cox, Robert. 1986. "Social Forces, States, and World Orders: Beyond International Relations Theory." In *Neorealism and Its Critics*, edited by Robert Keohane, 204–54. New York: Columbia University Press.

Crawford, Neta. 2002. *Argument and Change in World Politics: Ethics, Decolonization, and Humanitarian Intervention*. Cambridge: Cambridge University Press.

Cronin, Bruce. 2003. *Institutions for the Common Good: International Protection Regimes in International Society*. Cambridge: Cambridge University Press.

Daget, Serge. 1980. "A Model of the French Abolitionist Movement and Its Variations." In *Anti-Slavery, Religion, and Reform: Essays in Memory of Roger Anstey*, edited by Christine Bolt and Seymour Drescher, 64–79. Kent, UK: Wm. Dawson and Sons.

Dahbour, Omar. 2013. *Self-Determination without Nationalism: A Theory of Postnational Sovereignty*. Philadelphia: Temple University Press.

Daly, Erin. 2013. *Dignity Rights: Courts, Constitutions, and the Worth of the Human Person*. Philadelphia: University of Pennsylvania Press.

d'Anjou, Leo. 1996. *Social Movements and Cultural Change: The First Abolition Campaign Revisited*. New York: Aldine de Gruyter.

David, Roman, and Susanne Choi. 2005. "Victims on Transitional Justice: Lessons from the Reparation of Human Rights Abuses in the Czech Republic." *Human Rights Quarterly* 27 (2): 392–435.

David, Roman, and Susanne Choi. 2009. "Getting Even or Getting Equal? Retributive Desires and Transitional Justice." *Political Psychology* 30 (2): 161–92.

Davis, David Brion. 1984. *Slavery and Human Progress*. New York: Oxford University Press.

de Beauvoir, Simone. [1948] 1994. *The Ethics of Ambiguity*. Translated by Bernard Fretchman. New York: Citadel.

De Larrinaga, Miguel, and Marc Doucet. 2008. "Sovereign Power and the Biopolitics of Human Security." *Security Dialogue* 39 (5): 517–37.

Dickinson, Laura. 2003. "The Promise of Hybrid Courts." *American Journal of International Law* 97 (2): 295–310.

Donadio, Rachel, and Laurie Goodstein. 2009. "Pope Urges Forming New World Economic Order to Work for the 'Common Good.'" *New York Times*, 7 July. Accessed

19 January 2014. http://www.nytimes.com/2009/07/08/world/europe/08pope.html?ref=world.

Duffield, Mark. 2006. "Human Security: Linking Development and Security in an Age of Terror." In *New Interfaces between Security and Development: Changing Concepts and Approaches*, edited by Stephan Klingebiel, 11–38. Bonn: Deutsches Institut für Entwicklungspolitik.

Dunne, Timothy, and Nicholas Wheeler. 1996. "Hedley Bull's Pluralism of the Intellect and Solidarism of the Will." *International Affairs* 72 (1): 91–107.

Eagleton, Terry. 2010. *On Evil*. New Haven: Yale University Press.

ECCC (Extraordinary Chambers in the Courts of Cambodia). 2011. Internal Rules (Rev. 8). 3 August. Accessed 30 June 2012. http://www.eccc.gov.kh/sites/default/files/legal-documents/ECCC%20Internal%20Rules%20%28Rev.8%29%20English.pdf.

Eckel, Mike. 2012. "Is International Justice Finally Finding Its Footing?" *Christian Science Monitor*, 7 August. Accessed 16 August 2012. http://www.csmonitor.com/World/Global-News/2012/0807/Is-international-justice-finally-finding-its-footing.

*Edwards v. Attorney General of Canada*. 1930. AC 124, 1929 UKPC 86. Accessed 24 October 2013. http://www.chrc-ccdp.ca/en/browseSubjects/edwardspc.asp.

Emmers, Ralf. 2004. "Security Cooperation in the Asia-Pacific: Evolution of Concepts and Practices." In *Asia-Pacific Security Cooperation: National Interests and Regional Order*, edited by See Seng Tan and Amitav Acharya, 3–18. Armonk, NY: M. E. Sharpe.

Engster, Daniel. 2007. *The Heart of Justice: Care Ethics and Political Theory*. New York: Oxford University Press.

Enloe, Cynthia. 1996. "Margins, Silences, and Bottom Rungs: How to Overcome the Underestimation of Power in the Study of International Relations." In *International Theory: Positivism and Beyond*, edited by Steve Smith, Ken Booth, and Marysia Zalewski, 186–202. Cambridge: Cambridge University Press.

Enloe, Cynthia. 2000. *Bananas and Bases: Making a Feminist Sense of International Politics*. Berkeley: University of California Press.

Erlanger, Steven. 2011. "France Enforces Ban on Full-Face Veils in Public." *New York Times*, 11 April. Accessed 6 June 2012. http://www.nytimes.com/2011/04/12/world/europe/12france.html.

European Forum. 2014. "Kosovo." Accessed 10 January 2014. http://www.europeanforum.net/country/kosovo.

Falk, Richard. 1999. *Predatory Globalization: A Critique*. Cambridge: Polity.

Fanon, Frantz. 1963. *The Wretched of the Earth*. New York: Grove.

Fassin, Didier. 2010. "Ethics of Survival: A Democratic Approach to the Politics of Life." *Humanity: An International Journal of Human Rights, Humanitarianism, and Development* 1 (1): 81–95.

Feinberg, Kenneth. 2005. *What Is Life Worth? The Unprecedented Effort to Compensate the Victims of 9/11*. New York: Public Affairs.

Festa, Lynn. 2010. "Humanity without Feathers." *Humanity: An International Journal of Human Rights, Humanitarianism, and Development* 1 (1): 3–28.

Fierstein, Harvey. 2013. "Russia's Anti-Gay Crackdown." *New York Times*, 21 July.

Accessed 28 July 2013. http://www.nytimes.com/2013/07/22/opinion/russias-anti-gay-crackdown.html.

Fine, Robert. 2007. *Cosmopolitanism*. New York: Routledge.

Finnemore, Martha. 2001. "Exporting the English School?" *Review of International Studies* 27 (3): 509–13.

Fitzpatrick, Laura. 2010. "Why Do Women Still Earn Less than Men?" *Time*, 20 April. Accessed 24 June 2012. http://www.time.com/time/nation/article/0,8599,1983185,00.html.

Foucault, Michel. 1986. *The Care of the Self*. Vol. 3 of *The History of Sexuality*. Translated by R. Hurley. New York: Vintage Books.

Foucault, Michel. 2003. *Society Must Be Defended: Lectures at the Collège de France, 1975–1976*. New York: Picador.

Foucault, Michel. 2007. *Security, Territory, Population: Lectures at the College de France 1977–1978*. New York: Picador.

Fraser, Nancy. 2000. "Rethinking Recognition." *New Left Review* 3:107–20.

Fraser, Nancy. 1995. "From Redistribution to Recognition? Dilemmas of Justice in a 'Post-Socialist' Age." *New Left Review* I/212:68–93.

Frost, Mervyn. 1986. *Towards a Normative Theory of International Relations*. Cambridge: Cambridge University Press.

George, Vic, and Paul Wilding. 2002. *Globalization and Human Welfare*. New York: Palgrave.

Gennarini, Stefano. 2012. "Sexual Orientation and Gender Identity Still Divide UN Assembly." 21 November. Accessed 9 July 2013. http://www.turtlebayandbeyond.org/2012/homosexuality/sexual-orientation-and-gender-identity-still-divide-general-assembly/.

Gilbert, Alan. 1999. *Must Global Politics Constrain Democracy? Great-Power Realism, Democratic Peace, and Democratic Internationalism*. Princeton: Princeton University Press.

Glasius, Marlies, and Mary Kaldor, eds. 2006. *A Human Security Doctrine for Europe: Project, Principles, Practicalities*. New York: Routledge.

Goldhagen, Daniel Jonah. 1996. *Hitler's Willing Executioners: Ordinary Germans and the Holocaust*. New York: Vintage Books.

Gong, Gerritt. 1984. *The Standard of "Civilization" in International Society*. Oxford: Clarendon.

Goodrich, Leland, and Edvard Hambro. 1949. *Charter of the United Nations: Commentary and Documents*. Boston: World Peace Foundation.

Goodrich, Leland, et al. 1969. *Charter of the United Nations: Commentary and Documents*. 3rd ed. New York: Columbia University Press.

Gordon, Gregory. 2012. "The Trial of Peter Von Hagenbach: Reconciling History, Historiography, and International Criminal Law." 16 February. Accessed 23 May 2012. http://ssrn.com/abstract=2006370 or http://dx.doi.org/10.2139/ssrn.2006370.

Gottsegen, Michael. 1994. *The Political Thought of Hannah Arendt*. Albany: State University of New York Press.

Greenstock, Jeremy. 2008. "The Security Council in the Post–Cold War World." In *The United Nations Security Council and War: The Evolution of Thought and Practice since 1945*, edited by S. Vaughan Lowe et al., 248–62. New York: Oxford University Press.

Gross, Aeyal. 2007. "Queer Theory and International Human Rights Law: Does Each Person Have a Sexual Orientation?" *Proceedings of the Annual Meeting of the American Society of International Law* 101:129–32.

Guenther, Lisa. 2012. "The Living Death of Solitary Confinement." *New York Times*, 26 August. Accessed 17 February 2013. http://opinionator.blogs.nytimes.com/2012/08/26/the-living-death-of-solitary-confinement/?hp&gwh=43D7E55949665B69278006EA0AE68931.

Gurr, Ted Robert. 1969. *Why Men Rebel*. Princeton: Princeton University Press.

Gvosdev, Nikolas. 2013. "Kosovo and Serbia Make a Deal: Debalkanizing the Balkans." *Foreign Affairs*, 24 April. Accessed 10 January 2014. http://www.foreignaffairs.com/articles/139346/nikolas-k-gvosdev/kosovo-and-serbia-make-a-deal.

Halliday, Fred. 1992. "International Society as Homogeneity: Burke, Marx, Fukuyama." *Millennium: Journal of International Studies* 21 (3): 435–61.

Halperin, Morton, and David Scheffer. 1992. *Self-Determination in the New World Order*. With Patricia Small. Washington, DC: Carnegie Endowment for International Peace.

Hammarksjöld, Dag. 2005. *To Speak for the World: Speeches and Statements by Dag Hammarksjöld*. Stockholm: Atlantis.

Hannum, Hurst. 2002. "Rethinking Self-Determination." In *International Law and the Rise of Nations: The State System and the Challenge of Ethnic Groups*, edited by Robert J. Beck and Thomas Ambrosio, 214–49. New York: Chatham House Publishers of Seven Bridges Press.

Hannum, Hurst. 2011. "The Advisory Opinion on Kosovo: An Opportunity Lost, or a Poisoned Chalice Refused?" *Leiden Journal of International Law* 24 (1): 155–61.

Haque, Adil Ahmad. 2005. "Group Violence and Group Vengeance: Toward a Retributivist Theory of International Criminal Law." *Buffalo Criminal Law Review* 9 (1): 273–328.

Harbour, Frances. 1999. *Thinking about International Ethics: Moral Theory and Cases from American Foreign Policy*. Boulder, CO: Westview.

Hayden, Patrick. 2005. *Cosmopolitan Global Politics*. Burlington, VT: Ashgate.

Hayden, Patrick. 2009. *Political Evil in a Global Age: Hannah Arendt and International Theory*. London: Routledge.

Hegel, Georg Wilhelm Friedrich. 1952. *Hegel's Philosophy of Right*. Translated by T. K. Knox. London: Oxford University Press.

Held, David. 1995. *Democracy and the Global Order: From the Modern State to Cosmopolitan Governance*. Stanford: Stanford University Press.

Held, Virginia. 2006. *The Ethics of Care: Personal, Political, and Global*. Oxford: Oxford University Press.

Hicks, Donna. 2011. *Dignity: The Essential Role It Plays in Resolving Conflicts*. New Haven: Yale University Press.

Hirsh, David. 2003. *Law against Genocide: Cosmopolitan Trials*. London: Cavendish Publishing / GlassHouse.

Hiscocks, Richard. 1973. *The Security Council: A Study in Adolescence*. New York: Free Press.

Hobbes, Thomas. [1668] 1994. *Leviathan*. Edited by Edwin Curley. Indianapolis: Hackett.

Hobbes, Thomas. 1949. *De Cive, or The Citizen*. New York: Appleton-Century-Crofts.

Hoffmann, Matthew. 2009. "Is Constructivist Ethics an Oxymoron?" *International Studies Review* 11:231–52.

Hoge, Warren. 2008. "Intervention, Hailed as a Concept, Is Shunned in Practice." *New York Times*, 20 January. Accessed 5 June 2011. http://www.nytimes.com/2008/01/20/world/africa/20nations.html.

Holbrook, David, ed. 1990. *What Is It to Be Human? New Perspectives in Philosophy*. Aldershot: Avebury.

Honig, Bonnie. 1992. "Toward an Agonistic Feminism: Hannah Arendt and the Politics of Identity." In *Feminists Theorize the Political*, edited by Judith Butler and Joan Scott, 215–35. New York: Routledge.

Honneth, Axel. 1995. *The Struggle for Recognition: The Moral Grammar of Social Conflicts*. Cambridge: Polity.

Horkheimer, Max. 1974. *Eclipse of Reason*. New York: Seabury.

Howard, Rhoda, and Jack Donnelly. 1986. "Human Dignity, Human Rights, and Political Regimes." *American Political Science Review* 80 (3): 801–17.

HSU (Human Security Unit). 2006. *Human Security for All: Integrated Responses to Protect and Empower People and Their Communities: A Look at Nine Promising Efforts*. New York: United Nations. Accessed 18 June 2011. http://ochaonline.un.org/Reports/BookletHumanSecurityforAll/tabid/2187/language/en-US/Default.aspx.

HSU. 2009. *Human Security in Theory and Practice: Application of the Human Security Concept and the United Nations Trust Fund for Human Security*. New York: United Nations.

Hubbard, Ben. 2013. "Saudi Women Rise Up, Quietly, and Slide into the Driver's Seat." *New York Times*, 26 October. Accessed 27 October 2013. http://www.nytimes.com/2013/10/27/world/middleeast/a-mostly-quiet-effort-to-put-saudi-women-in-drivers-seats.html?ref=world.

Hubert, Don. 2004. "An Idea That Works in Practice." *Security Dialogue* 35 (3): 351–52.

Hudson, Heidi. 2005. "'Doing' Security As Though Humans Matter: A Feminist Perspective on Gender and the Politics of Human Security." *Security Dialogue* 36 (2): 155–74.

Human Rights Watch. 2013. *Between a Drone and Al-Qaeda: The Civilian Cost of US Targeted Killings in Yemen*. 22 October. Accessed 23 October 2013. http://www.hrw.org/reports/2013/10/22/between-drone-and-al-qaeda-0.

Hurd, Ian. 2007. *After Anarchy: Legitimacy and Power in the United Nations Security Council*. Princeton: Princeton University Press.

Hutchings, Kimberley. 2009. "Simone de Beauvoir." In *Critical Theorists and International Relations*, edited by Jenny Edkins and Nick Vaughan-Williams, 66–76. New York: Routledge.

ICC (International Criminal Court). 2002. *Rules of Procedure and Evidence*. Official Records ICC-ASP/1/3. International Criminal Court, New York. Accessed 19 May 2012. http://www.icc-cpi.int/NR/rdonlyres/F1E0AC1C-A3F3-4A3C-B9A7-B3E8B115E886/140164/Rules_of_procedure_and_Evidence_English.pdf.

ICISS (International Commission on Intervention and State Sovereignty). 2001. *The Responsibility to Protect*. Ottawa: International Development Research Centre.

ICJ (International Court of Justice). 1951. *Reservations to the Convention on the Prevention and Punishment of the Crime of Genocide.* Advisory opinion, 28 May. Accessed 27 June 2012. http://www.icj-cij.org/docket/index.php?sum=276&code=ppcg&p 1=3&p2=4&case=12&k=90&p3=5.

ICJ. 1975. *Western Sahara.* Advisory opinion. In *ICJ Reports 1975,* 16 October. Accessed 5 June 2014. http://www.icj-cij.org/docket/files/61/6195.pdf.

ICJ. 1986. *Frontier Dispute, Burkina Faso/Mali.* Judgment. In *ICJ Reports 1986,* 22 December, 554–651. Accessed 2 October 2010. http://www.icj-cij.org/docket/files/69/6447.pdf.

ICJ. 1992. *Questions of Interpretation and Application of the 1971 Montreal Convention arising from the Aerial Incident at Lockerbie (*Libyan Arab Jamahiriya v. United States of America*).* Judgment. Accessed 7 October 2010. http://www.icj-cij.org/docket/index.php?p1=3&p2=3&k=82&case=89&code=lus&p3=3.

ICJ. 1995. *East Timor (*Portugal v. Australia*).* Judgment, 30 June. Accessed 7 January 2014. http://www.icj-cij.org/docket/files/84/6949.pdf.

ICJ. 2004. *Legal Consequences of the Construction of a Wall in the Occupied Palestinian Territory.* Advisory opinion, 9 July. Accessed 8 January 2014. http://www.icj-cij.org/docket/files/131/1671.pdf.

ICJ. 2010. *Accordance with International Law of the Unilateral Declaration of Independence in Respect of Kosovo.* Judgment. Accessed 25 May 2012. http://www.icj-cij.org/docket/index.php?p1=3&p2=2&case=141&PHPSESSID=9cdce12836744fb 5695f7180f28df6c7.

ICJ. 2012a. *Questions Relating to the Obligation to Prosecute or Extradite (*Belgium v. Senegal*): Conclusion of the Public Hearings.* Press Release 2012/13, 21 March. Accessed 30 May 2012. http://www.icj-cij.org/docket/files/144/16953.pdf.

ICJ. 2012b. *Questions Relating to the Obligation to Prosecute or Extradite (*Belgium v. Senegal*).* Judgment, 20 July. Accessed 16 August 2012. http://www.icj-cij.org/docket/files/144/17064.pdf.

IGLHRC (International Gay and Lesbian Human Rights Commission). 2012. "Governments Condemn Extrajudicial Executions in Seminal UN Vote." 21 November. Accessed 3 September 2013. http://www.iglhrc.org/content/governments-con demn-extrajudicial-executions-seminal-un-vote.

Isaak, Robert. 1974. "The Individual in International Politics: Solving the Level-of-Analysis Problem." *Polity* 7 (2): 264–76.

Jackson, Robert. 1945. "Opening Statement for the Prosecution." Trial of the Major War Criminals before the International Military Tribunal. Accessed 21 May 2012. http://law2.umkc.edu/faculty/projects/ftrials/nuremberg/jackson.html.

Jacobi, Daniel, and Annette Freyberg-Inan, eds. 2012. "The Forum: Human Being(s) in International Relations." *International Studies Review* 14:645–65.

Jacobson, Harold. 1982. "The Global System and the Realization of Human Dignity and Justice." *International Studies Quarterly* 26 (3): 315–32.

Jaeger, Hans-Martin. 2007. "'Global Civil Society' and the Political Depoliticization of Global Governance." *International Political Sociology* 1 (3): 257–77.

Jaeger, Hans-Martin. 2010. "UN Reform, Biopolitics, and Global Governmentality." *International Theory* 2 (1): 50–86.

Janover, Michael. 2011. "Politics and Worldliness in the Thought of Hannah Arendt." In *Action and Appearance: Ethics and the Politics of Writing in Hannah Arendt*, edited by Anna Yeatman et al., 25–38. New York: Continuum.

Jaspers, Karl. [1948] 1995. "The Question of German Guilt." Reprinted in *Transitional Justice: How Emerging Democracies Reckon with Former Regimes*, edited by Neil J. Kritz, vol. 1, *General Considerations*, 157–71. Washington, DC: United States Institute of Peace.

Jeffrey, Renée. 2008. *Confronting Evil in International Relations: Ethical Responses to Problems of Moral Agency*. New York: Palgrave Macmillan.

Johnson, Carrie. 2013. "NGOs Call US Drone Program Illegal in Damning Reports." 22 October. Accessed 23 October 2013. http://www.npr.org/templates/story/story.php?storyId=239860348.

Johnstone, Ian. 2005. "The Power of Interpretive Communities." In *Power in Global Governance*, edited by Michael Barnett and Raymond Duvall, 185–204. Cambridge: Cambridge University Press.

Johnstone, Ian. 2008. "Legislation and Adjudication in the UN Security Council: Bringing Down the Deliberative Deficit." *American Journal of International Law* 102 (2): 275–308.

Jones, Roy E. 1981. "The English School of International Relations: A Case for Closure." *Review of International Studies* 7 (1): 1–13.

Judah, Tim. 1999. "History, Bloody History." *BBC News*, 24 March. Accessed 21 January 2011. http://news.bbc.co.uk/2/hi/special_report/1998/kosovo/110492.stm.

Kalman, Matthew, and Emma Reynolds. 2011. "The Eight-Year-Old Girl Called a Whore by Israel's Jewish Religious Hardliners." *Daily Mail*, 21 December. Accessed 6 June 2012. http://www.dailymail.co.uk/news/article-2078771/Israel-braced-protests-treatment-women-girl-8-spat-Jewish-extremists.html.

Kaplan, Morris B. 1997. *Sexual Justice: Democratic Citizenship and the Politics of Desire*. New York: Routledge.

Kateb, George. 2011. *Human Dignity*. Cambridge, MA: Harvard University Press.

Keck, Margaret, and Kathryn Sikkink. 1998. *Activists beyond Borders*. Ithaca: Cornell University Press.

Keene, Edward. 2002. *Beyond the Anarchical Society: Grotius, Colonialism, and Order in World Politics*. Cambridge: Cambridge University Press.

Kelman, Herbert. 1977. "The Conditions, Criteria, and Dialectics of Human Dignity: A Transnational Perspective." *International Studies Quarterly* 21 (3): 529–52.

Kempster, Norman. 2001. "CIA Files: Nazis Recruited to Spy during Cold War." *Houston Chronicle*, 28 April, 26A.

Kerim, Srgjan. 2008. Opening statement at the Thematic Debate on Human Security, United Nations Headquarters, New York, 22 May. Accessed 18 June 2011. http://www.un.org/ga/president/62/statements/humansecurity220508.shtml.

Kessler, Oliver. 2012. "World Society, Social Differentiation and Time." *International Political Sociology* 6 (1): 77–94.

Khaitan, Tarunabh. 2012. "Dignity as an Expressive Norm: Neither Vacuous nor a Panacea." *Oxford Journal of Legal Studies* 32 (1): 1–19.

Kim, Jung-Gun Kim, and John M. Howell. 1972. *Conflict of International Obligations and State Interests*. The Hague: Martinus Nijhoff.

Kim, Samuel S. 1984. "Global Violence and a Just World Order." *Journal of Peace Research* 21:181–92.

King, Gary, and Christopher Murray. 2001–2. "Rethinking Human Security." *Political Science Quarterly* 116:585–610.

Klabbers, Jan. 2006. "The Right to Be Taken Seriously: Self-Determination in International Law." *Human Rights Quarterly* 28 (1): 186–206.

Klotz, Audie. 1995. *Norms in International Relations: The Struggle against Apartheid.* Ithaca: Cornell University Press.

Knop, Karen. 2002. *Diversity and Self-Determination in International Law.* Cambridge: Cambridge University Press.

Knutsen, Elise. 2013. "Chad: Special Court on Hissene Habre Opens." *allAfrica*, 8 February. Accessed 28 March 2013. http://allafrica.com/stories/201302081496.html.

Kolakowski, Leszek. 2002. "What Is Left of Socialism." *First Things* 126:42–46. Accessed 25 May 2012. http://www.firstthings.com/article/2007/01/-what-is-left-of-socialism-15.

Kontorovitch, Eugene. 2009. "The Constitutionality of International Courts: The Forgotten Precedent of Slave Trade Tribunals." *University of Pennsylvania Law Review* 158:39–115.

Krasner, Stephen. 1999. *Sovereignty: Organized Hypocrisy.* Princeton: Princeton University Press.

Kuper, Andrew. 2006. *Democracy beyond Borders: Justice and Representation in Global Institutions.* Oxford: Oxford University Press.

Lahey, Kathleen. 1999. *Are We "Persons" Yet? Law and Sexuality in Canada.* Toronto: University of Toronto Press.

Lahey, Kathleen. 2010. "Same-Sex Marriage, Transnational Activism, and International Law: Strategic Objectives." *Proceedings of the Annual Meeting of the American Society of International Law* 104:380–83.

Lang, Anthony, and John Williams, eds. 2005. *Hannah Arendt and International Relations: Readings across the Lines.* New York: Palgrave MacMillan.

*Lawrence et al. v. Texas (Syllabus).* 2003. 26 June. Accessed 24 October 2013. http://www.law.cornell.edu/supct/html/02-102.ZS.html.

Lilla, Mark. 2013a. "Arendt and Eichmann: The New Truth." *New York Review of Books* 60 (18): 35–36, 45.

Lilla, Mark. 2013b. "The Defense of a Jewish Collaborator." *New York Review of Books* 60 (19): 55–57.

Linklater, Andrew. 1982. *Men and Citizens in the Theory of International Relations.* New York: St. Martin's.

Linklater, Andrew. 1996. "The Achievements of Critical Theory." In *International Theory: Positivism and Beyond*, edited by Steve Smith, Ken Booth, and Marysia Zalewski, 278–300. Cambridge: Cambridge University Press.

Linklater, Andrew. 1998. *The Transformation of Political Community.* Cambridge: Polity.

Linklater, Andrew. 2001. "Citizenship, Humanity, and Cosmopolitan Harm Conventions." *International Political Science Review* 22 (3): 261–77.

Linklater, Andrew. 2009. "Human Interconnectedness." *International Relations* 23 (3): 481–97.

Linklater, Andrew. 2010. "Global Civilizing Processes and the Ambiguities of Human Interconnectedness." *European Journal of International Relations* 16 (2): 155–78.

Linklater, Andrew. 2011. *The Problem of Harm in World Politics: Theoretical Investigations.* Cambridge: Cambridge University Press.

Linklater, Andrew, and Hidemi Suganami. 2006. *The English School of International Relations: A Contemporary Reassessment.* Cambridge: Cambridge University Press.

Lipschutz, Ronni. 1992. "Reconstructing World Politics: The Emergence of Global Civil Society." *Millennium: Journal of International Studies* 21 (3): 389–420.

Lipstadt, Deborah. 2011. *The Eichmann Trial.* New York: Schocken.

Lowe, Vaughan, et al., eds. 2008. *The United Nations Security Council and War: The Evolution of Thought and Practice since 1945.* New York: Oxford University Press.

Luard, Evan. 1976. *Types of International Society.* London: Macmillan.

Luard, Evan. 1990. *International Society.* Basingstoke, UK: Macmillan.

Lynch, Cecelia. 1999. *Beyond Appeasement: Interpreting Interwar Peace Movements in World Politics.* Ithaca: Cornell University Press.

MacFarlane, S. Neil, and Yuen Foong Khong. 2006. *Human Security and the UN: A Critical History.* Bloomington: Indiana University Press.

MacKinnon, Catharine. 2006. *Are Women Human? And Other International Dialogues.* Cambridge, MA: Belknap Press of Harvard University Press.

MacLean, Sandra, et al. 2006. *A Decade of Human Security: Global Governance and New Multilateralisms.* Burlington, VT: Ashgate.

Mahony, Liam, and Roger Nash. 2008. "A Framework for a Holistic Approach to UNSC Resolutions on Protection of Civilians, Children and Armed Conflict, and Women, Peace, and Security." Fieldview Solutions report prepared for the Swiss Mission to the United Nations. Accessed 12 January 2012. http://fieldviewsolutions.org/fv-publications/Holistic_approach_to_UNSC_resolutions_on_protection-Fieldview_Solutions.pdf.

Mann, Michael. 2005. *The Dark Side of Democracy: Explaining Ethnic Cleansing.* Cambridge: Cambridge University Press.

Marcuse, Herbert. 1955. *Eros and Civilization.* New York: Vintage Books.

Marcuse, Herbert. 1964. *One-Dimensional Man.* Boston: Beacon.

Marso, Lori. 2012. "Simone de Beauvoir and Hannah Arendt: Judgments in Dark Times." *Political Theory* 40 (2): 165–93.

Mason, Andrew. 2000. *Community, Solidarity, and Belonging: Levels of Community and Their Normative Significance.* Cambridge: Cambridge University Press.

*Massachusetts Board of Retirement v. Murgia.* 1976. 427 U.S. 307. Accessed 15 May 2012. http://caselaw.lp.findlaw.com/cgi-bin/getcase.pl?navby=case&court=us&vol=427&invol=307#313.

Mayall, James. 2000. *World Politics: Progress and Its Limits.* Cambridge: Polity.

McCarthy, Thomas. 2009. *Race, Empire, and the Idea of Human Development.* Cambridge: Cambridge University Press.

McCormack, Tara. 2007. "From State of War to State of Nature: Human Security and Sovereignty." In *Politics without Sovereignty: A Critique of Contemporary International Relations,* edited by C. J. Bickerton, P. Cunliffe, and A. Gourevitch, 77–92. London: UCL Press.

McCrudden, Christopher. 2008. "Human Dignity and Judicial Interpretation of Human Rights." *European Journal of International Law* 19 (4): 655–724.

McRae, Rob. 2001. "Human Security in a Globalized World." In *Human Security and the New Diplomacy: Protecting People, Promoting Peace,* edited by Rob McRae and Don Hubert, 14–27. Montreal: McGill University Press.

McRae, Rob, and Don Hubert, eds. 2001. *Human Security and the New Diplomacy: Protecting People, Promoting Peace.* Montreal: McGill-Queen's University Press.

*Medellin v. Texas.* 2007. 223 S. W. 3d 315. Supreme Court of the United States. Accessed 3 June 2014. http://www.law.cornell.edu/supct/html/06-984.ZS.html.

Meilaender, Gilbert. 2009. *Neither Beast nor God: The Dignity of the Human Person.* New York: New Atlantis Books.

Meron, Theodor. 2000a. "The Humanization of Humanitarian Law." *American Journal of International Law* 92 (2): 239–78.

Meron, Theodor. 2000b. "The Martens Clause, Principles of Humanity, and Dictates of Public Conscience." *American Journal of International Law* 94 (1): 78–89.

Mertus, Julie. 2007. "The Rejection of Human Rights Framings: The Case of LGBT Advocacy in the US." *Human Rights Quarterly* 29 (4): 1036–64.

Minow, Martha. 1998. *Between Vengeance and Forgiveness: Facing History after Genocide and Mass Violence.* Boston: Beacon.

Momigliano, Arnaldo. 1980. "A Note on Max Weber's Definition of Judaism as a Pariah-Religion." *History and Theory* 19 (3): 313–18.

Morgenthau, Hans. 1962. *Politics among Nations: The Struggle for Power and Peace.* New York: Alfred A. Knopf.

Moruzzi, Norma Claire. 2000. *Speaking through the Mask: Hannah Arendt and the Politics of Social Identity.* Ithaca: Cornell University Press.

MRG (Minority Rights Group International). 2008. *World Directory of Minorities and Indigenous Peoples—Colombia: Afro-Colombians.* Accessed 30 June 2011. http://www.unhcr.org/refworld/docid/49749d3cc.html.

Mulisch, Harry. 2005. *Criminal Case 40/61, the Trial of Adolf Eichmann.* Philadelphia: University of Pennsylvania Press.

Mundis, Daryl. 2001. "New Mechanisms for the Enforcement of International Humanitarian Law." *American Journal of International Law* 95 (4): 934–52.

Muthien, Bernedette. 2000. "Human Security Paradigms through a Gendered Lens." *Agenda* 43:46–56.

NATO (North Atlantic Treaty Organization). 1999. "NATO's Role in Kosovo." 15 July. Accessed 25 May 2012. http://www.nato.int/kosovo/history.htm.

Navari, Cornelia. 2011. "The Concept of Practice in the English School." *European Journal of International Relations* 17 (4): 611–30.

Nayar, Jayan. 2002. "Orders of Inhumanity." In *Reframing the International: Law, Culture, Politics,* edited by Richard Falk et al., 107–35. New York: Routledge.

Neumann, Iver. 2001. "The English School and the Practices of World Society." *Review of International Studies* 27 (3): 503–7.

Neumann, Iver B., and Ole Sending. 2010. *Governing the Global Polity: Practice, Mentality, Rationality.* Ann Arbor: University of Michigan Press.

Newman, Edward. 2004. "A Normatively Attractive but Analytically Weak Concept." *Security Dialogue* 35 (3): 358–59.

Nhema, Alfred. 2006. "The Organization for Social Science Research in Eastern and Southern Africa's Contribution to Human Security Research in Africa." In *A Decade of Human Security: Global Governance and New Multilateralisms*, edited by Sandra MacLean, 193–200. Burlington, VT: Ashgate.

Nijman, Janne Elisabeth. 2004. *The Concept of International Legal Personality: An Inquiry into the History and Theory of International Law*. The Hague: T. M. C. Asser Press.

Nino, Carlos Santiago. 1996. *Radical Evil on Trial*. New Haven: Yale University Press.

Nouwen, Sarah. 2006. "'Hybrid Courts': The Hybrid Category of a New Type of International Crimes Court." *Utrecht Law Review* 2 (2): 190–214.

Nussbaum, Martha. 2002. "Patriotism and Cosmopolitanism." In *For Love of Country?*, edited by Martha Nussbaum and Joshua Cohen, 3–17. Boston: Beacon.

Nussbaum, Martha. 2010. *From Disgust to Humanity: Sexual Orientation and Constitutional Law*. New York: Oxford.

Oberlietner, Gerd. 2005. "Human Security: A Challenge to International Law." *Global Governance* 11:185–203.

Ogata, Sadako. 2002. "From State Security to Human Security." Ogden Lecture, Brown University, 26 May. Accessed 3 June 2011. http://www.humansecurity-chs.org/activities/outreach/ogata_ogden.html.

Onuf, Nicholas. 1989. *World of Our Making: Rules and Rule in Social Theory and International Relations*. Columbia: University of South Carolina Press.

Ortega y Gasset, Jose. 1961. *History as a System and Other Essays Toward a Philosophy of History*. New York: W. W. Norton.

Ottawa Convention. 1997. *Convention on the Use, Stockpiling, Production, and Transfer of Anti-Personnel Mines and Their Destruction*. Accessed 25 May 2012. http://www.un.org/Depts/mine/UNDocs/ban_trty.htm.

Owen, Taylor. 2004. "Human Security—Conflict, Critique, and Consensus: Colloquium Remarks and a Proposal for a Threshold-Based Definition." *Security Dialogue* 35 (3): 373–87.

Owens, Patricia. 2007. *Between War and Politics: International Relations and the Thought of Hannah Arendt*. New York: Oxford University Press.

Parekh, Bhikhu. 2003. "Cosmopolitanism and Global Citizenship." *Review of International Studies* 29 (1): 3–17.

Parekh, Serena. 2008. *Hannah Arendt and the Challenge of Modernity: A Phenomenology of Human Rights*. New York: Routledge.

Paris, Roland. 2001. "Human Security: Paradigm Shift or Hot Air?" *International Security* 26 (2): 87–102.

Paris, Roland. 2004. "Still an Inscrutable Concept." *Security Dialogue* 35 (3): 370–71.

Passavant, Paul. 2007. "The Contradictory State of Giorgio Agamben." *Political Theory* 35 (2): 147–74.

Pasternak, Charles, ed. 2007. *What Makes Us Human?* Oxford: Oneworld.

Patterson, Matthew. 2005. "Global Environmental Governance." In *International Society and Its Critics*, edited by Alex J. Bellamy, 163–77. New York: Oxford University Press.

Penn, Dianne. 2013. "Human Rights Office Launches Free & Equal Campaign to Raise Awareness about LGBT Discrimination." *United Nations Radio*, 26 July. Accessed 29 July 2013. http://www.unmultimedia.org/radio/english/2013/07/

human-rights-office-launches-free-equal-campaign-to-raise-awareness-about-lgbt-discrimination/.

Phillips, Tom. 2011. "Uncontacted Tribe Found Deep in Amazon Rainforest." *Guardian*, 22 June. Accessed 6 June 2012. http://www.guardian.co.uk/world/2011/jun/22/new-tribe-discovered-amazon.

Pillay, Navi. 2010. "Ending Violence and Criminal Sanctions Based on Sexual Orientation and Gender Identity: Statement by the High Commissioner." *United Nations Human Rights: Office of the High Commissioner for Human Rights*, 17 September. Accessed 3 September 2013. http://www.ohchr.org/EN/NewsEvents/Pages/DisplayNews.aspx?NewsID=10717&LangID=E.

Pogge, Thomas. 2002. *World Poverty and Human Rights*. Cambridge: Polity.

*Prosecutor v. Anto Furundžija*. 1998. Case no. IT-95-17/1-T. Trial chamber judgment, 10 December. Accessed 30 June 2012. http://www.icty.org/x/cases/furundzija/tjug/en/fur-tj981210e.pdf.

*Prosecutor v. Dragoljub Kunarac et al.* 2001. Case no. IT-96-23-T & IT-96-23/1-T. Trial chamber judgment, 22 February. Accessed 26 March 2012. http://www.icty.org/x/cases/kunarac/tjug/en/kun-tj010222e.pdf.

*Prosecutor v. Dragoljub Kunarac et al.* 2002. Case no. IT-96-23 & IT-96-23/1-A. Appeals chamber judgment, 12 June. Accessed 30 June 2012. http://www.icty.org/x/cases/kunarac/acjug/en/kun-aj020612e.pdf.

*Prosecutor v. Drazen Erdemovic.* 1996. Case no. IT-96-22-T. Sentencing judgment, 29 November. Accessed 1 July 2012. http://www.icty.org/x/cases/erdemovic/tjug/en/erd-tsj961129e.pdf.

*Prosecutor v. Dusko Tadic.* 1995. "Decision on the Defense Motion for Interlocutory Appeal on Judgment." 2 October. Accessed 30 May 2012. http://www.icty.org/x/cases/tadic/acdec/en/51002.htm.

*Prosecutor v. Ferdinand Nahimana et al.* 2003. Case no. ICTR-99-52-T. Trial chamber judgment, 3 December. Accessed 30 June 2012. http://www.unictr.org/Portals/0/Case%5CEnglish%5CNahimana%5Cjudgement%5CSummary-Media.pdf.

*Prosecutor v. Jean-Paul Akayesu.* 1998. Case no. ICTR 96-4-T. Trial chamber judgment, 2 September. Accessed 22 May 2012. http://www.unictr.org/Portals/0/Case%5CEnglish%5CAkayesu%5Cjudgement%5Cakay001.pdf.

*Prosecutor v. Radislav Krstić.* 2001. Case no. IT-98-33-T. Trial chamber judgment, 2 August. Accessed 30 June 2012. http://www.icty.org/x/cases/krstic/tjug/en/krs tj010802e.pdf.

*Prosecutor v. Tihomir Blaškić.* 2000. Case no. IT-95-14-T. Trial chamber judgment, 3 March. Accessed 1 July 2012. http://www.icty.org/x/cases/blaskic/tjug/en/bla tj000303e.pdf.

*Prosecutor v. Zlatko Aleksovski.* 1999. Case no. IT-95-14/1-T. Trial chamber judgment, 25 June. Accessed 28 March 2012. http://www.icty.org/x/cases/aleksovski/tjug/en/ale-tj990625e.pdf.

Quinn, Kenneth. 1989. "The Pattern and Scope of Violence." In *Cambodia, 1975–1978: Rendezvous with Death*, edited by Karl Jackson, 179–208. Princeton: Princeton University Press.

Rabin, Robert, and Stephen Sugarman. 2007. "The Case for Specially Compensating the Victims of Terrorist Attacks: An Assessment." *Hofstra Law Review* 35:901–15.

Raghuram, Parvati, et al. 2009. "Rethinking Responsibility and Care for a Postcolonial World." *Geoforum* 40:5–13.

Rajagopal, Balakrishnan. 2003. *International Law from Below: Development, Social Movements, and Third World Resistance.* Cambridge: Cambridge University Press.

Reagan, Ronald. 1985. Second inaugural address. 21 January. Accessed 29 June 2011. http://www.bartleby.com/124/pres62.html.

Reilly, Niamh. 2007. "Cosmopolitan Feminism and Human Rights." *Hypatia* 22 (4): 180–98.

ReliefWeb. 2012. "ICC Trust Fund for Victims Assists over 80,000 Victims, Raises Reparations Reserve." 27 March. Accessed 30 June 2012. http://reliefweb.int/node/485620.

Resnick, Judith, and Julie Chi-hye Suk. 2003. "Adding Insult to Injury: Questioning the Role of Dignity in Conceptions of Sovereignty." *Stanford Law Review* 55 (5): 1921–62.

Results for the referendum of southern Sudan. 2011. Accessed 22 May 2012. http://southernsudan2011.com/.

Reus-Smit, Christian. 1999. *The Moral Purpose of the State: Culture, Social Identity, and Institutional Rationality in International Relations.* Princeton: Princeton University Press.

Reus-Smit, Christian. 2005. "The Constructivist Challenge after September 11." In *International Society and Its Critics*, edited by Alex J. Bellamy, 81–94. New York: Oxford University Press.

Rittberger, Volker. 2008a. "From the Westphalian Peace to Strategies for Peace in a Post-Westphalian Environment." In *Strategies for Peace: Contributions of International Organizations, States, and Non-State Actors*, edited by Volker Rittberger and Martina Fischer, 25–48. Opladen, Germany: Barbara Budrich Publishers.

Rittberger, Volker. 2008b. "Global Governance: From 'Exclusive' Multilateralism to Inclusive, Multipartite Institutions." Accessed 20 May 2013. http://tobias-lib.uni tuebingen.de/volltexte/2008/3672/pdf/tap52.pdf.

Robertson, Geoffrey. 2006. *Crimes against Humanity: The Struggle for Global Justice.* New York: New Press.

Robinson, Fiona. 1999. *Globalizing Care: Ethics, Feminist Theory, and International Relations.* Boulder: Westview.

Robinson, Fiona. 2009. "Feminist Ethics in World Politics." In *The Ashgate Research Companion to Ethics and International Relations*, edited by Patrick Hayden, 79–95. Burlington, VT: Ashgate.

Robinson, Fiona. 2011. *The Ethics of Care: A Feminist Approach to Human Security.* Philadelphia: Temple University Press.

[*Rome*] *Statute for the International Criminal Court.* 1998. http://untreaty.un.org/cod/icc/statute/romefra.htm.

Romero, Simon. 2008. "Talk of Independence in a Place Claimed by 2 Nations." *New York Times*, 1 February. Accessed 1 June 2011. http://www.nytimes.com/2008/02/01/world/americas/01colombia.html.

Rosand, Eric, Alistair Millar, and Jason Ipe. 2007. *The UN Security Council's Counterterrorism Program: What Lies Ahead?* New York: International Peace Academy.

Accessed 18 December 2011. http://www.ipacademy.org/media/pdf/publications/cter.pdf.

Rouner, Leroy, ed. 1992. *Selves, People, and Persons: What Does It Mean to Be a Self?* Notre Dame: University of Notre Dame Press.

SáCouto, Susana. 2012. "Victim Participation at the International Criminal Court and the Extraordinary Chambers in the Courts of Cambodia: A Feminist Project?" *Michigan Journal of Gender and Law* 18:1–63.

Said, Edward. 2004. *Humanism and Democratic Criticism*. New York: Columbia University Press.

Saiz, Ignacio. 2004. "Bracketing Sexuality: Human Rights and Sexuality: A Decade of Development and Denial at the UN." *Health and Human Rights* 7 (2): 48–80.

Salter, Mark. 2002. *Barbarians and Civilization in International Relations*. Sterling, VA: Pluto.

Sartre, Jean-Paul. 2007. *Existentialism as Humanism*. New Haven: Yale University Press.

Schachter, Oscar. 1983. "Human Dignity as a Normative Concept." *American Journal of International Law* 77 (4): 848–54.

Seidman, Steven. 1993. "Identity and Politics in a 'Postmodern' Gay Culture: Some Historical and Conceptual Notes." In *Fear of a Queer Planet: Queer Politics and Social Theory*, edited by Michael Warner, 105–42. Minneapolis: University of Minnesota Press.

Sennett, Richard. 1998. *The Corrosion of Character: The Personal Consequences of Work in the New Capitalism*. New York: W. W. Norton.

Sennett, Richard. 2003. *Respect, in an Age of Inequality*. New York: W. W. Norton.

Sennett, Richard. 2008. *The Craftsman*. New Haven: Yale University Press.

Sennett, Richard. 2012. *Together: The Rituals, Pleasures, and Politics of Cooperation*. New Haven: Yale University Press.

Sennett, Richard, and Jonathan Cobb. 1973. *The Hidden Injuries of Class*. New York: Alfred A. Knopf.

Sepúlveda-Amor, Bernardo. 2010. *Separate Opinion of Judge Sepúlveda-Amor*. Accessed 25 May 2012. http://www.icj-cij.org/docket/files/141/15997.pdf.

Shklar, Judith. 1982. "Putting Cruelty First." *Daedalus* 111 (3): 17–27.

Shklar, Judith. 1984. *Ordinary Vices*. Cambridge, MA: Harvard University Press.

Shklar, Judith. 1998. *Political Thought and Political Thinkers*. Edited by Stanley Hoffmann. Chicago: University of Chicago Press.

Simma, Bruno. 2010. *Separate Opinion of Judge Simma*. Accessed 25 May 2012. http://www.icj-cij.org/docket/files/141/15991.pdf.

Simmons, William Paul. 2011. *Human Rights Law and the Marginalized Other*. New York: Cambridge University Press.

Simpson, Gerry. 2007. *Law, War, and Crime*. Cambridge: Polity.

Smith, Christian. 2010. *What Is a Person? Rethinking Humanity, Social Life, and the Moral Good from the Person Up*. Chicago: University of Chicago Press.

Smith, Roger. 2007. *Being Human: Historical Knowledge and the Creation of Human Nature*. New York: Columbia University Press.

Sokoloff, Constantin. 2005. *Denial of Citizenship: A Challenge to Human Security*. New

York: United Nations. Accessed 25 September 2011. http://www.statelesspeoplein bangladesh.net/uploaded_files/studies_and_reports/DenialOfCitizenshipAChal lengToHumanSecurity.pdf.

Sontag, Susan. [1973] 2013. "The Third World of Women." In *Sontag: Essays of the 1960s and 70s*, edited by David Rieff, 769–99. New York: Library of America.

Special Tribunal for Lebanon. 2014. "About the STL: Defence Office." Accessed 17 January 2014. http://www.stl-tsl.org/en/about-the-stl/structure-of-the-stl/defence/ defence-office.

Stahn, Carsten. 2001. "Accommodating Individual Criminal Responsibility and National Reconciliation: The UN Truth Commission for East Timor." *American Journal of International Law* 95 (4): 952–66.

Sterio, Milena. 2013. *The Right to Self-Determination under International Law: "Self-istans," Secession, and the Rule of the Great Powers*. New York: Routledge.

Sterling-Folker, Jennifer. 2005. "Realist Global Governance: Revisiting *Cave! Hic Dragones* and Beyond." In *Contending Perspectives on Global Governance: Coherence, Contestation, and World Order*, edited by Alice Ba and Matthew Hoffmann, 17–38. New York: Routledge.

Suganami, Hidemi. 2005. "The English School and International Theory." In *International Society and Its Critics*, edited by Alex Bellamy, 29–44. Oxford: Oxford University Press.

Svendsen, Lars. 2010. *A Philosophy of Evil*. Translated by Kerri Pierce. Champaign, IL: Dalkey Archive Press.

Sylvester, Christine. 1994. *Feminist Theory and International Relations in a Postmodern Era*. Cambridge: Cambridge University Press.

Sylvester, Christine. 1996. "The Contributions of Feminist Theory to International Relations." In *International Theory: Positivism and Beyond*, edited by Steve Smith, Ken Booth, and Marysia Zalewski, 254–78. Cambridge: Cambridge University Press.

Szasz, Paul. 2002. "The Security Council Starts Legislating." *American Journal of International Law* 96 (4): 901–5.

Sznaider, Natan. 2011. *Jewish Memory and the Cosmopolitan Order: Hannah Arendt and the Jewish Condition*. Malden, MA: Polity.

Tadjbakhsh, Shahrbanou, and Anuradha Chenoy. 2007. *Human Security: Concepts and Implications*. London: Routledge.

Talmon, Stefan. 2005. "The Security Council as World Legislature." *American Journal of International Law* 99 (1): 175–93.

Taylor, Charles. 1989. *Sources of the Self: The Making of Modern Identity*. Cambridge, MA: Harvard University Press.

Taylor, Viviene. 2004. "From State Security to Human Security and Gender Justice." *Agenda* 59:65–70.

Teitel, Ruti. 2011. *Humanity's Law*. New York: Oxford University Press.

Tétreault, Mary Ann, and Ronnie Lipschutz. 2009. *Global Politics As If People Mattered*. Lanham, MD: Rowman and Littlefield.

Thomas, Caroline. 2004. "A Bridge between the Interconnected Challenges Confronting the World." *Security Dialogue* 35 (3): 353–54.

Thomson, Janice, and Stephen Krasner. 1989. "Global Transactions and the Consolidation of Sovereignty." In *Global Changes and Theoretical Challenges*, edited by Ernst Czempiel and James Rosenau, 195–219. Lexington, MA: Lexington Books.

Tickner, J. Ann, and Laura Sjoberg, eds. 2011. *Feminism and International Relations: Conversations about the Past, Present, and Future*. New York: Routledge.

Tieku, Thomas. 2007. "African Union Promotion of Human Security in Africa." *African Security Review* 16 (2): 26–37.

Tronto, Joan. 1993. *Moral Boundaries: A Political Argument for an Ethic of Care*. New York: Routledge.

True, Jacqui. 2011. "Feminist Problems with International Norms: Gender Mainstreaming in Global Governance." In *Feminism and International Relations: Conversations about the Past, Present, and Future*, edited by J. Ann Tickner and Laura Sjoberg, 73–88. New York: Routledge.

True-Frost, Cora. 2007. "The Security Council and Norm Consumption." *NYU Journal of International Law and Politics* 40 (1): 115–217.

UNDP (United Nations Development Programme). 1994. *Human Development Report, 1994*. New York: Oxford University Press. Accessed 21 June 2011. http://hdr.undp.org/sites/default/files/reports/255/hdr_1994_en_complete_nostats.pdf.

UN ECOSOC (United Nations Economic and Social Council). 2006. *Definition of Basic Concepts and Terminologies in Governance and Public Administration*. E/C.16/2006/4. Accessed 29 June 2011. http://unpan1.un.org/intradoc/groups/public/documents/un/unpan022332.pdf.

UNGA (United Nations General Assembly). 1960a. "Declaration on the Granting of Independence to Colonial Countries and Peoples." Resolution 1514 (XV). 14 December. Accessed 6 January 2014. http://www.un.org/ga/search/view_doc.asp?symbol=A/RES/1514%28XV%29.

UNGA. 1960b. "Principles Which Should Guide Members in Determining Whether or Not an Obligation Exists to Transmit the Information Called for under Article 73e of the Charter." Resolution 1541 (XV). 15 December. Accessed 4 January 2012. http://daccess-dds-ny.un.org/doc/RESOLUTION/GEN/NR0/153/15/IMG/NR015315.pdf?OpenElement.

UNGA. 1970. "Declaration on Principles of International Law concerning Friendly Relations and Co-operation among States in Accordance with the Charter of the United Nations." Resolution 2625 (XXV). 24 October. Accessed 7 January 2014. http://daccess-dds-ny.un.org/doc/RESOLUTION/GEN/NR0/348/90/IMG/NR034890.pdf?OpenElement.

UNGA. 1974. "Definition of Aggression." Resolution 3314 (XXIX). 2319th plenary meeting, 14 December. Accessed 30 May 2012. http://daccess-dds-ny.un.org/doc/RESOLUTION/GEN/NR0/739/16/IMG/NR073916.pdf?OpenElement.

UNGA. 1985. *Declaration on Basic Principles of Justice for Victims of Crimes and Abuse of Power*. A/Res/40/34. 40th session, 96th plenary meeting, 29 November. Accessed 19 May 2012. http://www.un.org/documents/ga/res/40/a40r034.htm.

UNGA. 1990. *Basic Principles for the Treatment of Prisoners*. A/Res/45/111. 45th session, 68th plenary meeting, 14 December. Accessed 22 December 2013. http://www.un.org/documents/ga/res/45/a45r111.htm.

UNGA. 2005. *World Summit Outcome.* A/Res/60/1. 24 October.

UNGA. 2010a. Press release. GA/10942. 20 May. Accessed 18 June 2011. http://www.un.org/News/Press/docs/2010/ga10942.doc.htm.

UNGA. 2010b. Press release. GA/10944. 21 May. Accessed 18 June 2011. http://www.un.org/News/Press/docs/2010/ga10944.doc.htm.

UNGA. 2012. *Follow-up to Paragraph 143 on Human Security of the 2005 World Summit Outcome.* A/Res/66/290. 25 October. Accessed 25 March 2013. https://docs.unocha.org/sites/dms/HSU/Publications%20and%20Products/GA%20Resolutions%20and%20Debate%20Summaries/GA%20Resolutions.pdf.

United Nations. 1948. *Universal Declaration of Human Rights.* Accessed 23 June 2012. http://www.un.org/en/documents/udhr/index.shtml.

United Nations–Bhutan. 2010. *From the Bottom Up: Empowerment and Protection to Strengthen Human Security in Bhutan; Civil Society Organization Best Practices and Lessons Learned.* Accessed 29 June 2011. https://docs.unocha.org/sites/dms/HSU/Outreach/Bhutan/047/Bhutan%20From%20the%20Bottom%20Up%20Broschure.pdf.

United Nations Office of the High Commissioner for Human Rights. 2013. "Fact Sheet: Criminalization." *Free & Equal: United Nations for LGBT Equality.* Accessed 28 October 2013. https://unfe-uploads-production.s3.amazonaws.com/unfe-34-UN_Fact_Sheets_v6_-_Criminalization.pdf.

United Nations Secretary-General. 2010. *Human Security: Report of the Secretary General.* A/64/701, 8 March.

UN PGA (United Nations President of the General Assembly). 2008. *Summary of the General Assembly Thematic Debate on Human Security.* 22 May. Accessed 1 July 2011. http://www.un.org/ga/president/62/ThematicDebates/humansecurity/summary.pdf.

Vaughan-Williams, Nick. 2009. "Giorgio Agamben." In *Critical Theorists and International Relations,* edited by Jenny Edkins and Nick Vaughan-Williams, 19–30. New York: Routledge.

Vertovec, Steven, and Robin Cohen, eds. 2002. *Conceiving Cosmopolitanism: Theory, Context, and Practice.* New York: Oxford University Press.

Vickers, Adrian. 2005. *A History of Modern Indonesia.* Cambridge: Cambridge University Press.

Vincent, R. J. 1986. *Human Rights and International Relations: Issues and Responses.* Cambridge: Cambridge University Press.

von Tigerstrom, Barbara. 2007. *Human Security and International Law: Problems and Prospects.* Portland, OR: Hart.

Waldron, Jeremy. 2012a. *Dignity, Rank, and Rights.* New York: Oxford University Press.

Waldron, Jeremy. 2012b. "How Law Protects Dignity." *Cambridge Law Journal* 71 (1): 200–202.

Waller, James. 2002. *Becoming Evil: How Ordinary People Commit Genocide and Mass Killing.* Oxford: Oxford University Press.

Waltz, Kenneth. 1959. *Man, the State, and War: A Theoretical Analysis.* New York: Columbia University Press.

Walvin, James. 1980. "The Rise of British Popular Sentiment for Abolition, 1787–1832." In *Anti-Slavery, Religion, and Reform: Essays in Memory of Roger Anstey,* edited by Christine Bolt and Seymour Drescher, 149–62. Kent, UK: Wm. Dawson and Sons.

Warner, Michael, ed. 1993. *Fear of a Queer Planet: Queer Politics and Social Theory.* Minneapolis: University of Minnesota Press.

Watson, Adam. 1982. *Diplomacy: The Dialogue between States.* London: Methuen.

Watson, Adam. 1990. "Systems of States." *Review of International Studies* 16 (2): 99–109.

Watson, Adam. 1992. *The Evolution of International Society.* London: Routledge.

Weinert, Matthew S. 2006. "Adolf Eichmann: Understanding Evil in Form and Content." *Human Rights and Human Welfare* 6:179–92.

Weinert, Matthew S. 2007. *Democratic Sovereignty: Authority, Legitimacy, and State in a Globalizing Age.* London: University College London Press.

Weiss, Thomas, et al. 2010. *The United Nations and Changing World Politics.* Boulder, CO: Westview.

Wellens, Karel, ed. 1990. *Resolutions and Statements of the United Nations Security Council (1946—1989): A Thematic Guide.* Dordrecht: Martinus Nijhoff.

Wheatley, Steven. 2005. *Democracy, Minorities, and International Law.* Cambridge: Cambridge University Press.

Wheeler, Nicholas. 2000. *Saving Strangers: Humanitarian Intervention in International Society.* Oxford: Oxford University Press.

Wheeler, Nicholas, and Justin Morris. 1996. "Humanitarian Intervention and State Practice at the End of the Cold War." In *International Society after the Cold War,* edited by Rick Fawn and Jeremy Larkins, 135–71. London: St. Martin's.

Wight, Martin. 1977. *Systems of States.* Leicester: Leicester University Press.

Wight, Martin. 1978. *Power Politics.* Leicester: Leicester University Press.

Wight, Martin. 1992. *International Theory: The Three Traditions.* Edited by Gabriele Wight and Brian Porter. New York: Holmes and Meier.

Williams, John. 2005a. "Hannah Arendt and the International Space In-Between." In *Hannah Arendt and International Relations,* edited by Anthony Lang and John Williams, 199–220. New York: Palgrave MacMillan.

Williams, John. 2005b. "Pluralism, Solidarism, and the Emergence of World Society in English School Theory." *International Relations* 19 (1): 19–38.

Williams, John. 2010. "The International Society—World Society Distinction." In *The International Studies Encyclopedia,* edited by Robert Denemark, 7:4562–78. West Sussex: Wiley-Blackwell.

Wintemute, Robert. 1995. *Sexual Orientation and Human Rights: The United States Constitution, the European Convention, and the Canadian Charter.* Oxford: Clarendon.

Wittgenstein, Ludwig. 1958. *Philosophical Investigations.* Translated by G. E. M. Anscombe. New York: MacMillan.

World Bank. 2014. "Kosovo Overview." Accessed 10 January 2014. http://www.world bank.org/en/country/kosovo/overview.

Yoshino, Kenji. 2007. *Covering: The Hidden Assault on Our Civil Rights.* New York: Random House.

Young, Iris Marion. 1990. *Justice and the Politics of Difference.* Princeton: Princeton University Press.

Young, Iris Marion. 2000. *Inclusion and Democracy.* New York: Oxford University Press.

Yusef, Abdulqawi Ahmed. 2010. *Separate Opinion of Judge Yusef.* Accessed 25 May 2012. http://www.icj-cij.org/docket/files/141/16005.pdf.

# Index